MASS AND ELITE

IN DEMOCRATIC ATHENS

Demokratia crowning Demos. Athenian public document relief adorning the Law against Tyranny (337/6 B.C.). (Courtesy of the American School of Classical Studies at Athens: Agora Excavations.)

MASS AND ELITE IN DEMOCRATIC ATHENS

Rhetoric, Ideology, and the Power of the People

BY

JOSIAH OBER

PRINCETON

UNIVERSITY PRESS

Published by Princeton University Press, 41 William Street,
Princeton, New Jersey 08540
In the United Kingdom: Princeton University Press, Oxford

All Rights Reserved

This book has been composed in Linotron Baskerville

Clothbound editions of Princeton University Press books
are printed on acid-free paper, and binding materials are
chosen for strength and durability. Paperbacks, although satisfactory
for personal collections, are not usually suitable for library rebinding

Printed in the United States of America by Princeton University Press
Princeton, New Jersey

Library of Congress Cataloging-in-Publication Data

Ober, Josiah.
Mass and elite in democratic Athens : rhetoric, ideology, and the
power of the people / Josiah Ober.
p.   cm.   Bibliography: p.   Includes index.
ISBN 0-691-09443-8 (alk. paper)
1. Athens (Greece)—Politics and government. 2. Political participation—Greece—
Athens. 3. Political leadership—Greece—Athens. I. Title.
JC79.A8O24 1989   306'.2'0938—dc19   88-25413

Second printing, with corrections, 1990

9 8 7 6 5 4 3 2

For my father, Nathaniel Ober,
whose praxis helped me to
formulate a hypothesis.

CONTENTS

PREFACE

Thanks to the influence of the dedicand, I had begun to think about the role of elite and egalitarian institutions in democratic society long before I first read the Attic orators. Yet I had been studying the orators for quite a while before the elitist tone of Demosthenes' comments on Aeschines in *On the Crown* struck my attention. That was ten years ago. Given this extended period of gestation, it is perhaps inevitable that my purposes and intentions in writing about mass and elite in Athens should be manifold. First, the book is meant to be a contribution to Greek history: an attempt to explain the social roots and internal functioning of the political system of an ancient city-state. I hope that many of those who consider the history and culture of fifth- and fourth-century Athens intrinsically interesting, as I do, will find this study valuable in formulating or reformulating their own assessments of classical Greece.

My other primary goals in writing the book may be less self-evident. Some historians of Greco-Roman antiquity, including myself, have embraced the technique of employing models devised by modern social scientists to help explain ancient society. When models are used crudely or mechanically, however, the results are unlikely to be persuasive. I propose that it is now time for students of the classics to take a dynamic approach to methodology and theory. A field that engages a relatively large number of scholars in studying a relatively small body of texts, and in which cross-disciplinary work is inevitable, presents an ideal environment for the production, refinement, and testing of critical theories and social models. And these models and theories may have relevance well beyond the study of the Greco-Roman world and its cultural products. The book is therefore intended as an example of a radical approach to classical history. I have combined a central tenet of *Annales*-School social history—the importance of understanding the "mentality" of ordinary people—with a major insight of modern literary theory: viewing texts as symbol-systems that must be understood in relationship to their receptors. The result is a reading of the political development of an ancient state that is more concerned with rhetoric and popular ideology than with constitutions, personalities, factions, or foreign relations. I hope to show that Athenian decision-making processes were coherent without being completely rational, that effective leadership coexisted with genuine popular sovereignty, and that ideological hegemony, while vitally important, was not a tool of the leisure class. In the end, I hope to demonstrate how a democratic political culture came into being and how it sustained and reproduced itself through the generation of rules (laws and political institutions) and discourse (especially public rhetoric). This demonstration should have some significance for students of political theory.

Deciding what conditions will foster stable democratic government and will reproduce democratic political culture is a matter of practical importance to all citizens of democratic states, as well as a matter for debate among theorists. But there are few historical examples of the independent evolution of a democratic political culture. Theory testing using modern democracies is problematic, since most are quite young, and their ultimate form remains unknown. Testing is further complicated by the tendency of modern political leaders to devise policy on the basis of theoretical constructs—analysis of the validity of Keynesian economics (for example) is arguably complicated by policymakers' attempts to implement it. Since the ancient Athenians were not influenced by modern political, social, and economic theory, their actions and discourse provide an empirical testing ground for models of democratic political behavior. Thus, as I wrote this book, I had in mind an audience that includes classicists, historians, and social and political scientists, as well as citizens concerned with the potential of democracy as a means of self-government and as a way of life.

Attempting to reach a broad audience requires some divergences from the traditional rhetoric of classical scholarship. I have cited in the notes various studies intended to aid the non-classicist (these appear with asterisks in the Select Bibliography) as well as more technical and specialized studies. In order to make the book accessible to those who do not read classical Greek, I have translated all Greek passages and have defined Greek terms at first use. Greek terms that are used frequently are listed in the index; the page on which the definition appears is indicated in boldface. In order to make the book's appearance less forbidding, I have transliterated Greek phrases. My translations of the Attic orators are often based on the generally quite readable Loeb Classical Library editions.

In the process of researching and writing this book I have contracted many debts, material and intellectual. Drafts of unpublished papers and articles were made available to me by Glenn Bugh, William Dray, Mogens Hansen, Carol Lawton, Carnes Lord, Paul Rahe, David Small, Barry Strauss, Robert Wallace, and Jack Winkler; much of this material has since appeared in print, but early access to their conclu-

sions saved me much time and trouble. The generous leave policy of
Montana State University, along with financial support from the Office of the Vice-President for Research and the Department of History
and Philosophy, made the project possible. Much of the primary research, hypothesis formulation, and writing were undertaken in
1983–1984, while I was a Fellow of the National Humanities Center.
Discussions there with scholars in a variety of disciplines were seminal
in the development of many of the ideas presented here. Among my
fellow Fellows, Michael Alexander, William Dray, Linda Kauffman,
Robert Lane, Gladys and Kurt Lang, and Helen North were particularly helpful. The penultimate draft of the manuscript was completed
in 1986–1987, while I was a visiting professor at the University of
Michigan. In Ann Arbor I benefited from conversations with Sally
Humphreys, Riet Van Bremen, and Chester Starr, among others.

I received expert and constructive criticism when I presented parts
of several chapters at department colloquia at Michigan and Montana
State and at larger conferences of classicists, historians, and political
scientists. Correspondence and discussion with Brook Manville, Robert Wallace, Mogens Hansen, and Jack Winkler saved me from errors
and helped to refine my thinking on early Athens, democratic institutions, and the relationship between public rhetoric and theater.
Among my severest and most influential critics have been my students
in Montana and Michigan; their frequent unwillingness to accept con-
ventional wisdom at face value is more of an inspiration than I suspect
they realize. Cynthia Kosso put in many hours verifying references
and saved me from any number of errors. Billy Smith, David Small,
and Nathaniel Ober read parts of the manuscript and made valuable
suggestions. Barry Strauss read a late draft in its entirety; I am very
grateful for his detailed and insightful commentary. The staff of
Princeton University Press has been very helpful throughout; special
thanks are due to Joanna Hitchcock (editor) and Nancy Moore (copy
editor). I must also acknowledge the contribution of the people of
Montana. They not only paid my salary for the past several years, they
taught me what it means to live in a society defined by an egalitarian
ethos. But my greatest debt, as always, is to Adrienne Mayor, with
whom I argued through virtually every idea in the book; I owe more
to her critical acuity, impatience with glib solutions, and broad reading
in comparative history and political theory than I can express in
words.

Bozeman, Montana
January 1988

ABBREVIATIONS

Ancient Authors and Texts

AP = *Athēnaiōn Politeia*
Aesch. = Aeschines
And. = Andocides
Ant. = Antiphon
Aristoph. = Aristophanes
Aristot. = Aristotle
  Pol. = *Politics*
  Rhet. = *Art of Rhetoric*
Dem. = Demosthenes
  Ex. = *Exordium*
Din. = Dinarchus
F = Fragment

Hdt. = Herodotus
Hyp. = Hyperides
Is. = Isaeus
Isoc. = Isocrates
Lyc. = Lycurgus
Lys. = Lysias
Plut. = Plutarch
Ps = Pseudo
Thuc. = Thucydides
Xen. = Xenophon
  Mem. = *Memorabilia*
  Hell. = *Hellenica*

Modern Works and Collections

Asterisks indicate works likely to be especially useful to non-classicists.

AJA = *American Journal of Archaeology*
AJAH = *American Journal of Ancient History*
AJP = *American Journal of Philology*
Belegstellenverzeichnis = E. C. Welskopf, ed., *Soziale Typenbegriffe im alten Griechenland und ihr Fortleben in dem Sprachen der Welt.* Vols. 1 and 2: *Belegstellenverzeichnis altgriechischer sozialer Typenbegriffe von Homer bis Aristoteles*, Berlin, 1985
Blass, *AB* = Friedrich Wilhelm Blass, *Die attische Beredsamkeit*, 2nd ed., 3 vols., Leipzig, 1887–1898
CJ = *Classical Journal*
CM = *Classica et Mediaevalia*
CPh = *Classical Philology*
CQ = *Classical Quarterly*
CR = *Classical Review*
Connor, *NP* = W. Robert Connor, *The New Politicians of Fifth-Century Athens*, Princeton, 1971
Davies, *APF* = J. K. Davies, *Athenian Propertied Families, 600–300 B.C.*, Oxford, 1971

*Davies, *DCG* = J. K. Davies, *Democracy and Classical Greece*, Stanford, 1978

Davies, *WPW* = J. K. Davies, *Wealth and the Power of Wealth in Classical Athens*, New York, 1981

Dover, *GPM* = K. J. Dover, *Greek Popular Morality in the Time of Plato and Aristotle*, Berkeley, 1974

FGrH = F. Jacoby, *Die Fragmente der griechischen Historiker*, Berlin, 1923–

*Finley, *AE* = M. I. Finley, *The Ancient Economy*, Berkeley, 1973.

*Finley, *DAM* = M. I. Finley, *Democracy Ancient and Modern*, New Brunswick, New Jersey, 1973

*Finley, *PAW* = M. I. Finley, *Politics in the Ancient World*, Cambridge, 1983

*Forrest, *EGD* = W. G. Forrest, *The Emergence of Greek Democracy: The Character of Greek Politics, 800–400 B.C.*, London, 1966

GRBS = *Greek, Roman, and Byzantine Studies*

Hansen, *AECA* = Mogens Herman Hansen, *The Athenian Ecclesia: A Collection of Articles, 1976–1983*, Copenhagen, 1983

HSCP = *Harvard Studies in Classical Philology*

Hignett, *HAC* = C. Hignett, *A History of the Athenian Constitution to the End of the Fifth Century B.C.*, Oxford, 1952

IG = *Inscriptiones Graecae*

JHS = *Journal of Hellenic Studies*

*Jones, *AD* = A.H.M. Jones, *Athenian Democracy*, Oxford, 1957

Kock, *CAF* = T. Kock, *Comicorum Atticorum Fragmenta*, 3 vols., Leipzig, 1880–1888

LCM = *Liverpool Classical Monthly*

Ober, *FA* = Josiah Ober, *Fortress Attica, Defense of the Athenian Land Frontier, 404–322 B.C.* Mnemosyne Supplement 84, Leiden, 1985

REG = *Revue des Études Grecques*

Rhodes, *CommAP* = P. J. Rhodes, *A Commentary on the Aristotelian 'Athenaion Politeia'*, Oxford, 1981

SEG = *Supplementum Epigraphicum Graecum*

SO = *Symbolae Osloenses*

Ste. Croix, *CSAGW* = G.E.M. de Ste. Croix, *The Class Struggle in the Ancient Greek World*, Ithaca, 1981

Strauss, *AAPW* = Barry S. Strauss, *Athens after the Peloponnesian War: Class, Faction, and Policy, 403–386 B.C.*, Ithaca, 1986

TAPA = *Transactions of the American Philological Association*

ZPE = *Zeitschrift für Papyrologie und Epigraphik*

MASS AND ELITE IN

DEMOCRATIC ATHENS

CHAPTER I

PROBLEMS AND METHOD

The form of political organization that evolved in the *polis* of Athens over the course of the sixth, fifth, and fourth centuries B.C. is one of the best known, most frequently evoked, but least well-understood legacies of the Greco-Roman world. Formidable stumbling-blocks stand in the way of a modern understanding of Athenian political life: the problems that arise because of our great chronological distance from classical Athens are compounded by our emotional proximity. Today the word "democracy" almost invariably carries a positive connotation. Democratic government—an anomaly in the fifth century B.C., an idea disparaged by ancient philosophers, and a term of abuse in eighteenth-century political debates—is now nearly universally accepted (at least in the public pronouncements of national leaders) as the most desirable form of human political organization.[1] Of course, not all modern proponents of democracy mean quite the same thing when they speak in its favor, and few citizens of any modern democratic state would be likely to find themselves in full agreement with an ancient Athenian's views of how a democracy should operate. But there is also some common ground.

A. Democracy: Athenian and Modern

The Greek word *dēmokratia* can be translated literally as "the people (*dēmos*) possess the political power (*kratos*) in the state." In ordinary discourse, "the people" meant for the Athenians, as for modern democrats, the whole of the citizen body, and citizenship was determined

[1] For a particularly nasty ancient portrait of the "democratic man" see Plato *Republic* 8.555b–569c with the comments of Ste. Croix, *CSAGW*, 70–71. On democracy in 18th-century political debates and its modern acceptance, see Finley, *DAM*, 9–10; cf. Richard Jenkyns, *The Victorians and Ancient Greece* (Cambridge, Mass., 1980), 14–15. On the near universal acceptance of democracy as an ideal, and on differing definitions of democratic, see Andrew J. Nathan, *Chinese Democracy* (New York, 1985), esp. ix–x, 224–32. Of course there are exceptions; the ruler of the state of Brunei on Borneo, Sultan Hassanal Bolkiah, is quoted (*Newsweek*, December 22, 1986, p. 24) as saying of democracy: "We tried it, and it didn't work."

by birthright rather than by property-holding.[2] Much of the appeal of
democracy in antiquity, as now, rested upon the attractiveness of two
closely related ideas: first, that all citizens, despite differences in their
socioeconomic standing, should have an equal say in the determination of state policy; second, that the privileges of elite citizens, and the
elite collectively, must be limited and restricted when those privileges
come into conflict with the collective rights of the citizenry, or the individual rights of non-elite citizens. I suppose that few modern advocates of democracy would find reason to quarrel with Demosthenes'
(24.171) characterization of the ethos of democratic Athens: compas-
sion for the weak, a prohibition against strong and powerful individuals acting violently toward other citizens, and a refusal to countenance either brutal treatment by the powerful of the mass of citizens
or subservience by the masses to the powerful.

Yet despite similarities in principle, there remain many significant
differences in practice. Modern democracies assume clear distinctions
between the concepts of the state, the citizenry, and the government.
The day-to-day business of a modern democratic government typically
is run by an elite, whose members provide the abstract entity of the
state with the experience and leadership necessary for its continued
existence. Some members of the governing elite are elected by the
people as their representatives. The people (the citizenry) thus delegate much of their political power to an elite (the government) whose
members are expected to make policy in the interests of the state.

In addition to elected representatives, the governing elite in a modern democracy normally includes executive officials, at least some of
whom are appointed rather than elected, and a professional judiciary.
The duties of each official in the government are relatively clear and
often legally defined and circumscribed. Furthermore, the functional
role of government officials in modern democracies has tended to be
quite clearly differentiated; hence, individual officials are expected to
fulfill leadership and administrative functions, but they are not nec-

---

[2] In elite discourse the term *dēmos* was sometimes used of the lower classes, rather
than of the entire citizen body. See the discussion of the term in Vlastos, "ΙΣΟ-
ΝΟΜΙΑ ΠΟΛΙΤΙΚΗ," 8 n. 1; Ste. Croix, "Character," 21–26; Whitehead, *Demes*,
364–68; Raaflaub, "Democracy, Oligarchy," 524 with n. 36, and below, I.B. The
argument of Sealey, "Origins," esp. 281, and *Athenian Republic*, esp. 91–106, 146–
48, that Athenian ideas of democracy can only be understood by disassociating
those ideas from the concept of "government by the people," seems to me fundamentally wrong; cf. below, VII.C. Nor am I persuaded by Sealey's claim (*Athenian
Republic*, 5) that the laws of Athens were written with a "standard citizen" in mind—
one who was considerably wealthier than the "average citizen" and whose values
and norms "determined the values and norms of behavior for the whole society."

essarily expected to be exemplars of every moral value held worthy by the society as a whole. Within the governmental organization itself, there is typically a fairly clear division of powers and responsibilities between legislative, executive, and judicial branches. The citizenry, whose only direct responsibility to the governance of the state consists in voting for officials, is ordinarily composed of both men and women. There is no large class of unfree persons, and in some modern democracies aliens are able to achieve full citizenship without undue difficulties.[3]

The Athenians, for their part, limited citizenship rights to freeborn males of Athenian ancestry. Women, slaves, and resident aliens, a majority of the total adult population, were excluded from participation in political life. As a consequence, Athenian "political society"—that is the community of franchise-holders—was less closely coextensive with the "whole society" than is the case in modern democracies. In the following pages I will analyze the rules and procedures—explicit and implicit—by which Athenian political society operated. I will attempt to show how its mode of political organization helped the Athenian polis to function as a society. But readers should bear in mind that there were many individuals living in Attica who were not direct beneficiaries of the social and political balancing act described here. Indeed, the achievement of a degree of social harmony among the citizens ensured that those without political rights would have less chance to exploit social disorder as a possible means of improving their own standing.

The political cohesiveness of the citizenry was partly a product of the oppression of noncitizen groups within the polis. Kurt Raaflaub suggests that "the success of the democracy in securing the loyalty and devotion of the vast majority of citizens rested largely on its insistence on a marked distinction between citizens (whatever their social status) on the one hand, and all categories of noncitizens on the other."[4] Although "rested largely" seems to me an overstatement, the group interest of the citizens vis-à-vis noncitizens undoubtedly provided the

---

[3] On the influence of elites and the responsibilities of the masses in modern democracies, see Marger, *Elites and Masses*, esp. 209–98. On differentiation, see Luhmann, *Differentiation*, 138–65, and below, III.D.3.

[4] Raaflaub, "Democracy, Oligarchy," 532, cf. 544 n. 93; "Freien Bürgers Recht," 44–46; Meier, *Anthropologie*, esp. 20–22; cf. Sarah B. Pomeroy, *Goddesses, Whores, Wives, and Slaves: Women in Classical Antiquity* (New York, 1975), 78. On the political position of Athenian women, see also Lacey, *Family*, 151–76; Cantarella, *Pandora's Daughters*, 38–51; Keuls, *Reign of the Phallus*. For slaves, see esp. Golden, "Slavery and Homosexuality," on the importance of drawing the psychic distinction between male youths (potential citizens) and slaves.

former with an inducement to cooperate among themselves. Fear (conscious and subconscious) of the "others" may also have persuaded Athenians to overlook some of the class and status inequities that existed among themselves.

Exclusion of "others" from the political sphere was, in sum, a very important factor in the coalescence of the political society of the Greek polis, and we will consider some of the ramifications of exclusivity for the Athenian citizen body's definition of itself below (esp. VI.C). But, in order to prove that exclusivity was the necessary and sufficient cause of the efficient functioning of Athenian democracy (viz., that democracy was a direct product of exclusion), a demonstration that Athenian treatment of resident noncitizens differed significantly from practices of nondemocratic Greek poleis would be necessary. Given the state of our evidence for social relations in poleis other than Athens, the matter is not amenable to rigorous empirical proof. It is notable, however, that democratic Athens did not engage in the sort of organized terrorism against its unfree population that pertained in Sparta.[5] Athenian laws and customs kept women in an inferior social position and denied their political existence. But Aristotle (*Pol.* 1300a4–8, 1322b37–1323a6) points out that boards of magistrates for controlling the behavior of women were suitable to aristocracies and unsuitable to democracies, since it was impossible to prevent the wives of the laboring (*aporoi*) citizens from going out in public.[6]

The exclusion of women, slaves, and foreigners from political rights must be faced by anyone who hopes to gain a fair understanding of classical Greek civilization. Oppression of noncitizens is, however, an insufficient explanation for the unique direction of Athenian sociopolitical development. The limitation of the franchise to freeborn males is certainly undemocratic by current standards, but to deny the name democracy to Athens' government, on the grounds that the Athenians did not recognize rights that most western nations have granted only quite recently, is ahistorical.[7] We may deplore the Athe-

---

[5] *Krupteia*: H. Jeanmaire, "La Cryptie lacédémonienne," *REG* 26 (1913): 121–50. Gouldner, *Enter Plato*, 33–34, suggests that Athenian slaves were, on the whole, better off than Spartan helots.

[6] On the development of boards of overseers of women, which apparently originated on Thasos, see B. J. Garland, "Gymnaikonomoi: An Investigation of Greek Censors of Women." (Ph.D. diss., Johns Hopkins University, 1981). Overseers of women are first attested at Athens in the last quarter of the fourth century, after the end of the democracy; Garland (11–45) suggests that the magistracy was introduced by Lycurgus in ca. 328–326, but the evidence for this date is no stronger than it is for the *communis opinio* of ca. 317, by Demetrius of Phaleron.

[7] Universal male suffrage was still a very rare phenomenon in modern western

nians' exclusivist attitude, but moral censure should not obscure our appreciation of the fundamental importance of the new democratic political order. For the first time in the recorded history of a complex society, *all* native freeborn males, irrespective of their ability, family connections, or wealth, were political equals, with equal rights to debate and to determine state policy.

The radical nature of Athenian democracy is clear when measured against the standards of the age in which it developed. Throughout ancient Greek history, oligarchy remained the most common form of polis government. According to Aristotle, who devoted much thought to the question of how to define various political regimes, an oligarchy pertains wherever there exists a property qualification for citizenship, so that the wealthy control the state (*Pol.* 1279b17–1280a4, 1309b38–1310a2; *Rhet.* 1365b31–33). But he notes elsewhere (*Pol.* 1317b39–41) that oligarchy is defined by birth (*genos*), wealth (*ploutos*), and education (*paideia*). Given the parameters of Greek political culture, it is less useful to ask why the Athenians failed to grant political rights to women, slaves, and foreigners, than to ask how the Athenians achieved political equality among the adult male citizens and restricted the political privileges of the elites.[8]

The Athenian form of political organization differed from modern democratic governments in that there was no entrenched governing elite and there were no elected representatives. Elections were considered potentially undemocratic, since they favored those with demonstrated ability (Aristot. *Pol.* 1273b40–41, 1294b7–9); most government officials were selected by lot. Lotteried officials had very limited powers; their office was generally collegiate, annual, and subject to judicial scrutiny. The key decision-making body of the Athenian state was the Assembly. Open to all citizens, the Assembly met frequently (forty times per year in the later fourth century) to debate and to decide

---

nations at the close of the nineteenth century; female suffrage was unknown before the twentieth. Cf. the survey in Bowles and Gintis, *Democracy and Capitalism*, 42–47, 56: ". . . the universal suffrage and civil liberties generally associated with liberal democracy simply did not exist in any country before World War I. It was only distantly approximated in a handful of nations."

[8] Cf. esp. Davies, "Athenian Citizenship," who points out the various more restricted alternatives by which citizenship might have been (and was, in other poleis) defined, cf. idem, *DCG*, 37–38; Ste. Croix, *CSAGW*, 283–84, "Character," 41; Finley, *PAW*, 9; Reinhold, "Human Nature," 24–25. Prevalence of oligarchy: Raaflaub, "Freien Bürgers Recht," 8. Assuming a total slave population of 40–80,000 (below, I.n.59), about 10,000 adult male metics, and a citizen population of ca. 30,000 (below, III.E.1), it is possible to suggest that the citizen population was about half of the total adult male population; but none of these numbers is secure.

state policy. Any citizen who could gain and hold the attention of his fellows in the Assembly had the right to advise them on national policy. As Plato (*Protagoras* 319d) put it, "Anyone may stand up and offer advice, whether he be a carpenter, a blacksmith, a shoe-maker, a merchant, a ship-captain, wealthy, poor, noble, or base-born. . . ." After debate, the assembled citizens voted on specific proposals; simple majorities therefore determined the state's policy. Each meeting's agenda was set by a Council (*boulē*) of five hundred citizens, chosen, like other magistrates, annually by lottery. Until the end of the fifth century, all decisions of the Assembly had the immediate force of law; at that time a procedure for judicial review was instituted. But the juries that reviewed some Assembly decisions, like all Athenian juries, were chosen from nearly the full spectrum of Athenian citizens: the juries were large (generally 200–1,500) panels of citizens over thirty years of age, who voted democratically on the verdict. The demos, its will expressed in both Assembly and in court rulings, was master of Athens. The roles of political leaders were also much less clearly defined and less differentiated from the social matrix than has been the norm in modern states. There was neither a formal division of powers within the government, nor any clear distinction between state, people, and government. Thus, if the Athenians were less inclusive than modern democracies in their citizenship policy, they were more egalitarian in their governmental organization. Athens was a direct democracy, a mode of state organization that seems not to exist in the modern world.[9]

Identification of some of the basic similarities and differences between Athenian and modern democratic principles and practice is im-

[9] Good introductions to the Athenian political structure include Gomme, "Working"; Hopper, *Basis*; Finley, "Athenian Demagogues," esp. 9–13; and Jones, *AD*, esp. 99–133. The most important ancient source for the constitution is the Aristotelian *Constitution of Athens*; see the extensive commentary by Rhodes, *CommAP*; cf. Hignett, *HAC*. More specialized studies on various government institutions will be cited in Chapters II and III. While the distribution of offices by lot was considered the distinctive constitutional feature of democracy (e.g., Aristot. *Rhet.* 1365b31–32), some officials were elected, notably the board of ten generals. Some elective financial offices had a property qualification, but this was to assure personal financial accountability, see Jones, *AD*, 48–49; Hignett, *HAC*, 224; Ste. Croix, *CSAGW*, 602 n. 21; Gabrielsen, *Remuneration*, 112–15. Hansen, *AECA*, 207–26, draws interesting parallels between the Athenian Assembly and some of the local cantonal assemblies (*Landsgemeinde*) of Switzerland. The parallel is, however, limited, since the cantonal assembly's sphere of competence is limited by the powers of the federal Swiss government, and the citizens of the cantons meet in assembly only once each year. Cf. also Woodhead, "ΙΣΗΓΟΡΙΑ," 132 n. 9.

portant. Much modern scholarship on ancient democracy has been marred by a tendency to overstress the similarities. As a result, because many modern western democracies are based on a pluralistic political party system within a parliamentary context, some scholars have distributed Athenian politicians into parties, whose platforms are delineated and whose successes and failures at the "polls" are laboriously charted and endlessly debated. The result is a thoroughly erroneous view of Athenian political life.[10] But if we overstress the differences and ignore similarities in principle, the study of ancient political activity becomes empty antiquarianism, sterile cogitation by specialists in dead languages, which can (and will) be ignored by those interested in current affairs.[11] This situation is not only regrettable but harmful. The Athenian example has a good deal to tell the modern world about the nature and potential of democracy as a form of social and political organization. Athens can serve as a corrective to the cultural chauvinist's argument that only the experience of the modern western world is of contemporary value. By clearly identifying both similarities and differences in principle and practice, we can make the Athenian democracy both explicable in its own terms and an accessible tool for political analysis and action by those who are, or would be, citizens of democratic states.

The Athenian democratic "constitution" (a convenient, if imprecise term to describe the formally recognized principles and practices of Athenian government) was undergirded by a belief system that

[10] Cf. the comments of Loraux, *Invention*, 1–14, concluding that "we no longer believe naively that we are the posterity whom the orators [of funeral orations] exhorted to remember Athens" (14). A notable example of the tendency to assume continuity of political forms is A. B. West, "Pericles' Political Heirs," *CPh* 19 (1924): 124–46, 201–28. For more recent assessments of Athenian political groups, see below, III.D.2.

[11] Meier, *Anthropologie*, esp. 7–26, 46, while making some extremely valuable observations, seems to me to overemphasize the gulf between ancient and modern political organization; cf. below, I.n.83. See also Ober, "Aristotle's Political Sociology," for a discussion of the assumption of Holmes, "Aristippus," that the lack of social differentiation in Greek poleis renders the experience of ancient politics irrelevant to the modern experience. Holmes' article contains pointed criticism of the theories of the school of political philosophy based on the ideas of Leo Strauss, whose members have tended to take the lead in advocating the usefulness of ancient political experience. A primary problem with the Straussian approach, from my point of view, is the assumption that only the philosophical products of elite culture are of contemporary value. I think the Athenian mode of political organization itself is at least as relevant to the modern world as anything Plato or Aristotle had to say about it.

stressed the innate wisdom and binding nature of group decisions, the freedom of the citizen, and the equality of all citizens. Freedom and equality were both limited and conditional, however: individual freedom was constrained by the necessity that the individual subordinate himself to group interests, and equality was limited to the political sphere. The Athenians never developed the principle of inalienable "negative rights" (freedom from governmental interference in private affairs) of the individual or of minorities vis-à-vis the state—a central tenet of modern liberalism. Nor were they convinced that social advantages would result from the equalization of property—an idea discussed by Greek philosophers and a cornerstone of Marxist sociopolitical theory.[12] In addition to inequalities in property-holding, the Athenians continued to live with inequalities of status on the basis of birth—the result of an aristocratic tradition—and of ability—the result of differences in natural gifts and educational opportunity. There were elites in Athens, and elite Athenians tended to compete with one another over anything they thought might enhance their personal standing. These contests were hard fought, because for every winner whose status was enhanced, there were inevitably losers whose standing was lowered.[13] Hence, there remained significant and unresolved tensions within Athenian political society which might have resulted in divisive conflict between community and individual, between mass and elite, between elite and non-elite individuals, and between members of the elites. The political power of the group threatened the liberty of the individual and the property of the wealthy; the wealth, status, and abilities of the elites threatened both the non-elite individual and the masses collectively; intra-elite contests threatened to undermine the stability of the entire society.

[12] On Athenian ideas of equality and freedom, and their limits and contradictions, see Aristot. *Pol.* 1281a39–b9, 1284a30–34, 1286a25–35, 1317a40–b16, 1318a2–10, *Rhet.* 1366a4; cf. Finley, "Freedom of the Citizen," esp. 13–14; Maio, "*Politeia*," esp. 19–20; Jones, *AD*, 45–50; Larsen, "Judgment," esp. 3–5; Arnheim, *Aristocracy*, 130–31, 156; Osborne, *Demos*, 9–10; and above all Raaflaub, "Freien Bürgers Recht," "Democracy, Oligarchy," *Entdeckung der Freiheit*, 258–312. On the misguided attempt to find a "liberal temper" in Greek political theory, see Holmes, "Aristippus," 115 (criticizing Havelock, *Liberal Temper*). On the difficulty of applying purely Marxist notions of class struggle and consciousness to the Athenian example, the best discussion is Ste. Croix, *CSAGW*, who believes that both did in fact pertain and frankly admits the difficulties of proving it; cf. Dover, *GPM*, 38–39; Finley, "Athenian Demagogues," esp. 6–8, 18; Ober, "Aristotle's Political Sociology." On the inability of either traditional liberal or Marxist theory to explain democracy adequately, see Bowles and Gintis, *Democracy and Capitalism*, 8–20.

[13] On aristocratic society as a contest society, see, for example, Gouldner, *Enter Plato*, 13–15, 45–55; cf. below, VI.A.

B. Elites and Masses

The relationship between elites and the mass of ordinary citizens within the context of Athenian political society is the central concern of the present study. The general definition of "the elite," as a relatively small subgroup of society whose members enjoy extraordinary advantages of one sort or another, is, however, too vague to be useful for analytical purposes. Modern sociological discussions of elites tend to use the term in one of two ways. First, "the elite" may refer to a cohesive ruling oligarchy that runs an organization or a state. In this study, such a group will be called a governing or ruling elite. The second modern definition of the elite is less specifically linked to political power: those members of society who are (1) much more highly educated than the norm (the educated elite), (2) much wealthier than the norm (the upper class or the wealth elite), or (3) recognized by other members of society as deserving privileges based on their birthright and/or by their performance (or avoidance) of certain occupations (the nobles, aristocrats, or status elite). The term "masses" can be used to refer to all members of society who are not members of an elite. But here we are concerned specifically with non-elite members of Athens' political community: citizens who had political rights but were otherwise "ordinary."[14] The Athenian citizen-masses are described in the ancient sources as to plēthos (the mass), hoi polloi (the many), or—more insultingly—ho ochlos (the mob).[15]

Perhaps the best ancient analysis of Greek mass-elite relations is Aristotle's Politics. Aristotle notes (Pol. 1291b14–30) that the free population of a polis can be subdivided into the mass of ordinary citizens (demos—note that this is a more restricted sense of the word than its usual meaning as "the entire citizenry") and the elite (gnōrimoi). The latter group, he continues, is characterized by the elements of wealth (ploutos), high birth (eugeneia), aretē (a difficult term to define, but generally meaning "virtue," or excellence), and cultural education (paideia).

Leaving aside the moral category of aretē, Aristotle's list parallels the constellation of elite attributes used by modern students of elites. The

---

[14] My definition of "masses" therefore excludes many persons (slaves, women, laboring-class metics) who would be included in a Marxist description of "the masses of Athens." For a discussion of modern definitions of mass and elite, see, for example, Mills, Power Elite, 13–18.

[15] See Belegstellenverzeichnis, s.vv. Of these, plēthos is perhaps the most ambiguous. For a discussion of its evolution from an institutional term for "majority" to a political synonym for "demos" to a sociological term for "the lower-class populace" (especially in elite writers), see Ruzé, "Plethos," 259–63; cf. Rhodes, CommAP, 88–89.

education/wealth/status list is repeated, with some variations, by Aristotle elsewhere and by some of the Attic orators.[16] The three primary elite attributes are described variously in the ancient sources. Wealth was (as in many modern societies) the clearest indicator of elite status. Membership in the wealth elite might be manifested either by demonstrated ownership of valuable possessions or by notable public and private generosity. Nobility was indicated by reference to birthright per se and by allusions to aristocratic pursuits, especially sports and contests. Nobles were expected to refrain from participation in degrading occupations, such as manufacturing or commerce, which the Greeks referred to as "banausic." Education, which might consist of formal training in philosophy or rhetoric, was demonstrated by mastery of literary culture and by the ability to speak persuasively in public.

The ancient definitions of elites and elite attributes are collectively similar enough to modern definitions to permit the use of modern analytical categories without immediate danger of anachronism. At least some of the theoretical foundations for a sociology of Athenian politics have been laid by scholars willing and able to use sociological models and categories in a careful and sophisticated manner.[17] G.E.M. de Ste. Croix's monumental *Class Struggle in the Ancient Greek World*, the most complete and rigorous Marxist assessment of ancient society ever attempted (at least in English), includes an analysis of the role of class in the Athenian democracy.[18] M. I. Finley, in a series of articles and monographs, has elucidated ancient, and especially Athenian, sociopolitical life based in part on Max Weber's studies of status and hierarchy.[19] Both class and status are useful analytical constructs, and an

---

[16] Aristot. *Pol.* 1289b27–1290a5, 1293b34–39, 1296b15–34, 1317b39–41, *Rhet.* 1360b19–30, 1378b35–1379a4, *Nicomachean Ethics* 1131a24–29; Dem. 19.295; Isoc. 19.36; Lys. 2.80, 33.2, 14.38–44. Cf. Seager, "Elitism," 7, for other references. Adkins, "Problems," 154, notes that there is a general tendency for ancient orators to list three virtues, rather than four or five, because of the pleasing "tricolor" effect this produces.

[17] P. Abrams, "Sociology and History (I)," review of R. Hofstadter and S. M. Lipset, *Sociology and History* (New York, 1968), in *Past and Present* 52 (1971): 118–25, has a stimulating and insightful discussion of the congruity of historical and sociological epistemology and the vital importance of conceptualization and hypothesis formation to historical inquiry. On the use of sociological models in ancient history, see the classic programmatic statement by K. Hopkins, "Rules of Evidence," review of F. Millar, *The Emperor in the Roman World*, in *Journal of Roman Studies* 68 (1978): 178–86; cf. Ste. Croix, *CSAGW*, 81–82; Finley, *Ancient History*, esp. 4–6, 60–66, 78–87; Shaw, "Social Science."

[18] *CSAGW*, esp. 283–300.

[19] Finley, *AE*, esp. 35–61, "Ancient City," *Ancient History*, esp. 88–90. In *PAW* (esp.

investigation of the consequences of status and class inequalities within the citizen population is vital to an understanding of Athenian political sociology. Yet neither Finley nor Ste. Croix succeeded in fully explaining the operational significance of the relations between ordinary and elite citizens in Athenian social and political life.

Modern philologists, not surprisingly, have been particularly interested in the educated elite of Athens, since it included the writers of virtually all surviving Athenian texts. Many classical scholars have supposed that major literary figures had a direct influence on society. The works of Werner Jaeger, especially his three-volume *Paideia* and his biography of Demosthenes, might be singled out as worthy exemplars of the philologists' emphasis on the importance of educated elites in Athenian political life.[20] But Jaeger's thought was not much influenced by sociology, and relatively little satisfactory work has been done by other students of Greek literature on the relationship between the actions taken by the Athenian masses and the ideas generated by the educated elite. While all studies that touch on ancient society implicitly deal with both elites and masses, the bibliography of titles that explicitly define the interaction of elite and mass as a key element for analysis of Athenian democracy is remarkably small.[21]

The relative paucity of works on mass-elite interactions in democratic Athens may be explained in part by the difficulty of accurately identifying Athenian elites. There were various general Greek terms for "elite"—besides "notables" (*gnōrimoi*), they could be called the "beautiful and good" (*kaloi k'agathoi*), "worthies" (*charientes*), the "excellent" (*aristoi*), the "happy" (*eudaimones*), the "prominent" (*chrēstoi*). The elites of ability, wealth, and status in a Greek polis (as elsewhere) tended to overlap, and it is sometimes difficult to determine whether those referred to by the various Greek terms are to be taken as the possessors of some particular elite attribute or of a broader constellation of attributes.[22]

1–10), Finley rather blurs the category of status, by using the term "class" in its place, while claiming (10 n. 29) not to have changed his primary analytical category. On the debate over whether status or class is the better analytical category for social analysis, see below, VI.A.

[20] Jaeger, *Paideia*, esp. III.84–85, *Demosthenes*.

[21] But see Seager, "Elitism"; Welskopf, "Elitevorstellung"; Bolgar, "Training." Finley, *DAM*, esp. 3–37; Davies, *WPW*, esp. 1–2; and Starr, *Individual and Community*, esp. 89–93, are also very sensitive to the interplay of mass and elite in Athenian political development.

[22] Cf. *Belegstellenverzeichnis*, s.vv. Finley, *PAW*, 2, considers these to be class terms. While wealth was often a common denominator between elites, this oversimplifies the situation.

The problem is compounded by the Athenian refusal to grant formal political privileges to the elite; indeed, the only subset of the citizen body to be normally and frankly granted a special constitutional position were the older citizens.[23] The members of the wealth elite were legally distinguished, less by extraordinary privileges than by their responsibility for undertaking extraordinary duties in terms of material contributions to the state.[24] Members of the birth elite might hold special priesthoods, but these do not appear to have been regarded as important privileges (see VI.B.2). The dominant egalitarian ideology discouraged Athenian elites from most forms of public display. Thucydides (1.6.3–4) notes that in conformity to contemporary Athenian taste the wealthy citizens led lives that were as much as possible like the lives of the ordinary people. Isocrates (3.16, in an oration not intended for mass consumption) praised monarchy because it allowed the elite individual (*chrēstos*) to avoid being mucked in (*pheresthai*) with the mass (*plēthos*), as was the tendency in democratic regimes. As we will see (below, IV–VI), elite Athenian litigants involved in private legal actions often attempted to obscure their status in court. Yet the Athenians were very much aware of the elites among them and were seldom really fooled by the elite citizen's attempt to cast himself in a demotic role. While the Athenians stuck by their conviction that all Athenians were political equals, they would have appreciated the irony of the pigs' revised slogan in George Orwell's *Animal Farm*: "All animals are equal, but some animals are more equal than others."[25]

Orwell's "animals more equal than others" were ultimately distinguished by their privileges in regard to dress and habitation, and they constituted a ruling elite. The existence of a similar ruling elite in democratic Athens has sometimes been assumed but never demon-

[23] See, for example, Thuc. 6.13.1, 8.1.3–4; Aesch. 2.22, 171, 3.2, 4; Hyp. 5.22. Athenian jurors had to be at least 30 years of age, as (most probably) did magistrates; see R. Develin, "Age Qualifications for Athenian Magistrates," *ZPE* 61 (1985): 149–59. Arbitrators had to be 60. Sommerstein, "Aristophanes," 320–21, notes that Old Comedy "displays a systematic bias in favour of older and against younger men." S. C. Humphreys, "Kinship Patterns in the Athenian Courts," *GRBS* 27 (1986): 89–90, points out that older relatives were preferred as supporting witnesses. Age status may have had some influence on the orators' claims that they had learned the history of the city from their elders; cf. IV.D.

[24] In the fourth century B.C. the ca. twelve hundred to two thousand citizens with personal fortunes of ca. one talent were expected to pay war tax; the three hundred or so with ca. three to four talents were liable to serve as trierarchs (warship outfitters) and to perform other liturgies. See below, III.E.1.

[25] G. Orwell, *Animal Farm* (New York, 1946), 112.

strated.[26] Elite citizens certainly took an active role in political affairs: generals and expert public orators typically came from elite backgrounds, and no Athenian politician was poor.[27] Yet, as Finley notes, "it would not have been easy for an ancient Athenian to draw the sharp line between 'we,' the ordinary people, and 'they,' the governmental elite, which has been so frequently noted in the responses of the present-day apathetic [citizen of a democratic state]."[28] The political advisers and leaders of the Athenian state (at least after Pericles) failed to develop the continuity of control of bureaucratic infrastructure, group cohesiveness vis-à-vis the masses, and means to control decision making and state policy, all necessary for the existence of a genuine ruling elite.

Finley's comment, cited above, was in response to the theories of the so-called elitist school of political theory. The elitist philosophers, notably Gaetano Mosca and Vilfredo Pareto, enunciated a view of political action that emphasized the tendency of powerful elites to evolve within and ultimately to control social institutions. Elite domination was made possible in part by the natural tendency of the strong to dominate the weak and in part due to the natural apathy of the numerically superior masses.[29] Mosca's and Pareto's work was amplified and strengthened by Robert Michels' very influential book *Political Parties*. Michels' primary thesis was the "Iron Law of Oligarchy": the inevitable tendency for oligarchies to evolve "in every kind of human organization which strives for the attainment of definite ends." For Michels, "democracy is inconceivable without organization," and organization, which leads to the development of a hierarchical bureaucracy, is itself the source of the "conservative currents" which "flow over the plain of democracy, occasioning there disastrous floods and rendering the plain unrecognizable." True direct democracy, in which simple majorities determined policy, was declared an impossibility in

[26] The existence of a ruling elite in Athens is assumed by, for example, Haussoullier, *Vie municipale*, 132–33; Larsen, "Judgment," 8; Perlman, "Politicians," esp. 340–41, and "Political Leadership," esp. 161–62; de Laix, *Probouleusis*, 174–77, 191–92; Mossé, "*Politeuomenoi*," 199.

[27] Jones, *AD*, 42; Finley, *AE*, 37. Cf. below, III.C.

[28] Finley, *DAM*, 64; on the absence of an institutionalized ruling elite at Athens, cf. ibid., 25–26, *Ancient History*, 97–98; Hopper, *Basis*, 18–19; Bolgar, "Training." Cf. below, VII.G.1.

[29] See G. Mosca, *The Ruling Class*, ed. and trans. E. and C. Paul (New York, 1962); V. Pareto, *The Mind and Society*, 4 vols., trans. A. Bongiorno and A. Livingston (New York, 1935, repr. 1963). For concise introductions to elitist political philosophy, see Marger, *Elites and Masses*, 63–86; Burnham, *Machiavellians*, 81–115 (Mosca), 171–220 (Pareto).

the long run because of physical factors (e.g., the physiological difficulty of even the most powerful orator making himself heard by a
crowd of 10,000 persons) and the inability of a collectivity to settle
major controversies between its members. Hence, Michels argued,
there was always the need for responsibility to be delegated to a group
of educated and able individuals, and this group would naturally
evolve into a ruling elite as they gained control of an increasingly complex bureaucratic apparatus. Michels' empirical basis for his Iron Law
was a study of early twentieth-century democratic socialist political
parties, but he believed that his Law applied to state organization as
well.[30]

Michels' Iron Law has become (at least implicitly) a central tenet of
modern political sociology and has suffered few effective empirical
challenges.[31] Neither Michels nor any other elitist philosopher is much
cited by students of the Athenian democracy, although I suspect that
some of the scholars who have assumed the existence of a ruling elite
in Athens were influenced (directly or indirectly) by their ideas.[32] Only
M. I. Finley seems to have recognized clearly that elitist theory offers
a challenge to our understanding of the Athenian democracy and that
the Athenian example in turn may offer an empirical challenge to the
general validity of Michels' Iron Law of Oligarchy. In *Democracy Ancient and Modern* and again in *Politics in the Ancient World*, Finley vigorously attacked the assumptions of elitist political theorists, especially
those who attempt to demonstrate that the existence of a ruling elite
in a democracy is not only inevitable, but desirable, and that the citizens of the democratic state are naturally apathetic.[33]

Finley realized that denying the existence of a cohesive ruling elite
at Athens required a reexamination of the nature of Athenian political
leadership. He concentrated on the upper-class political orators of the

[30] Michels, *Political Parties*, esp. 50–51, 61–77, 85–128, 333–71. The quotes are
from 50, 61–62. Cf. Burnham, *Machiavellians*, 141–68.

[31] Marger, *Elites and Masses*, 81. Mills, *Power Elite*, esp. 3–29, is an example of an
influential modern study which, while critical of some of the classical elitists, assumes the essential correctness of an elitist organizational model. Cf. Lipset, "Political Sociology," esp. 91; Washburn, *Political Sociology*, esp. 50–103. See also below,
VII.G.1

[32] See Connor, *NP*, 94 n. 11, for a rare example of an ancient historian citing
Michels; notably, the citation is approving (although it does not concern the Iron
Law of Oligarchy per se).

[33] Finley, *DAM*, esp. 7–16, *PAW*, esp. 139–40, cf. *Ancient History*, 97. For apathy
as good for democracy: Lipset, "Political Sociology," 95, with literature cited in n.
20. For other criticisms of classical elitist theory, see, for example, Bachrach, ed.,
Political Elites; Field and Higley, *Elitism*.

late fifth century—the "demagogues" (*dēmagōgoi*, literally "leaders of the people") who addressed the citizenry in the Assembly and law courts—identifying them as an essential structural element in the direct democracy's decision-making process. Finley's work on the demagogues was an important breakthrough, and the structural role of the political orators in the Athenian state has been further elucidated by other scholars.[34] Yet neither Finley nor subsequent scholarship has faced what appears to be a central dilemma inherent in the "structural demagogues" model: how and why did the Athenian demos come to accept as legitimate the political leadership of elite individuals who, moreover, referred explicitly to their elite attributes in public speeches? That the Athenian masses did accept members of various elites as leaders is undeniable, yet if the ideology of the democracy was fundamentally egalitarian, the existence of leaders who chose to identify themselves as elites must have led to considerable tension. And, since the educated and wealthy demagogues never evolved into a ruling elite, the frustration of their "natural" tendency and desire to rule must have been a source of further sociopolitical stress.[35] A major burden of this study will be to explain the ways in which the masses came to accept elite leadership and the means by which they limited the concentration of power in the hands of elite citizens without driving them into open opposition. Only when these ways and means have been clearly defined can we understand the practical significance, in terms of political theory and action, of using the Athenian example as an empirical challenge to the elitist argument that direct democracy is impossible.

C. Explaining Sociopolitical Stability

The identification of tensions between ordinary and elite Athenians, seen in the light of Michels' Iron Law of Oligarchy, leads to the question of how the Athenian direct democracy could have survived over a long period of time. For almost two hundred years, from the late sixth through the late fourth centuries, Athenians governed themselves more or less democratically. The only serious interruptions were two brief oligarchic coups in the late fifth century (411/10, 404/3), one established under the pressure of the Peloponnesian War,

[34] Finley, "Athenian Demagogues," cf. *DAM*, 3–37, *PAW*, 70–84. Among important studies building on some of Finley's ideas are Connor, *NP*; Strauss, *AAPW*.

[35] Cf. the discussion of Carter, *Quiet Athenian*, 10–17. On the natural desire of the elite to rule, see Aristot. *Pol.* 1283b34–1284b34; cf. Ober, "Aristotle's Political Sociology." See also below, II.F.6.

the other imposed by the victorious Spartans after the defeat of Athens in that war. In both cases, the Athenians promptly threw out the oligarchs and restored their accustomed government. Vastly superior military forces allowed the Macedonians to replace the Athenian democratic political order with an oligarchy in 322 B.C. But even after repeated demonstrations of Macedonian military might in the late fourth and early third centuries, the Athenians continued to struggle to restore democracy. The historical record forbids the notion that the stability of the democracy was the result of inertia or a historical fluke.

The question of democratic stability may be broken down into two intertwined problems. The first is how the Athenians were able to deal with existing inequalities, especially between rich and poor. Class tension was endemic in Greece and often contributed to the violent and disruptive political conflicts (*staseis*) that were common in the poleis of the archaic and classical periods.[36] The existence of the democracy itself provides only a partial solution to the problem of Athenian social stability. The democratic government indeed gave the poorer citizens a degree of protection against the property-power of their wealthy fellows and so moderated class antagonism.[37] But the elite litigant retained functional advantages over his ordinary opponent, and the poorer Athenian's envy and resentment of the social privileges enjoyed by the wealthy man were far from eliminated. Nor does the ex-

---

[36] Aristotle (*Pol.*, esp. 1265b10–12, 1296a21–32, 1302b24–25, 1303b13–17, 1304b20–1305a7) regards class tension to be among the greatest dangers facing the polis and devotes much space to recommendations of how tensions can be mediated, both on the ideological and material planes; cf. Ober, "Aristotle's Political Sociology." Ste. Croix, *CSAGW*, esp. 278–300, while tending to overemphasize the role of class at times, is the best and fullest treatment of the problem; cf. Fuks, "Patterns"; Vernant, "Remarks." For different views on the prevalence and importance of class tension in relation to political disorder and civil strife in archaic and classical Greece, see, for example, E. Ruschenbusch, *Untersuchungen zu Staat und Politik in Griechenland vom 7.–4. Jh. v. Chr.* (Bamberg, 1978): ideology and class tension played little part in civil strife; all conficts were between competing *hetaireiai* of aristocrats and were caused by foreign policy problems. Lintott, *Violence*, 34: tensions arose "from the fundamental inequality between rich and poor," but the relative "rareness of genuine class conflicts" is "their most striking feature"; cf. ibid., 272–73 for criticism of Ruschenbusch's position. Cf. also the discussion of the role of class in archaic Athenian history, below, II.C, D. For a catalogue and analysis of *staseis* of the fifth and fourth centuries, see H.-J. Gehrke, *Stasis. Untersuchungen zu den inneren Kriegen in den griechischen Staaten des 5. und 4. Jh v. Chr.* (Munich, 1985).

[37] On class struggle in the fourth century and the function of democracy in mediating it, see Ste. Croix, *CSAGW*, 284–87, 293–98; Vernant, "Remarks"; Fuks, "Patterns"; Rhodes, "On Labelling," 208; Wood, "Agricultural Slavery," 9–10, 13. Cf. the somewhat different view of the importance of the democratic political order of Meier, *Anthropologie*, esp. 18–21.

istence of the democracy in and of itself explain why the wealthy were not more active in agitating for a political position that would match their property-power and could guarantee the security of their goods against the poor.

The second problem is explaining how a direct democracy could function without institutionalized leadership. How did thousands of men, with no specialized knowledge or education, set a consistent and rational policy, over a long period of time, for a complex state? The solutions to these problems are key to understanding the political sociology of classical Athens. As S. M. Lipset noted, "If the stability of society is a central issue for sociology as a whole, the stability of a specific institutional structure or political regime—the *social* conditions of democracy—is the prime concern of political sociology." Lipset goes on to point out that "a stable democractic system requires sources of cleavage so that there will be struggle over ruling positions . . . but without consensus—a value system allowing the peaceful 'play' of power . . . there can be no democracy."[38] In order to answer the question of democratic stability, therefore, we need to explain the nature of the power of the Athenian people. Power is not simple; a proper explanation of the demos' *kratos* will have to embrace not only the more obvious elements of the franchise and the reality and threat of physical force but also authority and legitimacy, ideology and communication, interpersonal and intergroup relationships, reciprocity, and heterogeneity.[39]

How and why the Athenian democracy worked as well as it did is, I

[38] Lipset, "Political Sociology," 91–92; cf. ibid., 83: "The central concern of the study of politics is the problem of consensus and cleavage. . . ." On the origins of political sociology, see ibid., 84–91, citing Marx, Tocqueville, Weber, and Michels as the "founding fathers" of the field. Washburn, *Political Sociology*, 27, considers Weber the real inventor of political sociology, on the basis of the latter's recognition that political institutions are an independent source of social change. Cf. Shaw, "Social Science," 36–47, who criticizes narrowly functionalist sociological models on the grounds that functionalists cannot adequately explain social change or conflict and so tend to overemphasize and eulogize equilibrium. But an excellent argument can be made in structuralist terms for the desirability of an institutional equilibrium that is the product of a dynamic process of democratic change; see Bowles and Gintis, *Democracy and Capitalism*, 185–88.

[39] Among discussions of power I have found especially useful are Meier, *Anthropologie*, 32–35; Bachrach, ed., *Political Elites*, introduction: 2–5 (on the relationship between power and authority); Luhmann, *Differentiation*, 150–52 (power and decision making); Lipset, "Political Sociology," 105–107 (access); Washburn, *Political Sociology*, esp. 19–20 (discussion of Weber on legitimacy); Foucault, *History* 1. 41–42, 81–102 (relationality); Bowles and Gintis, *Democracy and Captitalism*, 92–120 (heterogeneity).

think, one of the original questions that led to the development by the
Greeks of self-conscious political theory.[40] It remains one of the major
questions of Greek history, and many answers have been proposed. A
complete survey of the literature is impossible here and would serve
little purpose, but some of the more recent lines of inquiry may be
sketched out briefly. Before proceeding I should point out that many
of the works that I will accuse here of having failed to provide a full
and adequate explanation for the workings of the Athenian sociopolitical order will be frequently and approvingly cited in later chapters.
Attempting a new understanding of Athenian democracy is indeed to
stand on the shoulders of those who are giants not only in terms of
their scholarship but because of their moral commitment to demonstrating the enduring importance of the question.

C.1 DENIAL OF THE REALITY
OF THE DEMOCRACY

The simplest way of explaining the survival of the Athenian political
order is to deny that true democracy ever existed at Athens, by asserting that the masses never held true political power. Lionel Pearson,
for example, argued in an article on Athenian party politics that until
the death of Pericles (in 429) the demos controlled only domestic policy, while more important questions of foreign policy were dealt with
by the board of ten generals. Pearson suggested that Pericles, who
served as a general for many years, became involved in domestic policy, and his intermixture of the two formerly discrete spheres led the
demos to dabble in foreign policy after his death. The result was anarchy and so "the old democracy was dead."[41] But there is simply no
evidence for the existence of discrete domestic and foreign spheres of
responsibility at Athens, and no evidence that the board of generals
ever had independent policymaking powers. Classical Athens never
fell into a condition even approaching anarchy for any extended period, and the government functioned more or less efficiently for well
over a hundred years after the death of Pericles. Pearson's argument

---

[40]See esp. Hdt. 3.80–82 with the comments of Ehrenberg, "Origins," 525; and
Connor, NP 199–206. Raaflaub, "Democracy, Oligarchy," 517–18 with n. 3, notes
that political thought "started early on" to deal with the exciting and unsettling
phenomenon of democracy. My conception of the relationship between sociopolitical praxis and political theory—that practice and ideology interact to create democracy and that theory is posterior—is somewhat different from that of, e.g.,
Meier, *Anthropologie*, 7–8, 17, 27–44, who assumes that the *idea* of democracy must
have preceded the practice. Cf. below, esp. II.E.

[41] Pearson, "Party Politics"; quote: 50.

was based on the *a priori* assumption that "if free speech and the power of the ecclesia had been extended to larger issues, it is unbelievable that the Athenian democracy could have remained intact for a century."[42] His article, therefore, is not really an explanation of why the democracy worked, but a speculation on what the nature of Athenian government must have been, based on the presumption that it could not have been truly democratic and functioned so well.

A more detailed, but equally unsatisfactory, argument against the existence of true democracy at Athens was developed by R. A. de Laix, in a book on the Athenian Council. De Laix argued that the Council was the "senior partner" in the government and thus the most important policymaking body. The Assembly, as junior partner, was normally responsible only for rubber-stamping preliminary decisions (*probouleumata*) made in the Council. The Council was dominated by aristocrats and the wealthy until the latter part of the fifth century, by "middle-class" politicians thereafter; these politicians were given a constitutional position in the state in the fourth century and served as a ruling elite.[43] Leaving aside "middle-class politicians" and their putative constitutional position, which will be considered below (I.C.5), the idea that the Council ruled Athens is fundamentally erroneous, as A. W. Gomme demonstrated in an article published some years before de Laix's book appeared. Gomme argued that the Assembly truly ruled Athens, noting that the major political speeches were delivered in the Assembly, not the Council, and he pointed out that a corporate body can only rule if there is a continuity of membership and a corporate identity.[44] Neither pertained in the case of the Athenian Council, whose membership changed annually. More recent scholarship has favored Gomme's general conclusion. Although the agenda-setting function of the Council was certainly a necessary element in the democratic decision-making process, and the Council was responsible for some technicalities of state business, the final and most important decision-making body was the Assembly, which frequently amended, replaced, or rejected outright, recommendations the Councilmen put forward.[45]

[42] Ibid., 49.

[43] de Laix, *Probouleusis*, esp. 139–42, 189–92. Cf. the other studies which assume the existence of a ruling elite at Athens, cited above, I.n.26. On the social composition of the Council, see below, III.E.3.

[44] Gomme, "Working." Cf. Marger, *Elites and Masses*, 82.

[45] Cf. Jones, *AD*, 111–22; Rhodes, *Boule*, esp. 78–87, 214–15. On de Laix's erroneous reading of the relationship of the Council to the democracy, see the important reviews by Connor, "Athenian Council," esp. 35–36; H. W. Pleket, *Mnemosyne*

C.2 CONSTITUTIONAL AND LEGAL EXPLANATIONS

M. I. Finley cited de Laix's study as an example of "falling into the
constitutional-law trap": the fundamental error of imagining that it is
possible to understand politics "by a purely formal . . . analysis of the
'parliamentary' *mechanics* alone."[46] M. H. Hansen has written extensively on the relationship between legislative enactment and policymaking; the division of powers among boards of "Lawmakers" (*nomothetai*), the peoples' courts, Assembly, and individual citizens; the
locus of sovereignty in the Athenian state; and in general on whether
the Athenian state of the fourth century was constitutionally a "radical" or "moderate" democracy. Hansen concludes that the democracy
was in general more "moderate" than it had been in the fifth century
and that, due to the division of powers between the Assembly and people's courts elaborated in the later fifth and early fourth centuries, the
Assembly lost its ultimate sovereignty.[47] The sovereignty issue has generated a good deal of discussion. Martin Ostwald agrees with Hansen
that as a result of constitutional reforms in the late fifth century, the
"sovereignty of law" replaced the political sovereignty of the people.
R. Sealey has argued that *dēmokratia* never implied popular sovereignty but rather meant "rule of law"; according to Sealey, Athens was
therefore a republic, not a democracy.[48] I will return to the issue of
sovereignty below (III.E.4, VII.C); suffice it to say here that much of the
recent discussion seems to have fallen into the "constitutional-law
trap." Attempts to define divisions of powers, to find a unitary locus
of sovereignty, and to enunciate a "rule of law" that was exterior, superior, and in opposition to the will of the people will not, I think,
help us to understand the nature of Athenian democracy, because the
Athenians themselves never acted nor thought along those lines.[49]

4th ser. 31 (1978), 328–33, esp. 331. Hansen, "History of the Athenian Constitution," 64, points out the rarity of the term *probouleusis* and notes that it is not attested as a technical constitutional term used by the Athenians.

[46] Finley, *PAW*, 56.

[47] See, for example, Hansen, *Sovereignty*, esp. 15–21 (an early and somewhat extreme statement of his position); cf. below, VII.C. Hansen, "Initiative and Decision,"
is a good summary of many of his ideas on the nature of Athenian government and
a strong statement of his "separation of powers" theory.

[48] Ostwald, *From Popular Sovereignty*, 497–524; Sealey, "Athenian Concept of
Law," *Athenian Republic*, esp. 146–48, 91–106. Cf. Harald Meyer–Laurin, *Gesetz und
Billigkeit im attischen Prozess*: Graezitsche Abhandlungen 1 (Weimar, 1965); Joachim
Meinecke, "Gesetzesinterpretation und Gesetzesanwendung im attischen Zivilpro-
zess," *Revue internationale des droits de l'antiquité*, 3rd ser. 18 (1971): 275–360.

[49] Discussions of the nature of Athenian law by Humphreys: "Evolution of Legal
Process," "Law as Discourse," "Social Relations," "Discourse of Athenian Law";

Laws and constitutional forms are indeed important, and I will turn to them often, because they both reflected and subsequently influenced the political attitudes of the Athenian populace. But the laws themselves may be less significant than the thought process that led to decisions about when laws should be enforced and when they should be ignored. A constitution remains, in Finley's words, "a surface phenomenon," and if we are to understand the reasons for Athenian sociopolitical stability, we must get beneath the surface, to the level of the society.[50]

C.3 EMPIRE

Finley himself, who thought deeply and seriously about the social roots of Athenian democracy, sought a solution to the stability question in the economic realm. The democracy was made financially possible and social tensions were lessened, he postulated, at least in part because of the existence of the Athenian empire (ca. 478–405 B.C.). The empire benefited both rich and poor citizens materially, the former by providing outlets for investment, the latter by providing land (in overseas clerouchies, that is, citizen-colonies) and occupation (as rowers in the Athenian navy). Moreover, since the state was able to draw on sources of revenue (especially in the form of tribute) from outside its own local resources, it could afford to pay poorer citizens to participate in the government (as jurors and magistrates) without the necessity of exerting excessive economic pressure (in the form of steep taxes) upon the upper classes.[51]

The general argument that Athenian democracy depended upon

Maio, "*Politeia*"; Osborne, "Law in Action"; Garner, *Law and Society*; and (with some reservations) Holmes, "Aristippus," 118–23, seem to me to come much closer to the ancient reality than more narrowly constitutionalist arguments.

[50] Finley, *DAM*, 23. Among various programmatic statements on the limited usefulness of constitutional study, see, for example, Finley, *PAW*, 7, 56–58, *Ancient History*, 99–103; Ehrenberg, "Origins," 546–47; Osborne, *Demos*, 64–65; Connor, *NP*, 4–5, "Athenian Council," 33, 39. Cf. the vigorous attack on the "juridico-discursive" conception of power by Foucault, *History*, I.81–91, 102, on the grounds that it concentrates too much on restrictions and limitations: "It is this image we must break free of, that is, of the theoretical privilege of law and sovereignty, if we wish to analyze power within the concrete and historical framework of its operation. We must construct an analytics of power that no longer takes law as a model and a code" (90).

[51] Finley, "Fifth-Century Athenian Empire"; cf. "Freedom of the Citizen," 21, *DAM*, esp. 48–50, *PAW*, 33–36, 111–14, 131–34, *Ancient History*, 84. Similar comments are made by, inter alios, Mahaffy, *Problems*, 16–17; Ste. Croix, *CSAGW*, 290–91; T. J. Galpin, "The Democratic Roots of Athenian Imperialism," *CJ* 79 (1983): 107–108.

the empire dates back to antiquity (cf. Ps-Xenophon and Thucydides, in particular). The major problem with the argument had been recognized well before Finley reopened the issue: democracy was restored in 403 after the collapse of the empire, and the state survived as a democracy without imperial revenues for over eighty years thereafter.[52] Finley was aware of this objection to the argument that the empire fueled the democracy, but he suggested that when the empire dissolved, the system was "so deeply entrenched that no one dared attempt to replace it. . . ."[53] Surely this begs the question. In the decade after the fall of the empire, the Athenians actually expanded the state's financial obligation of ensuring that poorer citizens could participate in the government, by introducing pay for attendance at Assembly meetings.[54] If imperial revenues had been the key factor in fifth-century stability, it seems highly unlikely that stability could be maintained for so long after the revenues were lost. Perhaps there never would have been a full-blown "radical" democracy at Athens without the empire to buffer the financial strains of its development, but we need some further explanation for the continued success of the democratic form of government in the fourth century. Indeed, Finley's identification of the social significance of the imperial revenues to the democratic state in the fifth century highlights the necessity of finding some different explanation for the stability of the Athenian social and political order in the period after 404 B.C.

C.4 Slavery

A second important economic argument is based on linking democracy with the prevalence of chattel slavery. M. H. Jameson, arguing for the existence of a large population of agricultural slaves in Attica, suggested that the participation of large numbers of rural citizens in the government would only have been possible if they owned slaves whose labor would provide them with the financial wherewithal to spend significant amounts of time in the city performing the duties of a citizen.[55] Jameson's argument (like Pearson's, above I.C.1) attempts not so much to explain the stability of the government as to demonstrate the existence of an institution by positing the impossibility of a stable democratic government without it.

Jameson's conclusions on democracy and slavery were endorsed by

[52] See, for example, Gomme, "Working," 13; Jones, *AD*, 5–10, Badian, "Marx in the Agora," 50.

[53] Finley, *DAM*, 49.

[54] *AP* 41.3; cf. below, II.G.

[55] Jameson, "Agriculture and Slavery."

Ste. Croix, who asserts that the existence of widespread agricultural slavery helps to explain the social stability of the democracy.[56] Before proceeding, the stability/slavery argument should be separated from extraneous considerations. Ste. Croix's concern with identifying a large population of agricultural slaves at Athens is conditioned by his desire to demonstrate empirically the validity of Marx's hypothetical ancient "slave mode of production," and by a need to explain in materialist terms the absence of overt class conflict in the best-documented state of Greek antiquity. The stability/slavery argument may, however, be made independently of Marxist theory; I emphasize Ste. Croix's discussion of the democracy-and-slavery issue because it seems to me the most sophisticated in the recent literature, not in order to knock down a Marxist straw man.[57] A broader, but separate, question is whether or not Greek civilization as a whole was "based on" slave labor. This question is of only peripheral significance to the present inquiry, since I am attempting to explain the apparent uniqueness of the Athenian political experience, not the general linkages between economic mode of production and culture.[58]

It is important to decide whether the issue of Athenian political stability is to be linked directly or indirectly to slavery. An indirect argument that slavery was important to Athenian government could be framed as follows: the existence of large numbers of slave laborers provided an economic surplus, part of which could be tapped by the state through taxation and used to finance the expenses of the democratic government. Given the certainties that (1) a significant (if not quantifiable) slave population existed in Athens, (2) slaves could generate a surplus (wealth above and beyond what they consumed), and (3) the state had the power to tax surplus wealth, this indirect argument cannot be disproved. But it does not necessarily tell us much about the roots of Athenian sociopolitical stability. If Jameson's conclusion is incorrect, and most slaves were owned by a relatively small group of wealthy men (whether citizens or resident aliens), the ques-

[56] Ste. Croix, CSAGW, 141–42, 284, 505–506.

[57] For the more general Marxist argument about slavery in the ancient economy, see Ste. Croix, CSAGW, 120–74, 226–43, 255–59, 504–505; Vernant, "Remarks." Among earlier, non-Marxist arguments linking the democracy to slavery, see, for example, Mahaffy, Problems, 16–17; E. Meyer, Kleine Schriften (Halle, 1924), 1.193–98 (cited by Finley, Ancient Slavery, 90).

[58] Among discussions of ancient Greece as a slave society, in addition to the studies cited in the previous note, see Gouldner, Enter Plato, 25–27; Finley, "Was Greek Civilization," Ancient Slavery (with voluminous bibliography); Chester G. Starr, "An Overdose of Slavery," Journal of Economic History 18 (1958): 17–32; C. N. Degler, "Starr on Slavery," Journal of Economic History 19 (1959): 271–77.

tion devolves to a financial one: how did rich men in Athens make their money? The answer to this question is of intrinsic interest, and various answers have been proposed, but it will not adequately explain either the social rapprochement between the Athenian elite and the mass of citizens or the processes of direct democratic decision making.[59]

In order to demonstrate that there was a direct and causal relationship between stable democratic government and slavery, we must prove that a large percentage of Athenian citizens owned slaves and thereby gained sufficient leisure to become actively involved in democratic government and acquired a vested interest in maintaining a stable social order that protected private property. The slave-owning population must be shown to include many of the non-elite Athenians who attended the Assembly, sat as jurors, and served as magistrates. Given that a majority of Athenians owned land and at least half the citizen population lived in rural areas (see below, III.E.1), it is also essential (as Ste. Croix recognized) to show that agricultural slavery was common.[60] Widespread slaveholding by neither non-elite Athenians nor by average Athenian farmers can be demonstrated. The available evidence was marshaled by Jameson and Ste. Croix, but neither was able to prove the matter empirically; other scholars have looked at the same body of evidence and have arrived at the opposite conclusion.[61]

[59] If it were demonstrated that no significant surplus could have been generated by a Greek polis without the use of slaves, Greek civilization would be shown to be based on slavery. But Wood, "Agricultural Slavery," 15, 21–31, shows that slaves were not necessary to produce wealth from Athenian land, since there were known ways of extracting a surplus from free labor. Finley, "Was Greek Civilization," 150–51, following Lauffer (Bergwerksklaven, II.904–906, who estimates ca. 90,000: 916 n. 5), guesses that there may have been a peak of 60,000–80,000 slaves in Attica during the fifth and fourth centuries and notes that this represents an average of three or four slaves per free household. But cf. the much lower estimate of ca. 20,000 slaves made by Jones, AD, 76–79. Certainly slaves were not so evenly distributed as Finley implies; at least a few very rich citizens owned hundreds, and Nicias was reported to own 1,000 (Xen. Poroi 4.14). On other sources of wealth of rich Athenians, see Thompson, "Athenian Investor"; Davies, WPW, 38–72.

[60] On landholding citizens and rural residence, see Audring, "Grundeigentum," "Grenzen"; Ober, FA, 19–23; Osborne, Demos, 47–63; cf. below, III.E.1.

[61] See especially Jones, AD, 10–20; Wood, "Agricultural Slavery," 16, 41–47. Finley, "Was Greek Civilization," 148–49, hedges on the degree of agricultural slavery that pertained in Greece, and (ibid., 163–64) flirts with the notion that democracy and slavery were linked, at least symbolically. But in Ancient Slavery, 90, he specifically rejects the link between slavery and democracy as "patently false," while accepting (ibid., 89 n. 60) Jameson's argument on the prevalence of agricultural slaves, an argument based on the false link! The empirical case for average citizens owning slaves, which hangs in part upon comments made by litigants in Athenian

I will attempt in the body of this study to disprove the presumptions on which Jameson and Ste. Croix grounded their *a priori* arguments for broad-based agricultural slave owning in Attica (that neither citizen participation, nor the absence of class conflict can be explained except by the assumption that many small holders owned slaves). Meanwhile their hypotheses may be set against the powerful argument that slave ownership would not have made financial sense to the average Athenian farmer in light of the smallness of plots and the seasonal nature of agricultural labor.[62] In sum, while the importance of slavery to Athenian society and economy should not be underestimated, no direct, causal relationship between chattel slavery and social stability or democratic decision making is demonstrable at Athens.[63]

C.5 MIDDLE-CLASS MODERATION AND THE RESOURCES OF ATTICA

Several scholars have argued that the stability of the democracy was due to the predominance of "middle-class" citizens in all important governmental bodies, especially in the Assembly and on juries. The question here is whether a large middle class, with identifiable class interests and with a strong political voice, actually existed in Athens. We do not possess the evidence to generate an accurate wealth/population curve for classical Athens, but Greek writers seem to have had no well-developed concept of a middle class. The sources typically

---

courts (e.g., Dem. 45.86), becomes even weaker in light of the habit of wealthy litigants of addressing lower-class jurors as their economic equals; see below, v.d.2.

[62] Audring, "Grenzen," 454; Ober, *FA*, 22–23; and esp. Wood, "Agricultural Slavery."

[63] A stronger indirect argument for linking Athenian slavery with democracy might be made on the parallel of colonial Virginia, where the growth of chattel slavery and the development of republican sentiment were simultaneous and apparently closely linked phenomena. Edmund S. Morgan, *American Slavery—American Freedom: The Ordeal of Colonial Virginia* (New York, 1975), esp. 363–87, emphasizes the importance to republicanism of political solidarity between upper- and lower-class free white males in Virginia and argues that the exploitation of slave labor by the upper class made this solidarity possible. The parallel, if fully developed, might yield important insights into the role played by slaveholding among the rich in the development among Athenian citizens of an ideological consensus which transcended class lines. But there are significant differences between the Virginian and Athenian examples. In Virginia, unlike Athens, the rural economy was overtly market oriented (ibid., 366); poor Virginians paid taxes (ibid., 366); and the free poor were relatively few in number (ibid., 366, 380, 386) and so posed no threat to the rule of the elite. I owe the Morgan reference to Billy G. Smith, to whom I am also indebted for a discussion on the slavery and democracy issue. Cf. also below, ii.c, vi.d.

speak of the "wealthy" and the "poor," meaning by the former the leisure class and by the latter those who were constrained to work for a living.[64] The Greek rich/poor terminological dichotomy suggests that the wealth/population curve was quite steep, but there would still be some individuals who would fall into the middle range in terms of wealth. One might legitimately ask how these "middling" citizens saw themselves in relation to the state, how they made their living, and to what extent they helped to stabilize Athenian society and the political process.

A.H.M. Jones, whose book *Athenian Democracy* helped to define the modern debate over the influence of a hypothetical "middle class" in Athens, argued for the existence of a middle class on the basis of a demographic analysis. Jones suggested that the size of the Athenian citizen population dropped sharply in the late fifth to the early fourth centuries, on the assumption that the poorest citizens were forced by economic constraints to emigrate after Athens' loss in the Peloponnesian War. The population thereafter, he argued, was very stable, about twenty-one thousand citizens. Of these, about six thousand had enough surplus income to pay war taxes (*eisphora*), and these taxpayers were the ones who saw to the government. Demographic factors, then, help to account for "the increasingly bourgeois tone of the fourth-century democracy."[65]

There was a population decline between 431 and 403, perhaps a very precipitous one. And the lower population probably did relieve some of the pressure of land-hunger and so may have contributed to social stability in the early fourth century. But it is unlikely that the population curve between 403 and 322 was as flat as Jones believed.[66]

[64] For an attempted wealth/population curve for Athens, see Davies, *WPW*, graph I (opposite 36). Davies' graph is hypothetical; for a realistic assessment of the difficulties involved in attempting a statistically meaningful assessment of wealth distribution in a premodern economy, see Smith, "Material Lives," "Inequality." On the Greek terminology of wealth, see below, v.A.1. On Aristotle's embryonic and incomplete notion of "middling citizens" and their place in his political analysis, see Ober, "Aristotle's Political Sociology."

[65] Jones, *AD*, esp. 8–10, 23–37, 80–93; quote: 10. For further discussion of Jones' "middle-class" argument, see below, III.E.2, 4; V.D.2.

[66] Gomme, *Population*, Table 1, p. 26, suggests a rise from ca. 22,000 in 400 to ca. 28,000 in 323. Hansen, "Demographic Reflections," argues that the fourth-century population was quite stable; cf. idem, *Demography and Democracy*, esp. 9–13, 65. Barry S. Strauss, "Demography and Democracy in Fourth-Century B.C. Athens" (Paper delivered at the Annual Meeting of the American Philological Association, December 30, 1986), has argued for a rather steeper rise in population. For the argument that lower population after the Peloponnesian War had major political consequences, see Strauss, *AAPW*, esp. 81. Cf. below, III.E.1.

Furthermore, the taxpaying contingent of the fourth-century population was much smaller than Jones assumed. J. K. Davies, after a careful study of the Athenian upper classes, has convincingly argued that only about twelve hundred to two thousand Athenians had fortunes of about one talent (6,000 drachmas) or more and that a fortune of roughly this size would be required to live a life of leisure and to be liable for payment of war taxes. The rest of the citizens had to work for their living. The leisure-class population of two thousand (maximum) was much too small to have numerically dominated Athenian egalitarian political institutions, such as the Assembly or courts.[67]

Even though the leisure class was too small to control directly the democratic government, a common occupational interest and so a common "moderate" political outlook might be presumed to exist among those who were less than leisure class but well above poverty level. S. Perlman, for example, who took the existence of a large "middle class" at Athens more or less for granted, argued that its members were heavily involved in commerce and that they constituted a cohesive political interest group large and influential enough to keep the state on an even keel through most of the fourth century.[68] The existence of a commercial middle class, with an interest in state support of trade and in competition for markets with foreign nationals, was denied a half-century ago by J. Hasebroek, who argued that most of those involved in large-scale trading at Athens were metics (resident foreigners). Hasebroek's thesis on the number of citizens involved in trade may have been overstated, but his general conclusion that there was no cohesive commercial class of citizens to influence state trade policy is surely correct.[69] While there were certainly a good number of Athenians who were directly and indirectly involved in commerce, no evidence suggests that these persons constituted anything like a "class"

[67] Davies, WPW, 28–35. See below, III.E.1, 2, 4.

[68] Perlman, "Politicians," esp. 327, "Political Leadership," esp. 162–66; cf. de Laix, Probouleusis, 174–77, 191.

[69] Hasebroek, Trade and Politics. Hasebroek's thesis was challenged by, inter alios, Gomme, "Traders and Manufacturers," in Essays in Greek History and Literature (Oxford, 1937), 42–66; Thompson, "Athenian Investor"; Marianne Hansen, "Athenian Maritime Trade in the Fourth Century B.C. Operation and Finance," CM 35 (1984): 71–92. But cf. E. Erxleben, "Das Verhältnis des Handels zum Produktionsaufkommen in Attica im 5. und 4. Jh. v.u.Z.," Klio 57 (1975): 365–98; and the various essays collected in Trade in the Ancient Economy, esp. Cartledge, "Trade and Politics." A compromise (citizen traders were few, but this was a function more of the complexity of the trade than of Athenian distaste for trade) was suggested by H. Montgomery, " 'Merchants Fond of Corn.' Citizens and Foreigners in the Athenian Grain Trade," SO 61 (1986): 43–61. Cf. also below, VI.D.2.

(however one wants to define the term), had well-defined political goals, or were sufficiently numerous to influence the tenor of Athenian politics.[70] Most Athenians no doubt lived at a level somewhere between affluence and abject poverty, but their class interest, insofar as they had one, was that of persons who had to work for a living and who viewed themselves in relation to, and sometimes in opposition to, the leisured rich.

Economic factors alone are inadequate to explain Athenian sociopolitical stability, but one must keep the economic background in mind while searching for other answers. The empire (in the fifth century) and a surplus-generating slave population were indeed important. Athens also had major natural resources. The rich silver mines of south Attica were especially lucrative, but clay beds, marble quarries, and adequate (if unexceptional) agriculture contributed to the state's wealth. The fine harbors of Piraeus attracted a large transit trade as well as a large metic population.[71] Each of these resources contributed to the financial base of the democratic state which benefited directly through leasing of silver mines, collection of taxes on metics, and port duties.[72] The larger the revenues that could be collected from these various public sources, the less need there was to tax the wealthy citizens in order to support the political activity of the poor, and so (at least potentially) the lower the level of social tension. But by the fourth century, Athens' revenue from the various public sources was insufficient to keep the state solvent. The revenues of empire were gone, and silver production, disrupted in the war, apparently remained depressed until the 340s.[73] Consequently, the rich citizens had to support the democratic state, ideally through voluntary contributions, otherwise through taxation. The Athenians' ability to

[70] On the uselessness of the concept of "middle class" as an analytical concept for ancient social and political history, see Finley, *PAW*, 10–11 with n. 31; Davies, *DCG*, 36; Ste. Croix, *CSAGW*, 71–72, 120–33. Demosthenes (e.g., 18.46, 24.165) seems to have no notion of a middle class.

[71] On the place of natural resources in the economy of Athens, see Isager and Hansen, *Aspects*, 19–106; Ober, *FA*, 13–31; Osborne, *Demos*, 93–126. On metics: Whitehead, *Ideology*. Finley, *PAW*, 16, notes the importance of the large total Athenian population and territorial base and the silver of Laurion in Athenian political development; cf. Jones, *AD*, 93–96.

[72] On the difficult problem of the state revenues from the silver mines, see Hopper, "Attic Silver Mines," "The Laurion Mines: A Reconsideration," *Annual of the British School at Athens* 63 (1968): 293–326. Cf. Ober, *FA*, 28–30 (with literature cited). On Athenian revenues in general, see Andreades, *History*, 268–363; cf. Burke, "Lycurgan Finances."

[73] Silver production down until 340s: Hopper, "Attic Silver Mines," 215–16, 250–52; Ober, *FA*, 28–29.

extract wealth from sources other than the citizenry may therefore have buffered social tensions in the fifth century, but those tensions were never eliminated, and the loss of public revenues might have exacerbated class feeling in the period after 404. Furthermore, the economic advantages of Attica do not help to explain the Athenians' success in policymaking by direct democratic means.

C.6 FACE-TO-FACE SOCIETY

Recognition of the failure of material factors to explain social stability adequately, or decision making at all, may have been what led Finley to characterize Athens as "the model of a face-to-face society": a society whose members knew each other intimately and interacted with one another closely.[74] This knowledge and interaction led to an informal, but intense, training in public, political life and allowed the members of the society to work together toward common goals in a way that would be impossible for a group of strangers. The concept of the face-to-face society was borrowed by Finley from Peter Laslett's studies of pre-industrialized English village life and may indeed have much to tell us about the processes of social integration on the local level. Recent work on the demes (villages, townships, or urban neighborhoods) of Attica has emphasized the importance of the deme as a unit in which relationships between citizens necessarily crossed class lines and so helped to unify the interests of elite and non-elite citizens.[75]

As a factor in *local* social stability, the integrative function of village life should not be underestimated. But Finley's face-to-face model has serious flaws when extrapolated to the polis level. The polis of Athens was very much larger than a village, and the Athenian state was not constituted as a federation of villages. In order for true social stability to obtain, the elite of Athens had to be reconciled to the masses of

[74] Finley uses the analogy of a modern university community: *DAM* 17. Finley hinted at the face-to-face concept in "Athenian Demagogues," 9, 13, but it was more fully elaborated in his "Freedom of the Citizen," 23, *DAM*, 17–18, *PAW*, 28–29, 82–83. Quote: *DAM*, 17. Finley's face-to-face model has been picked up by, inter alios, Holmes, "Aristippus," 121.

[75] Finley (*PAW*, 28 n. 9) cites chapter 10 of Laslett, *Philosophy, Politics and Society* (Oxford, 1956); cf. also Laslett, *The World We Have Lost: England Before the Industrial Age²* (New York, 1973), 55–83. Demes: Hopper, *Basis*; Daviero-Rocchi, "Transformations," 36–40, 44–45; Whitehead, "Competitive Outlay," *Demes* 68–69, 85, 226–233, 248; Osborne, *Demos*, 64–92. Roussel, *Tribu et cité*, 157, suggests a similar integrative role may have been played by the phratries. Cf. the stress placed by Tocqueville on local communities as units that could create and maintain both the political cleavage and the consensus necessary for a democratic society, discussed by Lipset, "Political Sociology," 87–88.

Athens, and reconciliations on a local level, although good practice and arguably a valuable metaphor for the participants, were insufficient. When a rich Athenian entered the people's court as a litigant, he could not count on having even a single fellow demesman on the jury, and the rest of the jurors were likely to be strangers, with no particular reason to feel especially grateful to him for benefactions he may have performed for his home village.[76]

If the model of the face-to-face society is limited in the social sphere, it is even less useful in the political sphere. The demes did not provide a training ground for politically ambitious citizens. No doubt the experience of the deme assembly and participation in the public life of the deme generally was useful for the political education of the ordinary Athenian (cf. below, IV.B.2), but the deme assemblies did not make major policy.[77] The real political work of the state was done in the "national" Council, Assembly, and courtroom, and here each citizen had a history of intimate interaction with only a very small percentage of the participants. Exact population figures are unobtainable, but there were probably at least twenty thousand to forty thousand Athenian citizens through most of the fifth and fourth centuries. Thucydides (8.66.3) emphasizes the populousness of the polis and the fact that the members of the Athenian demos were *not* known to each other (*dia to megethos tēs poleōs kai dia tēn allēlōn agnōsian*) in explaining the success of the coup of 411, by which date war losses had considerably reduced the size of the citizen body.[78]

In support of his face-to-face model, Finley adduced the testimony of Aristotle's discussion of the proper size for the ideal society in the *Politics*.[79] Aristotle first notes the physical difficulties imposed by a large citizen body—who had the ability to be herald, other than Stentor, the famous great-voiced herald of the *Iliad*? (the same acoustical

[76] Humphreys, *Family*, 9, "Social Relations," esp. 350, and "Evolution of Legal Process," discusses the ramifications for Athenian law of changing the locus of public judgment from the village, where participants *did* have face-to-face relations, to the city, where they did not. Osborne, *Demos*, 64–65, points out the inappropriateness of Finley's face-to-face model on the polis level, but errs by assuming that local interactions are sufficient to explain the democracy; cf. Ober, Review of Whitehead, *Demes* and Osborne, *Demos*.

[77] On deme assemblies, see Whitehead, *Demes*, 86–120. Significantly, there was no pay for attending deme assemblies, or even for the major deme magistrates: ibid., 161.

[78] On the population of Athens, see the studies cited above, I.n.66 and below, III.E.1. On war losses, see Strauss, *AAPW*, 179–82.

[79] Finley, *DAM*, 17. Finley cites only *Pol.* 1326b3–7, but lines 8–25 are also highly germane to the question.

problem also occurred to Michels, see above, I.B). Aristotle then states that the citizen body must be limited in size so that the citizens will get to know one another personally and so become familiar with one another's qualities. This is necessary because the citizens must be able to judge one another's suitability for holding state offices. Aristotle's discussion of the demographic organization of the ideal state is in fact a strong argument *against* explaining Athenian democratic process in face-to-face terms. While Aristotle never gives absolute figures for his ideal state's citizen population, this passage and others show that it was obviously intended to be much smaller than Athens, where, as we have seen, most citizens did not know one another well. Aristotle's ideal citizens are intended to be only a small fraction of the total population of the polis: a leisured ruling elite whose members would make their living by extracting the surplus value of the labor of a population of "natural" slave farmers and noncitizen craftsmen and merchants. Unlike the Athenians, Aristotle's ideal citizens therefore would be able to devote themselves full time to education, military training, and political activity and so would come to know one another intimately.[80]

Aristotle's comments demonstrate that the face-to-face model is not anachronistic when applied to Greek philosophical thought and that it might indeed have been regarded as an ideal. But that ideal did not and could not pertain in Athens, where there were relatively great numbers of citizens, most of whom necessarily spent the majority of their time engaging in remunerative, nonpolitical activities. Aristotle was well aware of this; whatever his practical goals in writing the *Politics*, his ideal society was not intended as a blueprint for reforming the existing Athenian citizen population.[81] Unlike the ideal city of the *Politics*, which was to be "easy to take in at a glance" (*eusunoptos*: 1326b24), Athens remained an "imagined community" in that no one had ever seen the entire demos assembled; it was a political society that existed at the level of law and of ideology but not of personal acquaintance.[82]

[80] *Pol.* Books 7 and 8, esp. 1326a5–b25, 1329a17–1330a33, 1332b29–33, 1337a21–26; cf. Ober, "Aristotle's Political Sociology."

[81] On Aristotle's goals in writing the *Politics*, see Lord, *Aristotle: Politics* (Introduction), *Education and Culture*, 30–33. Cf. the essays collected in Lord, *Essays*.

[82] I have borrowed the idea of "imagined community" from Anderson, *Imagined Communities*, a study of modern nationalism that has much to say about political societies generally. See esp. 15–16: A nation is *imagined* "because the members of even the smallest nation will never know most of their fellow-members, meet them, or even hear of them, yet in the minds of each lives the image of their communion." Anderson (ibid., 15–16) contrasts this sort of community to "primordial villages of face-to-face contact."

C.7 GENIUS, CORPORATE AND INDIVIDUAL

Occasionally, writers have fallen back upon quasi-mystical explanations to account for "The Athenian Miracle." Some of these, such as the virtues of the clear Athenian air as a tonic leading to clarity of thought, we may pass over without further comment. But serious scholars have suggested that the Athenians were somehow innately better suited to democracy than other men. Gomme, for example, proposed that the Athenians "had an almost unique genius for democratic politics."[83] While not wishing to impugn the influence in human affairs of individual genius, or to deny the possibility that a society could provide a particularly good environment in which genius might be manifested, I do not think the Athenians were inherently more democratic than other peoples. Since it seems unlikely that any human group possesses a genetic propensity toward democracy, it is misleading to rely on expressions like "unique genius for democratic politics."

Nor can the stability of the democracy be attributed to the action of any individual genius, although the influence of certain individuals in the development of the democracy is undeniable (see below, II). While Cleisthenes and Pericles (for example) did much to establish and further the democratic form of government, the democracy would not have long outlived the latter had the Athenians not already developed a strong and viable social basis for political action.[84] Any explanation for the survival of the Athenian state must take into consideration the post-Periclean period, when there was no directing "genius" controlling affairs. The Athenian democracy should not be viewed as a clock devised and wound up by a master technician.

The present study is justified both by the theoretical implications of the Athenian example for testing Michels' Iron Law of Oligarchy and by the inadequacy of previous explanations of the stability of the Athenian social system and the functioning of direct democratic decision making. Despite the great quantity and high quality of scholarship on Athenian history, the key to Athens' success in maintaining a political

[83] Gomme, "Working," 24–25. But his comment there that the "genius" is demonstrated by the fact that the rich, both *vieux* and *nouveaux*, were not only prepared to take part in Assemblies, but were convinced "to obtain by demagogic arts the power which previously they had claimed by right of wealth and birth," is typically insightful.

[84] The tendency to enshrine Cleisthenes as the founder-genius is exemplified by Ehrenberg, "Origins," esp. 540–43. Cf. the criticisms by Finley, *Ancient History*, 93–99, of the Weberian "ideal type" of charismatic domination-leadership for the Greek polis in general and the Athenian democracy in particular.

system unique in its own time and labeled an impossibility in ours has continued to elude students of the classical world. I would suggest that the failure may be attributed to the habits of looking for the key in familiar but wrong places and of using the wrong analytical tools. Most investigators have (whether consciously or not) employed the assumptions of political pragmatism, liberal pluralism, or materialism. Hence the key has been sought for the most part in the relationships between "politicians," in the constitutional realm of individual rights and the state's powers, and in materialistic explanations of various sorts. Each of these approaches has shed some light, but collectively they have obscured what I take to be the real key: the mediating and integrative power of communication between citizens—especially between ordinary and elite citizens—in a language whose vocabulary consisted of symbols developed and deployed in public arenas: the peoples' courts, the Assembly, the theater, and the agora. This process of communication constitutes the "discourse of Athenian democracy." It was a primary factor in the promotion and maintenance of social harmony, and it made direct democratic decision making possible.

D. Premises and Methods

In addition to assuming the fundamental importance to democracy of relations between mass and elite, this study is grounded in six interlocking premises: (1) that politics is a social phenomenon; (2) that a synchronic approach can validly be used to study the sociopolitical history of Athens in the period ca. 403–322 B.C.; (3) that every individual has opinions about human nature, morality, and politics, and that some opinions are common to many people in any given society; (4) that communication is symbolic and that symbols derive in part from ideology; (5) that an individual's decisions, judgments, and actions are based, at least in part, on ideology and communication; and (6) that formal rhetoric in general, and the corpus of Attic orations in particular, provide examples of symbolic communication and can be used to reconstruct social opinions and principles and therefore can help us to understand the ideology of the Athenian citizenry. These six premises, and my basis for adopting them, are stated more formally in the following paragraphs.

1. "Politics is a cultural phenomenon, embedded in society; it is impossible to understand the political decisions or actions of either masses or elite leaders outside of their social context."

While it has been suggested that Greek political thought and action can be can be understood in isolation from the social matrix of "private life"—indeed that the Greeks consciously chose to act according to political principles and to reject the private sphere—the value of looking at ancient politics in a social context has been adequately demonstrated by Finley, among others.[85] The close relationship between politics and social structure seems to be a central assumption of all ancient political philosophers; Aristotle's *Politics*, for example, is explicitly predicated upon a series of correlations between social groups and politics.[86]

2. "A synchronic approach can be valid when attempting a social historical analysis; and the period ca. 403–322 B.C. can be treated as a chronological unit for the purposes of analyzing mass-elite relations."

On the general relationship between synchronicity and analysis we may note the work of William Dray, a philosopher of history who has argued that when historians engage in analysis they refer to periods rather than moments and that historical writing (even supposedly "pure" narrative) is invariably analytical.[87] The social historian of antiquity typically deals with relatively long periods; an extreme example is R. MacMullen's *Roman Social Relations, 50 B.C.–A.D. 284*, which treats a period of over three centuries as a unit.[88] The justification for treating extensive eras as analytical units is typically the scarcity of useful sources, undeniably a factor for all periods of ancient Greek his-

[85] R. Sealey has repeatedly argued that the motivation of Athenian political actors was pragmatic and personal and that political change was not a function of social class conflict or tension; see, for example, his "Athens after the Social War," "Callistratos of Aphidna," *Athenian Republic*, 148. For an attempt to elevate political life above and separate it from the social matrix, see Paul A. Rahe, "The Primacy of Politics in Classical Greece," *American Historical Review* 89 (1984): 265–93. A somewhat similar approach is taken by Meier, *Anthropologie*, 7–26, but cf. also 40–44: the inseparability of society and politics. Embedded nature of politics in society: Finley, *PAW*, esp. 8–9; cf. Vernant, "Remarks," 73; Daviero-Rocchi, "Transformations"; Osborne, *Demos*, 8–10; Lipset, "Political Sociology," esp. 83; Washburn, *Political Sociology*, esp. 108; Foucault, *History*, 1. Humphreys, *Family*, 1–32, 61–75, is an excellent introduction to the question of the relationship between public political life and private life in Athens. She notes that a conscious attempt was made by the democratic polis to exclude the influence of private interests and loyalties from political contexts; but this is very different from claiming that private life was unimportant.

[86] Ober, "Aristotle's Political Sociology"; cf. the somewhat more extreme comments of Holmes, "Aristippus," esp. 116, who suggests that Plato and Aristotle (inter alios) made no distinction between state and society.

[87] W. Dray, "Narrative versus Analysis in History" (Paper read at North Carolina State University, 1983): idem, "On the Nature and Role of Narrative in History," *History and Theory* (1971): 153–71; idem, "Point of View in History," *Clio* (1978): 265–83. Cf. the comments of Humphreys, "Law as Discourse," 257–59, on the need to integrate structuralist and diachronic approaches.

[88] New Haven, 1974.

tory, although less so for fourth-century Athens than for many others (see below, I.E). The danger remains that a synchronic approach may treat a rapidly evolving society as static and thereby misrepresent the dynamic social reality. Hence, it is incumbent on historians to justify their assumptions that synchronic social analysis of a relatively long period can yield meaningful results.

Chapter II will trace the evolution of the constitutional and institutional relationship between mass and elite in the sixth through the fourth centuries B.C., but the detailed analysis of sociopolitical interaction in Chapters III–VII will concentrate on the period from the end of the Peloponnesian War to the end of Athenian independence after the Lamian War (403–322 B.C.). There seems no fundamental demographic problem with treating the period 403–322 synchronically, once we are aware of the probability that the Athenian citizen population grew during this period. We cannot demonstrate either the rate or steadiness of demographic growth, but it was in any case organic; there was no large new body of citizens added after 403 who might have imported radically different cultural or social assumptions.[89] Furthermore, despite some constitutional changes, the period can reasonably be treated as a unit in terms of political development, as it was by the contemporary author of the Aristotelian *Constitution of Athens* (*AP* 41.2). In terms of sources, the period is characterized by the corpus of Attic orators (cf. below, I.E); genuine legal and political orations are rare before this period and nonexistent after it. The subject matter of the orations varies, but there is no dramatic change in either form or general content over the course of the period. K. J. Dover, who analyzed Athenian "popular morality" on the basis of the orations and of Attic comedy, argued for a high degree of continuity in social attitudes from the late fifth through the late fourth centuries.[90] The corpus of speeches will provide my most important texts. While I have attempted to pay close attention to the chronological context of each text, I have come to a conclusion similar to Dover's: the attitudes toward the relations between mass and elite expressed in the speeches throughout this period seem quite consistent over time. I would not deny that those attitudes evolved in the course of the era, but a signif-

[89] Whitehead, "Thousand New Athenians," has argued that about a thousand metics were granted citizenship after the democratic revolution of 404/3, but this depends on a controversial reading of *IG* II² 10; see below, II.n.103. On the general tendency of the Athenians not to make many new citizens in the fourth century, see Hansen, "Demographic Reflections," and below, VI.C.2.

[90] Dover, *GPM*, esp. 30–32. For an alternative view, that there was rapid evolution in Athenian social attitudes from 380–330, see Davies, *DCG*, 165–87.

icant degree of ideological continuity can be demonstrated, and the
period can therefore be treated as a unit for purposes of sociopolitical
analysis.

3. "Each member of any given community makes assumptions about
human nature and behavior, has opinions on morality and ethics, and
holds some general political principles; those assumptions, opinions,
and principles which are common to the great majority of those members are best described as ideology."

Attempting to prove the first part of this statement rigorously would
take us much further into epistemology, moral philosophy, and cognitive psychology than I am prepared to go here; I hope most readers
will be willing to accept it at face value. My definition of ideology is
similar to that of Finley, who suggests that ideology is "the matrix of
attitudes and beliefs out of which people normally respond to the
need for action, . . . without a process of ratiocination leading them
back to the attitudinal roots or justification of their response . . . ," or
"the combination of beliefs and attitudes, often unformulated or subconscious and certainly neither coherent nor necessarily consistent,
which underlay . . . thinking and . . . behaviour."[91] Ideology is hence
distinct from philosophy and theory in that it is not necessarily clearly
articulated, logically consistent, or *consciously* employed in the decision-
making process. To speak of Athenian democratic ideology, then, is
not to assume the existence of a body of democratic theory; as has
often been pointed out, there was no philosophically articulated democratic theory in fifth- or fourth-century Athens.[92] On the other hand,
I follow Brent Shaw in defining ideology as "a more organized and
structurally consistent set of ideas" than mere prejudices.[93]

[91] Finley, *Authority and Legitimacy*, 17; cf. his discussions of ideology in *PAW*, 122–
41, *Ancient History*, 4–5.

[92] Jones, *AD*, 41–72, and Havelock, *Liberal Temper*, are notable examples of attempts to "reconstruct" democratic theory. The futility of this exercise is noted by
Finley, "Athenian Demagogues," 9, *PAW*, 124–25 with n. 7. Loraux, *Invention*, 173–
80, 204–206, finds it odd that the democratic Athenians failed to develop a coherent and systematic theory of democracy, but cf. Maio, "*Politeia*," 18–19 n. 7, who
states, correctly I think, that the lack of theory is not surprising, since "one defends
his faith vigorously . . . when it is under general attack; in fourth-century Athens,
the democratic faith was under no such attack."

[93] Shaw, " 'Eaters'," 5. Dover, *GPM*, while an important collection of materials on
Athenian social attitudes, seems to tend in the latter direction, to concentrate on
prejudices rather than integrated sets of ideas, and therefore to obscure important
nuances in Athenian attitudes that were used in political decision making. For a
general criticism of Dover's implicit assumption that because popular morality was
not rationally thought out, it was also completely without structure, see Adkins,
"Problems." The study of "Begriffsgeschichte" pioneered by C. Meier and his fol-

Ideology, therefore, consists of a set of ideas sufficiently well organized to facilitate decision and action. Political ideology is the subset of ideology that relates to the political sphere. P. C. Washburn offers a concise conceptualization of political ideology as "individuals' relatively stable, more or less integrated set of beliefs, values, feelings, and attitudes about the nature of human beings and society and their associated orientations toward the existing distribution of social rewards and the uses of power and authority to create, maintain, or change them."[94] Political ideology is therefore an important part of the interior context that will help a subject to judge and to formulate an appropriate response on the political plane to changes in the exterior environment. In short, it defines how one is likely to react to events.

The second part of the statement, that one may speak of an ideology common to most members of a community, may be more problematic but should need no elaborate defense. The very term "community" implies some minimal level of shared values, and a degree of commonality of values in every functioning society is assumed not only by modern sociologists but by ancient historians, philosophers, and orators.[95] The main problem comes in determining the extent and specificity of shared ideology. In particular, does ideology transcend the gulf between mass and elite? I agree with Chester G. Starr and other scholars that at least to some degree it must.[96] It is, however, dangerous to assume too much ideological continuity, and texts written by and for

---

lowers takes a middle ground between the study of popular ideologies and the traditional "history of ideas" approach; cf. the comments of Raaflaub, "Freien Bürgers Recht," 13.

[94] Washburn, *Political Sociology*, 234–67; quote: 261.

[95] See, for example, Aristot. *Rhet.* 1368b7–9: "law" (*nomos*) is either individual (*idios*), in which case it is written, or common (*koinos*); the latter is unwritten and is "that which everyone agrees is right" (*para pasin homologeisthai dokei*). On Isocrates' and Plato's notion of the ethos of a community, see Jaeger, *Paideia*, iii.119–20, ii.238; cf. Demosthenes 24.121 (cited above). The difficulty of recovering this "common law" or ethos is noted by Osborne, *Demos*, 66; Gruen, *Hellenistic World*, I.250.

[96] Starr, *Awakening*, 88–89, *Individual and Community*, 61. See also Finley, *PAW*, 124–26, "Was Greek Civilization," 154; Forrest, *EGD*, 21–36; Dover, *GPM*, 39–40 (overstating the case, I think). Washburn, *Political Sociology*, 245–46, cites J. Huber and W. H. Form, *Income and Ideology* (New York, 1973), who suggest that the ideology of privileged Americans is quite different from that of poor citizens. The rich tend to believe more than the poor that the economic system's rewards are distributed justly and that voting is meaningful. But Washburn (*Political Sociology*, 245–46) also notes that divergent social ideals have not been accompanied by overt sociopolitical conflict in part because particular "ideological differences are often submerged beneath apparent agreement with general American values."

elite audiences must be treated differently from texts written by the elite for mass audiences. Furthermore, we must attempt to discover the origins of Athenian political ideology and to locate its operational significance within the communication between Athenian citizen masses and elites. Is popular political ideology the result of a "trickle down" of ideas and values from the elite? Is it a product of the experience and self-definition of the masses? Whose interest does it serve? Many traditional Marxists (who regard ideology as the ideas of the dominant class, used to promote false consciousness among the lower classes) and some students of Greek aristocratic culture assume that ideology is indeed a creation of the elite. But my formulation, which has much in common with the view of ideology developed by the structural Marxist Louis Althusser, raises the possibility that ideology is the locus of a struggle between mass and elite conceptions and images, a struggle that has the potential to transform institutional structures.[97]

4. "Communication between members of a society, especially in the context of political decision making, will make use of symbols (metaphors, signs) which refer to and derive from ideology."

The theoretical basis for this statement ultimately derives from a semiotic model of cognitive psychology that assumes that the human mind works through the process of analogy by means of symbols or metaphors. Thought and perception, and therefore language, are symbolic and metaphoric; thus, communication is based on complex and intertwined symbolic references and cross-references. Communication is never simple, since symbols are not static and refer to other symbols. The meaning of words, sentences, images, and so on changes depending on the broader context, since the interpretation of any given symbol depends on associating it with other symbols. Semiotic theory therefore suggests that the meaning of a text lies not only in the writer's original intention but in its "discourse," which includes the text's structure and context as well as its content. The interaction be-

---

[97] Cf. the useful discussion of Loraux, *Invention*, 170, 330–37, and below, VII.G.2. For Althusser on ideology, see L. Althusser, *Essays on Ideology* (London, 1971), esp. 32–60 on the inseparability of the ideological from "the material" in human action and on the difference between ideology and ideological state apparatuses (educational and religious institutions, etc.). Cf. the discussion and criticism of T. Benton, *The Rise and Fall of Structural Marxism: Althusser and His Influence* (London and Basingstoke, 1984), esp. 45–49, 96–107: "Ideology [for Althusser] has its own reality, it is not reducible to 'consciousness' which may be 'true' or 'false,' so that ideological struggle may now be thought of as itself 'real' struggle to transform institutional structures and social practices, rather than as an exercise in the 'correction of illusions' " (106).

tween receptor (reader or auditor) and text is also part of discourse, since each reader construes the text's meaning according to his or her own symbol-network.[98]

The general principle of communication as discourse should raise few problems for anyone who agrees that the interpretation of a metaphorical message is affected by the frame of reference employed by both sender and receiver and by the relationship between them. Herodotus (5.92) provides a good example of this process in the story of Periander, tyrant of Corinth, who sent a messenger to Thrasybulus of Miletus to learn the secrets of a successful tyranny. Thrasybulus refused to speak to the messenger of political matters, but took him for a walk through a grain field where he lopped off the heads of the tallest stalks with his stick. The baffled messenger reported back to Periander that he had failed to learn anything useful and described the walk in the field. Periander immediately grasped the meaning and proceeded to put the lesson into action by eliminating the most prominent citizens of Corinth. Thrasybulus' metaphorical message was inexplicable to the messenger, who lacked a proper frame of reference. Periander understood it because he shared a common frame of reference with Thrasybulus. But the message remains subject to different interpretations—did Thrasybulus advise killing the highest people, or suppressing them in some other way? Of course the message might have been "read" very differently by someone with a different frame of reference, for example an agronomist.

5. "An individual's decisions, actions, and judgment of his or her fellows will be based, at least in part, upon ideology and symbolic communication."

I suggested in point 3 that the Athenian citizens, like members of other communities, shared a common ideology. Expressed, like all other ideas, in terms of groups of symbols, this ideology provided a common metaphorical frame of reference—a mutually agreed upon "internal context"—by which the citizenry responded to events or ideas. Hence, a public speaker attempting to persuade the citizenry to act in a certain way might employ metaphors referential to that common ideology, in the hope of evoking a specific response from his audience. The text of every oration was a matrix of many symbols that operated at various levels, and no speaker could anticipate exactly how

[98] J. Culler, *The Pursuit of Signs: Semiotics, Literature, Deconstruction* (Ithaca, 1981), is a good general introduction. Bowles and Gintis, *Democracy and Capitalism*, 152–63, is an excellent discussion of the relationship of discourse to social struggle. For the relationship of semiotic theory to systems theory in a political context, see Luhmann, *Differentiation*, 166–89.

each member of the audience would react to each symbol. The expert
public orators of Athens were extremely skilled at manipulating symbols, but communication is not completely dependent on conscious attempts by a speaker to evoke a specific response in his auditor. Much
of the communication that went on between the orator and his audience may have operated at an unconscious level, but it was no less
significant for that.

The idea that Athenian social and political decisions, actions, and
judgments were the products of ideology and discourse functioning
within the environment of the democratic political order and in response to external events is the central organizing principle of this
study. The employment of an analysis based on communication and
discourse seems justified in light of the failure to explain the democracy by theories that assume that Athenian political action and social
relations were motivated largely by a rational assessment of clearly
understood alternatives. This rationalist assumption has tended to
lead to Finley's "constitutional-law trap." I am in agreement with those
who have argued recently that the study of constitutional arrangements and other formal institutions is a dead end and that without an
understanding of the attitudes and values that created and maintained
institutions, ancient social and political life will remain indecipher-
able.[99] Therefore, while recognizing the danger that Goethe notes in
Faust (lines 577–79), of the *Zeitgeist* being a mere reflection of the mind
that perceives it, I hope that a study of the Athenian climate of opinion—of ideology and discourse—may offer some new insights into
Athenian political and social life.

6. "Formal rhetoric in general, and the corpus of Attic orations in
particular, provides examples of the symbolic communication of point
4; and hence for reconstructing the ideology of point 3; and therefore
for understanding the Athenian citizens' decisions, judgments, and actions in regard to their fellows."

Recent critical theory has concentrated on the concept of rhetoric,
the form in which content is cast, as an important principle that can
be usefully applied to any text, literary or otherwise.[100] The form of
any text may well help to reveal the ideology of the society that produced it, but I am not in the position of having to prove that general

---

[99] E.g., Connor, "Athenian Council," 33, 39; Finley, *Authority and Legitimacy*; Maio,
"*Politeia*," 19 with n. 9 (citing Finley, *DAM*); Whitehead, *Demes*, 251. Cf. above, I.nn.
49, 50.

[100] For an early statement along these lines, see Bryant, "Aspects II"; cf. C. Per-
elman, *The Realm of Rhetoric*, trans. by William Kluback (Notre Dame, Indiana,
1982), esp. 153–62.

proposition, since the ancient sources most important to my argument are rhetorical in the more narrow, traditional sense of the term.

E. Rhetoric

The corpus of Attic orators provides a particularly valuable set of texts for analysis of mass-elite ideology. Most ancient texts were written by elites, specifically for an elite readership. Many of these "elite/elite" texts deal with the question of relations between mass and elite, but the attitudes and opinions that Thucydides or Plato, for example, attributed to the Athenian citizen masses were conditioned by their own elite frame of reference and that of their probable audience. While elite authors may not have intended to mislead their expected audience of elite readers about popular ideology, they were not directly accountable to non-elite critics. The orators were certainly members of the elite (see below, III.C), but they wrote most of their speeches for oral delivery to a mass audience, generally either a large jury or an Assembly. Furthermore, the overt purpose of most orations was to persuade the mass audience to act—specifically, to vote—in a particular way. As Aristotle clearly recognized, an orator who wishes to persuade a mass audience must accommodate himself to the ethos—the ideology—of his audience. He must therefore in general speak well of what the audience thinks is good and ill of what the audience thinks is evil. He will present his own behavior and character as conforming to the values of his audience, his opponent's as failing to conform.[101] The tendency of orators to say whatever they believed might please their audience was considered reprehensible by elite political philosophers, who thought a speaker's responsibility was to say what is true and necessary, not what is pleasant.[102] But at the practical level of discourse in

[101] Accommodating oneself to the audience's opinions: Aristot. *Rhet.* 1367b7–12, 1390a25–27, 1395b1–11, 1395b27–1396a3, 1415b28–32; presenting one's own character and behavior as proper and one's opponent's as improper: *Rhet.* 1377b20–1378a3, 1415a28–1415b1, 1416a4–1417a8. See also the similar comments by the closely contemporary Ps–Aristotle *Rhetoric for Alexander* 29.1436b16ff., 34.1439b15–36, 1440a25–b1; 37.1441b36–1442a14, 1443b14–21, 1444b35–1445a29, with the discussion of Sattler, "Conception of *Ethos*," esp. 56–60. Cf. the succinct statement of Bryant, "Rhetoric," 413: the function of rhetoric is "the function of adjusting ideas to people and of people to ideas."

[102] E.g., Aristot. *Rhet.* 1354a1–31, 1395b27–1396a3; 1404a1–8; Plato *Gorgias* 452c–454b, 462b–c, *Phaedrus* 260a, *Republic* 6.493a–c; Thuc. 2.65.8–12; Isoc. 1.36. The political orators themselves attacked this habit; see below, VII.E.4. Modern admirers and students of rhetoric have attempted to refute the charge that rhetoric is mere flattery; see Jaeger, *Paideia*, II.71; Bryant, "Aspects I." Cf. also III.D.2.

the courtroom and the Assembly, the orator had to conform to his audience's ideology or face the consequences: losing votes or being ignored.

When addressing a mass audience, the Athenian orator used symbols, in the form of modes of address and metaphors, that derived from and referred to the common ideological frame of reference of his listeners. At least some metaphors became standardized and can be described as *topoi*. Rhetorical topoi were repeated by different orators over time; they were therefore familiar but certainly not empty of content. Indeed, topoi were reiterated precisely because of their symbolic value and demonstrated power to influence an audience. It would be reductionist to suppose that every comment in an oration derives immediately from popular ideology, but we may suppose that skilled and experienced speakers would avoid making comments that they thought were likely to contradict deeply held popular convictions.[103] It is therefore possible to analyze the collected orations of the Attic orators to discover the sorts of symbols that were employed frequently and to reconstruct the political ideology of the citizen masses on the basis of these symbols.[104]

In the absence of a large collection of texts written by ordinary Athenians and for a mass audience, analysis of rhetoric offers our best hope for understanding the ideological roots of Athenian political organization and action. But only a small fraction of the speeches delivered in Athens were ever published, and probably less than 10 percent of these have survived. Furthermore, the corpus does not offer a random sample of Attic oratory.[105] The selection we have is, however, a

[103] Aristotle (*Rhet.* 1403b9–13) points out that persuasion results from the three proofs: (1) the judges are affected in some way, (2) they consider the speaker to be of a certain character, or (3) something is demonstrated. The last is not necessarily ideology-dependent. Adkins, "Problems," 145–47, notes that there may be a general flow of philosophical and other "non-popular" ideas into the orators' speeches; no doubt this is so, but cf. below, VII.G.2. It is also necessary to keep in mind that ideology is complex and (relative to philosophy) inconsistent; the orator may appeal to different aspects of popular ideology as it suits his purposes. Consider the different treatment of the rich in Dem. 20 and 21—the former in support of a rich man's privileges, the latter an attack on a rich man's hubris.

[104] On this general method, see Ober, *FA*, 5–6; cf. Dover, *GPM*, esp. 6; Davies, *DCG*, 124; Finley, "Freedom of the Citizen," 10; Loraux, *Invention*, 176: ". . . the only texts genuinely inspired by democratic thinking are those of the fourth-century orators. . . ." On the importance of looking at groups of documents collectively, see Finley, *Ancient History*, 44–45 (speaking of epigraphy).

[105] Over 1,700 speeches were attributed in antiquity to the ten best known Attic orators alone: Bonner, *Lawyers*, 4. Of this number we have about 140 (see Appendix). On the very small number of deliberative speeches preserved, see Hansen,

particularly valuable subset of the universe of all Athenian orations. We seldom know whether a particular speech was successful or not, but the surviving corpus contains primarily the works of extraordinarily skillful and successful orators, men whose reputations, and sometimes lives, rested upon their ability to manipulate symbols to good advantage. Furthermore, most (perhaps all) of the extant legal orations were prepared by and/or for elite litigants. Although it would be very instructive to know how a non-elite Athenian litigant addressed a jury, a reasonable assumption is that the elite litigant, facing a mass jury, had a particularly pressing need to appeal to a common ideology.

In most cases we can assume that the orator's primary motive for using any given rhetorical tactic is selfish—the desire to persuade the members of his audience to vote in his favor. Yet, as I will argue, speeches delivered by elite Athenians to mass audiences had a social function that transcended the individual motives of the speakers. Along with drama in the theater and gossip in the streets, public oratory, in the courts and the Assembly, was the most important form of ongoing verbal communication between ordinary and elite Athenians. Formal rhetoric was therefore a primary means by which mass-elite relations could be discussed publicly. Communication may be both a means to an end and an important end in itself. Through oratory the underlying political ideology was manifested in specific sets of symbols and thus was made operative at the level of collective action. Therefore, public rhetoric not only helps us to define Athenian political ideology, it was instrumental in the regulation of mass-elite relations for the Athenians themselves.

The approach I have suggested offers the advantage of treating rhetorical texts at the level of image and appearances, which were recognized by Aristotle (*Rhet.* 1404a1–12) as the defining characteristics of practical rhetoric.[106] Modern students of Athenian history, when they have used rhetoric for anything beyond mining speeches for nug-

---

"Two Notes on Demosthenes." For theories about how lost speeches might have differed in form from the corpus speeches, see, for example, Adams, "Demosthenes Pamphlets," 15–16, who suggests that lost extemporaneous deliberative speeches would contain more personal comments than the few we have, which were all apparently written in advance. Bonner, "Wit and Humor," suggests that lost forensic speeches which were not written by logographers may have made more use of humor than the existing speeches.

[106] Thus, there is no *a priori* reason to assume that an orator's description of, for example, his opponent's motives was intended to correspond to an objectively verifiable reality, as there is, for example, reason to suppose that Thucydides' descriptions of events were. Cf. the comments of Cawkwell, *Philip*, 19; cited approvingly by Finley, *Ancient History*, 81.

gets of information regarding events, have often taken a literalist approach, supposing that speeches are a more or less accurate mirror of
social and political reality. This has, I think, led to some fairly serious
errors. On the one hand, there is the tendency to take (for example)
Demosthenes' description of Aeschines' background at face value. But
perhaps more damaging (because less obviously misdirected) is the assumption that (for example) when wealthy litigants address jurors as
economic equals, the jurors must have been wealthy.[107] I will attempt
to demonstrate in the body of this study that a litigant may cast both
himself and the jury in roles that are at variance with reality. But that
does not necessarily mean that speakers were consciously attempting
to deceive or that jurymen were gullible. Rather, oratorical discourse
stimulated two kinds of responses. Not only did it reveal a social or
political reality, but it also produced a response at the level of image
and symbol. The juryman who was treated as wealthy by the litigant
might temper the action he would otherwise have taken on the basis
of existing class or status inequality, by operating on the level of the
symbolic equality that the litigant proposed. Once again, we must keep
in mind the interactive and dynamic nature of the texts we hope to
understand.

The orators I cite most often in this study—Lysias, Andocides, Isocrates, Isaeus, Demosthenes, Aeschines, Hyperides, Dinarchus, and Lycurgus—all flourished between 404 and 322 B.C. We know by far the
most about the life of Demosthenes, because of the large number of
speeches preserved under his name and because of Plutarch's *Life of
Demosthenes*. The social backgrounds of the orators, insofar as they can
be reconstructed, are considered in Chapter III(C). We also have some
rather scanty fragments of speeches by these and other orators from
the same period, but fragments are somewhat less useful than whole
speeches since the context is usually lost.

From the second half of the fifth century we have the speeches recorded in Thucydides' *History* and several speeches and rhetorical exercises by the logographer and oligarchic mastermind, Antiphon.
None of these was demonstrably written for presentation to a mass
audience, but they purport to be real and take the form of genuine

---

[107] See below, III.E.4. The errors of a piecemeal approach to literature generally
are pointed out by Shaw, " 'Eaters'," 25–26, who emphasizes the need to reach beneath the surface of the text for "a comprehension of the dynamics of the whole
mental structure behind it." Loraux, *Invention*, esp. 338, is a fine example of a study
that refuses to treat texts (in this case funeral orations) as a simple description of
reality.

speeches. Of particular interest among the Thucydidean speeches are Pericles' Funeral Oration, the speeches delivered to the Athenian Assembly (by Pericles, Cleon, Diodotus, Alcibiades, and Nicias), and the speeches of the Syracusan politicians Hermocrates and Athenagoras before the democratic Assembly of Syracuse (see Appendix). The relationship of the speeches in Thucydides to the speeches actually delivered (and in the cases of the Funeral Oration and Athenian Assembly speeches, at least, there can be little doubt that originals really were delivered) has been much debated, but no scholarly consensus on the issue has emerged.[108] I have attempted to avoid basing statements about Athenian ideology on passages from fifth-century speeches alone. On the other hand, the ideological underpinning sometimes seems very similar to that of genuine fourth-century orations, and some conclusions about fourth-century ideology may be extrapolated back at least as far as the latter part of the fifth century.

Aristotle (*Rhet.* Book 3) subdivided rhetoric into deliberative (political decision making), forensic (legal), and epideictic (display); the different conditions under which each type of speech was delivered affected the rhetorical tactics of the speaker and are detailed in Chapter III. Deliberative speeches include those delivered in the Assembly and Council. The surviving forensic speeches may be subdivided into those prepared for political trials (usually written and delivered by an expert politician) and those for private trials. The latter sort was usually written by a professional speechwriter (logographer), then memorized and delivered by his wealthy client.[109] Display speeches include public funeral orations—which were delivered before a mass Athenian audience—and speeches prepared by professional rhetoricians as examples of eloquence—which were not. Some of the latter merge into the category of political pamphlets, which were probably meant to be read privately or aloud to a small elite audience. Also contained in the corpus are some letters and nonpublic texts.

Each of the various subgenres may be treated somewhat differently for ideological analysis. Among epideictic speeches, the public funeral orations can be used to look at general ideological notions but are often less useful than deliberative and forensic speeches for the par-

---

[108] The literature on this question, much of which hinges on the interpretation of Thuc. 1.22, is vast. For an introduction to some of the main lines of the debate, see Kennedy, "Focusing of Arguments," 131–35; Andrewes, "Mytilene"; P. A. Stadter, ed., *The Speeches in Thucydides* (Chapel Hill, 1973).

[109] See Lavency, *Aspects*, esp. 195–98; Usher, "Lysias."

ticular purpose of analyzing mass-elite relations.[110] Some epideictic
speeches, such as Isocrates' *In Praise of Helen*, seem to be purely es-
thetic; I have not made much use of these. Epideictic speeches written
as political pamphlets must be used with considerable care, as they fall
into the category of elite/elite literature. Many of Isocrates' speeches
are of this sort. On the other hand, in at least some of his pamphlet/
speeches, Isocrates seems to have hoped to influence a fairly broad
spectrum of Athenian opinion, and these speeches often share at least
some of the ideological presuppositions of speeches written for mass
audiences.[111] As in the case of the speeches of Antiphon and Thucydides, Isocrates' pamphlets will be used primarily to reinforce arguments drawn on the basis of less problematic material. The same general considerations apply to Plato's *Apology of Socrates*.

Deliberative and forensic speeches are, collectively, the most useful,
but the various subcategories may serve somewhat different purposes.
Private trial orations are important for investigating social relations.
Deliberative and political trial orations, which I will refer to generically
as "political rhetoric," also refer to the social background, but they are
particularly informative about the relationship between elite politicians and their mass audiences. The divergences between the rhetorical tactics employed by private litigants and politicians have much to
tell us about the role of the politician in the Athenian state.

Debate over the authorship of some speeches stretches back to antiquity. Many of the private trial speeches assigned in the manuscripts
to Lysias and Demosthenes, for example, have been attributed by
scholars to other authors. In some cases the argument for different
authorship is very strong, in others considerably less so.[112] But the au-

[110] For a thorough treatment of public funeral orations, see Loraux, *Invention*,
who warns (11) against the error of considering them a simple subset of epideictic
oratory.

[111] For a review of the literature on Isocrates' political opinions and intentions,
see Ober, "Views," 119 n. 4; R. A. Moysey, "Isocrates' *On the Peace*: Rhetorical Exercise or Political Advice?" *AJAH* 1 (1982): 118–127 (arguing for the latter position).

[112] For a review of some major controversies, see Dover, *GPM*, 8–10. Dover, *Lysias*, attacks the authenticity of many of the speeches in the Lysian corpus partly on
the grounds that they are written in different styles with different voices. But Aristotle (*Rhet.* 1408a25–32) implies that the good speechwriter must be able to imitate
the speaking patterns of his clients, noting that the "rustic" (*agroikos*) will speak
differently from the "educated man" (*pepaideumenos*). Cf. C. D. Benson, *Chaucer's
Drama of Style: Poetic Variety and Contrast in the Canterbury Tales* (Chapel Hill, 1986),
esp. 20–22, who shows that Chaucer used strikingly different poetic styles and
voices in the various Tales. Some of the forensic speeches in the Demosthenic corpus were certainly not by Demosthenes, but in all likelihood, all were written by

thorship, especially of private trial orations, is seldom of great moment to my argument. As long as the speech in question was actually written for delivery to a mass audience during the period we are concerned with, it can be used for ideological analysis. I have assumed throughout that the speeches as we have them are similar in content and organization to the form in which they were delivered. Some speeches were no doubt revised before publication, but in general the revision probably was not serious enough to affect the argument materially.[113]

The date of delivery of many speeches can be determined quite closely on the basis of internal or external evidence. Others, which are less precisely datable, can be bracketed within a decade or so.[114] Once again, although chronological context may be very significant in some instances, the synchronic assumption I have made above (I.D, point 2) may justify using speeches that cannot be precisely dated. The synchronic assumption is also important when we consider the uneven distribution of speeches across the period 403–322. For example, among dated speeches, we have an average of over twice as many per annum in the period 355–338 (2.2) as in 377–356 (1.0), and 14 of the total of 17 fourth-century Assembly speeches date to the former period (Appendix: Table 1). The Appendix lists the speeches of the corpus by author, according to the traditional numbering system. The subgenre and date (if known) of each speech is indicated, along with any contextual considerations (in terms of authorship, chronology, and so on) that appear to me to be particularly relevant.

---

fourth-century orators; see, for example, Hansen, 'Apagoge', 145, citing the communis opinio on this issue.

[113] Argument from probability suggests that political orators and logographers would be unlikely to publish speeches (which, at least in the case of Demosthenes were published in his own life: Plut. Demosthenes 11) that were wildly different from the speeches they delivered, for fear of being mocked by their opponents for it, or losing clients if they were found out. In some cases we can cross-reference, by looking at speeches delivered by opponents, e.g., Dem. 19 and Aesch. 2; Dem. 18 and Aesch. 3. Statements about what an opponent will say are not proof of revision: cf. Aristot. Rhet. 1418b9–11. Burke, "Character Denigration," 128 with n. 46, suggests that the contents of major political trial speeches may have been made public in advance. On the general question of relationship of text to original speech, see Kennedy, Art of Persuasion, 206; Adams, "Demosthenes Pamphlets"; Usher, "Lysias"; Hansen, "Two Notes on Demosthenes"; E. M. Carawan, "Erotesis: Interrogation in the Courts of Fourth-Century Athens," GRBS 24 (1983): 209–226.

[114] On dates for speeches, see, in general Blass, AB; Jebb, Attic Orators; Schaefer, Demosthenes; Wyse, Isaios; Dover, Lysias; Kennedy, Art of Persuasion; Sealey, "Dionysius"; and the introductions to the Loeb and Budé editions. Cf. Appendix.

F. Other Primary Sources

While rhetorical texts provide my primary source material, a variety of other sorts of texts will be cited. Among ancient philosophical treatises, the most important for our purposes are Aristotle's *Politics* and *Rhetoric*. Aristotle's analyses of political sociology in the *Politics* and of the purposes, strategies, and conditions of public oratory in the *Rhetoric* are extremely valuable, both for his insights into mass-elite relations and for the context of those relations. In many ways, Aristotle was hostile to democracy and he wrote for an elite audience. Nevertheless, he was very aware of the power of mass ideology. His theoretical analysis of "radical" democracy provides a counterpoint to my own reading.[115]

Tragedy and comedy, like public orations, were written for presentation to a mass audience (cf. below, III.E.6). The theater offered a forum in which Athenians could attempt to explain themselves to themselves and could comment upon their own society.[116] The Attic dramatists worked on a broader canvas and dealt with a wider range of human (and divine) relationships than did the orators, and the function and goals of playwrights may not have been been explicitly and immediately political.[117] The dramatist hoped to please the audience and stood to gain (in terms of fame and prizes) if he succeeded in doing so, but his life and career were not placed as obviously on the

[115] On Aristotle's view of the democracy, Strauss, "Aristotle"; Finley, *PAW*, 125–26. On the intended function and audience of the *Politics*, see the works by C. Lord, cited above, I.n.81. On the *Rhetoric*, see Lord, "The Intention of Aristotle's '*Rhetoric*'," *Hermes* 109 (1981): 326–339; Arnhart, *Aristotle*. Riley and Riley, "Mass Communication," 538–39, 541 n. 15, 545 n. 33, note that modern mass communication theory is an elaboration of the basic principles set down by Aristotle, although they suggest (563–69) that modern models stress the interactive nature of communication more than did Aristotle.

[116] This new approach to drama in a social and institutional context is exemplified by Winkler, "Ephebes' Song"; Zeitlin, "Thebes"; S. Goldhill, "The Great Dionysia and Civic Ideology," *JHS* 107 (1987): 58–76; and other papers collected by Winkler and Zeitlin, edd., *Nothing to Do with Dionysus*. Comedy has long been recognized to have strong roots in social commentary; see, for example, Ehrenberg, *People of Aristophanes*. But the complexities of the comedian's commentary on society have sometimes been obscured by modern scholars' tendency to view comedy as simple fun; cf. the critical assessment of J. Henderson, "The Demos and the Comic Competition," in Winkler and Zeitlin, edd., *Nothing to Do with Dionysus*.

[117] For the long-standing debate over Aristophanes' political views and intentions, see D. M. McDowell, "The Nature of Aristophanes' *Akharnians*," *Greece and Rome* 30 (1983): 143–62, and other recent studies discussed by Ian C. Storey, "Old Comedy 1975–1984," *Echos du Monde Classique*, n. s. 6 (1987): 2–9, 36–37. On the politics of tragedy, see essays in Euben, ed., *Greek Tragedy and Political Theory*.

line as were those of the political orator. Moreover, the playwright did not confront the audience in his own person. Drama, therefore, may not offer as direct and clear a commentary on the relations between mass and elite as rhetoric. Yet many of the symbols, metaphors, and plot structures of Attic tragedy and comedy are clearly informed by tensions between mass and elite, and dramatic texts can help to elucidate those tensions and the means by which they were mediated. The relative scarcity of citations of tragedy and comedy in this study is not due to a belief that the potential of drama to explicate Athenian political sociology is limited; to the contrary, the potential is so great that a separate study would be required to treat the subject of the political sociology of Attic drama with the seriousness that it deserves.[118]

Historiography and biography are important for gaining an appreciation for the context of mass-elite relations, and some historians, notably Thucydides, have much to say on the matter. The *Lives* of Plutarch (especially those of Pericles, Demosthenes, and Phocion) contain valuable material, although we must keep in mind that Plutarch's purpose in writing was moral rather than historical or sociological (see Plut. *Alexander* 1). A particularly useful source of both historical and constitutional material is the *Constitution of Athens* (*Athēnaiōn Politeia*), probably written by a student of Aristotle. Other historical sources (e.g., Herodotus) will figure prominently in Chapter II. Once again, it is essential to remember that ancient historiography and biography were written by and for elite audiences. While we cannot hope to understand mass-elite relations on either a social or a political plane without the ancient historians' description of the events that provided the environment in which mass-elite relations developed, we must view their testimony as to the whys and wherefores of those relations with considerable caution.[119]

The major category of "nonliterary" texts that can be brought to bear on the history of democratic Athens, namely, inscriptions, will play a relatively small role in this study. However, individual inscriptions often clarify legal questions, and the form, vocabulary, content, and iconography of public inscriptions, when viewed collectively, may help to elucidate some of the theories that will be advanced in the following pages. Once again, the potential contribution of epigraphy and

[118] For a preliminary discussion of some of the issues involved, see J. Ober and Barry S. Strauss, "Drama, Political Rhetoric, and the Discourse of Athenian Democracy," in Winkler and Zeitlin, edd., *Nothing to Do with Dionysus*.

[119] For a good example of a sophisticated literary approach to historiography, see Connor, *Thucydides*. See ibid., 13–17 for an introduction to Thucydides' elite audience and his goals in relationship to the goals of the orator.

iconography to mass-elite relations is considerable and deserves more space than can be devoted to it here.[120]

In sum, this volume is not a constitutional history of Athenian government, a history of Athenian politicians and their dealings, or the general "social and economic history of classical Athens" to which J. K. Davies considered his *Athenian Propertied Families* a prolegomenon.[121] It is not intended to replace either of the first two categories of investigation. I hope that it will contribute to the larger enterprise of the third category by explaining how political sociology contributed to social stability and how direct democratic decision making was facilitated through mass-elite communication.

In the course of the investigation, a number of themes will recur. Besides the central problem of masses and elites, we will be concerned with the related dichotomies of individual/community, personal liberty/political consensus, and sovereignty of law/sovereignty of popular will. Chapter II deals with the historical development of the Athenian elites and masses in the context of, and as an influence on, the evolving democratic constitution from the sixth through the fourth centuries B.C. Here, coverage will necessarily be selective and will concentrate on what M. Foucault called "the history of that which renders necessary a certain form of thought."[122] Chapter III considers the nature of the relationship between public speaker and his audience, similarities and differences between private Athenian citizens and expert politicians, and the various forums of political debate and communication. Chapters IV–VI deal with how the elites of ability, wealth, and status were treated in Athenian rhetoric, in an attempt to understand both the strategies of Athenian speakers and the operational significance of oratory in state and society. Chapter VII suggests some general conclusions about the role of rhetoric and ideology in the maintenance of social harmony and in the processes of democratic decision making at Athens.

---

[120] The very significant contribution epigraphical iconography can make to the study of the democracy is demonstrated by Lawton, "Iconography."

[121] Davies, *APF*, xxx–xxxi.

[122] "Monstrosities in Criticism," *Diacritics* 1 (1971): 60, cited in Connor, *Thucydides*, 26.

CHAPTER II

HISTORY OF
THE ATHENIAN "CONSTITUTION":
A DIACHRONIC SURVEY

The institutional history of Athens has been rewritten many times since the late fourth century B.C. when Aristotle sketched it briefly in the *Politics* (1273b33–1274a21), perhaps on the basis of the fuller treatment in the *Constitution of the Athenians* prepared under his direction.[1] Many aspects of the Athenian constitution, including the nature of its ultimate form, are still hotly debated, but the main lines of development are tolerably clear. Happily, the personal motivations and long-term intentions of lawmakers—the subjects of much of the modern debate—are seldom at issue here. For the present argument, neither the long-term goals sought by Cleisthenes or Pericles (for example) nor the private political agendas involved in their reforms are of primary importance. Rather, we are concerned here with how the evolving relationship between mass and elite was institutionalized and how constitutional development in turn contributed to changes or encouraged stability in the political sociology of Athens. The institutional organization of the state was in part a product of evolving Athenian political ideology, but it also contributed to the environment in which political ideology developed, as well as providing the formal structure through which the citizenry acted in response to the stimulus of external events.

A. Introduction

The period from ca. 600 to 400 B.C. saw dynamic changes in the political organization of Athenian society, and the period was therefore characterized by relatively frequent and significant institutional adjustments. Struggles within the elite, both between various sub-elites and between individual politicians, resulted in the initial reforms that led to the development of a political environment conducive to the

---

[1] On the authorship of the *AP* and its relationship to the *Politics*, see Rhodes, *CommAP*, 58–63, with references cited.

growth of democratic ideology. Consequently, by the late sixth century, the evolving realization among the masses that their collective power could be used to improve their own position became a major factor in the form the constitution would take. The changes that will concern us may be roughly grouped under the following headings: (1) What did it mean to be a citizen of Athens? Who was to be a citizen? And by what means were new members to be included in the citizen group? (2) What was the form (in terms of method, place, and frequency of meeting) and social composition of the decision-making bodies that determined state policy? (3) Who had the power to propose measures to the decision-making bodies, and who had the right to debate those measures once they had been proposed? What was the social standing of the proposers and debaters? (4) What were the limitations upon the implementation of decisions? And what was the form and social composition of the limiting bodies? (5) What was the social standing of those responsible for carrying out decisions? How were they selected? And how extensive were their powers? (6) What was the social standing of those responsible for legal judgment? What was the basis of their judgment?[2]

The period from the early sixth to the late fifth centuries was, generally speaking and especially in its second half, one in which the masses gained more political power vis-à-vis the elite. By 400 B.C. there were no property qualifications for citizenship, and socially heterogenous subsets of the citizen body were responsible for enrolling new members, subject to review by the entire citizenry. The primary decision-making bodies were the citizen Assembly, the legislative bodies of Lawmakers (*nomothetai*), and the popular courts. All of these bodies met openly; the Assembly and courts met frequently. Assembly meetings were open to all citizens; boards of Lawmakers and juries were selected randomly and by lot from the citizen body. The agenda of the Assembly was determined by the Council, whose members were selected annually, by lot, from the entire citizen population; discussion in the Assembly was open, and every citizen had the right to take part in it, although normally members of the elite took the most active part. The decisions of the Assembly were subject to review only by the people's courts. The decisions of the courts were final. Most offices of the state were open to all citizens and were filled annually, by lot; most

---

[2] These categories are admittedly artificial and derive, at least indirectly, from modern theories of the divison of governmental powers; cf. above. I do not mean to imply that this is the sort of categorization the Athenians would have used; but it may help to give some form to our picture of the evolving institutional relationship between mass and elite.

magistrates' powers were strictly limited by law and by their colleagues, since magistrates usually served on boards. The performance of every magistrate was subject to legal audit in the people's courts. Virtually all important legal judgments were by popular juries who decided legal disputes on the basis of Athenian law and their own ideological predilections. Furthermore, state pay for most forms of government service made participation in the government accessible to ordinary citizens. The institutional bases for elite control of the state had been, in most instances, eliminated or severely weakened. Athens had achieved full democracy.

In comparison to the preceding 200 years, the period ca. 400–322 seems to have been relatively stable and to have required few major structural adjustments. Both mass and elite were sufficiently content with their respective positions to obviate the need for constitutional overhauls. My contention is that the earlier period was one in which the Athenians were seeking a balance between the positions of mass and elite and that by the later period the balance had been struck. The burden of this chapter will be to sketch the evolution of the relationship between mass and elite in the earlier period and to demonstrate the relative institutional stability of that relationship during the later.

B. Before Solon: Birth Elite

An egalitarian ethos of some sort may have operated in the pre-polis society of the early Dark Ages (ca. 1100–900), a period during which there may have been little economic surplus and a relatively low level of sociopolitical differentiation—and for which there are no texts, other than the problematic Homeric epics.[3] But both surpluses and social differentiation seem to have increased markedly from ca. 900 to 600, so that by the early sixth century there were clear distinctions between masses and elites in Athens.[4] The ruling elite of the seventh century was defined by descent; its members may be characterized as

[3] Cf. Donlan, *Aristocratic Ideal*, 18–25, 178, who investigates Homeric society in an attempt to recover "the profoundly rooted legacy of egalitarianism from the tribal past" (178). I do not agree, however, that this was the key factor in the erosion of "class pretensions" in the fifth and fourth centuries. For Homer as a source for Dark Age Greek social and political life, see M. I. Finley, *The World of Odysseus²* (London, 1978).

[4] On economic development and the growth of social inequality in the early archaic period, see Starr, *Economic and Social Growth*; cf. Snodgrass, *Archaic Greece*, esp. 143–48; Murray, *Early Greece*, 38–68. On changing attitudes in literature, see Donlan, *Aristocratic Ideal*, 26–51.

aristocrats or nobles.[5] They were (at least in later years) known collectively as the *Eupatridai*: those born from noble fathers.[6]

We do not know exactly how this noble elite was organized. Certainly, each nobleman regarded himself as a member of an *oikos*, a family unit that included direct linear ancestors and, in some sense, a line of future descendants.[7] Every noble was certainly closely linked to members of other aristocratic *oikoi* through marriage connections and secondary degrees of kinship. It appears unlikely, however, that these various networks of extended kinship connections were formally organized into units resembling Roman clans (Latin: *gentes*). Many of the details of the elaborate system of clans (*genē*), which later Athenians imagined had existed in the archaic period, were the product of fourth-century (and later) speculation. But inter-*oikos* cooperation was undoubtedly an important political factor in early Athens.[8] Nobles may have dominated the phratries ("brotherhoods"), although phratries certainly included non-noble members; indeed in the early period, all Athenians probably belonged to a phratry.[9] The *Eupatridai*

[5] On the relationship of birth to political power in early Greece, see Starr, *Individual and Community*, 59–63; cf. the cautionary comments of Finley, *PAW*, 45. For a fuller definition of nobility see below, VI.A.

[6] *Eupatridai*: *AP* 13.2; Plut. *Theseus* 24–25. Thucydides (1.13.1) notes that before the tyrannies, Greek poleis were typically ruled by "ancestral kings" (*patrikai basileiai*) who ruled by fixed prerogatives (*epi rhētois gerasi*). Cf. Wade-Gery, "Eupatridai"; Rhodes, *CommAP*, 72, 74–76; Roussel, *Tribu et cité*, esp. 55–58. Figueira, "Ten Archontes," 454–59, quite rightly objects to describing the *Eupatridai* as a caste and notes that wealth as well as nobility would have been a prerequisite for political power. But his argument that "*Eupatridai*" was a label devised by members of an anti-tyrant Pedion "party" for themselves, as part of an unsuccessful early sixth-century attempt to *create* a caste system, is no more convincing than other attempts to reconstruct archaic "political parties."

[7] For a good introduction to the concept of the *oikos* as both a kinship and an economic unit, see Humphreys, *Family*, 1–21, 31–32.

[8] The place of the *genē* in archaic Athenian social and political history has been clarified by Roussel, *Tribu et cité*, 51–87; and Bourriot, *Recherches* (cf. Bourriot's summary in *Information Historique* 37 [1975]: 228–236), who conclude that, with the exception of a few groups with sacerdotal associations, the notion of the *genos* as an extremely ancient clan association, or a quasi-state possessing property and constituting all descendants of a single male ancestor, is a myth of modern historiography. See also below, VI.B.1.

[9] On Athenian phratries, see Hignett, *HAC*, 55–60; Roussel, *Tribu et cité*, 139–56, esp. 146–47 (not limited to aristocrats); M. Golden, " 'Donatus' and Athenian Phratries," *CQ* 35 (1985): 9–13; Finley, *Ancient History*, 91. Rhodes, *CommAP*, esp. 68–71, 258, follows A. Andrewes (in *JHS* 86 [1961]: 1–15), in arguing that all Athenians belonged to phratries and that before Cleisthenes the phratry was important as an institution that defined citizenship.

cannot be linked with the four Ionian tribes into which Attica's population was subdivided before the Cleisthenic reforms.[10]

How the nobles legitimated or exercised their power is impossible to determine exactly. Politically, they appear to have inherited the powers of the royal house; according to Athenian tradition the last king of Athens was deposed some time around 700 B.C. He was replaced with a college of annually selected archons, ultimately nine in number: an eponymous official ("the" *archōn*), a war leader (*polemarchos*), a "king" (*basileus*) who performed the religious rituals that required royal participation, and six officials who had legal responsibilities (*thesmothetai*). Neither the means by which archons were selected nor the relationship between archons and other institutional structures of the pre-Solonian government is known. Reasonable assumptions, however, are that the *Eupatridai* controlled the archon-selection process and that Eupatrid leaders foregathered from time to time, either formally or informally, as a council to advise the year's archons. An Assembly of some sort presumably existed, perhaps limited—de facto or de jure—to those who served as heavy-armed warriors. At any rate, the Assembly was not powerful, and it must have been called by the magistrates only in order to rubber-stamp decisions previously arrived at by the ruling elite.[11]

It appears that *Eupatridai* effectively dominated the major magistracies and hence that the government was largely or entirely controlled by the nobility. The aristocrats were probably able to consolidate their hold on the political power in the state by their control of state religion, and we may presume that the important rituals by which the gods were propitiated and their will was made manifest could only be performed by noble priests.[12] Perhaps the most important element in

[10] On the early Ionian tribes of Attica, see Hignett, *HAC*, 50–55; Rhodes, *CommAP*, 67–71; Roussel, *Tribu et cité*, 193–208.

[11] On the pre-Solonian political order, see Hignett, *HAC*, 47–85; Rhodes, *CommAP*, 79–118; Humphreys, "Evolution of Legal Process," 231–37; Carawan, "*Apophasis* and *Eisangelia*," 116–18. Earlier accounts of the Eupatrid government will probably have to be corrected in light of the conclusions of Wallace, *Areopagos*, chapter 1, who argues vigorously against the theory that the Eupatrids ruled through a powerful Areopagus council. But Wallace also notes (*Areopagos*, chapter 1) that there may well have been a standing committee which met in the Prytaneion to advise the archons. The "Constitution of Draco" of *AP* 4.2–5 is a fiction: K. von Fritz, "The Composition of Aristotle's *Constitution of Athens* and the So-Called Dracontian Constitution," *CPh* 49 (1954): 74–93.

[12] Aristocratic control of state religion: Davies, *WPW*, 105–114 (accepting the reality and power of archaic *genē*); Roussel, *Tribu et cité*, 65–78, esp. 70: "Tout semblerait donc d'indiquer que les corporations religieuses qui en vinrent à être appelées génè étaient les associations constituées à l'époque historique, d'abord au sein

the aristocrats' ability to dominate early Athenian society, however, was their control of much of the economic surplus. The aristocrats were undoubtedly among the richest members of society; their wealth was largely in land, although some of them may have been involved in trade or manufacturing, at least indirectly. Their property-power, in conjunction with their control of religion and the offices of the state, presumably gave the aristocrats the authority that maintained their political power. Most members of the lower classes were probably in some sense "clients" of rich men: often in debt to them and in awe of them. The ideological basis of aristocratic control would have been a "politics of deference," based on the respect the lower classes felt for the birth, offices, and wealth of the nobility.[13]

But the aristocrats were not the only wealthy men in early Athenian society. By the later seventh century, if not before, there was a noticeable group of individuals who were rich but not noble-born. They were called, by some nobles at least, *kakoi*. This might mean only baseborn, but it had an aspect of moral censure as well; we might translate it as "the nasty men."[14] In the late seventh century a noble named Cylon attempted to establish himself as tyrant (*turannos*: the Greek term did not have negative moral connotations in the seventh century but meant simply "sole ruler"). Cylon's attempted coup was put down by force, apparently by the concerted action of the other nobles and their clients. Shortly thereafter a code of law was written down by a certain Draco. We may guess that both Cylon's attempted coup and Draco's

d'une aristocratie s'organisant dans la Cité naissante pour assurer son monopole sur les principaux cultes. . . ." Cf. the overly cautious comments of Finley, *PAW*, 93–94. On the democratization of state religion in the course of the fifth century, see Ostwald, *From Popular Sovereignty*, 137–71.

[13] On the power of wealth in early Athens, clientage, and deference, see esp. Finley, *PAW*, 44–45 (speaking specifically of the sixth century); Roussel, *Tribu et cité*, 57; Rhodes, "Political Activity," 133. On trade as a source of wealth for archaic aristocrats, see C. Reed, "Maritime Traders in the Ancient Greek World: A Typology of Those Engaged in the Long-Distance Transfer of Goods by Sea," *Ancient World* 10 (1984): 31–44; cf. Humphreys, *Anthropology*, 165–70; Cartledge, "Trade and Politics." On the concept and function of clientage, see Saller, *Personal Patronage*, 1, 3–4 (with literature cited), who notes that patron-client relations are invariably reciprocal, personal, and asymmetrical. For a good discussion of deference to political elites in relationship to the concepts of power, authority, coercion, and influence, see J. B. and R. R. Gilsdorf, "Elites and Electorates: Some Plain Truths for Historians of Colonial America," in D. D. Hall et al., edd., *Saints and Revolutionaries: Essays on Early American History* (New York, 1984), 207–44.

[14] On the *kakoi* in general: Starr, *Economic and Social Growth*, 123–28. *Kakoi* in the Theognid corpus of the sixth century: Adkins, *Moral Values*, 37–46; the problem of "status incongruence": Gouldner, *Enter Plato*, 16–17.

law code may have been the result of tensions within the upper classes of Athens; but it is unclear whether the tensions resulted from squabbling within the noble ruling elite or from differences between the *Eupatridai* and *kakoi* who wanted greater political power in the state.[15]

Neither Cylon's revolt nor the new law code necessarily had much to do with those at the lower end of the social spectrum, the working poor. These were subsistence farmers for the most part, at least some of whom were unable to maintain their families on the produce of their own lands and so had fallen into debt and bondage to the wealthy. The status of the bondmen was indeterminate: they were of Athenian ancestry, perhaps members of phratries, tribes, or both, but were no longer free.[16] Were they to be regarded as "citizens"? Probably few of the wealthy bothered themselves with this point. The general notion of the citizen (*politēs*) as "one of us"—a full member of a society, in whom social rights and duties inhered—was old, although "citizenship" per se was not of much functional political or economic significance in the late seventh century.[17] But the question of who was

[15] Cylon: Thuc. 1.126.3–12; Hdt. 5.71; *AP* 1; Plut. *Solon* 12; cf. Hignett, *HAC*, 86; Rhodes, *CommAP*, 79–84. Draco's law code: see Hignett, *HAC*, esp. 305–311; R. S. Stroud, *Drakon's Law on Homicide* (Berkeley, 1968); Rhodes, *CommAP*, 109–18; M. Gagarin, *Drakon and Early Athenian Homicide Law* (New Haven, 1981); idem, *Early Greek Law*, 86–89, 112–116.

[16] The status and economic condition of the Athenian lower classes before Solon must be extrapolated from his reforms. See Plut. *Solon* 14–15.1 and esp. the fragment of Solon's poem on his reforms quoted in *AP* 12.4, with Rhodes, *CommAP*, 174–78. Cf. Ehrenberg, *From Solon to Socrates*, 56–62, and the literature cited below, II.n.20. On the difficult problem of defining the status of debt-bondmen see Finley, "Debt Bondage," "Between Slavery and Freedom"; Beringer, " 'Servile Status'," "Freedom, Family, and Citizenship"; Raaflaub, *Entdeckung der Freiheit*, 29–54.

[17] For early Greek ideas on freedom and citizenship as relating to the idea of belonging to a community, see esp. Beringer, "Freedom, Family, and Citizenship." Sealey, "How Citizenship and the City Began" (cf. *Athenian Republic*, 124–25), denies that the concept of citizen (*politēs*) was more than "embryonic" before the early fifth century; but this conclusion is based on what appears to me to be an excessively legalistic view of citizenship. Cf. the early use of the term *Athēnaios* for a resident of Attica (e.g., *Iliad* 2.551); the term surely suggests that some (at least) of those who lived in Attica viewed themselves as constitituting an identifiable group of persons who were in some way different from those who were not *Athēnaioi*. On the importance of Solon's law code in strengthening the idea of citizenship: Gagarin, *Early Greek Law*, 139–40; Meier, *Anthropologie*, 16–18 (cf. 28–32), who sees Solon as rather more self-consciously on the side of the masses than I do. On the importance and meaning of citizenship, see also Aristotle, *Pol.* Book 3, with the discussion of C. Mossé, "Citoyens actifs et citoyens 'passifs' dans les cités grecques: Une approche théorique du problème," *REG* 81 (1979): 241–49. The origins and development of Athenian citizenship are the subject of an important forthcoming book by P. B. Manville, *Origins of Athenian Citizenship* (Princeton, 1989).

"one of us" and what that meant might well have been a matter of growing concern to the lower classes, who otherwise were really no different from foreign-born slaves.[18] The poor stood outside the political structure of the state. They had no forum for political action and probably had little political consciousness and therefore few political ambitions. Besides simple survival, their main concern must have been over what we may call their status (cf. below, vi.a): they wanted to be better than slaves, and so they desired certain protections (e.g., from debt-bondage) that might be expected to inhere in the status of citizen.

C. Solon: Wealth Elite and Masses

Perhaps spurred by a quickening pace of economic growth, social tensions were exacerbated in the course of the seventh century, and matters came to a head in 594 B.C., with the appointment of Solon as archon with extraordinary powers to reform the state.[19] We know little about the mechanism by which he was appointed, but we must assume that his appointment was with the agreement of the ruling birth elite, who presumably recognized the need for sociopolitical compromise. Many reforms were attributed to Solon in antiquity, and arguably not all of them were genuine. But the two key reforms that concern us are quite securely attested: the rectification of the position of Athenians who had fallen into debt-bondage and a change in the prerequisites for holding the major offices of the state.[20] In these reforms Solon used constitutional amendments to make changes both in the mem-

[18] On the economic and social role of slaves in archaic Greece see, for example, Humphreys, *Anthropology*, 161–64; Raaflaub, *Entdeckung der Freiheit*, 60 with nn. 133 and 134. The existence of an inter-state slave trade is demonstrated by the Athenian debt-bondmen who had been sold abroad as slaves and were brought back by Solon: *AP* 12.4.

[19] On the date of Solon's reforms I follow R. Wallace, "The Date of Solon's Reforms," *AJAH* 8 (1983): 81–95. For an alternate dating: R. Develin, "Solon's First Laws," *LCM* 9.10 (December 1984), 155–56. Among other discussions of Solon's reforms I have found particularly useful: Hopper, "Solonian 'Crisis' "; Ellis and Stanton, "Factional Conflict"; Starr, *Economic and Social Growth*, 181–87; Gallant, "Agricultural Systems"; Hignett, *HAC*, 86–107; Forrest, *EGD*, 143–74; Ehrenberg, *From Solon to Socrates*, 62–76; Adkins, *Moral Values*, 47–57. Cf. other discussions cited in Rhodes, *CommAP*, 118–79.

[20] Debt-bondage and legislation on it: *AP* 6, 12.4; Plut. *Solon* 15.2–16.4; Cf. Finley, "Debt-Bondage," esp. 156–57; Raaflaub, *Entdeckung der Freiheit*, 54–65. Distribution of citizens into wealth classes and their relation to political power: *AP* 7–8, 12.3; Plut. *Solon* 16.5–19; cf. Rhodes, *CommAP*, 119.

bership of the ruling elite and in the social and political relationships between mass and elite.

The change in membership of the ruling elite was fairly straightforward. Solon instituted prerequisites for officeholding based directly on economic class. The Athenian populace was divided into four census classes, each with specific political privileges. Membership in each group was defined by an individual's wealth, based on a standard derived from annual agricultural production: *pentekosiomedimnoi* (500 measures), *hippeis* (300), *zeugitai* (200), and *thētes* (less than 200). The central offices of the state, the archonships, were open only to the members of the one or two highest census classes.[21] An elite of wealth, which would be both larger and more permeable to new members, thus replaced the nobility of birth as the exclusive governing elite. The institutionalization of the wealth elite made possible political mobility and thus facilitated the circulation of elites which Pareto considered essential to stable elite rule. Financially successful Athenians would automatically be coopted into the ruling elite, while financial failures would drop out of it. The membership of the new ruling class therefore would be sensitive to economic change; the absence of disparity between economic position and access to political power might defuse intra-elite tension considerably.[22]

For those at the other end of the spectrum, Solon's reforms resulted in a rigidification of sociopolitical status as a function of birth. Existing debts were forgiven, and debt-bondage was permanently eliminated in Attica. Athenian debt-slaves were freed and those who had been sold abroad were brought back. There is much debate about what the

---

[21] *AP* 7.3 (". . . assigning offices to members of each [of the top three classes] according to the level of their assessment"), 8.1 (treasurers from the first class only), 26.2 (archonship opened to the third class in 457/6); cf. Rhodes, *CommAP*, 148, 330, for the debate over whether Solon opened the archonship to only the first class, or to the first two classes. For the significance of this reform, see also Ehrenberg, "Origins," 538 (with bibliography of older literature); Finley, *PAW* 12–14; Starr, *Individual and Community*, 78–79. Frost, "Toward a History," 66, notes that the acropolis dedications of the late sixth century prove the existence of an elite of wealth, not birth. W. R. Connor, "Tribes, Festivals, and Processions: Civic Ceremonial and Political Manipulation in Archaic Greece," *JHS* 107 (1987): 47–49, suggests that the origins of the property classes should be sought in the marching order of a public procession celebrating the dedication of the "first fruits" of the year's harvest.

[22] The possibility of upward mobility (and the existence of census classes) is proved by the dedication of Diphilus, who rose in status from a *thēs* to the ranks of the *hippeis*: *AP* 7.4; cf. A. E. Raubitschek, *Dedications from the Athenian Acropolis* (Cambridge, Mass., 1949), no. 372. Circulation of elites: V. Pareto, *The Rise and Fall of the Elites* (Totowa, New Jersey, 1968); cf. Marger, *Elites and Masses*, 66.

economic intent or impact of this reform might have been; but, while interesting, the question is not terribly relevant here and has tended to obscure the simple fact that Solon's debt-bondage reform formally defined the Athenian citizenry. The distinction between citizen and slave was now made clear, explicit, and (in the normal course of events) unbridgeable. No matter how serious his failure financially, the citizen need not fear the ultimate status-humiliation of becoming a slave in his own home territory. Yet this reform might potentially serve to worsen the lower-class citizen's economic position in the long run by reducing his "capital." He lost his ability to use his person as collateral, to trade his freedom for the minimal economic security enjoyed (as it were) by the slave. The poorest citizens had exchanged potential economic advantage for status security, their personal position for a position in society.[23]

The status-reform legislation which defined certain minimal rights as inherent in citizen birth was presumably enacted in part because of agitation by the lower classes themselves. Whether or not they saw clearly the consequences of giving up their bodily "capital," apparently the lower-class Athenian citizens desired to have the distinction between themselves and the slaves clarified and legalized. The cancellation of debts cost the wealth elite something in financial terms, and there were complaints on this score (*AP* 11.2, 12.4). But the reform was also to the long-term advantage of the elite. The statutory creation of an impassable barrier between citizen and slave ensured the continued existence of a large body of persons who stood between the elite and the slaves and who could be expected to side with the former. The

---

[23] My analysis of the significance of Solon's reforms of the lower classes differs from those who believe he was primarily worried about feuding aristocrats (e.g., Sealey, "Regionalism"; Ellis and Stanton, "Factional Conflict"), and from those who see him as attempting to improve the economic condition of the lower classes (cautiously: Hignett, *HAC*, 88; with more emphasis on class struggle: Ste. Croix, *CSAGW*, 278–83). My scenario has elements in common with Beringer, "Freedom, Family, and Citizenship," 53; Gallant, "Agricultural Systems" (although I think he takes the economic primitivism argument too far, and underestimates the seriousness of debt-bondage); and esp. Raaflaub, *Entdeckung der Freiheit*, 60–65, who emphasizes the immediate ideological and long-term political importance of the new distinction between the status of citizens and unfree foreigners. It is worth noting that status reform is not invariably welcomed by peasants. R. Edelman, *Proletarian Peasants: The Revolution of 1905 in Russia's Southwest* (Ithaca, 1987), 70, 82, points out that the serfs of southwestern Russia were angered by the Manifesto of 1861, which "freed" them, because it did not give them land and in fact took away their traditional feudal rights (e.g., to use pastures and forests). The Athenian peasants may not have been fully content with their grants either, but Solon was looking for a workable balance, not full social justice.

elite were thus protected from the potential consequences of a hyper-polarization of society. If the Athenian masses fell into a position of status equality with the slave population, there would be a manifest danger of creating a homogenous lower class. And if that large lower class became conscious of its collective power, it could mean the end of the existing social order. Therefore, many among the elite may well have decided that the trade-off was to their advantage; the creation of a citizen mass, secure in its status, allowed the rich to exploit their for-eign-born slaves as vigorously as they wished, with less fear of class revolt.[24]

Whatever else he may have had in mind, Solon's two major socio-political reforms were apparently designed to alleviate social tension by redefining the rights and privileges of different groups in society. By loosening the ties of birth at the top of the social order and strengthening them at the bottom, Solon could reasonably hope to achieve long-term social stability. There is no necessary reason to sup-pose that he had "democratic" leanings: coopting the rich *kakoi* into the ruling elite eliminated them as potential leaders of the masses against the nobles and gave a political dimension to the common class interests of the wealthy. Defining the rights of citizenship in terms of personal freedom severed the interests of the poor from those of the foreign slaves. The resulting order was one in which the position of the ruling elite was strengthened, both by making it more permeable and by eliminating a possible threat to its survival.[25]

The tradition about the political changes instituted by Solon for the

[24] A somewhat analagous situation existed in the antebellum American South, where the desirability of maintaining a community of interests between lower- and upper-class white males contributed to the willingness of the wealthy slave owners to tolerate high levels of petty crime against property by their poor white neigh-bors; see Wyatt-Brown, "Community." Cf. R. H. Sewell, *The House Divided: Section-alism and Civil War, 1848–1865* (Baltimore, 1988), 13–14, for the social function of slaves as a "mudsill." Note that in the American situation the legal status of the free lower-class citizenry was not threatened, but the slave owners still dreaded the con-sequences of lower-class white interaction with black slaves. Cf. the symbolic link between slavery and democracy noted by Finley, "Was Greek Civilization," 163–64: above, 1.n.61.

[25] I do not, of course, mean to imply that Solon was acting according to an un-derstanding of elitist theory, any more than he was from democratic theory. Rather, Solon acted as Michels et al. supposed any elite naturally would, to protect his own and his group's privileged position in society. On the symbolic context of the image (esp. in *AP* and Solon's poems) of Solon's standing between opposing armies (which does *not* mean he was "middle class" or that he favored a "moderate" political order), see N. Loraux, "Solon au milieu de la lice," in *Aux origines de l'hel-lénisme . . . Homage à H. van Effenterre* (Paris, 1984), 199–214.

Assembly and the people's court is less secure, but the reported changes fit quite well with the assumption that Solon was attempting to establish a sociopolitical order in which the privileges of the elite would be secured by granting minimal rights to the poor. Solon either opened or left open the Assembly to *thētes* and set up a council of 400 to prepare motions for the Assembly.[26] Access to the Assembly for the *thētes* would be part and parcel of the definition of citizenship: citizens were those who were allowed to attend the Assembly. The reform (if so it was) would have had little practical effect, since the *thētes* would not have the option of speaking in the Assembly, and probably few would attend its infrequent meetings. Besides, the agenda of the Assembly would be prepared by the new council, which would (presumably) be controlled by the reorganized ruling elite of wealth. Archons, now probably elected by the Assembly, became, upon completion of their year's term, members of a reorganized Areopagus council which was apparently given general oversight of the laws of the state (*nomophulakia*). The Areopagites were to ensure that magistrates obeyed the laws and that measures passed in Assembly were in accordance with the laws.[27] Since the Areopagites were ex-archons, and so from the top one or two property classes, the wealth elite would have an institutional means to control any independent tendencies that might be manifested by the citizenry in Assembly.

Solon also established a new court (perhaps simply the Assembly sitting as a court) to which citizens could appeal rulings of magistrates. We do not know how the new court was constituted, but it is unnecessary to assume that the court was either intended or able to limit the collective power of the elite.[28] In all of these arrangements there is a

[26] Solonian Assembly open to *thētes*: *AP* 7.3. It is not clear whether Solon opened the Assembly to *thētes* (as some have assumed) or *left* it open. Solon's poem cited by *AP* 12.1 suggests he did not reduce the *thētes*' political position, but it does not say whether they were given any new political rights; cf. Rhodes, *CommAP*, 140–41, 172, 174–75; Raaflaub, "Freien Bürgers Recht," 29–30. Council of 400: *AP* 8.4, Plut. *Solon* 19.1–2; cf. Hignett, *HAC*, 92–96 (arguing against its existence); Rhodes, *CommAP*, 153–54 (for its existence); Rhodes, *Boule*, 208–209 (with bibliography: 208 n. 2); cf. Sealey, "Probouleusis," 266–67. There is no direct evidence for the social composition of this council, but presumably its members (like archons) were selected from the higher property classes.

[27] Archons elected: Aristot. *Pol.* 1273b35–1274a3, 1274a15–18, 1281b32–34; but cf. *AP* 8.1 with Rhodes, *CommAP*, 146–48. Areopagus' new powers: Wallace, *Areopagos*, chapter 2, esp. 2.ii.a. I do not, however, agree with Wallace's conclusion (ibid., chapter 2.ii) that the motive behind Solon's political reforms was to eliminate oligarchy and to give real power to the demos.

[28] *Dikastēria* open to *thētes*: *AP* 7.3. Citizens allowed to appeal to *dikastēria*: *AP* 9; Plut. *Solon* 18.3–7; cf. M. H. Hansen, "The Athenian *Heliaia* from Solon to Aris-

common thread of emphasizing the unity of the citizen body and, thereby, the unity of all Athenians' interests, without sacrificing any of the real political power of the wealth elite. Emphasis on the unity of the citizenry had tremendous long-term consequences and ultimately helped to undercut the political position of the upper classes. But neither Solon nor his contemporaries could have foreseen that result. The emphasis on common interests may indeed be seen as an example of elite manipulation of ideology, intended to persuade the masses to accept a social order that legitimized and so perpetuated elite rule.[29]

D. Pisistratus and the Aspirations of the Demos

By the middle third of the sixth century, there was further disruption in the Athenian state, culminating in 546 with Pisistratus' successful bid (after two false starts) to establish himself as tyrant. Our sources for the conditions that led to Pisistratus' takeover are meager and subject to different interpretations, but there is little reason to suppose that mass-elite conflict was a primary contributing factor. Pisistratus' tyranny may have been the outgrowth of intra-elite rivalries; there seems to have been little actual participation by the masses in any of his three coups.[30] The immediate effects of the establishment of Pisis-

totle," *CM* 33 (1981–82): 9–47; Sealey, *Athenian Republic*, 60–70; Humphreys, "Evolution of Legal Process," 237–39, 242–47; Ostwald, *From Popular Sovereignty*, 9–15; Osborne, "Law in Action," 40–42. Wallace, *Areopagos*, chapter 2.ii, suggests that Aristotle (*Pol.* 1274a15–18, 1281b32–35) is correct in stating magistrates were scrutinized not by the Areopagus council but by the demos. If this is correct, it is a striking example of *potential* mass power, but this would only be a truly democratic reform if we assume that the Assembly was able to act independently, as it apparently was not. Cf. Hignett, *HAC*, 96–98; Carawan, "*Eisangelia* and *Euthyna*," esp. 168, 182, 188, 191, 207–208.

[29] On elite manipulation of popular ideology to secure mass support for a social order in which the elite rule, see Marger, *Elites and Masses*, 307–309; cf. below, VII.n.65. Note that this is a more restricted use of the term ideology than the one I employ elsewhere; cf. I.D. Once again, Solon was not necessarily acting cynically, but simply to secure what he felt was the best possible social order under the circumstances.

[30] Pisistratus and tyranny at Athens: *AP* 14–16; Hdt. 1.59.4–64. Among modern accounts, see esp. Andrewes, *Greek Tyrants*, 100–15; H. Berve, *Die Tyrannis bei den Griechen*, 2 vols. (Munich, 1967), I.47–77, II.543–63; C. Mossé, *La tyrannie dans la Grèce antique* (Paris, 1969), 49–78. For a good review of the evidence for the Pisistratid period, see Frost, "Toward a History"; cf. Hignett, *HAC*, 110–23; Rhodes, *CommAP*, 189–240. On the orgins of the tyranny, I am in closer agreement with those who emphasize intra-elite factionalism (e.g., Sealey, "Regionalism"; Hopper,

tratus as master of Athens were probably much more clearly felt by the elite than by ordinary citizens. Some of his opponents were driven into exile, and their lands may have been confiscated. Some land may have been turned over to the use of lower-class citizens, as a way of gaining favor for the new political order.[31] Pisistratus furthermore seems to have attempted to break the ties between members of the elite and mass in the countryside. He is reported to have advanced loans to needy farmers (*AP* 16.2), and he established circuit courts to try petty disputes in rural areas. The ordinary rural Athenian would now no longer have to turn to the local "big man" for financial aid and legal decisions. The establishment of circuit courts generated gratitude toward the tyrant but also must have led to a closer identification of the rural citizenry with the machinery of the state.[32]

Perhaps most significantly, however, Pisistratus attempted to legitimate his own position by fostering closer ideological identification of the citizenry as a whole with the Athenian state. Pisistratus and his sons symbolically emphasized the commonality of the heritage of all Athenians by various measures, including the renovation of the great temple of Athena Polias on the Acropolis and other public building projects, the formalization and expansion of the Panathenaic Festival, and the sponsorship of tragic theater as part of the Festival of Dionysus, which now became a major national affair, celebrated annually in the city. Since Pisistratus also emphasized the links between himself and the state, the overall result seems to have been a considerable degree of popularity for his personal rule, perhaps approaching what is now called a "cult of personality."[33]

Like Solon, Pisistratus realized the potential power of ideological integration of the populace as a source of support for the existing order. But as an indirect consequence of Pisistratus' "propaganda," the mass of citizens also formulated a clearer notion of the abstractions of "Athens" and "the Athenians," and consequently a greater meaning was attached to Athenian citizenship. The Athenian masses were increas-

---

" 'Plain,' ") than those who emphasize class conflict (e.g., Ste. Croix, *CSAGW*, 278–83).

[31] Exiles: Hdt. 1.64.3 (rather overstating the situation in the case of the Alcmaeonidai); possible land grants: Hignett, *HAC*, 114–15; Rhodes, *CommAP*, 214–15.

[32] *AP* 16.5; circuit courts as an attack on local patronage: Finley, *PAW* 46–47; cf. Hignett, *HAC*, 115.

[33] Building program: Boersma, *Athenian Building Policy*, 11–27. For Pisistratus' attempts to encourage identification with the state as a prop for his rule, see esp. Forrest, *EGD*, 175–89; On the origins of tragedy as an attempt to promote civic unity, see Winkler, "Ephebes' Song," esp. 45–46.

ingly conscious of themselves not just in relation to inferior status groups within the state but in relation to other peoples and to the Athenian state itself. Citizenship was no longer simply protection from ultimate status degradation, but something much more positive and potentially more politically meaningful.

In terms of constitutional development, the Pisistratid period seems to have been fairly conservative; the tyrant and his successors (his sons) maintained the Solonian constitutional forms. The Assembly continued to meet, presumably advised by the council of 400, and the courts continued to arbitrate legal disputes.[34] Behind the constitutional facade stood the tyrants, and they retained true political power. Many members of the old ruling elite would see the sham, and some may have refused to play the relatively meaningless game of constitutional government. But among the masses, who had never been allowed real power, the change from the rule of the wealth elite to the rule of the tyrant may have been perceived as a positive one. While the masses had no more real power than before, the effective control by elites of their "clients" must have declined as the tyrant worked to weaken the hold of deferential behavior patterns, publicly humiliated his enemies, and emphasized ideological bonds that cut across class lines. Hence, elites may have become, in the eyes of the ordinary citizens, less significant, less legitimate as rulers, less impressive individually. Mass awe for the elite was being replaced by awe for the state. The state was, on one level, Pisistratus the benevolent tyrant and on another level, "The Athenians"—all citizens. The ultimate result was the beginnings of what W. Eder has called the "civilian self-consciousness" of the Athenian demos.[35]

After the death of Pisistratus in 525, the elite opposition became better organized, and his heirs proved unable to contain it. Led by the Alcmaeonid family, the opposition ultimately persuaded the militarily powerful Spartans to depose his son Hippias in 510 B.C. The Spartans may have hoped to benefit from this situation through installing a governing elite favorable to themselves. But the situation proved too volatile for them to handle, and what appears to be open civil war broke out in the years between 510 and 508. Within the Athenian elite, the struggle was apparently between the aristocratic Alcmaeonidai on the one hand and the aristocratic Isagoras (archon in 508/7) and a pro-

[34] "Constitution" under Pisistratus: Hdt. 1.59.6; Thuc. 6.54.6; cf. Hignett, *HAC*, 115–17.

[35] W. Eder, "The Role of Archaic Tyranny and Monarchy in Creating 'Political' Identity" (Paper delivered at the Annual Meeting of the American Philological Association, December 28, 1983). Cf. Starr, *Individual and Community*, 85–86.

Spartan group on the other. But the struggle soon involved the ordinary citizens. For perhaps the first time, action by the Athenian masses was a direct factor in changing the political direction of the state.[36]

E. Cleisthenes' *Isonomia*

The major difference between the struggle of 510–508 and previous power struggles in Athens was that by 510 the ordinary Athenians were sufficiently self-conscious to act in concert. We cannot tell whether or not the masses played any significant part in either agitating against or supporting Hippias. But once the tyrant had been deposed, they were free agents; their former loyalties to the House of Pisistratus could potentially be attached to someone else. That person would have to pay close attention to the growing awareness of the ordinary citizens of themselves as Athenians. He who would lead the newly politicized masses must cast himself into the role of the leader of the Athenian people. Cleisthenes the Alcmaeonid saw the opportunity that the pro-Spartan stance of Isagoras (Hdt. 5.70.1) had virtually thrust into his hands. The Spartans, speakers of a foreign dialect, were non-Athenian outsiders with no business in Athens. The citizens would be likely to support anyone who exploited their sense of themselves as Athenians. As Herodotus (5.66.2) notes, Cleisthenes took the demos into his *hetaireia* (faction or close-knit friendship group).

In order to gain and hold the loyalty of the masses, Cleisthenes built upon their growing political consciousness by advocating a series of constitutional reforms emphasizing the bonds between the citizens and providing for widespread popular participation in the affairs of the state. This announced program presumably included at least some of the reforms he ultimately enacted (below, II.E.1–3). Isagoras responded by recalling the Spartans who expelled Cleisthenes and his closest supporters from the city. Isagoras was apparently acting on the assumption that once its head had been cut off, the serpent of Cleisthenes' mass *hetaireia* would die. He failed to reckon with the degree to which the citizenry had become politicized and the unified mass action which this politicization allowed. Incited by the *boulē* (Hdt. 5.72.2, AP 20.3: probably the council of 400, possibly the Areopagus), the

---

[36] Fall of Pisistratidai and civil war up to the reforms of Cleisthenes: AP 17–19. Assassination of Hipparchus: Hdt. 5.55–61, 6.123.2; Thuc. 1.20.2, 6.54–59. Ousting of Hippias: Hdt. 5.62.2–65. Cf. Hignett, *HAC*, 124–26; Ehrenberg, *From Solon to Socrates*, 88–90; E. David, "A Preliminary Stage of Cleisthenes' Reforms," *Classical Antiquity* 5 (1986): 1–13.

people rose up against the outsiders and their minions, besieging the Spartan garrison on the Acropolis. The Spartan commander surrendered, and the outsiders left Athens; Isagoras apparently went with them.

Cleisthenes returned in triumph; he was the hero of the hour. The atmosphere was no doubt euphoric, but the future was a frightening prospect to anyone able to see beyond the immediate success. If Cleisthenes were to make anything of permanent value—for himself, his political allies, or the Athenian state—out of the highly fluid situation, he had to act quickly. The Spartans could be expected to retaliate sooner rather than later. In order to meet the threat, public order was essential, but Athens must have been in a condition of near anarchy. The power of the ruling elite, based largely on the deferential habits and lack of political consciousness of the masses, had been shattered by the tyrants and the revolution. No organized group within the state could hope to exert authority by coercion or impose order by force. The only way to fashion a constitutional structure that would frame the Athenians' newly discovered mass power was by using the existing momentum of growing political consciousness to move forward: to reemphasize the unity of the group, its coherence as a group, and its united political will. Lacking authority, then, Cleisthenes resorted to a politics of consensus. His constitutional reforms created the most democratic state the Greek world had ever seen, but that is by no means proof that he was a democrat at heart. Whether he was an idealist or an opportunist, democratic visionary or clever political manipulator, is, for our purposes, immaterial. The key point is that he saw the exigencies of the moment clearly and moved quickly to design and implement a new constitutional order that was elegant in its essential simplicity and functional efficiency.[37]

[37] The main ancient sources for Cleisthenes are *AP* 20–22; Hdt. 5.66, 5.69–73.1. Among other discussions of Cleisthenes and his reforms I have found particularly useful are Ehrenberg, "Origins," *From Solon to Socrates*, 90–103; Hignett, *HAC*, 124–58; Lewis, "Cleisthenes"; Kinzl, "Athens," 202–10; Andrewes, "Kleisthenes' Reform Bill"; Meier, *Entstehung des Politischen*, 91–143; Whitehead, *Demes*, 3–38; Rhodes, *CommAP*, 240–72. F. J. Frost, "The Athenian Military Before Cleisthenes," *Historia* 33 (1984): 283–94, points out that there was probably no effective mobilization system before 508, and he rightly emphasizes the urgent need for an efficient military system in light of the Spartan threat. But the attempt by P. Siewert, *Die Trittyen Attikas und die Heeresreform des Kleisthenes* (Munich, 1982), to show that Cleisthenes' reforms were specifically designed to facilitate mobilization fails to explain the location of demes or their organization into trittyes; see G. R. Stanton, "The Tribal Reform of Kleisthenes the Alkmeonid," *Chiron* 14 (1984): 1–41, esp. 3–7. I have adapted the concept of democratic forms as a way to achieve consensus from Zuck-

E.1 CITIZENS, DEMES, AND CONSENSUS

Like Aristotle in the *Politics* (1274b32–1275a2) 170 years later and Solon 85 years before, Cleisthenes began with the definition of the citizen. The Athenian citizenry would now be a self-defined body. Each
existing citizen was instructed to register in one of 139 deme centers;
normally this would be his home village or neighborhood of the city.
The exact process by which demes were identified, and how much factional politics had to do with deciding which villages achieved deme
status, remains unclear, but these issues are not really relevant for our
purposes in any event.[38] Hereafter, the members of each deme were
responsible for coopting new members by voting upon them in deme
assemblies, which were open to all demesmen. The demesmen were to
determine, on the basis of their knowledge of their neighbors,
whether a new applicant for citizenship, normally presented to the
deme assembly at age eighteen by his father, was a legitimate son of
an Athenian father, who was himself a registered member of the
deme. The official name of the newly enrolled citizen was cast in the
formula "x of deme y."[39] Every citizen was directly dependent upon
his fellow citizens for his primary political identity, and his very name
symbolically reiterated his dependence upon them.

The bonds of mutual interdependence between citizens were now
based on an assumption of political equality. This assumption tended
to weaken the old bonds of deference which had been based on class
and status inequality, because the new ties cut across the horizontal
strata of birth and wealth. The scion of the haughtiest noble house
was—at the emotionally charged moment at which his political life began, when he crossed the divide from boy to full citizen—voted into
the demos by the decision of his ordinary neighbors. Democratic vot-

---

erman, "Social Context"; I am indebted to Billy G. Smith for the reference and for
his insightful comments on Zuckerman's thesis. For further discussion of the relationship between authority and sovereignty (popular and otherwise), see Bowles
and Gintis, *Democracy and Capitalism*, 181–82.

[38] In assuming that demes were originally identified as registration centers,
rather than as geographical regions, I follow W. E. Thompson, "The Deme in Kleisthenes' Reforms," *SO* 46 (1971): 72–79; Andrewes, "Kleisthenes' Reform Bill";
Whitehead, *Demes*, 27–30. For the alternative thesis see, recently, M. K. Langdon,
"The Territorial Basis of the Attic Demes," *SO* 60 (1985): 5–15. On what constitutes
a deme and how many there were: Traill, *Political Organization*, 73–103. On the
word "deme" (*dēmos*) and its relationship to demos = the people, see Whitehead,
Demes, 365–68.

[39] Nomenclature, registration method, deme assemblies: Whitehead, *Demes*, 69–
72, 97–109, 258. On the significance of the reform for the idea of the citizen, see
esp. Meier, *Entstehung des Politischen*, esp. 129–38, *Anthropologie*, 12–13.

ing on new citizens and on affairs of local interest furthermore emphasized and promoted consensus: since all had a say in the assembly, each demesman was morally bound by its decisions. Consensus decision making therefore created and then reinforced the new sociopolitical order and made up for the lack of a fully operative deferential social order or a coercive governmental authority. In this respect, the situation in the Attic demes of the late sixth and early fifth centuries B.C. is similar to that of Massachusetts towns in the late seventeenth and early eighteenth centuries of our era. As Michael Zuckerman has shown in a revealing study of the social context and meaning of democratic political process in colonial New England, Massachusetts townsmen employed a wide franchise and democratic forms, not out of any theoretical preference for democracy (indeed the elite of the period generally despised the principle of democracy), but because of a lack of any external authority capable of enforcing order.[40]

E.2 COUNCIL AND ASSEMBLY

Consensus decision making in the deme assemblies, where everyone knew everyone else, would prepare the citizenry for the leap to the national level of state decision making (cf. below, IV.B.2). Thus, the demes were the basis of Cleisthenes' reforms of the decision-making process at the national level. Each deme annually sent a fixed number (based on its population) of individuals to serve on the new advisory Council of 500, which replaced the Solonian council of 400. The new Council, like the old, was responsible for developing the agenda for each meeting of the Assembly and for dealing with sundry matters of state business.[41]

We do not know how the original delegates were chosen in the demes; very possibly they were chosen by election (see below, II.F.1). If so, the local notables, who had more leisure and perhaps some political experience, would probably have been the first to be sent forward. The early Councils may therefore have been dominated by elite Athenians, but all delegates would have been chosen by the demo-

---

[40] Zuckerman, "Social Context." The use of an assembly to disseminate information and to generate consensus on problematic issues has Homeric parallels; see Starr, *Individual and Community*, 18–21; Ruzé, "*Plethos*," 248–49. On the function and procedure of pre-democratic assemblies in general: Ste. Croix, *Origins*, 348–49.

[41] On the organization and powers of the Cleisthenic Council, see Rhodes, *Boule*, esp. 208–10. Connor, "Athenian Council," 38–39, believes the early Council may have had rather wider legal powers than Rhodes supposes; see also Woodhead, "ΙΣΗΓΟΡΙΑ," esp. 138–39.

cratic deme assemblies; Councillors owed their office not to birth- or class-right but to the masses at home. And, given that service was limited to a maximum of two annual terms, demographic realities made it inevitable that the numerical domination of the Council by the Solonian wealth elite would soon have been diluted (see below, III.E.3). While never construed as "local representatives," the new Councilmen were much more closely tied to the masses than the members of the old council of 400 had been.

In meetings of the Council, the delegates had to cooperate with individuals from all over Attica; no longer would the government be directly controlled by a small cadre of urban political specialists, as it had been in the past.[42] The 500 members of the Council were considerably more numerous than the average deme assembly, but they were broken up for many purposes into prytanies, "tribal" groups of fifty. The system of grouping the 139 demes into thirty trittyes ("thirds") and the trittyes into ten tribes (*phulai*) ensured that these subgroups of the Council included a broad geographical cross section of the citizenry.[43] In prytany and in plenary Council, the Councillors had to make important decisions, and this required cooperating with strangers. Those strangers were, however, fellow Athenians and political equals, and these had become important criteria. The ideological ties of similarity that now united the Athenians allowed the Councillors to perform the same sort of morally binding, democratic decision making in Council that they had performed when deciding on local affairs in the more intimate and familiar forum of the deme square. Thus the Council served important social and educational functions: transferring to the level of the state government the habits of consensual political action that integrated the citizenry and stabilized the social order at a local level.

The final step was for the demos as a whole to vote upon decisions. Scholars sometimes assume that Cleisthenes introduced freedom of debate (*isēgoria*) in the Assembly and Council.[44] If he did so, he may

[42] Urban elite: Hopper, *Basis*, 7; cf. Osborne, *Demos*, 64–92.

[43] An average-sized deme assembly might have had between 150 and 250 potential voters (total population of ca. 30,000 divided by 139 demes = 216). The grouping of demes into *phulai* and trittyes: *AP* 21; cf. Traill, *Political Organization*, esp. 56–58, 64–72; Whitehead, *Demes*, 17–23. On the operation of tribal prytanies in the Council, see Rhodes, *Boule*, esp. 16–25. Hansen, "History of the Athenian Constitution," 64, suggests that the agenda of the Assembly was drawn up by the Council prytanies.

[44] J. D. Lewis, "Isegoria at Athens: When Did it Begin?" *Historia* 20 (1971): 129–40, makes a rather weak case for a Solonian introduction and Cleisthenic reinstatement. The fullest and best argument for the Cleisthenic introduction is Raaflaub,

truly be regarded as the founder of the democracy. But encourage-
ment of open debate by Cleisthenes seems unlikely. The key element
for his new order was the assertion of collective responsibility for decisions that could not be enforced by external authority. This desirable
end might have been achieved through the Assembly's voting on motions presented by the Council without much, or any, debate. Indeed,
the legitimacy of publicly airing differences of opinion and dissension
implied by *isēgoria* runs directly counter to the consensual spirit of
Cleisthenes' deme reform. When all citizens are thinking alike, when
the individuals in the community are bound by consensus, there is no
need for open political debate.[45]

How extensively Cleisthenes used selection by lot for offices of the
government remains uncertain.[46] There is no necessary reason to assume he would have favored the lot in principle. He did not undercut
the oversight powers of the council of the Areopagus,[47] abandon
property qualifications for officeholding, or introduce pay for government service. Without extensive use of the lot, open debate, or pay for
service, and with the maintenance of property qualifications, the elites
could certainly hope to retain control of the state through elected
magistracies, control of debate in the Council and Assembly, and the
powers and moral authority of the Areopagus. They would be more
accountable to the masses than their predecessors, but their position
might be all the more secure for the legitimacy they would achieve
through mass support.

E.3 OSTRACISM

One other Cleisthenic reform adds much to our understanding of the
symbolic relationship between Athenian mass and elite in the late sixth
and early fifth centuries: the institution of ostracism.[48] The Athenian

---

"Freien Bürgers Recht," 28–34, who suggests that Cleisthenes introduced at least
the *possibility* of public speech by members of the hoplite class; see also Forrest,
EGD, 202; Loraux, *Invention*, 409 n. 22; E. Will, "Bulletin historique," *Revue Historique* 238 (1967): 396–97. But cf. II.n.59.

[45] Cf. below, VII.B. Zuckerman, "Social Context," 526–27, 538–44, notes that in
colonial Massachusetts town meetings, the aim of the vote was endorsement, assent,
and accommodation, not disputation or deciding between real alternatives: "neither
conflict, dissent, nor any other structural pluralism ever obtained legitimacy . . ."
(526–27).

[46] See, for example, Badian, "Archons," 21–27; Rhodes, *Boule*, 6–7, *CommAP*,
251; Hansen, "Demos, Ecclesia," 142–43; Finley, *PAW*, 48.

[47] Rhodes, *Boule*, 201, 209–10. See also below, II.F.1.

[48] For ostracism, its origins and purposes, see D. Kagan, "The Origin and Purposes of Ostracism," *Hesperia* 30 (1961): 393–401; Ehrenberg, "Origins," 543–45

people were given the opportunity each year to decide whether or not
to hold an ostracism; if a quorum of 6,000 voted to hold one, the Assembly would foregather, and each citizen would scratch on a pot-
sherd—or have a literate fellow citizen scratch for him—the name of
the man he most wanted to see expelled from the city. He did not
need to indicate why he wanted the individual expelled; motives no
doubt varied. The ballots were collected, and the "winner" was forced
into exile for ten years.

Any number of possible intended functions have been suggested for
this peculiar institution, but in the context of consensual politics its
symbolic meaning, at least, becomes clear: ostracism was a way of expelling from the community any individual who threatened the national consensus, especially by publicly advocating ideas or acting in
ways that threatened the values of political society.[49] Ostracism also
served as a public demonstration of the binding nature of democratic
decisions on an individual. As was the case in citizen registration in the
deme, the masses judged and imposed their collective will upon individuals. The ostracized citizen was morally, as well as legally, bound by
the will of the people; their decision might be arbitrary and irrational,
but he was obliged to obey it. However, the ostracized Athenian was
not permanently excluded from the community. Having obeyed the
will of the people, having accepted the consensual covenant that
bound all members of the state, the ostracized man was allowed eventually to return to the group, with his citizenship, as well as his status
and property (i.e., his primary elite attributes) intact.

Ostracism clarifies the central message of Cleisthenes' reforms at
both the local and state levels: "We Athenians are all in this together;
we all take part in decisions; and we are all bound to support mutually
agreed-upon solutions. Active dissent is unacceptable, but he who accepts decisions that are not in his favor remains part of the group."
The political slogan of Cleisthenes' reform, the name of his new order,
seems to have been *isonomia*, a word that may have been coined by
Athenian aristocrats as an anti-tyrannical catchphrase. If so, Cleis-

with n. 71; Hignett, *HAC*, 159–66; E. Vanderpool, "Ostracism at Athens," in *Lectures in Honor of Louise Taft Semple*, 2nd series, 1966–70 (Norman, Oklahoma, 1973),
215–70; R. Thomsen, *The Origin of Ostracism: A Synthesis* (Copenhagen, 1972); J. J.
Kearney and A. Raubitschek, "A Late Byzantine Account of Ostracism," *AJP* 93
(1972): 87–91; Roberts, *Accountability*, 142–44. On the link between ostracism and
envy: Gouldner, *Enter Plato*, 57–58.

49 This aspect of ostracism might be compared to the practice in colonial Massachusetts of "warning out" (i.e., expelling) social misfits: Zuckerman, "Social Context," 537–38.

thenes gave the term a new meaning, which was defined by Gregory Vlastos as "political equality maintained through the law and pro- moted by the law."[50] The Athenians of 508/7 might have interpreted *isonomia* even more broadly, as "equality of participation in making the decisions (laws) that will maintain and promote equality and that will bind all citizens equally." But the practice of ostracism might have had an ancillary and more pointed symbolic message for the Athenian citizenry: no member of the elite, no matter how powerful he might seem, was safe from the ire of the masses. Whoever Cleisthenes designed the weapon to be used against, those who ended up ostracized were members of the elite. The experience of arbitrarily expelling a prominent citizen, for the simple and sufficient error of standing out too obviously from the group, was an important lesson in the collective power of the masses to impose upon elites a degree of conformity to popular conceptions of proper public behavior.[51]

F. Fifth Century

In the eight decades that elapsed between Cleisthenes' reforms and the death of Pericles (429 B.C.), most remaining institutional bastions of elite political privilege were dismantled, and the collective political power of the masses was enhanced.[52] Hence, the analogy with the

[50] G. Vlastos, "Isonomia," *AJP* 74 (1953): 337–66, "ΙΣΟΝΟΜΙΑ ΠΟΛΙΤΙΚΗ." Cf. Ehrenberg, "Origins," 530–37; Ostwald, *Nomos*, esp. 119–20, 137–60, *From Popular Sovereignty*, 27; Meier, *Anthropologie*, 29; Whitehead, *Demes*, 37–38 (following Ostwald); Raaflaub, *Entdeckung der Freiheit*, 115–17. My own reading of the use of the term by Cleisthenes is perhaps closest to that of H. W. Pleket, "Isonomia and Cleisthenes: A Note," *Talanta* 4 (1972): 63–81, and requires a looser definition of *nomos* than pertained in the fourth century (see below, II.G). But *nomos* was not clearly defined as written "constitutional" law even in the mid-fifth century; cf. J.A.S. Evans, "Despotes Nomos," *Athenaeum*, n. s. 43 (1965): 142–53, for the concept of *nomos* in Herodotus.

[51] Cf. the story (Plut. *Aristides* 7.5–6) of the famous politician Aristides being asked by an illiterate citizen to inscribe his own name on a sherd; when queried, the citizen stated he was tired of hearing Aristides called "The Just" all the time. The story says something about Athenian literacy and Aristides' reputation for honesty, but also about the sources of resentment the elite would now have to contend with. Pearson, "Party Politics," 44, correctly notes that ostracism also implies the rejection of the notion of desirable and legitimate organized opposition; this may be another argument against its originator's being interested in *isēgoria*.

[52] For the constitutional development of this period, see *AP* 22–27, with Rhodes, *CommAP*, 283–344; Carawan, "*Eisangelia* and *Euthyna*"; cf. Hignett, *HAC*, 159–260; Ostwald, *From Popular Sovereignty*, 28–83, who emphasizes the importance of the regularization of and popular control (through the elaboration of the *heliaia* into *dikastēria*) of the *euthunai* and *dokimasia* procedures.

town meetings of colonial Massachusetts breaks down: the Athenians turned the corner from the use of democratic forms that created order in the absence of external authority to the creation of a state in which active public debate over real alternatives preceded genuine decision making by the masses. Without abandoning consensus as an ideal or developing any real conception of democratic pluralism, the Athenians developed means of operating on the basis of majoritarian as well as communitarian principles and ways to permit and legitimize dissent in the context of political discussion.[53] Whereas in colonial Massachusetts franchise democracy occupied a peripheral position in terms of social organization, for the Athenians, democracy and equality became central organizing principles of their social as well as of their political order.[54]

F.1 CONSTITUTIONAL REFORMS TO CA. 440

The first major post-Cleisthenic reform seems to have come in 487, with the introduction of a lottery for the selection of archons and probably for other magistrates, including the Councillors, as well. The origins of the lottery for selecting individuals to perform various tasks may have been religious, and both Solon and Cleisthenes may have used lot selection for some magistracies. But beginning in 487/6 the nine archons and (perhaps) the secretary of the *thesmothetai* were chosen by lot from a much larger group of men (*prokritoi*: at least 100 and perhaps as many as 500) who had been "pre-elected" either by the tribes or by the demes. Although the archonship remained the legal preserve of the wealthy, this reform had a significant long-term impact on the ability of the elite to control the institutional apparatus of the state.[55] Politically ambitious elites now must have found it more

[53] Ruzé, *"Plethos,"* 247–59, demonstrates that the idea that the majority will can legitimately bind the minority without endangering the community is nonexistent in Homer, fully developed in Herodotus and Aeschylus, and at least incipient in some of the texts in between.

[54] Peripheral position: Zuckerman, "Social Context," 535. Hansen, *AECA*, 208, notes that the New England town meeting is too small a forum to provide a true parallel to Athenian direct democracy. This is an important point, especially in light of the "face-to-face" argument (above, I.C.6), but I think the question of the difference in the *function* of democracy in the two societies is as fundamentally important as the difference in scale. Seventeenth-century England seems to have turned the same corner from politics of consensus to a politics of debate and decision, although the institutional context was very different: see M. Kishlansky, *Parliamentary Selection: Social and Political Choice in Early Modern England* (Cambridge, 1986).

[55] Archons by *prokrisis* and lot: *AP* 22.5, with the discussion of Rhodes, *CommAP*, 272–74, on the numbers of *prokritoi* and the question of whether they were elected by demes or tribes. Importance of sortition to democracy: Hdt. 3.80. Cf. Ehren-

difficult to gain powerful positions in the government by a display of their abilities, family backgrounds, or wealth.

Since many persons had to be pre-elected each year, some nonentities and incompetents must have ended up in important magistracies. Moreover, even those who were personally able did not necessarily have the network of connections within the elite that major magistrates might have been expected to have had in the sixth century. Officeholders could no longer automatically call on a cadre of politically experienced friends and kinsmen for help in making and carrying out decisions. In short, with the introduction of the lot, magistrates might find it more difficult to function effectively as the political arm of a cohesive ruling elite. As a result, there seems to have been a gradual weakening of magisterial power and influence, and magistrates tended to become more closely tied to the authority of central decision-making bodies: the Areopagus, Council, and Assembly.[56]

A generation later, in 462, an important, if somewhat obscure, series of reforms crippled the direct political power of the elite. A certain Ephialtes led a movement to strip the "extra powers" from the Areopagus council. While we do not know exactly what this meant in practice or what Ephialtes' motive might have been, the Areopagus probably lost some of its legal powers, including the authority to review and set aside as "unconstitutional" decisions of the Assembly.[57] Assuming

---

berg, "Origins," 528; Hopper, Basis, 7; and esp. Headlam, Election, 4–12, 19–26. Badian, "Archons," esp. 9; Kinzl, "Athens," 215–22; and Carawan, "Eisangelia and Euthyna," 207–208, point out that the reform was not originally self-consciously democratic, and it may even have been intended to strengthen the position of the elite by limiting intra-elite fighting over offices. But by the time of Aristotle (Pol. 1274a5, 1294b7–9) the lot was considered specifically democratic. Sortition was also being used in the demes by the mid-fifth century (Whitehead, Demes, 114–16); unfortunately we do not know how people arranged to have their names put in the hat (Whitehead, Demes, 320–21). Carter, Quiet Athenian, 17 with n. 26, suggests that all fifth-century magistrates were chosen from wealthy prokritoi, but there is no evidence for the institution after 458/7: Hansen, "ΚΛΗΡΩΣΙΣ."

[56] After 487 it is rare to hear of archons taking political initiatives similar to that of Themistocles (archon in 493), who began the fortification of Piraeus (Thuc. 1.93.3). For the date, see W. W. Dickie, "Thucydides 1.93.3," Historia 22 (1973): 758–59. Badian, "Archons," demolishes the argument that the reform was a result of a plot to break the power of the archons in favor of the stratēgoi; but I think he underestimates its long-term political significance. Cf. also Sealey, Athenian Republic, 128–29; Gabrielsen, Remuneration, 116, 139 with n. 35; Whitehead, Demes, 319–20, who notes the difficulty of planning a career of magistracies on either local or city level, given the use of the lot.

[57] Ephialtes' reforms: AP 25.2; Plut. Pericles 9–10, Cimon 15.2–3. Cf. Hignett, HAC, 193–213; Rhodes, Boule, 202–207; Davies, DCG, 70–72; Ostwald, From Popu-

this is correct, the decision-making powers of the Assembly were no longer limited by a body that was sociologically more narrowly constituted than the demos itself: the elite no longer had an institutional means to veto the decisions of the masses. The Areopagus was still the preserve of the wealth elite, but it now played a considerably reduced political role in the state.

The reduced powers of the Areopagus left the Council of 500 as the only institutionalized advisory group in the state. The Council's agenda-setting function and its recommendations (*probouleumata*) to the Assembly became consequently more important. But it would be wrong to see the Council as acting as a brake on the Assembly. Rather, the Council served an empowering function, ensuring that a fairly broad cross section of the demos (which had been selected randomly by lot), rather than a narrow elite, would determine the agenda of Assembly meetings and make suggestions on policy. If the Council, with its popular base, had not set the agenda, the Assembly would be relatively powerless: those who did gain control of the agenda could have stopped any move that threatened their institutional position, simply by ensuring that threatening proposals never came before the people. As Peter Bachrach has pointed out, "an elite not only wields an inordinate amount of power in making decisions to initiate, approve, or veto policies within the scope of his influence, but he also exercises a great amount of power by *preventing* issues from being publicly considered that might threaten his interests."[58] Unlike the Areopagus, the Councillors had no corporate identity and so no institutional position to protect and no collective private agendas to advance. They could be expected to bring all those matters before the Assembly that were of concern to the citizenry.

Within a few years after 462, two other vitally important innovations made possible the full political participation of ordinary citizens at every level of the government. One was the introduction—or at least a greater emphasis upon—*isēgoria*, the right of all citizens to speak on matters of state importance in the Assembly.[59] Raaflaub has argued

---

lar Sovereignty, 47–81; and esp. Wallace, *Areopagos*, chapter 3.iii, iv. For a different perspective, see Sealey, "Ephialtes."

[58] Bachrach, *Political Elites*, introduction: 6 with n. 11 and literature cited. The idea that the Council was set up as an independent center of power (which then declined) was advanced by Bonner, *Aspects*, 4; and Woodhead, "ΙΣΗΓΟΡΙΑ," esp. 133. On the relationship between Council and Assembly, see Rhodes, *Boule*, 64–81, 210–15; cf. Hignett, *HAC*, 237–44; Headlam, *Election*, 56–63.

[59] Date: Griffith, "Isegoria"; followed by Woodhead, "ΙΣΗΓΟΡΙΑ," 131. On the meaning of the term cf. also Forrest, *EGD*, 202; Loraux, *Invention*, 175; and below, VII.B.

convincingly that the origins of the *concept* of *isēgoria*, as equal opportunity *among the nobles* to speak, must be sought in the context of pre-
Cleisthenic, intra-elite competition.[60] But the pre-Cleisthenic noble
was likely to hold an official position (e.g., as an Areopagite) that gave
him the legal or traditional (it does not really matter which) privilege
of addressing the citizenry in formal Assembly. With the ongoing
fragmentation of the institutional bases of Athens' political elites, the
Assembly gained power and became a primary locus for competition
between potential leaders. But since by now most offices were certainly
filled by lot, the politically ambitious elite might not be able to secure
an official position that would give him the right to speak to the Assembly. The result was a conviction in elite circles that a greater freedom of political debate was a good idea.

Isēgoria was later considered by the Athenians to be a cornerstone of
democracy, and so it was. Probably most Athenian citizens—even
those who attended the Assembly regularly—never exercised their
right to speak there. But *isēgoria* changed the nature of mass experience of the Assembly from one of passive approval (or rejection) of
measures presented, to one of actively listening to and judging the
merits of complex, competing arguments.[61] Skill in public speech became an increasingly important leadership skill, since all major matters of state policy were decided on the basis of speeches delivered in
the Assembly. The political life of the citizen became much more intense and personally meaningful, as he was forced to think about and
choose among the various policy options presented to him. From a
forum to ensure that responsibility for decisions would be collective
and so morally binding upon the citizenry, the Assembly became the
focus of public political discussion, debate, and decision.

Two particularly important developments in the years immediately
following 462 were the lowering of property qualifications for officeholding and the introduction of pay for government service.[62] In

---

[60] Raaflaub, "Freien Bürgers Recht," 23–28, citing the name of Isagoras, opponent of Cleisthenes.

[61] Cf. Raaflaub, "Freien Bürgers Recht," esp. 43; Woodhead, "ΙΣΗΓΟΡΙΑ," 131.

[62] Lowering of property qualifications for archons in 457/6: *AP* 26.2. Pay for archons: *AP* 29.5, 62.2; for jurors and *bouleutai*: below II.nn.64, 67. Cf. Hignett, *HAC*,
219–21; Buchanan, *Theorika*, 14–22; Finley, *DAM*, 19 (sortition and pay for office
were the "linchpin" of the democratic system); Ste. Croix, *CSAGW*, 289 (the introduction of pay for office was, with the possible exception of the reforms of 462/1,
the most important democratic innovation of 507–322). Markle, "Jury Pay," 271–
72; and Loraux, *Invention*, 409 n. 28 (with literature cited) note that the importance
of pay is demonstrated by attacks upon this institution by the oligarchs in 411 and

457/6 all offices, including the archonships, were opened to the *zeugi-tai*—who were not members of the leisure class. The magistracies of Athens collectively would no longer reflect even a randomly selected cross section of the wealth elite but were open to a large percentage of the citizen population, indeed, perhaps, to the entire citizenry. By the fourth century, at any rate, no attention was being paid to property qualifications at all; even *thētes* could be, and were, officeholders.[63] The constitutional change was made meaningful by the provision of state pay for officeholders. Now, for the first time, those who had to work for a living could afford to dedicate significant amounts of time to state service. Since most offices were dispensed by lot, we may assume that from here on in many of the officeholders of Athens were ordinary citizens. Just how important this development was to the actual ruling of the state is unclear, since most offices were not centers of great responsibility or power. Assuming that pay for Councillors was introduced at the same time, however, the reform undoubtedly had considerable impact on the social composition of the vital agenda-setting body.[64]

The symbolic value of ordinary citizens conducting all levels of state business must have been considerable. The awe that an Athenian might feel upon confronting a magistrate (e.g., the *basileus*, about some problem to do with religion) would now be a function of the office itself, not of the private status of the officeholder. Awe would therefore be ascribed to the reflected grandeur of the state, which the magistrate in some sense symbolized. The dislocation of elite status from the awe-inspiring (assuming they were so) figures of the state's official representatives thus tended to lower the potential influence of the elite collectively over the minds of the masses. The deference that the non-elite citizen might feel toward the elites on account of their high birth and wealth was no longer reinforced by seeing them in the trappings of state authority.

In 451/0 a new law, advocated by Pericles, limited citizenship to those who could demonstrate that they were sons of Athenians on their mother's as well as their father's side. Formerly, sons of non-

---

in later elitist texts. Davies, *DCG*, 69, emphasizes the symbolic significance of the reform.

[63] Census classes ignored: *AP* 7.4; cf. Gabrielsen, *Remuneration*, 112–13. Even in the late fourth century, the Treasurers of Athena were selected from the top census class (*AP* 47.1; cf. Gabrielsen, *Remuneration*, 111–12), but this may be explained by the Athenian concern with assuring personal financial accountability: above I.n.9. On the major financial *archai* of the later fourth century, see below, II.G.

[64] Pay for Councillors (in 411): Rhodes, *Boule*, 13–14, 214; cf. below, III.E.3.

Athenian mothers had been allowed to become citizens. The immediate concern prompting the reform may have been the tendency of Athenian clerouchs (for whom see below, II.F.2) to marry foreign women while abroad. The many clerouchies of the mid-fifth century provided an unprecedented opportunity for lower-class Athenians to marry non-Athenian women; before the clerouchies, this option had been for the most part restricted to the more mobile members of the elite.[65] Upon the implementation of the new citizenship law, the Athenian citizen body became, in theory, a closed set; there would be no further admixture of such foreign sympathies and tendencies as could be transmitted (in the Athenian imagination) through bloodlines. The long-term symbolic effect of endogamy was to reemphasize the Athenian belief in the superiority of pure Athenian descent and in the inheritability of the characteristics that the citizens now felt marked the true Athenian: native intelligence, quickness, patriotism, public-spiritedness, innate love of equality, and respect for the traditions of the state.[66]

This major series of post-Cleisthenic reforms culminated in the 440s with the introduction of state pay for the jurors in the people's courts.[67] Once again sponsored by Pericles, jury-pay allowed the working citizens to sit as jurors. This effectively established the masses as the legal judges of all citizens' behavior. Now the elite individual who fell afoul of the laws, or into a dispute with another citizen, would have to face a jury dominated by ordinary citizens (cf. below, III.E.4). The upper-class litigant's life, his conduct, his attitudes, would be the subject of close scrutiny by those whose property, social status, and education were much inferior to his own. Since jurors were free to vote their own consciences, he would be judged by *their* standards, which might be different from his own. The introduction of pay in the law courts gave the masses the same sort of control over private behavior and the interpretation of law that they had over state policy. By the

[65] Plut. *Pericles* 37.2–5; Sealey, *Athenian Republic*, 23–25. Cf. Patterson, *Pericles' Citizenship Law*, esp. 96–115; Hignett, *HAC*, 343–47; Humphreys, *Family*, 24–25, suggests that the law was intended to prevent the elite from making international dynastic marriages that could lead to the use of private relationships to manipulate foreign policy. On the importance for the reform in defining the Athenians' image of themselves, see Loraux, *Invention*, 150; cf. below, VI.C.

[66] These virtues are emphasized by Pericles in the Funeral Oration (Thuc. 2.35–46); cf. Loraux, *Invention*.

[67] Pay for jurors: *AP* 27.4; Plut. *Pericles* 9.2–3; cf. Hignett, *HAC*, 219–21, 342–43. Davies, *DCG*, 68–69, notes that the uniformly conservative ancient tradition ignores the functional effect of this reform and attributes it purely to tactical maneuvering on Pericles' part.

440s, if not before, *dēmokratia* became the standard term to describe the Athenian form of government, and the demos indeed possessed the political power in the state.[68]

F.2 CONTEXT OF REFORM

The factors, internal and external, that contributed to the Athenians' success in turning the corner to a true democracy, in which genuine decisions between real alternatives were made openly by the masses, are certainly complex. No single cause seems likely to provide a sufficient explanation, and it is difficult to assess the relative weight that should be assigned to each of various factors that came into play. One important factor is Cleisthenes' constitutional arrangement itself. Rather than divorcing local political organization from state government, Cleisthenes devised a means for transferring the experience of achieving political consensus at the deme level to the level of state policymaking. While the intent of the lawmaker may not have been true democracy, democratic political ideology, developed locally, was therefore transferred to the national Assembly. As Zuckerman notes in the conclusion to his article on Massachusetts town meeetings,

> ironically, local politics may have been democratic indeed, at least in the limited terms of political participation, since a politics of consensus required consultation with most of the inhabitants in order to assure accord. In little towns of two or three hundred adult males living in close, continuing contact, men may very well have shared widely a sense of the amenability of the political process to their own actions and attitudes, and the feeling of involvement may well have been quite general.[69]

[68] Meier, *Entstehung des Begriffs*, 44–69, esp. 48–49, argues that the term came into general use in the 440s, but cf. Ehrenberg, "Origins" (with idem, *From Solon to Socrates*, 209 with n. 44: correction on the date of Aeschylus' *Suppliant Women*), arguing for a date earlier in the fifth century; M. H. Hansen, "The Origin of the term *dēmokratia*," *LCM* 11.3 (March 1986): 35–36, suggests that *dēmokratia* was the original name of Cleisthenes' constitutional order. Sealey, "Origins," argues (in my opinion wrongly) that the term was without positive connotation before 404/3. Sealey's argument is based in part on reading Pericles' discussion of *dēmokratia* in the Funeral Oration (Thuc. 2.37.1) as "apologetic." I think Vlastos, "ΙΣΟΝΟΜΙΑ ΠΟΛΙΤΙΚΗ," 8 n. 1, 28–31, with 29 n. 2, gets closer to the true meaning of this passage.

[69] Zuckerman, "Social Context," 544. Cf. Bowles and Gintis, *Democracy and Capitalism*, esp. 134, 138–40, 150–51, on the importance to the development of democratic political culture of the existence of smaller democratic communities, which stand between the individual and the state, and wherein individual citizens can learn to "do democratic politics" (139), and so "constitute . . . or reaffirm themselves as persons and groups with particular and desired attributes" (138).

In colonial Massachusetts, there were distinct limits to how far that sense could operate beyond the level of the township. But in the Council and Assembly organization developed by Cleisthenes, "a sense of the amenability of the political process" by the masses quickly had a major impact on the political direction of the Athenian state.

Among the external events that helped to hasten the evolution of the democratic order was the experience of the Persian Wars (490–479). In 490 a numerically inferior Athenian army pushed a Persian army off a beachhead at Marathon in northeastern Attica. Athenian determination was again tested in 480–479 when Persian armies marched through Greece and occupied Attica. The Athenians withdrew, choosing to abandon their land rather than surrender or be slaughtered attempting to defend it. The Athenian evacuations of Attica demonstrated, to themselves as well as to the rest of the world, that they were truly a nation and not simply inhabitants of a particular territory. Their sacrifice and fortitude contributed to national unity, pride, and sense of purpose.

Marathon was a victory for the heavy-armed hoplites. But victory in the war also depended on naval actions. Shortly after the first evacuation in 480, the Persian navy was dealt an overwhelming defeat at Salamis, off Athens' coast. Other Greek states contributed to the Greek fleet, but the plurality of the ships, as well as the strategic plan, were Athenian. Athens' ships were manned by lower-class oarsmen. The naval victory at Salamis, by which Athens and ultimately all Greece were saved, was a victory of the lower echelons of the Athenian masses—the poorest citizens, who had insufficient funds to purchase infantryman's armor. Hence, both hoplites and oarsmen contributed to the victory, and after the war had been won, those who had helped to save the state were in a position to demand a fuller share in it.[70]

In the aftermath of the Persian Wars, Athens organized and headed a Naval Confederacy, whose aim was to punish the Persians and prevent the reestablishment of Persian sea power in the Aegean. By mid-century, the Confederacy had become an Athenian empire, and the

[70] The most important ancient source for the Persian wars is Herodotus, esp. Books 6–8. Cf. Burn, *Persia and the Greeks*, for the Greek point of view; A. T. Olmstead, *History of the Persian Empire* (Chicago, 1948), 151–61, 248–61, for a valiant attempt to reconstruct the Persian. The link between democracy and sea power: Aristoph. *Wasps* 1093ff.; [Xen.] *Constitution of Athens*, 1.2; Aristot. *Pol.* 1274a12–15, 1304a21–24, 1321a5–14, 1327a40–b15. Cf. J. F. Charles, "The Anatomy of Athenian Sea Power," *CJ* 42 (1946): esp. 87; Romilly, *Rise and Fall of States*, 33; Ober, "Views," 129; Loraux, *Invention*, 213. For the elite counter-notion of the state as a "republic of hoplites": Vidal-Naquet, "Tradition de l'hoplite"; cf. Loraux, *Invention*, 155–71.

military contributions of the allies had become an outright tribute to Athens. Eventually Athens' "allies" lost the right to mint their own currency, and various legal actions were transferred to Athenian courts. The overseas empire ensured that sea power would remain vital to Athenian national security and thus that the lower-class rowers would remain essential to the state. Meanwhile, the empire proved a great financial asset. In addition to the tribute there were the citizen-colonies, the clerouchies, established in various parts of the empire, which provided poorer Athenians with land allotments. The legal activity generated by the laws compelling imperial subjects to try cases in Athens must have demanded a large pool of jurors, who were paid by the state. Hence, the empire helped create both the climate in which the masses were able to exert pressure for democratization, and the financial wherewithal to pay for citizen participation in government. Maybe full democracy would have emerged without the Persian Wars and the empire, but the external developments of the period were nevertheless conducive to continued growth in mass political consciousness and helped to buffer the financial impact of democratization upon the elite.[71]

F.3 ELITE LEADERSHIP

The tendency to democratization was never effectively blocked by the elites; indeed, elites provided the leadership for the reforms. Rich and well-born Athenians competed vigorously, sometimes savagely, with each other for political influence, and they used appeals to the masses as ploys in their ongoing political struggles.[72] This pattern of behavior is not surprising in light of the degree to which the aristocratic ethos emphasized competition. Since archaic times, Greek nobles had competed at everything from tossing wine dregs at targets when attending drinking parties to state politics. And they competed specifically with one another; in order for the victory to be sweet, it had to be over a properly aristocratic opponent (cf. above, I.A, below, VI.A). As long as the masses had been politically quiescent, intra-elite competition had had relatively little effect on the political direction of the state; the

[71] Athenian empire: Meiggs, *Athenian Empire*; clerouchies: Brunt, "Athenian Settlements." On the links between empire and democracy, see esp. Finley, "Fifth-Century Athenian Empire"; cf. above, I.C.3.

[72] Among the many studies of politics in the first two-thirds of the fifth century, see esp. Connors, *NP*; contrast E. Ruschenbusch, *Athenische Innenpolitik im 5. Jh. v. Chr.* (Bamberg, 1979), who denies that ideology had *any* part in fifth-century politics and attributes all constitutional development to factionalism and the evolving demands of foreign policy.

contests had served to determine who among the elite held the reins of power but did not challenge the hierarchical power structure of society. However, once the lower classes became sufficiently politically aware to be a factor in political struggles, that is, by the time of Cleisthenes, the elites recognized mass ambitions as a new weapon to use against each other. As a result, politically ambitious elites actively sponsored democratizing reforms; this gained influence for themselves in the state and, just as important, discomfited their opponents.

The masses were therefore never without leaders who, driven more by a competitive ethos than by theoretical principles regarding the rightness of equality or by love of the people, contributed their considerable abilities, experience, and connections to the development of true democracy. Ironically, as the elites gained victories over their enemies by sponsoring democratic reforms, there were fewer and fewer institutions that they could control directly. The series of democratizing reforms dismantled the magisterial apparatus that had been the institutional basis for collective elite rule in the pre-Cleisthenic period. By mid-century, most offices meant little, provided for no continuity of authority, and were open to all; major policy decisions were now being made in the open by mass bodies.

In the absence of institutions that would allow them to exercise power directly, elites had to become more overtly "politicians." After all, the masses still needed leaders, experienced men who could think through the best policy for the state and who would be willing to take a leading role in advocating that policy in the Council and Assembly. There were various ways a rich and well-born man could acquire a political reputation in the earlier fifth century; these have been documented by W. R. Connor and J. K. Davies. Politicians of this period depended on *hetaireiai* of elite relatives and friends who could serve as political helpers. An aspiring politician might also engage in ostentatious public display of his wealth and ancestry; victories in the various Panhellenic games provided an opportunity for bragging about both. Wealthy politicians could resort to a "politics of largesse"—giving money and other kinds of material support to their neighbors or providing in some material way for the good of the demos as a whole.[73] In short, the politician of the earlier fifth century tended to depend

---

[73] Connor, *NP*, 18–22; Davies, *WPW*, 96–99, 114–20. Cf. Finley, *PAW*, 39–40; Meier, *Anthropologie*, 14–15; Whitehead, *Demes*, 305–13. Stanton and Bicknell, "Voting in Tribal Groups," 76–77, argue that in the fifth century the Assemblymen were grouped according to tribe and trittys, and they speculate that this arrangement would facilitate control by aristocratic leaders of their local clients; cf. below III.n.72.

upon relationships that had much in common with the forms of deference and clientage that obtained in the pre-Pisistratus period. The Athenian politician of the earlier fifth century appealed to the demos, but he did so through symbols of wealth and birthright that would have been familiar to his sixth-century ancestors.

By the third quarter of the century, however, the developing ideology of the Athenian masses was making the established road to a political career more problematic. The Athenians became increasingly suspicious of the old symbols of aristocratic and class power, and they began to look askance at elites who seemed to prefer the company of their social peers to that of ordinary citizens. As the Athenian demos took closer control of the organs of government, the masses were more willing and able to exert effective pressure upon the elites to conform to increasingly clear, popular notions of proper social and political behavior. Connor suggests that Pericles was among the first politicians to recognize this trend and so to distance himself from the normal social round of the elite citizen.[74]

F.4 PERICLES

Pericles, who was both rich and well born, was the outstanding political figure of Athens between ca. 450 and his death in 429.[75] His eminence was due to his accurate assessment of the ideological climate of Athenian opinion, his clever and restrained use of the one major elective office left in Athens (the generalship), his rhetorical skill, and his willingness to call upon the abilities of a newly emerging "educated elite." The generalship, which had become an important magistracy during and after the Persian Wars as a result of Athens' constant military activity, provided Pericles with continuity in an institutionalized position of both symbolic and constitutional power. He was reelected general each year between 443 and 429, a record that demonstrates his continuing popularity with the voting population. Whether or not he held an official "first generalship," and so had greater legal authority than the other nine annually elected generals, there can be little doubt that his continuity in office made him de facto chairman of the board.[76] As a prominent general, Pericles was expected to address the

[74] Connor, *NP*, 57, 119–22, emphasizing the account of Plut. *Pericles* 7.4.

[75] Main ancient sources: Thuc. 2.13–65; Plut. *Pericles.* Wealth and family: Plut. *Pericles* 3.1, 7.1; cf. Davies, *APF* 11811. Among the many studies of Pericles, see esp. Connor, *NP*.

[76] On the powers of the *stratēgos ex hapantōn*, see the contrasting views of M. H. Jameson, "Seniority in the *Strategia*," *TAPA* 86 (1955): 63–87; E. S. Staveley, "Voting Procedure at the Election of *Strategoi*," *Ancient Society: Studies to Ehrenberg*, 275–

citizens in the Assembly and Council on military affairs and foreign policy. His continuity of office had, at least by the 430s, lent him considerable moral authority. Furthermore, he was able to use his influence with the other generals to avoid the calling of Assemblies for extended periods.[77] Pericles thus had at least a vestige of the "nondecision power" (the term is Bachrach's: see above, II.E.2) that had characterized the ruling elite in the days of the council of 400. Pericles could not prevent decision making indefinitely, but he could use his general's right to call, or not to call, emergency Assemblies according to his own reading of short-term changes in the climate of public opinion.

Pericles could never have achieved his position of eminence in the generalship, however, if he had not had other abilities; he was probably very good at finances and was a brilliant military strategist (if not a great tactician), but most important was his skill in rhetoric. Pericles was surely not the first Athenian politician to have a way with words, but he seems to have paid more attention to the power of public speech than any Athenian public figure before him. The historian Thucydides son of Olorus, who admired him tremendously, makes it clear that Pericles' authority in the state was to a large degree a function of his command of rhetoric: he was "the first of the Athenians, the most powerful in speech and in action" (1.139.4: *prōtos Athēnaiōn, legein te kai prassein dunatōtatos*; cf. 2.65.9; Plato *Phaedrus* 269e). Thucydides claims to reproduce three of Pericles' speeches: the Funeral Oration and two Assembly speeches (see Appendix). These are the earliest speeches by an Athenian politician that have any reasonable claim to being close to the original. This must not be entirely an accident of preservation: political rhetoric, the child of *isēgoria*, had only recently been recognized as a discipline worthy of study and practice. Pericles was no doubt a fine natural orator, but his natural abilities were certainly honed by self-conscious practice and preparation and perhaps by formal education.[78]

88; Fornara, *Board of Generals*; Bloedow, "Pericles' Powers." Generals were generally wealthy: Osborne, *Demos*, 70 with n. 17, and literature cited.

[77] Generals address Assembly and Council: Rhodes, *Boule*, 44–46; de Laix, *Probouleusis*, 148. On the limited access of other non-*bouleutai* to meetings: Hignett, *HAC*, 242–43. Pericles avoids calling Assemblies: Thuc. 2.22.1. The constitutional mechanics of arranging this are discussed by J. Christensen and M. H. Hansen in *CM* 34 (1983), 17–31; Bloedow, "Pericles' Powers."

[78] On the sophists and the origins of political rhetoric, see Pilz, *Rhetor*, esp. 13; Wilcox, "Scope," 128–42; Bolgar, "Training," 38–40; Kennedy, *Art of Persuasion*, 26–70; Ostwald, *From Popular Sovereignty*, 237–50. Pericles' speaking style and education: Plut. *Pericles* 4–6, 8, 15.3, citing Damon, Zeno, and Anaxagoras as influ-

According to Thucydides (2.65.8), Pericles did not attempt to gain influence with the demos by constantly speaking of pleasant things, but rather he sometimes opposed mass desires. No doubt this was true, as it must be true of all orators who hope to accomplish anything beyond ephemeral applause (see below, VII.E.4). But in his Funeral Oration, Pericles certainly played upon and emphasized the themes of Athens' glorious history, its great destiny, the citizens' unity, and their superiority to outsiders.[79] Similar themes recurred in his legislation (e.g., the Citizenship Law), his foreign policy—which emphasized imperial expansion, control of allies, and challenges to the other great powers—and his sponsorship of the great building program on the Acropolis.[80] Like Pisistratus before him, Pericles stressed the unity of citizens and state, and he encouraged the Athenians to see in himself the symbolic embodiment of the latter.[81]

Pericles was by no means free of the competitive attacks which all politically active members of the Athenian elite must expect. His opponents tried various ways to undermine his standing with the people, but he proved relatively immune to their ploys. His demonstrated loyalty to the cause of mass power, his general's authority, and his rhetorical skill retained the people's ear. Thus Pericles was able to rid himself of the presence of the most serious of his rivals by persuading the demos to ostracize them. His last major opponent in the political arena, Thucydides son of Melesias, apparently attempted to unify the old elites against Pericles, whom he clearly saw as a danger to their collective interests. Pericles' demonstrated ability to win every round in the ongoing competition for power and influence threatened to take the fun out of the game of political rivalry. The elites finally were persuaded to act in concert to protect their privileges. But it was too late. Thucydides' political plan—which included having elites sit together in the Assembly so that they could vote, heckle, and exert their moral authority over the mass as a cohesive group—failed. He was ostracized, perhaps in 443; the elite opposition to Pericles and to the

---

ences upon both his thought and speaking style. Cf. Eupolis F 94.5–7 (Kock, *CAF* I, 281) with the comments of Buxton, *Persuasion*, 12–13.

[79] Thuc. 2.35–46, cf. 1.70.6, 2.60.2–3. Cf. also Loraux, *Invention*.

[80] Building program: Plut. *Pericles* 8.2, 12–14. Cf. Boersma, *Athenian Building Policy*, 65–81; R. Meiggs, "The Political Implications of the Parthenos," *Greece and Rome*, Suppl. to vol. 10 (1963): 36–45; Wycherley, *Stones*, index, s.v. 'Perikles, building program.'

[81] Cf. the story, reported by Plutarch (*Pericles* 14.1), that when the Athenians complained of the cost of his building program, Pericles offered to pay for it himself and to have the inscriptions amended to say "of Pericles" rather than "of the Athenians."

rule of the masses went underground. Thucydides son of Melesias is often regarded as the first true party politician, but he appears rather to have pinned his hopes on the resurgence of a politics of deference. Unfortunately for him, the Athenian people were no longer willing to tolerate an assertion of collective privilege by the elite.[82]

According to the historian Thucydides (2.65), by the 430s Pericles was more than just a leader of the people, he was the true ruler of Athens: while in name the state was a democracy, in reality it was a monarchy. This somewhat overstates the case. Thucydides' portrait of Pericles suggests that the latter acted in magnificent isolation, was prescient in his understanding of political realities, and autocratic in his relations with the demos. The portrait may in fact reflect Thucydides' own youthful vision of the great man, but it must owe much to the historian's desire to contrast him with his political successors, whom Thucydides despised.[83]

Pericles had, as we have seen, limited his ties with the old elite as a way of demonstrating personal solidarity with the demos. But he was not necessarily quite so isolated as Thucydides implies. He was apparently able to draw on the talents of an intellectual circle. Many of the members of what might be called the "educated elite" of late fifth-century Athens are shadowy, but Pericles' friends included at least some of the sophists, experts in political manipulation who were flocking to Athens from other Greek poleis. The circle included artists and architects who worked on the great Acropolis projects and the various other public buildings, secular and religious, that Pericles sponsored in the city and countryside. Among Pericles' closest associates was the educated courtesan Aspasia, whom Plato makes the speaker of his pseudo-Funeral Oration (*Menexenus*) and whom Pericles' enemies said was the power behind the throne. The group included, at least collaterally, Socrates, a close friend of Pericles' ward Alcibiades. This group

[82] The son of Melesias may have been a relative of the historian: Finley, *Thucydides*, 28–29, 33. For the political career of the son of Melesias, see Plut. *Pericles* 11, 14; cf. H. T. Wade-Gery, "Thucydides the Son of Melesias," *JHS* 52 (1932), 205–27; Davies, *APF* 7268, with literature cited. Party politics: e.g., Roberts, *Accountability*, 149–50. Krentz, "Ostracism," demonstrates the tenuousness of the traditional date of 443 (based on Plut. *Pericles* 16.2) but his alternative (437 or 436) is not significantly more likely.

[83] See my comments in "Thucydides," esp. 182. Cf. M. H. Chambers, "Thucydides and Pericles," *HSCP* 62 (1957): 79–92; Jones, *AD*, 62–64; Finley, "Athenian Demagogues." Loraux, *Invention*, 190 with 418 n. 127, suggests that Pericles did exercise de facto authority but only within the framework of democratic institutions.

was probably not cohesive, but it may collectively have acted as a sort of brain trust for Pericles.[84]

Pericles' educated friends, whatever their relationship to him, were seldom in the public eye and a liability when they were. They helped to create the intellectual atmosphere in which a new generation of Athenian political leaders grew up, but most members of the educated elite, which included metics and women, necessarily remained on the fringes of political society. They were very important in the political development of Athens in that they served, directly or indirectly, as advisers and teachers of politicians, but they did not openly participate in the governance of the state.

The Athenian conviction that only native-born Athenian males were worthy of fulfilling political roles in the state ensured that many of the most sophisticated intellects in the city remained liminal figures: in society, but never of it. The most enduring political legacy of the fifth-century educated elite was the formalization of the theory and practice of rhetoric. Pericles' skill in manipulating images, especially through speech, had helped him to develop an intimate and personal relationship with the demos. After his death, rhetorical education quickly became essential background preparation for the Athenian politician.

As Connor has pointed out, Pericles was a transitional figure.[85] By wealth and birth he belonged to the old elite. Yet his ties were not to the old elite or even, at least publicly, to the new educated elite, so much as they were to the demos itself. Pericles seems to have gone further than any previous politician in both promoting, especially through pay for jurors, and personally accepting the power of the people to determine the public behavior of their leaders. Rhetoric and acknowledgment of mass control over public behavior were intimately connected: rhetoric provided the means not only to promote policy and to "oppose" the people but also to demonstrate to them one's own conformity to mass ideology. This sort of acknowledgment is not easy to pinpoint in the speeches Thucydides puts in Pericles' mouth, and Pericles himself may not have fully exploited the link between popular ideology and rhetoric.[86] But by his withdrawal from elite society, his

---

[84] Pericles' circle and their functions: esp. Plut. *Pericles* 4–6, 8, 13, 24 (Aspasia), 31.2, 32, 36, 37.1, 38.3–4. On the unique circumstances leading to legal actions against some of this group just before and during the Peloponnesian War, see Frost, "Pericles, Thucydides," 394–95; Krentz, "Ostracism," 502–503; Dover, "Freedom"; Finley, *DAM*, 85–86; Ostwald, *From Popular Sovereignty*, 191–98.

[85] Connor, *NP*, esp. 119–28.

[86] Here we face the difficulty of Thucydidean editing. Even if we assume that the

sponsorship of pay for jurors, and his demonstration of the power of rhetoric, he laid the groundwork for an approach to politics that permanently altered the relationship between political elites and the Athenian masses.

No politician after Pericles ever quite replaced him. None succeeded in combining his continuity of military office—the source of much of his moral authority—with his rhetorical skill, his fine ability to read the people's mood, his command of the details of finance, and his strategic insight. Some elements of this constellation of attributes were, to be sure, the result of what can fairly be called genius. But the break between Pericles and his political successors was not as sharp as Thucydides implied. The differences between Pericles and later Athenian politicians cannot be attributed entirely, or even primarily, to deliberate differences in political methods, social background, or innate character. Rather, the differences were the results of refinements and elaborations by subsequent political leaders upon Pericles' rhetorical method of allying himself with the demos and of changes in external circumstances. Pericles may have been a unique political genius, but he inhabited a unique historical moment; his successors, genius or otherwise, had to contend with somewhat different circumstances.[87]

F.5 Demagogues and Generals

At the time of Pericles' death, Athens was involved in the epic struggle with Sparta later called the Peloponnesian War (431–404 B.C.). The war made tremendous demands upon the Athenian people, and along the way it changed the framework in which Athenian political leaders operated. Particularly significant for long-term political development was the bifurcation of Pericles' road to power. Many of the best Athenian generals in the Peloponnesian War (e.g., Demosthenes and Lamachus) seem not to have been accomplished orators, and the great orators (e.g., Cleon and Hyperbolus) typically did not have a background of military leadership. This tendency toward political specialization may be attributed in part to Pericles' discouragement of potential rivals and to the exigencies of the war itself. None of the generals known to have served with (or under) Pericles seems to have been very

---

speeches in Thucydides' text are substantively as delivered, the historian may have played down (or deleted) the passages that seemed too demagogic; cf. above, I.E.

[87] Cf. Finley, "Athenian Demagogues"; Connor, NP, esp. 139–98; Ostwald, From Popular Sovereignty, 199–224. Davies, DCG, 111–113, and WPW, 126–27, suggests that the old elites did not provide the competent financial management that Athens now required and notes that rhetorical ability, unlike wealth and cult associations, is not directly inheritable.

politically active before 429; we might guess that Pericles encouraged the careers of competent military men who did not show much political flair.

After his death, the conflict broadened and the traditions of agonal battle, with its set forms and unspoken rules of engagement, were abandoned or modified. Strategies and tactics became more complex, demanding skilled and experienced commanders.[88] The "new warfare," with its greater emphasis on strategic planning, made it essential that the Athenians elect generals on the basis of military ability; the Athenians could not often afford the luxury of taking a chance on glib but inexperienced field commanders such as Cleon (Thuc. 4.27.3–29.1). Furthermore, campaigns in distant theaters of operation required generals to be away from the city for long periods of time, out of contact with the demos. Consequently, most Athenian generals after Pericles did not have the political background, the rhetorical skill, or the time to serve as active leaders of the people.

Indeed, the particular abilities and character traits specific to oratorical and military success were quite different. In the years after the war, Andocides (3.34) noted that a general was required by military concerns to keep his plans secret and to practice deception, even upon his own men, but that an ambassador (read: politician) must never be secretive or tricky and must refer everything to the demos. Isocrates (15.131) noted that the haughtiness (*megalophrosunē*) of the famous fourth-century general Timotheus was an advantage to him in the generalship but caused him difficulties in his dealings with the demos. These considerations applied in the last part of the fifth century as well. Though there was never a complete split between the military and the political spheres, and there were generals who addressed the Assembly in the late fifth (e.g., Nicias and Alcibiades) and in the early fourth centuries (e.g., Thrasybulus and Conon), only Phocion, in the second and third quarters of the fourth century, achieved a continuity in office and concomitant moral authority matching that of Pericles. But Phocion proved much inferior to Pericles as an orator and as a reader of the Athenian climate of opinion. Aeschines may have had him in mind when he stated that generals who had done good deeds for the polis might well complain of ill treatment, since lack of speaking skills led to an inability to describe their accomplishments well in public. Meanwhile their opponents, who were able speakers, could

---

[88] Pericles' fellow generals: Fornara, *Board of Generals*, 48–55 (lists of known *stratēgoi* from 443/2 to 429/8); Holladay, "Athenian Strategy." New forms of warfare: Ober, *FA*, esp. 32–50.

make themselves appear benefactors of the state despite having done nothing worthwhile.[89]

The prominent political leaders of Athens in the period from the death of Pericles to the end of the democracy in 322 were skilled, often formally trained, orators, but they typically lacked the institutional power base the generalship had provided for Pericles. Cleon, the first politician to come to the fore after 429, was from an upper-class family but not of the aristocratic birth elite; to what extent this influenced his outlook is hard to say.[90] What is certain is that he lacked Pericles' institutional position. Cleon based his career squarely on gaining and keeping the support of the masses by demonstrating his ideological solidarity with them. He went Pericles one better in publicly renouncing all of his former friends, in order to show that he was, as Aristophanes mockingly but quite accurately put it, a lover only of Demos.[91] Cleon showed his love through rhetoric; the speech Thucydides (3.37–40) gives him in the Mytilenean Debate is a masterpiece of persuasive speaking. We do not know how closely the speech mirrors the one Cleon actually delivered in 427, but we may guess that the strikingly egalitarian tone was true to Cleon's form, and that this tone was imitated by other would-be political leaders.

F.6 COUNTER-REVOLUTION

The demagogues' speeches emphasizing the rectitude of mass ideology and popular rule found favor with the demos but deeply disturbed many elites. The war had already led to direct taxation of the rich (by 428/7: Thuc. 3.19.1). Egalitarian ideology might bring worse—possibly demands for property confiscations. On the other hand, the elites had reason to hope that the current stress on political equality was superficial. The success that Alcibiades enjoyed in the Assembly debates of 415, after openly bragging of his wealth and ancestry (Thuc. 6.16.1–4), seemed to demonstrate that the masses could still

[89] Aesch. 3.229. Cf. Plut. *Phocion* 7.3, 8.2; Aristot. *Pol.* 1305a10–15. On the split between orators and generals in the late fifth and fourth centuries, see Perlman, "Politicians," 347–48, "Political Leadership," 169–72 (emphasizing the example of Phocion); Hopper, *Basis*, 10–11; Connor, *NP*, 143–47; Davies, *WPW*, 120–25; Finley, *PAW*, 59, 67. Roberts, *Accountability*, 171–73, warns against the danger of over-stressing the split. For the career of Phocion, see Gehrke, *Phokion*.

[90] Finley, "Athenian Demagogues," 16, assumes that their non-noble origins gave post-Periclean politicians a different outlook.

[91] Aristoph. *Knights*, esp. 732–34; cf. Thucydides 3.36.6, 4.27.5–28.5, 21.3; *AP* 28.3; Plut. *Nicias* 8.3; Theopompus (*FGrH* 115) F 92. On the career and rhetorical methods of Cleon, cf. esp. Finley, "Athenian Demagogues"; Connor, *NP*, 91–101. His wealth and family: Davies, *APF* 8674.

be swayed by elite status symbols. The aristocrats and wealthy men who had been driven into the political underground by Pericles still cherished political ambitions and were unwilling to degrade themselves in front of the mob. The strains of war, the success of the demagogues, and the career of Alcibiades spurred both elite fears of unrestrained mass rule and hopes of return to an order based on deference and political inequality.[92] When the opportunity for a coup arose in the context of a military/financial crisis in 411, they were ready. In a well-orchestrated campaign of terror and propaganda, a group of oligarchically minded elites seized control of the government.[93]

The counter-revolutionaries publicly announced that the new regime would be a moderate oligarchy. Pay for public service would be eliminated, but 5,000 citizens would remain technically eligible for office. In reality all power was retained by a much narrower elite of 400 men who believed that to allow 5,000 citizens to participate in the government would be outright democracy (Thuc. 8.92.11). The oligarchy soon collapsed. The 400 could not agree on what direction the state should take, the heavy-armed infantrymen became suspicious after rumors circulated that the oligarchs intended to surrender to Sparta, and the oarsmen of the Athenian fleet, stationed on the island of Samos, refused to acknowledge the legitimacy of the new government. As the oligarchs began losing their grip, various of their number started to court the masses, each attempting to become "the first leader of the demos" (*prōtos prostatēs tou dēmou*: Thuc. 8.89.3). The elite had proven unable to establish a stable, nondemocratic form of government in the face of their own tendency to intra-class competition, strong Athenian patriotism, and the developed political consciousness of the lower classes of Athenian political society. While revealing the depth of tensions within Athenian society, the failure of the oligarchic coup demonstrated the great strength of democratic ideology.[94]

[92] The political pamphlet by "The Old Oligarch" ([Xen.] *Constitution of the Athenians*) gives a good idea of the complaints an elite of the later fifth century (the exact date is disputed) had against the democracy. Cf. Finley, *DAM*, 73; Ostwald, *From Popular Sovereignty*, 188–91.

[93] The oligarchic coup: Thuc. 8.48.3–98; terror: Thuc. 8.65.2. Cf. Gomme et al., *Historical Commentary*, ad locc. On the organization of the oligarchs, see Calhoun, *Athenian Clubs*; Connor, *NP*, 25–29, 197.

[94] Disagreement among the oligarchs: Thuc. 8.89–92; infantrymen and rumors: Thuc. 8.92.5–93.1; fleet at Samos: Thuc. 8.72–74, 81–82. Cf. Gomme et al., *Historical Commentary*, ad locc.; Ostwald, *From Popular Sovereignty*, 344–95. G.E.M. de Ste. Croix, "The Constitution of the Five Thousand," *Historia* 5 (1956): 1–23 (cf. *CSAGW*, 291–92), argued that the "intermediate government" that served as a transition between the oligarchy of the 400 and the restoration of full democracy was

Athens lost the Peloponnesian War in 404. The victorious Spartans set up a puppet government headed by thirty members of the Athenian elite, a government which would meet a fate similar to the coup of 411. Once again, a broad program leading to moderate oligarchy was advertised and abandoned; once again the inability of the elite to act cohesively, the patriotic feelings of the Athenians, popular resentment against both the Spartans and their quislings, and the ability of the masses to act with a unitary will under the command of elite leaders who rejected the new order doomed the oligarchic government. In 403 the Athenians reestablished their democratic government and proclaimed a general amnesty: national unity would be reasserted by a legal requirement that all Athenians—at least in their public actions in the Assembly and court—forget the events of the immediate past. As in 508/7 the reestablishment of social order required a strong emphasis upon consensus and harmony.[95]

G. Fourth Century

In 403 the democracy was restored. But was it, in form or spirit, the "radical" democracy of the later fifth century? Certainly, changes were made in the organization and status of Athenian law. The process of reforming the legal system had begun in the later fifth century and continued into the 390s and beyond. The first major change, probably dating to 427–415, was the institution of the procedure of *graphē paranomōn*, whereby the proposer of a decree passed in Assembly could subsequently be tried in court for having proposed a measure contrary to democratic principles and to Athens' laws.[96] But what were the laws? This problem was addressed in 410/09 when a commission was established to collect and publish all existing laws. The job proved rather larger and more complex than anyone anticipated and was not

basically democratic, on the grounds that only the right to stand for offices, not the right to vote in Assembly, was restricted. This view is disputed by Vlastos, "ΙΣΟ-ΝΟΜΙΑ ΠΟΛΙΤΙΚΗ," 20–21 n. 6; P. J. Rhodes, "The Five Thousand in the Athenian Revolution of 411 B.C.," *JHS* 92 (1972): 115–27.

[95] Thirty tyrants and amnesty: Xen. *Hell.* 2.3.11–4.43; *AP* 34–41.1 (with Rhodes, *CommAP*, 415–82); Diodorus Siculus 14.3–6, 32–33; cf. Lys. 12, 13; Isoc. 18. Among modern studies see Hignett, *HAC*, 285–98, 378–89; Krentz, *The Thirty*; Cloché, *Restauration*; Funke, *Homónoia und Arché*, 1–73; Strauss, *AAPW*, 89–120; Ostwald, *From Popular Sovereignty*, 460–96.

[96] *Graphē paranomōn*: first securely attested in 415: And. 1.17; see esp. Wolff, *Normenkontrolle*; Hansen, *Sovereignty*; Sealey, "Athenian Concept of Law," *Athenian Republic*, 49–50; Ostwald, *From Popular Sovereignty*, 125–29, 135–36.

fully completed until 399.[97] Soon after the restoration of the democracy in 403, the Athenians recognized that the recently collected and
published laws did not constitute an adequate statutory basis by which
to govern the state. A procedure had to be established to make new
laws. The *graphē paranomōn* had already implicitly recognized that decisions by the Assembly were subject to review against a legal standard,
and so it would not do to have the Assembly itself simply pass laws at
will. Instead, a complicated procedure for review of existing laws and
establishment of new laws by boards of Lawmakers (*nomothetai*) was
instituted (ca. 403–399). As a result, a clear distinction was drawn between *nomoi* and *psēphismata*, with *nomoi* being those laws of a general
nature and of permanent standing that had been passed by a lawmaker of the past (e.g., Solon) or by one of the new boards of Lawmakers, and *psēphismata* being those decrees that ordinarily dealt with
immediate issues and did not necessarily establish legal precedent; the
latter were passed by the Assembly.[98]

A great deal of significance has been attached to this series of reforms; they have been described as "the great watershed in Athenian
constitutional development in the classical period."[99] The development of a procedure that appears to separate the Assembly from legislation has furthermore been considered to mark a break with the
"radical" democracy of the fifth century. The restored democratic political order is thus sometimes described as "moderate."[100] However,
these reforms are not a watershed in the terms of political sociology.
The *nomothetai* were apparently selected randomly by lot either from
the entire demos or from those on the rolls as jurors. They were cer

[97] Harrison, "Law-Making"; cf. A. L. Boegehold, "The Establishment of a Central
Archive at Athens," *AJA* 76 (1972): 23–30; Sealey, *Athenian Republic*, 35–41, 45–46;
Ostwald, *From Popular Sovereignty*, 405–11, 414–20.

[98] Harrison, "Law-Making"; MacDowell, "Law-Making"; Hansen, "*Nomos* and *Psephisma*," "Did the *Ecclesia* Legislate," "Athenian *Nomothesia* [1980]," "Athenian *Nomothesia* [1985]"; Rhodes, "Athenian Democracy," 305–306, "*Nomothesia*"; Gabrielsen, *Remuneration*, 47–49; Ostwald, *From Popular Sovereignty*, 511–22; Sealey,
"Athenian Concept of Law," 294–95, *Athenian Republic*, 41–45, arguing that the procedure was instituted between 399 and 382/1.

[99] Whitehead, *Demes*, 287; cf. Garner, *Law and Society*, 131–44, who argues for "a
deep shift in the place of law in Athenian society, a change which is partially obscured by superficial continuities" (131).

[100] Moderate democracy (vel sim.): Hansen, "Misthos"; Larsen, "Demokratia,"
45–46, "Judgment," 7; Sealey, "Athenian Concept of Law," *Athenian Republic*, 134–
38; Ostwald, *From Popular Sovereignty*, 522–24. Contra: Gabrielsen, *Remuneration*,
35–44 (with literature cited); Rhodes, "Athenian Democracy," 320–21 (although cf.
323: "the positive enthusiasm for democracy which we find in the second half of
the fifth century had gone"). Cf. below, VII.G.

tainly paid for their service (Dem. 24.21). In the one instance in which their numbers are known (Dem. 24.27), the board was made up of 1,501 Lawmakers, including all 500 Councillors. Since juries and the Council represented a wide cross section of the citizen population (below, III.E), there is every reason to suppose that the boards of Lawmakers were intended to, and did, reflect the social composition of Athenian political society.[101]

The constitution of the restored democracy retained all the major institutions that had guaranteed the ability of the common people to take an active role in governing the state: the Cleisthenic organization of the demes, the relationship between the Council and Assembly, *isēgoria*, the selection of magistrates and jurors by lot, and the provision of pay for office and for jury service.[102] An attempt in 403/2 to limit the franchise to property owners was rejected, as was a proposal to broaden the franchise by granting citizenship to slaves who had helped in the revolution against the Thirty.[103] The Athenians thus reasserted both political equality among citizens and the exclusivity of the citizen body. The defeat of both measures must be seen in terms of the determination of the Athenians to promote consensus: limiting the franchise would ease the state's financial burdens but would exacerbate class tensions. Allowing slaves to be citizens would deny the

---

[101] Cf. MacDowell, "Law-Making," 67–69. Hansen, "Athenian *Nomothesia* [1985]," 363–65, argues that throughout the fourth century the *nomothetai* were selected by lot from the pool of potential *dikastai*. Against this is Rhodes, "*Nomothesia*," 57, who suggests that in the 350s they were selected from all Athenians. The only sociological difference is that the former group excluded citizens between the ages of eighteen and twenty-nine; cf. below, III.E.4. Harrison, "Law-Making," 35, notes succinctly (and, I think, correctly): "The Athenians in fact regarded sworn *dikasts* as effective representatives of the *demos*. Why not also sworn *nomothetai*?"

[102] On the fourth-century constitution generally: *AP* 42–69 with Rhodes, *CommAP*, 493–735. On the question of pay for office, Hansen, "Misthos," is refuted by Gabrielsen, *Remuneration*; but cf. also M. H. Hansen, "Perquisites for Magistrates in Fourth-Century Athens," *CM* 32 (1980): 105–25. On the supposed reintroduction of *prokrisis* in lottery selection of magistrates, V.L.S. Abel, *Prokrisis* (Königstein, 1983) is refuted by Hansen, "ΚΛΗΡΩΣΙΣ"; cf. the review of Abel's book by P. J. Rhodes in *Gnomon* 57 (1985): 378–79.

[103] Decree of Phormosios to limit citizenship to property owners: Lys. 34. Decree of Thrasybulus to grant citizenship to metics and slaves who had aided in the revolt successfully indicted by a *graphē paranomōn*: *AP* 40.2; Xen. *Hell.* 2.4.25; on these, and other measures related to citizenship, see Ostwald, *From Popular Sovereignty*, 503–509. Whitehead, "Thousand New Athenians," argues that the fragments of *IG* II² 10 should be restored in such a way as to show that ca. 1,000 metics who had helped in deposing the Thirty were given full citizenship in 401. But cf. P. Krentz, "Foreigners Against the Thirty: *IG* 2² 10 Again," *Phoenix* 34 (1980): 298–306, who argues that citizenship was probably not granted to the honorees of the inscription.

linkage between patriotism and citizen blood. *Homonoia*, "same-mind-edness," demanded both equality and exclusivity.

One important constitutional measure, passed some time between 403 and 399, may be regarded as completing the "radical" democratic revolution of the fifth century: the introduction of pay for attendance at the Assembly. Although probably limited to the first several thousand citizens to show up for each meeting, this provision allowed working citizens to take a full part in the decision-making process without suffering loss of income.[104]

Both Aristotle (*Pol.* 1274a7–11) and the author of the Aristotelian *Constitution of Athens* (41.2) regarded the Athenian democracy of the fourth century as the furthest development, the *telos* of the democratic form of political organization. These assessments seem perverse when viewed in "capital-C Constitutional" terms of "rule of law" and of the Assembly's "sovereign" right to make decisions without review. But the description of the democracy of the fourth century as most fully developed, most extreme, even most "radical" makes a good deal of sense from the point of view of political sociology. In terms of the relative powers of mass and elite in the state, no meaningful "moderation" of the democracy was brought about by the constitutional reforms of the late fifth and early fourth centuries. The relative political standing of mass and elite within the political community, not abstract questions of divisions of powers or of the relation of laws to decrees, determined for the authors of the *Politics* and the *Constitution of the Athenians*—as well as for Thucydides, the "Old Oligarch," and the Athenians themselves—just how democratic Athens really was.[105]

Reestablishing full democracy, while expanding the financial responsibility of the state to ensure the possibility of participation by citizens of all classes, was a challenging undertaking. Athenian society had become badly polarized in the late fifth century; consensus had indeed been lost and might not return immediately simply because it had been proclaimed in the Amnesty Decree of 403. Class tensions remained high. The Athenians had lost the revenues of empire which had buffered the financial strain of democratic government upon the

---

[104] *AP* 41.3, cf. 62.2 with Rhodes, *CommAP*, 491–92, "Athenian Democracy," 307. See also below, III.E.2, 4.

[105] The combination of the passages cited above with Aristot. *Pol.* 1292a3–37, 1298b13–16, seems clearly to indicate that Aristotle saw the Athenian democracy as one in which demagogues and decrees (rather than Laws) ruled and that he saw Athens as an example of the most extreme form of democracy. Cf. Hansen, *Sovereignty*, 13–14; Strauss, "Aristotle." On the importance of political sociology to Aristotle: Ober, "Aristotle's Political Sociology."

elite. Furthermore, at least in the immediate postwar period, state revenue from other sources of public income (e.g., the silver mines) was much reduced.[106] Consequently, the members of the wealth elite would be expected to pay for rebuilding Athens' military might and for the expenses of the democratic state. The tax-paying rich would now at least indirectly subsidize the poor, who received pay for state service. The rich would get no greater political power or legal protection as a result; indeed, with state revenues down, the poor might be more tempted than ever to use their political power to squeeze the rich through stiff fines levied in the courts. For their part, the poor could not really forget that many of the rich had supported the oligarchic counter-revolutions of the late fifth century. Lower-class resentment and distrust of the upper classes was demonstrated by the decision to reduce state support for the Athenian cavalrymen—the latter among the wealthiest citizens and united in their support for the oligarchs.[107]

Furthermore, the postwar world was a challenging one in terms of foreign policy. The Athenian Assembly now had to make very complicated decisions. The diplomatic and military situation was fluid; the question was no longer how to beat the Spartans but whether to make an alliance with them or against them. Athens faced dangerous rivals: Sparta, a resurgent Thebes, the expansionist dynasts of Asia Minor, and finally Philip of Macedon. Warfare continued to increase in complexity and was becoming potentially much more destructive to the economic bases of the polis. If Athens was to counter potential threats, much less regain her position as a great power in the Mediterranean world, the Assembly had to come up with a foreign policy that was simultaneously realistic, flexible, and consistent. The rebuilding of the navy and the construction of a series of fortifications to defend the land frontiers gave a measure of protection against sneak attack but added to the financial strain.[108] The question of how effective leader-

[106] State revenues down: Gluskina, "Spezifik," 425–29; Ober, *FA*, 13–31; Strauss, *AAPW*, esp. 53–54; cf. the somewhat more optimistic view, in regard to agriculture at least, of Hanson, *Warfare and Agriculture*, 111–43. Silver mines: above, I.C.5.

[107] Class tensions: J. Pečírka, "The Crisis of the Athenian Polis in the Fourth Century B.C.," *Eirene* 14 (1976): 5–29, esp. 10; Strauss, *AAPW*, esp. 55–59; Daviero-Rocchi, "Transformations," esp. 36, 40–41; Ste. Croix, *CSAGW*, 298–99; Markle, "Support." Cavalry reform and its social context: below, V.A.4 with n. 24. Hansen, "Did the Ecclesia Legislate," 32, 37, suggests that the money saved by lowering the cavalrymen's allowance was used for providing small (one obol/day) pensions to poor and disabled Athenians and to children of citizens who died fighting the oligarchs.

[108] Complexity of diplomacy: P. Cloché, *La politique étrangère d'Athènes de 404 à 338 av. J.C.* (Paris, 1934); Ryder, *Koine Eirene*; D. J. Mosley, "On Greek Enemies Becom-

ship and decision making could be achieved within the context of egalitarian direct democracy was not academic; without effective leadership the state's chances for survival appeared slim.

In short, there were considerable strains upon democratic Athens in
the immediate postwar period, and these strains were not significantly
relieved by external circumstances down to 322. The financial picture
was better in the 340s, but the diplomatic situation had reached a
frenzy of complexity.[109] Thus, the social stability and effective democratic decision making that in fact characterized Athens in the period
from the end of the Peloponnesian War down to the end of the Lamian War in 322 cannot be taken for granted. In the fifth century, a
series of major adjustments in the institutional relationships between
mass and elite in a context of economic plenty helps to explain the
relative lack of overt social conflict. Effective leadership was provided,
first by elites who played upon the eagerness of the demos for reform,
then by Pericles. Between 403 and 322 Athens had no empire, no major sociopolitical reforms, no Pericles—and also no oligarchic coups,
no demands for redistribution of wealth, and no collapse of the Assembly's ability to guide the state.

None of the various constitutional changes made in the course of
the fourth century seem to have contributed substantively to the maintenance of either social stability or effective leadership. Various
changes in the duties of the *nomothetai* were made as part of the ongoing attempt to streamline the lawmaking process, but none seems
particularly significant.[110] Citizenship policy remained basically that of
451/o; there was no major revision in the political body's definition of
itself.[111] There were a few procedural changes in the operation of the
Council, but these did not change the essential nature of the relationship between the Council and Assembly.[112] Similarly, there were some

---

ing Allies," *Ancient Society* 5 (1974): 43–50 (esp. 48). Navy: Jordan, *Athenian Navy*;
and esp. G. L. Cawkwell, "Athenian Naval Power in the Fourth Century," *CQ* 34
(1984): 334–45; cf. Ste. Croix, *CSAGW*, 292–93 with literature cited in n. 37. Bor-
der fortifications: Ober, *FA*.

[109] Finances improved: Dem. 10.37–38; cf. Cawkwell, "Eubulus." Diplomacy su-
percomplex: see, for example, the articles collected in Perlman, ed., *Philip and Athens*; Hammond and Griffith, *History* index s.v. Athens *and* Athenians.

[110] MacDowell, "Law-Making"; cf. the refinements of MacDowell's scheme suggested by Hansen, "Athenian *Nomothesia* [1980]," "Athenian *Nomothesia* [1985]";
Rhodes, "*Nomothesia*."

[111] Osborne, *Naturalization*, esp. IV.152, 155–64; Whitehead, *Demes*, 97–109. Cf.
the comments of Is. 6.47, 8.43; Dem. 57.30–32, and below, VI.C.

[112] Rhodes, *Boule*, 218–19, "Athenian Democracy," 307–308, 314, 321; Connor,
"Athenian Council," 36–38.

changes made in the court system; among these was the introduction of lottery machines which made jury tampering more difficult. This reform reasserted the desirability of jurors being drawn from a broad cross section of the populace.[113]

Perhaps more substantive was a decree, passed by Demosthenes in the 340s, that seems to have given the Areopagus council authority to investigate certain classes of criminal action. Demosthenes apparently advocated the reform on a platform of "the ancestral constitution" (*patrios politeia*), which had been an oligarchic watchword in the late fifth century. What might be called "conservative" political ideas may have had a part in the reform, but it is best viewed as a tactical ploy in the squabbles of elite politicians. The reform does not seem to have limited the authority of the people's courts. Furthermore, in passing this decree, the people ignored constitutional niceties regarding the functional difference between *nomos* and *psēphisma* and frankly reasserted the authority of the demos in Assembly.[114] When, shortly after the loss at Chaeronea to Philip (338 B.C.), the people suspected that the Areopagus might be a source of anti-democratic plots, a *nomos* against Tyranny threatened the Areopagites with suspension if they were caught engaging in counter-revolutionary actions.[115] The sculptural relief that decorates the inscription depicts the personification of Demos being crowned by the female deity Demokratia.[116] The implication is

[113] Jury-selection system of the later fourth century: *AP* 63–66. Introduction of the *klērōtērion* (lottery machine) to avoid jury tampering in the early fourth century: Rhodes, "Athenian Democracy," 315–18; *klērōtēria* were later (ca. 370–360) used for magistrates as well: ibid., 318–19; Whitehead, *Demes*, 270–90. On the machine itself: S. Dow, "Aristotle, the Kleroterion, and the Courts," *HSCP* 50 (1939): 1–34. Other judicial reforms included changes in pre-trial procedure: Rhodes, "Athenian Democracy," 315; the introduction of public arbitrators (citizens over 60): ibid., 315–16; the provision of a special court for trials of commercial cases involving metics: Cohen, *Maritime Courts*; a possible transfer of *eisangelia* procedure from the Assembly to the courts in ca. 355: Hansen, "How Often"; centralization of the "circuit court" judges in the city in 403/2: Whitehead, *Demes*, 264. Perhaps this last reform should be associated with pay for Assembly attendance; rural citizens coming to town for the Assembly might settle their petty legal cases on the same day.

[114] Areopagus reform of 340s: Larsen, "Judgment," 8–9; Perlman, "Political Leadership," 167–69; Hansen, "Did the *Ecclesia* Legislate," 38 with n. 24; Rhodes, "Athenian Democracy," 319–20 with n. 105; and esp. Wallace, "Undemocratic Ideology," and *Areopagos*, chapters 4.ii.c, 7.ii; Carawan, "*Apophasis* and *Eisangelia*," 124–40.

[115] Anti-tyranny law of 337/6: *SEG* 12.87, 15.95. Cf. Ostwald, "Athenian Legislation Against Tyranny"; Larsen, "Judgment," 9; Rhodes, "Athenian Democracy," 319–20; Wallace, *Areopagos*, chapter 7.ii.

[116] Demos crowned by Demokratia: frontispiece; for discussion of this monument

inescapable that the Lawmakers who passed the *nomos* were popularly regarded as embodying the will of the demos.

The most serious internal threat to the rule of the people in the fourth century may have been the evolution of the bureaucracy that dealt with state finance. Finances had become very complex by mid-century, and the democracy's survival depended upon the state's continued ability to come up annually with enough cash to pay for the functioning of the government. Various changes were made in the way moneys were collected and distributed to the magistrates responsible for dispensing them.[117] But these were less significant in their implications than the development in the 350s and 340s of a centralized financial office in the hands of the elected directors of the Theoric Fund (*AP* 43.1). Under Eubulus, the Directorship of the Theoric Fund became an important elective office, although how much actual political power, authority, or influence it actually conferred is unclear.[118] Certainly Demosthenes complained that Eubulus and his cronies were too influential in the state, but the facts that he *could* complain publicly and that Demosthenes rose to political prominence at least in part in opposition to Eubulus and his policies are important correctives to any notion of an all-powerful financial director.[119] In the 330s and 320s, Lycurgus and some of this friends seem to have had a similarly close hold on Athenian finances, although the exact nature and scope of their official position are unclear. Once again, there is no evidence that they constituted a genuine ruling elite.[120] The basic principle of Athenian finance remained taxation of the leisure class by the state and distribution of state funds by lotteried or elected officials. Perhaps in the long run the financial offices truly would have provided an institutional basis for the evolution of an oligarchy on Michels' model. Perhaps the Athenians would have found ways to limit this tendency. We will never know, since the democratic government was overthrown by the Macedonians in 322.

In sum, there were various constitutional adjustments made in the period between the Peloponnesian and Lamian Wars, but there were

---

and its significance, see Raubitschek, "Demokratia," 238; Rhodes, "Athenian Democracy," 322; Lawton, "Iconography."

[117] Summarized by Rhodes, "Athenian Democracy," 309–312.

[118] Eubulus and the Theoric fund: Cawkwell, "Eubulus"; Larsen, "Judgment," 7; Perlman, "Political Leadership," 174–75; Rhodes, "Athenian Democracy," 312–14, 322; Hansen, "*Rhetores* and *Strategoi*," 157.

[119] Cf. the comments of Rhodes, "On Labelling," 209–10.

[120] For Lycurgus and the "Lycurgan period" generally, see Reinmuth, "Spirit"; Mitchell, "Lykourgan Athens"; Will, *Athen und Alexander*, 48–100; and esp. Humphreys, "Lycurgus," with literature cited.

no major changes in the sociology of Athenian politics. There were no compromises made with the basic principles of the political equality and exclusivity of the citizen body, of the lottery, or of pay for state service. Financial offices may have been tending to evolve into an environment that could have bred a new ruling elite, but no governing elite had emerged by 322. Compared with the fifth century, the fourth century is remarkable less for its constitutional evolution than for its social and political stability. Despite the internal tensions and external strains, the Athenians did not modify the basic principles of egalitarian direct democracy in the fourth century. This lack of fundamental change is why the author of the Aristotelian *Constitution of the Athenians*, written about 325 B.C., treats the period after 403 as a single constitutional epoch (*politeia*). Constitutional reform does not provide an explanation for the nature of fourth-century democracy. In order to understand how the democratic state maintained its social stability and political direction in the fourth century, we must look more closely at the underpinnings of Athenian political sociology, at the forms and forums of communication between mass and elite.

CHAPTER III

PUBLIC SPEAKERS AND
MASS AUDIENCES

If the key to social and political stability in democratic Athens is to be sought in communication between the Athenian elites and the masses, we must decide as best we can who was sending and who was receiving messages, what form messages took, and in what contexts the communication took place.

A. Mass Communication

Only after we have formed an idea of the participants in and the contexts of public communication can the actual content of the messages be properly assessed. Thus, before we can hope to understand the sociopolitical significance of the rhetorical texts available to us—the corpus of Attic orations—we must fill in some of the background in terms of the orators themselves, the nature and rules of the forums in which they spoke, and the audiences they addressed. We must also keep in mind that the communication was always reciprocal. The speaker obviously communicated messages to his audience, but the audience communicated to the speaker as well: immediately through direct verbal intervention (e.g., catcalls) and nonverbal signals (e.g., restlessness), at a short remove through voting, and at a greater remove through their subsequent behavior toward the speaker. We can begin to construct an adequate framework for the analysis of public political discourse and the nature of Athenian democracy only if we recognize that public communication between Athenian elites and masses was a dynamic and interactive process, undertaken in different forums but within a relatively stable ideological and social environment.[1]

B. Classes of Public Speakers:
Rhetores and *Idiōtai*

The orators represented in the corpus make a clear distinction between public speakers who were politicians and those who were not. A

[1] On the reciprocal nature of public speech, see Riley and Riley, "Mass Commu-

plurality of the orations (59 of 132) were delivered by individuals who, as far as we know, did not have great political ambitions. The legal actions in which they were involved are roughly equivalent to modern American civil suits. Texts of this sort are generally referred to as "private orations" and are classified as "I" speeches in the Appendix. On the other hand, a number of speeches were delivered by, or written for, politically active citizens, and these speeches were overtly intended to further their careers. The most important for our purposes are those listed in the Appendix as "E," "P," and "R" speeches: orations delivered in the Assembly and "public" legal actions brought by politicians (*rhētores*) against political opponents.

B.1 "RHETOR" AND OTHER TERMS FOR POLITICIAN

The expert orator/politician was a well-recognized figure in fourth-century Athens, and there was a wide variety of terms to describe him. The most common term was *rhētōr*. In the mid-fifth century this was apparently a legal term for one who proposed a motion in the Assembly; by the later fifth and through the fourth century it was ordinarily used of individuals recognized as active political experts: those who addressed the Assembly frequently and who competed in political trials with other *rhētores*.[2] As it is normally used in oratory, the term "rhetor," by itself, seems to be more or less value-neutral.[3] But it could certainly be used in negative contexts. Aeschines (3.253) called Demosthenes the "rhetor-man" who was responsible for all the evils of the city. Elsewhere (2.74), he refers to the "rank-ordered" (*suntetagmenoi*) rhetores who ignore the safety of the city. Similarly, Demosthenes (22.37) could speak of the entrenched (*sunestēkotōn*) rhetores who supported the evil Androtion. More vigorously yet, Demosthenes (23.201) discusses the "damnable and god-hated rhetores" who sold public honors as if they were nothing. In *On the Crown* (18.242) Demosthenes caps a tirade of insults against Aeschines with a claim that

nication," 537–78, esp. 563–68. Buxton, *Persuasion*, 10–18, points out the importance of public debate in Athenian political life.

[2] Common fourth-century use: e.g., Lys. 31.27; And. 3.1; Dem. 24.123, 51.20, 58.62; Aesch. 2.176, 3.231. As a technical term: *IG* I³ 46 (= I² 45), line 21; cf. Harrison, *Law*, II.204 n. 1. The fullest discussion of the term and its origins remains Pilz, *Rhetor*, with whom I am in substantial agreement on the common meaning of the term, although not on its negative connotation; see III.n.3. See also Wilcox, "Scope," 127–28; Connor, *NP*, 116–17; Hansen, " 'Politicians'," 39–49.

[3] Neutral: Wilcox, "Scope," 127–28 (citing Dem. 21.189, 18.280); Hansen, " 'Politicians'," 36–37, 46–49. Negative uses of 'rhetor': e.g., Dem. 23.184–85; Isoc. 8.129–31; Hyp. 4.33–36.

his opponent was a counterfeit (*parasēmos*) rhetor, whose cleverness was useless to the polis. This last suggests that the genuine rhetor might be expected to use his abilities for the good of the polis.

Other terms for politicians also reflect their primary role as addressers of the public. The political orators are often simply referred to as "the speakers" (*hoi legontes*).[4] An orator could also be alluded to as one who was able or clever at public address (*deinos, dunamenos legein*). Frequently this was intended to have a negative connotation.[5] Yet if an orator wanted to praise himself, he might refer to himself, as did Demosthenes (18.320), as "the most able speaker" (*kratista legōn*). Some other descriptions of public speakers refer to their advisory and leadership roles. Vying in popularity with rhetor as a standard term for political orator was *politeuomenos*. "He who is actively involved in the affairs of the polis" might be a safe general translation, but "politician" serves as well.[6] Variants include *to politeuesthai*, the infinitive form of the same root word (Dem. 22.47), and *to politeuesthai kai prattein*, "the engagement in politics and action" (Dem. 18.45). Ps-Lysias (6.33) claims that Androtion was preparing to engage in politics (*ta politika prattein*) and that he already spoke as a demagogue (*dēmēgorei*) and gave advice (*sumbouleuei*); the passage introduces two other terms associated with Athenian public speakers. The words *dēmagōgos* and the closely related *dēmēgoria* (public and, by extension, demagogic speaking) were often used by an orator of his political enemies.[7] But both terms could also be used in a more positive sense. The speaker in Lysias 16 claimed that he had to "speak out in public" (*dēmēgorēsai*: 16.20) in order to protect his own interests. Hyperides (5.17) claimed that a just demagogue (*dikaion dēmagōgon*) should be the savior of his polis. Demosthenes (19.251–52) mocked Aeschines for attempting to mimic the prose style of Solon and others who had served as public speakers (*dēmēgorountōn*) in the past. By the fourth century, Solon was widely

[4] E.g., Lys. 18.18, 28.9, 29.6; Dem. 1.28, 22.37, 24.198, 25.41.

[5] *ho deinos legein*: Lys. 12.86; Isoc. 21.5; *thrasus kai legein deinos*: Dem. 22.66; *dunamenos legein*: Lys. 14.38, 30.24; *dunasthai legein*: Din. 1.113; *deinos demiourgos logōn*: Aesch. 3.215; *hoi deinotatoi*: Dem. *Ex.* 45.2.

[6] E.g., And. 2.1; Dem. 3.31, 10.70, 19.285, 23.4, *Ex.* 42.1; Aesch. 3.235. Cf. Mossé, "*Politeuomenoi*." Hansen, " 'Politicians'," esp. 37, argues that the term 'politician' is best avoided in discussions of Athenian politics. It is certainly important to keep in mind the differences between modern and ancient "politicians," but I have continued to employ the term for want of a better one.

[7] E.g., Lys. 25.9; Dem. 22.48, 51.9; Din. 1.99, 113; cf. Ostwald, *From Popular Sovereignty*, 201–203. *Dēmagogos* derives from *dēmos* and the verb *agō* (to lead); *dēmēgoria* from *dēmos* and the verb *agoreuō* (to speak in public assembly), but the two root verbs are themselves closely related.

regarded as the Father of the Democracy, and so the description of him as a public speaker, even in the context of Demosthenes' parody of Aeschines, suggests that the term could be given positive connotations.[8] Similarly, Lysias (27.10) suggested that the duty of "good demagogues" (*dēmagōgoi agathoi*) was to give generously to the state in times of emergency.

The term "advisor" (*sumboulos*) was typically a positive one and seems to have become particularly popular with the orators of the latter part of the fourth century. Hyperides (5.28) notes that even after Chaeronea, the demos did not reject the rhetores but used them as advisors and public advocates (*su[mboulois] . . . kai s[unēgorois]*). Demosthenes (58.62), on the other hand, claimed that no one would consider Theocrines and his friends to be good men and advisors (*sumboulous kai agathous*: note that *agathos* here has an aristocratic connotation as well). Aeschines (3.226) warns against those who attempt to stop thoughtful men from giving advice. Dinarchus sums up the public position of the orators by arguing (1.72) that those who advise and lead (*hoi sumbouloi kai hēgemones*) were responsible for all the good and ill that befell the polis. He contrasted (1.40) the current crop of politicians with the worthy advisors and leaders of previous generations.

The politicians of Athens could be referred to as "leaders": *dēmagōgoi* (literally "they who lead the demos"), or *hēgemones*, ("they who lead") (Din. 1.40, 72, 74). The prevalence of descriptive terms that emphasize their speaking ability and their advisory function, however, suggests that public speech was a major aspect of their leadership role. We may contrast the etymologies of modern English terms for leaders, such as president, governor, chairperson, director. Speaking ability may be part of the arsenal of a modern political leader, but his or her power will typically be exercised largely outside of public view and as a direct function of the office he or she holds.[9] The vocabulary of political activism in Athens reveals that direct public communication was the primary locus of whatever power, authority, or influence the Athenian rhetor might hope to exercise.

The frequency and casualness with which many of the terms were used in the plural furthermore suggest that the rhetores were a recognizable "set" of men who played a special role in the political life of

---

[8] On the myth of Solon as father of the democracy, see, for example, Mossé, "Comment."

[9] Modern political leadership as behind-the-scenes power: e.g., Mills, *Power Elite*, esp. 229–35. But cf. Michels, *Political Parties*, 98–100, on the importance of excellence in oratory to political leadership in the modern democratic state.

the polis.[10] Demosthenes (4.1, cf. *Ex.* 55.2), for example, could refer to them as "the accustomed speakers" (*hoi eiōthotes*). We do not know how many individuals would be in the set at any one time, but the number is likely to have been quite small. "Membership" required virtually full-time participation in politics, a great deal of native ability, and (usually) specialized and expensive training. It was potentially lucrative (V.G.2) but also very dangerous (III.B.2). M. H. Hansen has suggested that perhaps only ten to twenty "professional" politicians would have been active at any given time; this may be a bit too low, but I think it is the right order of magnitude; probably, less than one hundred full-time political experts operated in Athens from 403 to 322 B.C.[11]

B.2 LEGAL STANDING OF RHETORES AND *Idiōtai*

The expert politicians were not a legally defined group. They tended to speak frequently in the Assembly, but this was a privilege granted them by the goodwill of the demos, not a legal prerogative. Aeschines (1.27) states clearly that no Athenian was forbidden to speak in the Assembly because of his social status or poverty, but rather all citizens were especially and repeatedly invited to come to the speakers' platform (*bēma*) if they wished to address the demos. By the mid-fifth century, all Athenian citizens possessed the right of *isēgoria* (above, II.F.1), and by law no Athenian had any greater right than any other to address the Assembly. If most citizens did not speak up in public, choice or habit, not legal restriction, was the reason.[12] Demosthenes (22.30) claimed that Solon himself had noted that most Athenians did not speak in public, although they had a right to do so.

Part of the rhetor's role in the Assembly was to secure passage of decrees (*psēphismata*) binding on the citizens. Thus he could be compared to the *nomothetai* who passed the general laws (*nomoi*) also binding on the citizenry. Lysias (31.27) could ask "what rhetor . . . or *no-*

[10] On the orators as a recognizable group, see Cloché, "Hommes politiques"; Ehrenberg, *People of Aristophanes*, 351; Perlman, "Political Leadership," "Politicians"; Seager, "Lysias," 177; Finley, *PAW*, 140.

[11] Hansen, "Number of *Rhetores*." Cf. Buxton, *Persuasion*, 14–16, who argues that "a fairly small group of individuals tended to dominate matters in the assembly . . .," citing Mark Hobart's anthropological study of public assemblies in Bali, where a few villagers are designated "speech-specialists" and comprise "an informal élite" with high prestige and extensive influence in assembly and in the community generally.

[12] As the comments of Euripides *Suppliants* 430–42, and Plato *Protagoras* 319d (quoted above, I.A), make clear. See also Finley, *DAM*, 24–25 and *PAW*, 139–40; cf. above, II.F.1.

mothetēs could have anticipated" (with a *psēphisma* or *nomos*) the crime of a citizen absenting himself from a crisis? But the right to propose a decree was open to any citizen. Despite the general dominance of the expert orators in public debate on major issues, ordinary citizens also raised their voices in the Assembly and proposed motions to the demos.[13] Isocrates' student in the *Panathenaicus* (12.248) states that in Athens sometimes the wisest speakers miss the point, and one of the ordinary citizens "deemed of little account and generally ignored" comes up with a good idea and is judged to speak the best. The ambiguity of the standing of the expert orators is suggested by arguments over how often a good rhetor should address the people. Aeschines (3.216–20) turned Demosthenes' charge that Aeschines seldom spoke in Assembly against his opponent, by implying that speaking constantly was an oligarchic trait. In oligarchies, only he who rules (*ho dunasteuōn*) addresses the people, whereas in democracies whoever so wished (*ho boulomenos*) could speak whenever it seemed right to him.

There is no evidence that the expert orators ever secured any legal privileges vis-à-vis the rest of the citizens, but they *were* subject to various laws as a consequence of their public actions. Demosthenes (10.70) states that the politician Aristomedes should know that the life of ordinary citizens (*idiōtai*) is a safe one but that of politicians (*politeuomenoi*) is dangerous, implying that the latter could expect to face legal prosecution. Demosthenes (24.192–93) argues that all law was divided into two types: that which concerned private life (*peri tōn idiōn*) and that which concerned the duties to the polis of anyone who wished to act as a politician (*politeuesthai*). Demosthenes claimed that it was to the advantage of the mass of citizens that the former class of laws be lenient but the latter harsh, so that the politicians would not be able to act unjustly to the masses (*adikoien tous pollous*). The proposer of a decree in the Assembly could be indicted by the procedure against unlawful decrees (*graphē paranomōn*); he who proposed an unlawful law could face a charge of having done so (*graphē nomon mē epitēdeion theinai*); he who spoke against the public interest due to having taken a bribe could be indicted according to the *eisangelia* (treason trial) procedure.[14] There was also a scrutiny procedure that applied specifically

---

[13] Hansen, "Number of *Rhetores*," adduces some statistics to suggest that some 700–1,400 individuals proposed decrees in the period 355–322. Although I do not find the statistical argument particularly convincing, he is certainly correct to argue that many Athenians who cannot be identified as "political experts" did propose decrees.

[14] On the types of procedure available, see Hansen, " 'Politicians'," 39–41. *Graphē paranomōn*: above, II.G with n.96. *Graphē nomon mē epitēdeion theinai*: Hansen, *Sover-*

to speakers in the Assembly (*dokimasia rhētorōn*), forbidding any citizen who had mistreated his parents, failed to perform his military duties properly, prostituted himself, or squandered his inheritance from addressing the demos. Our best evidence for the last procedure is Aeschines (1.28–32) who indicted the rhetor Timarchus on the prostitution clause.[15]

The existence of the *dokimasia rhētorōn*, Hyperides' (especially 4.7–8) discussion of provisions of the *eisangelia* procedure referring to rhetores and generals, and other testimonia (see III.D.1) have led M. H. Hansen to conclude that the term 'rhetor' was used in the fourth century as a legal/constitutional term for proposers of laws and decrees and for those who brought public actions in the courts.[16] In fourth-century Athenian legal terminology, 'rhetor' may have retained a specific technical meaning, but there is no reliable textual proof that it did.[17] The term is not used in any inscribed law or decree after the mid-fifth century (and only once then). The law cited by Aeschines in his action against Timarchus was attributed to Solon, but we have no way of knowing when the *dokimasia rhētorōn* process was actually first put into place. It was evidently very rare by the fourth century.

Hyperides' discussion (4.7–8) of the *eisangelia* procedure as it applied specifically to rhetores (*ē rhētor ōn mē legēi* . . .) was in the context of a speech in which he consistently emphasized the distinction between ordinary citizens—*idiōtai*—and the recognized set of expert public speakers—rhetores. When he quoted the law, he attempted to make it appear as if it was specifically written to apply to the expert

---

eignty, 44–48; Wolff, *Normenkontrolle*, 40ff. Eisangelia: below, III.n.75. For other sorts of public actions, see Hansen, '*Apagoge.*' *Pace* de Laix, *Probouleusis*, 189–90; and Perlman, "Politicians," 354, the *rhētorikē graphē* mentioned by Harpokration and other late texts certainly refers to the *graphē paranomōn*: Hansen, " 'Politicians'," 39–41.

[15] See also Harrison, *Law*, II.204–205; MacDowell, *Law*, 174; Hansen, " 'Politicians'," 40–41.

[16] Hansen, " 'Politicians'," 39–42, but he also (48–49) notes the "gap" between the supposed constitutional use of the term and its common use and suggests (49) that this must be attributed to the "gap between the constitution and how it works."

[17] Aeschines (1.33–34) mentions a *nomos* passed in 346/5 which appointed by lot the members of one tribe at each meeting of the Assembly to keep order. He suggests that this was specifically to control the rhetores (cf. Aesch. 3.4; Dem. 25.90). But the "law" included in the text (Aesch. 1.35) is a forgery, and (*pace* Hansen, " 'Politicians'," 40) there is no way of knowing what either the wording or the original intent of the law might have been. For differing views of the seating arrangements this *nomos* would have entailed, see Hansen, "Athenian Ecclesia and the Assembly-Place," 246–48; Stanton and Bicknell, "Voting in Tribal Groups," 58–65; and below, III.D.1.

political orators, as opposed to the ordinary citizens. Hyperides was exploiting the ambiguity between the old legal meaning of the term rhetor—which in the mid-fifth century had apparently been "decree-proposer"—and the everyday meaning of the term as it was used in oratory and would be understood by the jurors. He implied that there really was a legal difference between the expert politician and the ordinary citizen and so tried to show that his opponent had done a great injustice by indicting the innocent *idiōtēs* Euxenippus with a procedure (*eisangelia*) intended only for use against rhetores: "Although he is an *idiōtēs* your prosecution of him classifies him as a rhetor" (4.30; cf. Aesch. 3.214). Once again, the term *idiōtēs* had a common meaning in the fourth century: one who was an ordinary citizen and not a political expert.[18] But all Athenian citizens who were not serving in magistracies or on juries were *idiōtai*, if we are to accept Lycurgus' (1.79) definition. He stated that the *politeia* consists of three parts: the office-holder (*archōn*), the juryman (*dikastēs*), and the *idiōtēs*. Aeschines (2.181), one of the best known politicians of the mid-fourth century, could claim with a straight face to be both an *idiōtēs* and a middling citizen (*metrios*).

There was no legal difference between the expert politician and the ordinary citizen, except that the former was more likely to engage and to have engaged in activities, for example, proposing decrees and laws, that made him liable to legal action. As we have seen, all Athenian citizens had a right to speak in the Assembly and many decrees—especially those of an honorary nature—seem to have been proposed by "non-experts."[19] But there was certainly a *perceived* difference between the ordinary citizen and the political expert in fourth-century Athens, as Hyperides' comments, cited above, clearly attest. Like Aeschines, Demosthenes (22.25–27) considered the *metrioi* and *idiōtai* to be more or less synonymous, but he contrasted these folk with the powerful and bold (*deinoi, thraseis*)—the expert politicians. He suggested that there were different sorts of legal actions appropriate to each sort of citizen: public actions that might offer greater rewards but also carried

---

[18] E.g., Aesch. 3.233. Occasionally (e.g., Dem. 18.45) *hoi idiōtai* was used to describe the leisure class in contrast to *hoi polloi*; cf. Mossé, "*Politeuomenoi* et *idiōtai*." The rhetor/*idiōtēs* dichotomy may help to explain the *apragmōn* topos: cf. below IV.n.37.

[19] Political activity by *idiōtai*: Hansen, "Numbers of *Rhetores*," "*Rhetores* and *Strategoi*," 159–80 (catalogue), and " 'Politicians'," esp. 45–46 with n. 37. Cf. the much greater emphasis on the distinction between *idiōtēs* and rhetor assumed by Dover, *GPM*, 25–26; Perlman, "Politicians," 328–30.

greater risk, and private actions that ordinary citizens could undertake without risking their status or property.[20]

The *functional* difference between the expert politician and the "amateur" who might propose an honorary decree, but was likely to avoid hot issues, was in part a consequence of the increased risk that political activity brought in its wake. The maze of legal difficulties in which the proposer of a controversial decree might find himself would be enough to scare most citizens away from the bema during intense debate over major issues.[21] The general opprobrium that might follow upon a failed policy decision was also a consideration. The orator who spoke in favor of a policy that went wrong might later be regarded as a convenient scapegoat by the Assemblymen who had themselves voted for the policy, as Thucydides (8.1.1) and Demosthenes (1.16) both noted. Fear of legal difficulties and of the resentment of their fellows by most Athenians, even those who were active Assembly-goers and cared deeply about political affairs, rendered the experts a structural necessity in the Athenian system of government; without them there would be few bold and original policy initiatives.[22]

C. Elite Status of Public Speakers

Because of the risks that actively debating or proposing major new policy in the Assembly entailed, and because it was not necessary for the average citizen to engage in high-risk public legal actions, the most common public forum in which the Athenian *idiōtēs* spoke was the law court, in the course of defending or prosecuting a private lawsuit (*dikē*). The Athenians had a reputation for being an especially litigious folk (cf. Aristophanes, *Wasps, Clouds*), but we do not know how com-

[20] Cf. the seminal discussion of this passage by Osborne, "Law in Action," 42–44.

[21] An extreme case: Dem. 18.171. Connor, *NP*, 23, suggests that Diodotus, Cleon's opponent in the Mytilenean debate, was an ordinary citizen, a "temporary politician" outraged by the issues at hand. But if the speech Thucydides puts in Diodotus' mouth is in any way indicative of the speech he actually delivered, he must have been a master of sophistic rhetoric. R. A. Knox, " 'So Mischievous a Beaste'? The Athenian *Demos* and Its Treatment of Its Politicians," *Greece and Rome* 32 (1985): 132–61, lists some of the evidence for the legal "destruction" of Athenian politicians and argues that the high mortality rate among active politicians was damaging to the function of the democracy since, inter alia, it kept some citizens from engaging in politics. But see below, VII.E.5.

[22] Montgomery, *Way to Chaeronea*, esp. 66–95, provides a good introduction to the important political role played by the political orators in the polis, along with an assessment of the rhetorical tactics they used to demonstrate to the demos the legitimacy of their position in the decision-making process. Contrast the more legalistic approach to initiative of Hansen, "Initiative and Decision," 359–65.

mon it was for an average Athenian to find himself involved in a law-suit. On the other hand, we can probably assume that members of the Athenian elites, especially the wealth elite, were quite likely to get involved in legal actions, and it is the elite Athenian litigant who is represented in the preserved private orations. The internal evidence of the speeches frequently demonstrates that the speaker is a member of the leisure class, although some defendants prevaricated about the extent of their personal wealth (see v.D.2). Furthermore, most, if not all, of the surviving private orations were written by professional speech writers—logographers. The logographers' fee scales are not known, but once again, a safe assumption is that the common Athenian could not afford to buy an oration of a quality comparable to the average of those preserved in the corpus.[23]

Whether the speakers who commissioned and delivered the extant private orations should be considered members of an educated elite is debatable. On the one hand, we can probably assume that they would, as a function of their upbringing, have been better educated than the average Athenian.[24] On the other hand, probably relatively few of them had formal training in philosophy or rhetoric; the former was very rare in any case, and those who had been trained in the latter would presumably not have had to resort to logographers. The problem is complicated by the tendency of the private litigant to understate his ability and experience at public speaking (see IV.C.3). At least some private litigants can be assigned to the birth elite, on the basis of their own statements.

The elite status of the expert politicians who wrote and delivered speeches for political trials and for Assembly debates is quite clear. While we do not have adequate biographical data to determine as much as we might like about their backgrounds, a few generalizations are possible. First, they were, by definition, members of an elite of ability. Skill in public address was sine qua non for the politician. This meant not only skill at putting words together but also in putting them across. Isocrates, one of the most brilliant prose writers of classical Athens, was forced to forgo a political career because his voice was not

[23] On logographers and their clients, see Kennedy, *Art of Persuasion*, 126–45; Lavency, *Aspects*; Dover, *Lysias*, 148–74; Usher, "Lysias."

[24] As Wilcox, "Scope," 130–31, and "Isocrates' Fellow Rhetoricians," 174–75, points out, only the rich could afford higher education; cf. Finley, *PAW*, 28; Raaflaub, "Democracy, Oligarchy," 529–30. See also Jaeger, *Paideia*, III.120–21, for the idea (in Plato and Isocrates) that the length of an individual's education should be proportional to the extent of his parents' wealth.

strong enough to carry to a large audience.[25] The orator's native ability was necessarily sharpened by practice. According to Plutarch (*Dem.* 5–8, 11), Demosthenes listened to other orators (especially Callistratus of Aphidna), practiced his skills in private trials (against his guardians), received advice from other orators (notably Eunomus), and took a lesson in declamation from the comic actor Satyrus. He undertook vigorous physical training of various sorts, including declaiming while exercising and with his mouth full of pebbles. The story that he spent long hours in an underground study, with his head half-shaved to force himself to keep his nose to the grindstone because of embarrassment over his appearance, may be apocryphal, but it catches the spirit of the level of dedication necessary to become an effective political speaker in the competitive political atmosphere of fourth-century Athens.

In many cases, the prospective political orator must have sharpened his skills through formal training in rhetoric. Plutarch (*Dem.* 5.4–5) records the tradition that Demosthenes studied with Isaeus, because he could not afford Isocrates' fee. But Plutarch had read other accounts as well. He notes that Hermippus cited certain anonymous memoirs that stated that Demosthenes was a student of Plato. According to Plutarch, Hermippus also cited Ctesibius for the story that Callias the Syracusan and certain others secretly provided Demosthenes with the rhetorical system of Isocrates and Alcidamas. None of this, with the possible exception of the lessons with Isaeus, seems, on the face of it, very likely. Most can probably be attributed to ancient speculation, based in part on stylistic analysis.[26] Regrettably, our biographical tradition is equally confused and contradictory (if not as rich) concerning the educational backgrounds of most of the other famous *rhetores*, and it is nonexistent for the less well known. The Pseudo-Plutarchian *Lives of the Ten Orators* makes various speculations, which are sometimes contradictory, about who studied with whom, but on the whole, this evidence is useless.[27]

[25] Isoc. 5.81–82; cf. Aristot. *Rhet.* 1414a16–17, cited below, III.E.2. On the importance of natural ability in relation to training for the orator: Isoc. 13.14–15 with Jaeger, *Paideia*, III.63.

[26] For discussions of the ancient testimonia on Demosthenes' rhetorical education, see Blass, *AB*, III.1.10–20; Jaeger, *Demosthenes*, 31–32.

[27] He states that Isocrates studied under Prodicus, Gorgias, Teisias, and Theramenes (cf. Jaeger, *Paideia*, III.48–49, 314 n. 35) and that Isaeus may have studied under Isocrates (837D). Demosthenes supposedly did not have the cash to pay Isocrates his 1,000-dr. fee (837D–E), but he paid the huge fee of 10,000 dr. to Isaeus for private lessons (837F; cf. 844C). Aeschines is reported in one version to have studied with Isocrates and Plato (840B), according to another version with Leoda-

Nevertheless, we are faced with two undoubted facts: that the texts left us by the political orators display a great deal of rhetorical sophistication and that schools of rhetoric existed in fourth-century Athens. Isocrates' school was the most famous. The program of study there supposedly lasted up to four years, and Isocrates was said to have charged a flat fee of 1,000 drachmas for the course. Both figures are suspect, but he did have students, they did study for a considerable period, and they did pay him well enough that he was able to recoup his family fortune which had been destroyed in the Peloponnesian War. Both he and his son were liturgists, if unwilling ones.[28] Furthermore, as S. Wilcox has demonstrated, Isocrates and his fellow rhetoricians taught political rhetoric.[29] Although no doubt some aspiring logographers attended the rhetoricians's classes and legal rhetoric was surely included in the curriculum, most students of the fourth-century rhetoricians, as of the fifth-century sophists, probably studied rhetoric because they had political ambitions.[30] Thus, although not all the students of Isocrates and other rhetoricians were Athenian citizens or went on to successful political careers, a reasonable assumption is that many of the expert politicians of fourth-century Athens sharpened their rhetorical skills as students of the late fifth-century sophists and later at formal schools of rhetoric. Moreover, given that formal higher education in Athens was relatively rare and limited for the most part

mas (840B), and yet elsewhere with no one at all (840F; other late sources are discussed by Kindstrand, *Stylistic Evaluation*, 68–75, who concludes that Aeschines in fact had no formal training). Lycurgus and Hyperides are supposed to have studied under both Plato and Isocrates (841B, 848D; cf. Davies, *APF*, p. 518). Dinarchus is reported to have studied under Theophrastus and later under Demetrius of Phalerum (850C). For the similarly dubious ancient biographical tradition on famous Greek poets, see Mary R. Lefkowitz, *The Lives of the Greek Poets* (Baltimore, 1981).

[28] The amount of his fee is mentioned by Ps-Plutarch *Lives* 837D–E; Plut. *Demosthenes* 5.4. Both may have picked up the reference from Dem. 35.40–43. His personal fortune: Davies, *APF* 7716. For rather speculative discussions on Isocrates' school, see R. Johnson, "A Note on the Number of Isocrates' Students," *AJP* 78 (1957): 297–300; idem, "Isocrates' Method of Teaching," *AJP* 80 (1959): 25–36. Cf. Jaeger, *Paideia*, III.46–70.

[29] Wilcox, "Scope," and "Isocrates' Fellow Rhetoricians," also discusses the close relationship between the schools of rhetoric of the fourth-century and the fifth-century sophists; cf. Jaeger, *Paideia*, III.102–103. Demosthenes himself may have taught rhetoric, which would help to explain the relatively large number of Assembly speeches he published: Blass, *AB*, III.1.34–35; Adams, "Demosthenes Pamphlets," 11 with n. 2.

[30] Pilz, *Rhetor*, 13; Wilcox, "Scope," esp. 128–31; Bolgar, "Training," 38–40. Wilcox, "Isocrates' Fellow Rhetoricians," 175, 182–84, rather grudgingly admits that some forensic oratory must have been taught in the schools, but he suggests that even that would be mostly for political action.

to either philosophy (as Plato defined it) or rhetoric, we may guess that the political experts formed a relatively significant percentage of the "educated elite" of the fourth-century Athenian citizen body.[31]

Formal education in rhetoric was especially important for the aspiring Athenian politician because of the lack of ways in which he could gain a practical education in politics. Scholars once commonly assumed that holding offices and generally being politically active at the local level, in one's deme and tribe, provided the up-and-coming politician with his first political experiences.[32] But recent detailed studies of the Athenian demes have disproved at least part of this assumption. Prosopographical analysis of individuals active in deme affairs, especially the demarchs, has shown that there is no link between local political activity and "national" political activity; indeed the two spheres of activity appear to have been mutually exclusive. None of the known rhetores can be demonstrated to have been actively involved in the public life of his home village either before or after beginning his political career.[33] Once again, this provides a strong contrast to the modern politician, who typically begins his or her career at a local level and frequently maintains close ties with local supporters throughout his or her rise to national prominence. The lack of a federated structure of government and the relative insignificance of most offices in the Athenian state made the Assembly and people's courts unparalleled institutions. He who would be a politician at Athens must address the Assembly and become active in the courts, but prior experience in local politics was of relatively little use in these activities.

The political orators were also members of the Athenian elite of wealth. In general, a wealthy Athenian was statistically much more likely than the common citizen to be overtly politically active.[34] In 1983

---

[31] See Bolgar, "Training," 42–47, who decries the failure of both the philosophical and rhetorical schools to produce students who could form an effective ruling elite. See also M. S. Warman, "Plato and Persuasion," *Greece and Rome* 30 (1983): 48–54.

[32] E.g., Haussoullier, *Vie municipale*, 133; Hopper, *Basis*, 16.

[33] Whitehead, *Demes*, 236–41 and esp. 315–24; cf. Osborne, *Demos*, 83–87, who fails to prove that the deme was the "unavoidable channel for political activity" (189). Cf. above, I.c.6.

[34] By "overtly politically active citizen" I refer to those who fulfill the criteria for inclusion on Hansen's list, below III.n.35. I do *not* intend to imply that citizens who were not "overtly active" were apathetic or uninterested in politics. To the contrary, I would suggest that a great many citizens who never addressed the Assembly, served as generals, or brought a public legal action, nonetheless regularly attended the Assemblies and sat as jurors, partook in all the other normal activities of a citizen, and cared deeply about their polis.

M. H. Hansen published a list of all Athenians who are known to have held a generalship, addressed the Assembly, proposed a decree or law, or were involved in a public legal action, between 403 and 322 B.C.[35] Some 30 percent (114) of these individuals are listed by Davies in *APF* as liturgists and so had family fortunes of ca. three to four talents or more. Both Hansen's and Davies' lists are subject to unquantifiable variables, and the 30-percent figure is probably too low. According to Davies' estimates, which I accept, liturgists were only about one or two percent of the total Athenian citizen population in the fourth century. Furthermore, a number of the citizens on Hansen's list were probably in the leisure class, even if they were not liturgists, since the liturgical class constituted only about 15–30 percent of the leisure class (see below, III.E.1). Even allowing for a large margin of error in any or all of these numbers, the general conclusion that, relative to their numbers in the total citizen body, the leisure class was heavily overrepresented in the set of all overtly politically active citizens is secure.[36]

If the "overtly politically active" citizen was likely to be wealthy, so *a fortiori* was the expert politician. Hence, not surprisingly, many of the well-known politicians of fourth-century Athens are listed as liturgists in Davies' *APF*: for example, Andocides (828), Androtion (913), Apollodorus (11672), Callistratus (8157), Demades (3263), Demosthenes (3597), Hegesippus (6351), Hyperides (13912), Lycurgus (9251), Meidias (9719), Timocrates (13772). Some politicians, such as Demosthenes, clearly came from wealthy families. Others, for example, Demades and Aeschines, may have made their fortunes in the course of their careers. The question of the early careers of many orators is complicated by the tendency of politicians to denigrate opponents by implying that their fortunes had been made in an unsavory manner (see V.F.2–3). But in every known case, by the time an orator was a recognized political expert—by the time he was addressing the Assembly frequently on major issues and involving himself in high-visibility, public legal actions—he was unquestionably a member of the leisure class. The general impression of politicians as a wealthy group is rein-

[35] Hansen, "*Rhetores* and *Strategoi*," a total of 368 names. Cf. the less inclusive lists of Cloché, "Hommes politiques"; Roberts, "Athens' Politicians," which are restricted to individuals I would describe as politicians or political experts.

[36] The general tendency of the wealthy to be active in city politics is mirrored by their tendency to be active at the deme level, as proposers and receivers of honors from their demesmen—although *not* as demarchs or other regular deme magistrates. See Whitehead, *Demes*, 236–41, "Competitive Outlay"; Osborne, *Demos*, 66–68, 83–87. The latter's conclusion (68) that "still in the fourth-century political power lay effectively with a rather restricted and wealthy social group" is, however, not warranted.

forced by hyperbolic rhetorical statements, such as Demosthenes'
(23.208) comment that those who transact the public business have
such great fortunes that their private houses are grander than public
buildings and that some of them own more land than "all of you [ju-
rors] in this court put together." Such statements were intended to
have a specific impact on juries and cannot be taken at face value, but
they exaggerate rather than falsify the reality of the situation. Demosthenes implies here that great personal wealth was unseemly in a political leader, but, given that being a politician in fourth-century Athens was a full-time affair, being a member of the leisure class was
virtually a prerequisite.[37] And, as Demosthenes points out elsewhere
(22.27), the poor man simply could not afford to risk the high fines
that were levied on losers in certain public legal actions.[38]

A considerably weaker link joins the rhetores to the birth elite, at
least if we limit the latter to those who were members of a *genos* (see
below, VI.B). Lycurgus was of the *genos* of the Eteoboutadai; Hegesippus and his brother Hegesandros, who can also be considered a politician (cf. Hansen's list), were of the Salaminioi. Some scholars have
suggested that Demosthenes and Androtion may have been *gennētai*,
although this is far from certain.[39] But, as we shall see (VI.E.1), even
politicians such as Aeschines, who were certainly not *gennētai*, were eager to stress their connections with aristocrats and their own aristocratic pursuits.

D. Politics and Political Organization

In sum, the expert politicians of fourth-century Athens were not legally defined, and there are no fixed criteria by which we can include
or exclude marginal figures from the set. But the rhetores were easily
recognized by their contemporaries and could be spoken of collectively. They were relatively few in number, invariably elite in wealth
and ability, usually so in education, and occasionally were *gennētai*.
Many of the expert rhetores held lotteried offices from time to time,

[37] Full time: Demosthenes (19.226) describes politicians as "those who live their
lives for you and covet your honors." Cf. Larsen, "Judgment," 8; Jones, *AD*, 55;
Perlman, "Politicians," 333–36 with n. 38; Finley *AE*, 37 and *PAW*, 37. For an assessment of the ways by which a lower-class Athenian might climb to a position of
wealth and political influence, see Rhodes, "Political Activity," 142–44.

[38] Cf. Osborne, "Law in Action," esp. 42–43.

[39] See MacKendrick, *Athenian Aristocracy*, 14–15 (Hegesandros and Hegesippus),
22–23 (Lycurgus), index s.nn. (Demosthenes and Androtion).

as any other citizen might.[40] But, with the exception of Eubulus and Lycurgus in the financial *archai*, they did not normally hold consecutive magistracies. Their political influence was not dependent upon local constituencies, elective offices, or constitutionally granted powers.

D.1 RHETORES AND *Stratēgoi*

The orators are occasionally referred to in speeches as if they were the equivalent of elected magistrates. This is implicit in the reference of Lycurgus (F V.1a [Conomis] = F A.2.1 [Burtt]) to the three types of *dokimasia*: one to which archons submit, another for rhetores, and a third for generals (*stratēgoi*). Lycurgus is apparently referring here to the procedure used by Aeschines against Timarchus, discussed above (III.B.2). Like Aeschines, Lycurgus is exploiting the confusion between the common use of the term rhetor and its legal meaning. More problematic is a testimony by Dinarchus (1.71) to the effect that the laws (*nomoi*) declare that any rhetor or general must have legitimate children and own land in Attica if he is to be considered "worthy of the demos' trust" and that only then will he be "worthy to lead the demos" (*axioun proestanai tou dēmou*). If this were an accurate paraphrase of a law, we would have to assume that those who addressed the people were subject to a property qualification and that they were legally equated with the generals. Dinarchus does not, however, quote the *nomoi* in question, and his phraseology, which emphasizes who should be seen as worthy to lead the people, does not seem to reflect, even indirectly, Athenian legal discourse. In the absence of any other evidence for this sort of restriction on public address (taking rhetor here to mean anyone who addressed the Assembly) and in the face of the other testimonies that seem specifically to exclude the possibility of a property qualification, Dinarchus' testimony should not be taken as evidence for the existence of a written law requiring that public speakers have legitimate children and own property.[41]

Dinarchus' comment should be viewed in the context of the general tendency of the orators to treat rhetores and *stratēgoi* as fulfilling par-

---

[40] See Roberts, "Athens' Politicians," who certainly shows that, *pace* Gomme, "Working," 16, Athenian politicians often held offices in the course of their careers.

[41] Cf. Aesch. 1.171 (discussed above, III.B.2) and the testimonia cited in III.n.12. Rhodes, *CommAP*, 511, discusses the Dinarchus passage, concluding that the requirements are "probably survivals from the archaic state," although he also notes that "a law concerning ῥήτορες is not likely to be earlier than the end of the fifth century." Hansen, "History of the Athenian Constitution," 62, agrees with Rhodes' discussion of this passage.

allel functions and as constituting collectively a set of "the politically powerful," who were contrasted with the set of "the *idiōtai*." Hyperides, for example, claims (5.24) that the wrongdoing of *idiōtai* is less serious than that of rhetores and *stratēgoi*. As we have seen (III.B.2), he urged the prosecutor of Euxenippus to leave innocent *idiōtai* alone and "wait for a rhetor or a *stratēgos* to commit a crime" (4.27). In a similar vein, Dinarchus (3.19) exhorted the jury to demonstrate to all men that the demos had not been corrupted along with certain of the bribe-taking rhetores and *stratēgoi*. Demosthenes (18.171) emphasizes that after Philip's occupation of Elatea in 339, no one but he was willing to come to the bema, despite the fact that "all the *stratēgoi* and all the rhetores were present." The parallelism is particularly clear in a comment of Aristotle (*Rhet.* 1388b17–18), who states that the *archontes* who were able to do good for many were the *stratēgoi*, the rhetores, and generally all those who were powerful. *Stratēgoi* were constitutional magistrates, rhetores were not, as Aristotle certainly knew. The conflation of the rhetores and *stratēgoi* by Aristotle and by the orators describes a political reality, not a constitutional fact.[42]

Certainly, fourth-century rhetores had much to do with Athenian military policy, and some generals, such as Phocion, addressed the Assembly with some frequency. But, as was suggested above (II.F.5), the dual road to political power taken by Pericles had begun to bifurcate shortly after his death, and the distinction between political and military experts was quite clear in the fourth century. Aristotle noted (*Pol.* 1305a10–15) that the "demagogues" of his day tended to be skilled in rhetoric and not in military affairs; generals tended to be the opposite.[43] Precisely because of their differing areas of expertise and their common concern with both state policy and personal political survival, generals and orators tended to work closely together. Generals needed skilled speakers to help in impeachment trials—to which they were very commonly subjected in the fourth century—and to propose legislation providing the funds necessary to carry out military campaigns mandated by the Assembly. The political orator needed cooperative generals to enthusiastically pursue military actions in support of his own long-range foreign policy objectives. Generals, along with other

[42] Cf. Dem. 23.184 and Hansen, "*Rhetores* and *Strategoi*," for other testimonia. Hansen, " 'Politicians'," suggests that the "politicians" (a term he would prefer not to use) of Athens were the rhetores (construed constitutionally) and *stratēgoi*. Cf. Perlman, "Politicians," 353–54, who suggests that public opinion saw the orators as holding "a position similar or identical with that of the strategi."

[43] Hansen, " 'Politicians'," 49–52, emphasizes the "sharp" distinction between the roles of rhetores and *stratēgoi*.

orators, also made good character witnesses (*sunēgoroi*) at public trials, although the other side might attempt to discredit them. Dinarchus (1.112) assured his audience that any rhetor or *stratēgos* who might speak in Demosthenes' favor was guilty of bribe-taking himself. In *Against Ctesiphon* (3.7) Aeschines urged the jurors not to allow themselves to be influenced by intercessions of generals favorable to Demosthenes' cause, claiming that the generals had for a long time been co-workers (*sunergountes*) with certain orators and as such were outraging the state.[44]

The symbiosis between generals and orators was clearly important to the functioning of the post-Periclean Athenian government, and no doubt certain generals and orators did tend to act as "co-workers." Furthermore, orators clearly cooperated with other orators on specific issues and sometimes over fairly long periods of time. A politician commonly called upon friendly rhetores as *sunēgoroi* when he was involved in a public trial, and political legal actions were often aimed at those rhetores known to be actively supporting one's political opponents (e.g., Aeschines' actions against Timarchus and Ctesiphon). But we must resist the tendency to make too much of these relationships. As I have suggested above (I.B, II.G), the politicians and generals of the fourth century did not constitute a ruling elite. The limited amount of cooperation between orators and between orators and generals was more than overbalanced by the intensity of their competitions with one another. Whatever authority they wielded was dependent upon the people's continuing approval: *stratēgoi* faced reelection each year and trial at anytime; rhetores were judged each time they stood up in the Assembly and each time they were engaged in a public legal action.

D.2 POLITICAL GROUPS VERSUS INDIVIDUAL LEADERSHIP

The relations between orators and generals were not even remotely similar to modern party politics. Recent research on the political groupings of Athenian politicians and generals has shown the error of the party model for Athenian politics. There is no longer much scholarly enthusiasm for tracing the fortunes of hypothetical oligarchic and democratic "parties," and one now finds fewer references in the

---

44 Cf. Lys. 14.21; Dem. 12.19. Aeschines is making a pun on *sunēgoroi*: character witnesses. On the generally close cooperation between rhetores and *stratēgoi*, see Perlman, "Politicians," 347–48; Hansen, " 'Politicians'," 52–55. On character witnesses at Athenian trials, see Harrison, *Law*, II.158–60; Humphreys, "Social Relations," esp. 335–38 (rhetores and *stratēgoi* as *sunēgoroi*).

professional literature to organized conservative, moderate, and radical interest groups than was once the case. Most specialists in fourth-century politics would, I think, agree that such political groupings of orators and generals as can be demonstrated to have existed were fluid, although there is still not much agreement about the relative importance of principle, pragmatism, friendship, and family relations in the mutations of Athenian political factions.[45] The shifting alliances, whatever their bases, between political and military experts were certainly a factor in the public life of fourth-century Athens, and continuing research in the area should help to further clarify the situation. But the intense scholarly interest in defining parties, groups, and factions has tended to divert attention from other, perhaps more important, political realities.

The relationships between elite speakers and generals would certainly be the central feature of Athenian political life if the political and military experts constituted a ruling elite, but they did not. Their relations would also be of key importance if political groups commanded loyal mass followings, but they did not. The recent investigations into Athenian group politics have demonstrated clearly that no Athenian political faction had an organized or consistent popular constituency. The masses in the end, made and broke the politicians who constituted the factions. Thus, an exclusive emphasis on political groups is misdirected; it concentrates attention on ephemeral and epiphenomenal intra-elite relations and distracts our attention from the relationship between elites and masses that was the central reality of Athenian political life. Finley's comments on the demagogues are apropos.

> A man was a leader solely as a function of his personal, and in the literal sense, unofficial status within the Assembly itself. The test of whether or not he held that status was simply whether the Assembly did or did not vote as he wished, and therefore the test was repeated with each proposal.[46]

[45] The best recent study of fourth-century political groups is Strauss, *AAPW*, esp. 11–14. Among other useful discussions, see, for example, J. de Romilly, "Les modérés Athéniens vers le milieu de IVᵉ siècle: Échos et concordances," *REG* 67 (1954): 327–54; Cloché, "Hommes politiques"; Sealey, "Athens after the Social War," "Callistratos"; Perlman, "Politicians," 349–53, and "Athenian Democracy and the Revival of Athenian Imperial Expansion at the Beginning of the Fourth Century B.C.," *CPh* 63 (1968): 257–67; P. Harding, "Androtion's Political Career," *Historia* 25 (1976): 186–200; Roberts, *Accountability*, 55–83; Rhodes, "On Labelling." Humphreys, *Family*, 2–3, notes the relative unimportance of kinship and personal friendship in democratic politics.

[46] Finley, "Athenian Demagogues," 15, cf. *PAW*, 63–64.

When he addressed the Assembly or court, the orator stood alone, before the people. Thus Demosthenes (18.171), in describing his great moment in 339, does not say "the anti-Philip faction alone was able to field a credible spokesman" or anything of the kind. To have made such a claim would have been counterproductive, even if Demosthenes thought of those who shared his foreign policy views as his faction. The Athenians expected an individual politician to state his personal opinion on any given subject in open debate with other individuals of differing opinions. The suggestion that a politician was actively supported by powerful cronies was frequently used as an argument *against* his credibility.[47] As we shall see, the political orator was typically eager to portray himself as belonging to various elite status groups but never as belonging to an organized group of politicians that advocated special interests. The demos in the Assembly and the juries in the people's courts voted for or against the proposer of a decree or a litigant on the basis of his and his opponent's verbal arguments and perceived worth as citizens.

The most important political linkages in democratic Athens were not between politicians and generals but between public speakers and mass audiences. The key position of the individual demagogue in the political process and the key importance of rhetoric in Athenian decision making were well understood and heartily disapproved of by the elitist writers of late fifth- and fourth-century Athens. Among their objections to the demagogues was that the latter did not appeal in their speeches to the rational intellect but to irrationality, in the form of the baser emotions and ingrained prejudices of their audiences.[48] This general argument was reformulated by Max Weber, who characterized Athenian political leadership as of the "charismatic" type,

---

[47] E.g., Lys. 14.23; Dem. 21.139–40, 208–10, 213, 23.206; Aesch. 3.188, 255; Din. 1.99; cf. below, VII.F.1. Demosthenes' famous comment (2.29) to the effect that the Athenians conduct their politics by "symmories," each led by an orator with a *stratēgos* under him and three hundred others to do the shouting, must be read in this light and in light of the ideal of *homonoia*: below VII.B; cf. also Montgomery, *Way to Chaeronea*, 23–25. Recently, the group-politics model has been questioned; see esp. Meier's stimulating essay, "Les groupements politiques dans l'antiquité classique," in *Anthropologie*, 45–62. Meier argues that the political identification of the Athenians made parties unnecessary and undesirable, so that factions were always seen in a negative light.

[48] E.g., Aristot. *Rhet.* 1404a1–8, *Pol.* 1291b29–1292a38; Plato *Republic* 493a–d. Cleon was often considered to have been the originator of this evil: see II.n.91. Among modern discussions see Sattler, "Conceptions of *Ethos*"; Solmsen, "Aristotle"; Wilcox, "Scope," 145–48; J. de Romilly, *Magic and Rhetoric in Ancient Greece* (Cambridge, Mass., 1975), 25–32, 37–43 (Plato on rhetoric); Arnhart, *Aristotle*. Cf. ancient criticisms of rhetoric as flattery of the people: I.E, VII.E.4.

based on emotional appeals.[49] M. I. Finley, arguing against both the ancient critics of the democracy and against Weber, has disputed this categorization and asserted that the demagogues did not compete for leadership solely on the basis of emotional appeals but rather through "substantive promises" which they were expected to fulfill. Finley argues for an "instrumental view of politics" which locates the explanation for the workings of Athenian leadership "in the area of programmes and politics" rather than in the "mystical 'faith' " that Weber stressed. Finley concludes his essay on Weber and the Greek city-state by arguing that "to dismiss the Greek *polis* in general and Athens in particular as irrational does not advance our understanding."[50]

Finley is certainly correct to attack as simplistic and misleading a purely charismatic view of Athenian leadership and to point out the overemphasis of the ancient critics on demagogic appeals to base emotions. But Finley himself seems to go too far in the other direction. His eagerness to debunk the critics of the democracy leads him to overrationalize the nature of the Athenian orator's appeal to his audience. If good programs and sound policy were sufficient to achieve a position of leadership in Athens, Demosthenes and the other rhetores wasted a great deal of their own and demos' time, expending as they did much time and effort in perfecting their rhetorical style and in writing and delivering highly crafted speeches in which discussion of substantive proposals did not predominate. A careful reading of the oratorical corpus will not sustain the idea that the success of the Athenian politician was based on a purely instrumental approach. Rather, we should seek a middle ground between Weber's charismatic emotionalism and Finley's instrumental rationalism. And the middle ground can be sought in what I have described (I.D) as ideology. The successful orator was one who could consistently and seamlessly combine ideas drawn from mass ideology with moral principles and pragmatism in presenting a workable policy, a defense of his policy, or an attack on the policy of an opponent. The Athenian voter in the Assembly or courtroom did not react in a predictable and simplistic manner to obvious appeals to his baser emotions. But neither was he a logician

[49] See Finley, *Ancient History*, 93 with n. 21, for bibliography. Weber's charismatic model for Athenian leadership is accepted by Montgomery, *Way to Chaeronea*, 92–93. See also Michels, *Political Parties*, 64–65, 93–102.

[50] Finley, "Max Weber and the Greek City-State," in *Ancient History*, 88–103: quotes are from 98–99, 103. For a discussion of "instrumental" (instructional/informational) and "expressive" (emotional) communication, see Riley and Riley, "Mass Communication," 571–72.

or a purely pragmatic political analyst, who assessed and measured options on the basis of a purely rational calculation of interests.

When he entered the Assembly place or courtroom, the Athenian citizen was no doubt aware of his duty to the laws and customs of his state, of the importance of his decisions to his own and Athens' present and future interests. But he did not and could not check his ideological baggage at the gate. As a juror he swore: "I will listen impartially to both plaintiff and defendant, and I will cast my vote strictly on the basis of evidence that is relevant to the case."[51] But, if the extant orations are any guide, he construed relevance quite broadly and never thought of excluding his general impression of the speakers or litigants as citizens. When the time came to cast his ballot or to raise his hand, the citizen-voter evaluated the merit of the arguments on either side as best he could, but his judgment involved weighing them against not only the laws and the state interest but also his ideological presuppositions. Orators were well aware of the interplay of pragmatism, principle, and ideology in the minds of their audiences, and they designed their speeches accordingly (cf. Aristot. *Rhet.* 1354b4–11, 1375a27–31). The ideological content of Athenian orations should not, however, necessarily be construed as the product of cynical calculation on the part of the speakers. The line between personal character, legal and moral principles, and political ideology, though of considerable interest to Aristotle in the *Rhetoric*, was not, I think, particularly clear to most speakers or to their audiences in fourth-century Athens.[52] This lack of clarity is, at least in part, due to the relatively low level of political role differentiation that pertained in fourth-century Athens.

D.3 POLITICIANS AND ROLE DIFFERENTIATION

In a series of important essays, Niklas Luhmann has argued that one of the key sociological and political realities of modern industrial society is a very high level of role differentiation. Thus the modern politician's actions, undertaken while performing his political role in the government, are judged by criteria different from those employed

---

[51] Adapted from Dem. 24.149–51 by Lipsius, *Recht und Rechtsverfahren*, 152–53 n. 56; cf. Bonner and Smith, *Administration*, II.152–56; Maio, "*Politeia*," 43.

[52] Aristot. *Rhet.*, esp. 1355b25–1358a35, and Book 2, passim. Cf. Sattler, "Conceptions of *Ethos*," esp. 63–64; Arnhart, *Aristotle*, esp. 9–10, 112–14. Solmsen, "Aristotle," points out that before Aristotle's late fourth-century treatise, ethical arguments had not been subjected to independent analysis, since the emphasis of rhetoricians was on parts of the speech, rather than on the abstract nature of persuasion.

when he is perceived as acting as a private individual. His political and social roles are, therefore, differentiated in his own mind and in the minds of the other members of his society. As a corollary, Luhmann suggests that in simple societies there is a very low level of differentiation and that, therefore, the political leader will be judged by ordinary social values; his role as leader is not differentiated from his role as citizen.[53] Athens was certainly not a simple society, and the difference between *idiōtai* and rhetores stressed by the orators suggests that *some* role differentiation did indeed pertain and that it was of operational significance.[54] But the recognition that Athenian political roles were rather less differentiated from the social role of the average citizen than has often been the case in modern societies helps to explain the relative lack of interest shown by the Athenians in separating policy proposals from the individual character and behavior of the proposer, legal culpability from immoral behavior, or abstract political principles from popular ideology.

The demos judged a politician's policy at least in part by reference to his character, to his worth as a citizen. Hence, if a politician hoped to have his policy suggestions greeted with sympathy by the demos, it was incumbent upon him to demonstrate to the demos his personal worth. If he could undermine the demos' faith in the character of his adversary, he could undercut that adversary's policy initiatives as well. The degree of emphasis that both rhetorical manuals and the preserved orations place upon character defense and character assassination has sometimes disturbed modern readers, who have come to expect a greater degree of role differentiation between public and private lives than pertained in fourth-century Athens.[55] But character assassination appeared perfectly natural and quite correct to the relatively undifferentiated Athenians. Certainly there were limits, and concentrating completely on character to the exclusion of substantive discussion of the issues (legal or policy) at hand might alienate an audience. But the process of *dokimasia rhētorōn* specifically recognized the intimacy of the relationship between character and policy. In his prosecution of Timarchus, Aeschines (1.30) attributes the origin of the

[53] Luhmann, *Differentiation*, esp. 139–42, 146. For other aspects of role differentiation at Athens, see Humphreys, *Anthropology*, 250–65, *Family*, 21: ". . . the society of classical Athens was only at the beginning of the process of differentiation leading to complex modern societies. . . ."

[54] Holmes, "Aristippus," tends, I believe, to overemphasize the undifferentiated character of polis society; see Ober, "Aristotle's Political Sociology."

[55] Cf. Sattler, "Conceptions of *Ethos*," 55–56, 60–61; Kennedy, *Art of Persuasion*, 229. See, in general, Burke, "Character Denigration."

process to the lawmaker's conviction that no man "could be a rascal (*ponēros*) in his private life (*idiai*), but an excellent man (*chrēstos*) in public affairs" (*dēmosiai*). Later in the speech, he commented (1.179) that the laws were losing force, and the democracy was being destroyed because "you [jurors] sometimes recklessly accept mere speech (*logos*) that is unsupported by a good life" (*aneu chrēstou biou*). The stress on the necessity of good character for good political action led quite naturally to the politician's life as a whole being open to public scrutiny. For the expert Athenian politician, politics was a full-time occupation, not only because of the time consumed in perfecting rhetorical skills and the risks he undertook in the courts, but because his every action was public property and would be judged against the standard of popular morality. His family, early career, and personal relationships would all count for or against him in the courtroom and Assembly.

E. Public Forums of Debate and Communication

The forums of Athenian public life, at which the individual Athenian citizen might meet, communicate with, judge, and be judged by his fellows included the Assembly, the courts, the Council, the agora, and the theater. While courtroom and Assembly speeches form the bulk of the rhetorical corpus, speeches in the other public forums must be taken into consideration as well. In order to form an opinion on the political significance of the communication between mass and elite generally, we must try to understand the nature of communication in each public space, and this requires some background on the political function of each forum, the social composition of the audience, and the rules and procedures governing the actions of both senders and receivers of messages. We should first look briefly at Athenian economic and geographic demography and at the cost of living in fourth-century Athens. These will be significant variables in our assessment of the composition of mass audiences.

E.1 DEMOGRAPHY AND SUBSISTENCE

The most elementary demographic data needed are, of course, the size of the total population of Attica and the number of Athenian citizens. Unfortunately, neither is easily determined. There has been a good deal of interest in the demography of fourth-century Athens, which has concentrated on the size of the citizen body. But there is, as yet, no consensus, and scholars using the same limited data have come up with rather different answers. We will, however, not go very far wrong if we suppose that for most of the fourth century the citizen population was in the area of 20,000–30,000 (perhaps somewhat less in the immediate postwar decades) and that the total population of Attica was in the area of 150,000–250,000.[56] For our present purposes, no greater precision is really necessary, even if it were theoretically possible. In any event, the citizen population was in all likelihood never much more than about 15 to 20 percent of the total population, or half the adult male population; but, as suggested above (I.A; cf. II.F.1), the percentages are less important for understanding the nature of ancient democracy than is the absence of any property qualification for full political participation.

Lack of agreement among scholars also exists on the relative size of the Athenian wealth elite. J. K. Davies has, I believe correctly, defined the wealthiest citizens of Athens as the liturgy-paying class and has determined that a minimum size for a liturgical fortune was three to four talents (18,000–24,000 drachmas). I also accept his argument that in the fourth century there were about 300–400 liturgy payers.[57] Davies has also, once again in my opinion correctly, suggested that a fortune of about one talent (6,000 drachmas) was necessary to place a family in the leisure class, that a total of about 1,200–2,000 citizens (and their families, perhaps 4,800–8,000 persons total) were leisure class, and that the leisure-class citizens were those who paid the occasional war tax (*eisphora*).[58] The considerably higher figures suggested by other scholars for the size of the leisure class seem to me to be based on erroneous notions of the size and distribution of the slave population (see I.C.4), the probable rate of return on investments, and the cost of living and of maintaining a family fortune.[59]

---

[56] See esp. Strauss, *AAPW*, 70–86; Hansen, "Demographic Reflections," *Demography and Democracy*, with literature cited; cf. I.n.66. Among older accounts Gomme, *Population*, idem, "The Population of Athens Again," *JHS* 79 (1959): 61–68; and Mossé, *Fin de la démocratie*, 139–85, are still useful. Cf. above, I.C.5.

[57] Davies, *APF*, xx–xxx, *WPW*, 9–37.

[58] Davies, *WPW*, 6–14, 28–35, esp. 28 (one talent for leisure class status, citing Dem. 42.22), 34–35: ca. 1,200 in the leisure class. Cf. Mossé, "Symmories," 37; and E. Ruschenbusch in *ZPE* 31 (1978): 275–84, who suggest that there were about 1,200 liturgy-payers, and that these were identical to the *eisphora*-payers; P. J. Rhodes, "Problems in Athenian *Eisphora* and Liturgies," *AJAH* 7 (1982): 1–19, esp. 8, who argues that there were about 1,200 liturgy-payers and somewhat more than this, perhaps 2,000, *eisphora*-payers. On the organization of the *eisphora*, see below, V.A.3.

[59] Ste. Croix, "Demosthenes' TIMHMA," 33, accepted as very plausible the figure of ca. 6,000 citizen *eisphora*-payers, which had been suggested by Jones, *AD*, 9–10. Brun, *Eisphora*, 19–22, cf. 64–65, 68–73, supposes that there were some 6,000–9,000 *eisphora*-payers (including metics), that responsibility extended to those with fortunes of 2,000–2,500 drachmas, and that therefore most *eisphora*-payers could

Hence, the leisure-class citizens composed somewhere in the region of 5 to 10 percent of the citizen population. The other 90 to 95 percent of the citizens would have had to work, at least part time, to support themselves and to contribute to the support of their families.[60] Of these laboring citizens, a total of perhaps 7,000–8,000 possessed property amounting to about 2,000 drachmas or more and so were of hoplite status. A good many of these "middling" citizens would be subsistence farmers who were able to feed themselves and their families from the production of their farms.[61] The remainder of the citizen population would have included poorer subsistence farmers—some of whom would have to supplement their agricultural production with other income from wage-labor or labor-exchange—and urban residents who might own small shops or family-labor manufactures or

not be considered rich. The figure of ca. 6,000 payers is accepted by Markle, "Jury pay," 282, who attempts (295–97) to demonstrate that these 6,000 citizens (and their families) *would* be leisure class. Markle argues that a fortune of 2,500 drachmas would free a family from the necessity of laboring. This seems to me quite impossible. Thompson, "Athenian Investor," calculates, quite optimistically, that investment in land could return up to 8 percent per annum. Investments in slaves, mines, and overseas trade were more profitable but also more risky, and land surely formed the bulk of the property of most Athenians between the lowest and highest classes. Eight percent per annum would yield 480 dr. on a talent's worth of land; 200 dr. on 2,500 dr. worth of land. But a good part of the family's fortune would probably not be financially "productive" (e.g., the house and the land it sat on, property given for dowries) and considerable reserves would need to be retained for emergencies (e.g., legal entanglements, crop failures, tax assessments). It seems unlikely that a family with a fortune of a talent (6,000 dr.) would realize a disposable income of much over a drachma a day. It hardly seems likely that an income of substantially less than this would qualify a family as leisure class, since the expenditure by aspirants to the leisure class for food and other consumed goods would presumably be well above the subsistence level (e.g., wheat rather than barley, meat, better qualities of wine and oil, more and better clothing; cf. Lys. 32.20: a guardian who reckoned the *trophē* of two boys and a girl at five obols a day—albeit his opponent claims this was an inflated figure). All this suggests that the speaker of Dem. 42.22 was not exaggerating when he claimed that to live on a fortune of 4,500 dr. is not easy.

[60] *Pace* Gabrielsen, *Remuneration*, 126, the tendency of elite writers to equate the *penētes* with the demos as a whole is not significant in this context; cf. below, v.a.1 on the terminology of wealth.

[61] On hoplite status, see Jones, *AD*, 142 n. 50. On subsistence farming, see Ober, *FA*, 19–28, with literature cited; G. Audring, "Über Grundeigentum und Landwirtschaft in Attika wahrend des 4. Jh. v.u.Z.," *Klio* 56 (1974): 445–56; cf. Ste. Croix, *CSAGW*, 208–18. The average grain production of Attica, a key factor in the subsistence-farming question, is often grossly underestimated; see P. Garnsey, "Grain for Athens," in Cartledge and Harvey, edd., *Crux: Essays Presented to Ste. Croix*, 62–75.

who might work as hired laborers. Wages for laborers seem to have been in the range of between one and two and a half drachmas per day in the fourth century, although the significance of these figures is open to question.[62] At the bottom of the economic ladder were the truly indigent, citizens without real property and perhaps unable to work. At least some of these received direct state support.[63]

We should also consider briefly the geographical distribution of the citizenry. By use of the bouleutic quotas, a fairly good idea of the geographic distribution of citizens in 508/7, at the time of the Cleisthenic establishment of the deme system, may be obtained. But, since deme membership was hereditary, these quotas do not tell us as much as we should like about the actual distribution of population in the fourth century. Robin Osborne has calculated that, according to the bouleutic quotas, some 39 percent of Athenians lived further than 24 km. (15 mi.) from the city. This distance would represent a trip from home village to city of at least four hours each way on foot—and longer by slow-moving ox cart. Even in mid-summer, therefore, citizens at this remove would be unlikely to make the round trip in a single day.[64] Presumably, some members of rural demes had moved to the city since the time of Cleisthenes, but Thucydides (2.16.1) notes that before the Peloponnesian War the majority of Athenians lived in the countryside; this was most probably still the case in the fourth century.[65] Presumably, a significant number of citizens, then, still lived far

---

[62] See, in general, Y. Garlan, "Le travail libre en Grèce ancienne," in Garnsey, ed., *Non–Slave Labour*, 6–22; and E. C. Welskopf, "Free Labour in the City of Athens," in ibid., 23–25; cf. A. Fuks, "*Kolonòs místhios*: Labour Exchange in Ancient Athens," *Eranos* 49 (1951): 71–73; Wood, "Agricultural Slavery," 23–24. Wages for skilled laborers at the end of the fifth century seem to average about one drachma per day. See R. H. Randall, "The Erechtheum Workmen," *AJA* 57 (1953): 199–210, which is similar to military pay at the time (Thuc. 3.17.3). In the late fourth century, wages seem to be in the range of 1½ to 2½ dr. per day; see Markle, "Jury Pay," 293; Rhodes, *CommAP*, 691. The figures are problematic in that they are widely separated chronologically, are in the context of work on religious monuments (hence some workers may accept lower wages as a sort of liturgy), and are specific to the building trades.

[63] *AP* 49.4; Lys. 24; cf. Rhodes, *CommAP*, 570; Hansen, *Demography and Democracy*, 18–19; Buchanan, *Theorika*, 1–3, 38–48.

[64] Osborne, *Demos*, 68–72, 88. The suggestion of Hansen, "Political Activity," that there may have been a reassessment of bouleutic quotas in ca. 403/2, is not convincing. Ox carts as basic form of transport: A. Burford, "Heavy Transport in Classical Antiquity," *Economic History Review*, 2nd series 13 (1960): 1–18; speed: D. W. Engels, *Alexander the Great and the Logistics of the Macedonian Army* (Berkeley and Los Angeles, 1978), 14 with n. 15 (ca. 2 m.p.h. and generally good for only about 5 hrs. per day).

[65] According to Dionysius of Halicarnassus' *hupothesis* to Lysias 34, only 5,000

enough from the city to make it inconvenient for them to visit the city
without planning on an overnight stay.

Many imponderables are present in the attempt to calculate the av- *cost*
erage cost of living in fourth-century Athens, especially if we assume
that much of the Athenian economy was at the level of autarkic subsistence, barter, and exchange.[66] Housing was no doubt a significant
factor for a poor urban citizen who must rent his lodgings but not for
the rural resident who owned his home outright. For a citizen living
in the charcoal-burning region north of Acharnai, fuel would not cost
much, if anything; it might be expensive in the city.[67] There was no
doubt a considerable difference between the annual clothing costs of
the sheep-owning rural citizen whose wife was a weaver and the citizen
who purchased similar items in the agora. The one variable that can
be pinned down is the cost of grain, which was the basic source of both
calories and protein for most Athenians. The cost of both wheat (six
drachmas per *medimnos*) and barley (three drachmas per *medimnos*) was
fairly stable in fifth- and fourth-century Athens. Modern statistics on
subsistence diets suggest that a family of four would need to consume
a minimum of about twenty-three medimnoi of wheat or about
twenty-eight of barley in a year to achieve a basic subsistence level of
existence. Thus the fixed minimum annual cost for the family's basic
food commodity, assuming that cheaper barley was the most common
food of the poor, was about eighty to ninety drachmas—assuming the
family was able to buy in bulk. The per diem expense would have been
about a quarter drachma, or under two obols.[68]

Athens were landless in 403. Of course, not all landed Athenians lived in the country, but many did. The theory that by the early fourth century the land of Attica
was concentrated in the hands of a few wealthy citizens, most fully elaborated by
Mossé, *Fin de la démocratie*, 39–67, 133, has now been discarded by most scholars;
see Ober, *FA*, 20–22, with literature cited. Hansen, "Political Activity," 234–35, argues rather tentatively for a migration of significant proportions to the city, but he
admits that quantification is impossible.

[66] The extent to which ancient Greek economies were monetarized is not known,
but I tend to agree with scholars who suppose that they retained many primitive
features. See, in general, Finley, *AE*, esp. 123–49, and the essays collected in *Trade
in the Ancient Economy*.

[67] Charcoal burners: Aristoph. *Acharnians* (chorus); cf. And. F III.1 (Maidment).
The wealthy Phaenippus, owner of the largest known estate in fourth-century Attica, used six donkeys to ship wood (possibly timber, but more probably for fuel) to
the city, from which his opponent claimed he gained a profit of more than twelve
dr. per day: Dem. 42.7, with R. Meiggs, *Trees and Timber in the Ancient Mediterranean
World* (Oxford, 1982), 205–206.

[68] For the calculations, see Ober, *FA*, 24–25; cf. the similar figures arrived at by
Markle, "Jury Pay," 277–280: cost of grain per family = ca. 1.65 obols. For a fuller

E.2 ASSEMBLY (*Ekklēsia*)

In the latter part of the fourth century, there were normally four meetings of the Assembly per prytany, for a total of forty meetings each year (*AP* 43.3); the set number *may* have been thirty meetings per year in ca. 355–346; previously no more than one meeting per prytany may have been mandated, although as many as necessary could be called to deal with emergencies.[69] Meetings were typically held in the Pnyx, a theater-like area built and used exclusively for meetings of the Assembly. Assemblies could, however, be held elsewhere, especially in the theater of Dionysus (*AP* 42.4). The fourth-century Pnyx (period II) could comfortably seat about 6,000 to 8,000 persons, and Hansen has argued that an average meeting in the fourth century would have had an attendance of 6,000 or more citizens; it is possible, although I think it unlikely, that entrance was restricted to the first 6,000 citizens to arrive.[70] Thus, those present at any given Assembly probably represented between one- and two-fifths of the total citizen population—a remarkably high turnout, if one considers the frequency of meetings.[71] Seating may have been according to tribe and (at least in the fifth century) by trittys. A *nomos* of 346/5 (Aesch. 1.33; above, III.B.2) called for the members of one tribe to maintain order at each meeting

---

discussion of ancient grain consumption, see L. Foxhall and H. A. Forbes, "Σιτομετ-ρεία: The Role of Grain as a Staple Food in Classical Antiquity," *Chiron* 12 (1982): 41–90.

[69] Hansen, "How Often," and Hansen and Mitchel, "Number of Ecclesiai," argue that in the mid-fourth century the number of *ekklēsiai* per prytany was fixed at four (for a few years before this at three), and no more than this could legally be called. *Contra*: Rhodes, *CommAP*, 521–22; Markle, "Jury Pay," 274 with n. 18; Edward M. Harris, "How Often Did the Athenian Assembly Meet?" *CQ* 36 (1986): 363–77. Hansen replies to Harris in "How Often Did the Athenian *Ekklesia* Meet. A Reply," *GRBS* 28 (1987): 35–50.

[70] Excavations on the Pnyx: H. A. Thompson et al. in *Hesperia* 1 (1932): 90–217, 5 (1936): 51–200, 12 (1943): 269–383. On the dates of the three periods, see summaries in Thompson and Wycherley, *Agora*, XIV.48–52; H. A. Thompson, "The Pnyx in Models," *Hesperia* Suppl. 19 (1982), 134–47; R. A. Moysey, "The Thirty and the Pnyx," *AJA* 35 (1981): 31–37; Stanton and Bicknell, "Voting in Tribal Groups." Numbers in attendance: Hansen, "How Many," "Athenian Ecclesia and the Assembly-Place"; Stanton and Bicknell, "Voting in Tribal Groups," 68–69. Restricted entry: Hansen, "Athenian Ecclesia and the Assembly-Place," 243–44, "The Construction of Pnyx II and the Introduction of Assembly Pay," *CM* 37 (1986): 89–98; Krentz, *The Thirty*, 63; *contra*: Rhodes, "Athenian Democracy," 307. Meetings in the theater of Dionysus: *AP* 42.4 (regularly to review the ephebes); Thuc. 8.93–94 (extraordinarily in 411/10); cf. W. A. MacDonald, *The Political Meeting Places of the Greeks* (Baltimore, 1943), 47–61.

[71] Osborne, *Demos*, 65, 91, emphasizes the significance of the fact that not all citizens attended regularly, but contrast Raaflaub, "Freien Bürgers Recht," 39–41.

of the Assembly, and these men may have taken their seats in the front of the auditorium, by the bema. Otherwise there were no privileged seating arrangements. The seating was egalitarian: rich and poor, elite and commoner sat together in a socially undifferentiated mass (cf. Theophrastus *Characters* 26). Access to the meeting was controlled by entry gates.[72] This facilitated the payment of citizens in attendance. By the late 390s at least the first several thousand citizens to arrive received a stipend of three obols; by the 320s pay for attendance had been raised to one drachma for the ordinary meetings and 1½ drachmas for the ten annual principal meetings.[73]

A meeting of the Assembly began early in the morning and opened with a prayer to the gods. Then the president of the meeting (selected by lot from among the *bouleutai*) presented the issue for discussion, according to the agenda set by the Council. If the Councilmen had formulated a recommendation on the issue, it would be read in the form of a proposal to the Assembly. The president would then ask (through the herald) who of the Athenians had advice to give. After the debate (if any) he conducted the vote. Voting was normally by show of hands, but in exceptional circumstances it was by ballot.[74] If the measure passed, it became a decree (*psēphisma*) which had the force of law unless and until it was successfully challenged as having contravened the established *nomoi*, through the conviction of the proposer by the people's court (in a *graphē paranomōn*, see above, II.G). At least until the mid-350s the Assembly might also sit as a jury to hear impeachments for major public offenses (*eisangeliai*), but this seems to have been quite rare, and only one preserved oration (Lys. 28) was written for a trial heard by the Assembly.[75] Hansen has argued con-

---

[72] Tribal seating: Staveley, *Greek and Roman Voting*, 81–82; cf. Boegehold, "Toward a Study," esp. 374. *Contra*: Hansen, "How Did the Athenian *Ecclesia* Vote?" 135–36. Stanton and Bicknell, "Voting in Tribal Groups" (a reply to Hansen), argue for subdivision by tribe and trittys in Pnyx I and II and by tribe in Pnyx III. Stanton and Bicknell's arguments (80–86) for trittys divisions in Pnyx II seem to me inadequate. Entry gates: Hansen, "Two Notes on the Pnyx."

[73] Introduction and amount of ecclesiastic pay: *AP* 41.3; see also Markle, "Jury Pay," 273–76; above, II.G. In the late 390s, when Aristophanes wrote the *Ecclesiazusae* (see lines 183–88, 289–310, 383–95; date: Strauss, *AAPW*, 143 with 149 n. 85) payment was limited to a certain number who arrived early. On the rise in the amount of pay, see also below, III.E.4.

[74] See, in general, Staveley, *Greek and Roman Voting*, 83–87; Boegehold, "Toward a Study"; Hansen, "How Did the Athenian *Ecclesia* Vote?"

[75] For differing views on the evolution of *eisangelia* procedure in the fifth and fourth centuries see Hansen, *Eisangelia*, esp. 37 with n. 2; Rhodes, "ΕΙΣΑΓΓΕΛΙΑ"; Roberts, *Accountability*, 15–17, 21–24; Hansen, "Eisangelia. A Reply"; Carawan, "*Eisangelia* and *Euthyna*."

vincingly that a typical meeting would last about half the daylight hours.[76]

⌐ The Assembly represented the Athenian citizen body gathered together with the specific duty and intention of determining state policy. Any citizen in good standing could attend meetings of the Assembly, and his vote was equal to the vote of each other citizen in attendance. The Assemblymen could be and often were addressed as *ho dēmos*— they were, symbolically, the Athenians; their decisions were the decisions of the Athenian state.[77] The Assemblyman was not the representative of a constituency or special interest group. He voted as he saw best, according to his own ideological presuppositions and in the best interests of his state and of himself. The directness of the decision-making procedure makes it important to determine whatever we can about the social makeup of the Assembly. If its social composition was, typically, dramatically different from that of the citizen body as a whole, this would have a considerable bearing upon our reading of the nature of the arguments made by politicians in Assembly and of the decision-making system of the democracy as a whole.[78]

Some scholars have assumed that most citizens who attended Assembly meetings were quite wealthy or at least were members of a hypothetical "middle class."[79] But, if the demographic analysis suggested above (III.E.1) is anywhere near correct, no Assembly could have been numerically dominated by the leisure class, since there were not more than 2,000 leisure-class citizens, and surely not all of them attended any given meeting. Assuming an average Assembly attendance of 6,000 or more, we must suppose that 4,000 or more of them were Athenians who had to work for a living. The mythical "middle class" of Athens was dealt with above (I.C.5). But we should at least consider the argument that many poorer Athenians were excluded from the Assembly (and from the jury-courts) because the state reimbursement was insufficient to replace wages and too low to support a family. M. M. Markle, in an article that vigorously disputes the idea that the rich dominated either the Assembly or the juries, has attempted to

[76] Hansen, "Duration."

[77] On 'demos' as a synonym for *ekklēsia*, see Hansen, "Demos, Ecclesia," 130–31. On the question of the sovereignty of the Assembly, see below, III.E.4, VII.C.

[78] The fullest discussion of this point is Ernst Kluwe, "Die soziale Zusammensetzung der athenischen Ekklesia und ihr Einfluss auf politische Enstscheidungen," *Klio* 58 (1976): 295–333, "Nochmals zum Problem: Die soziale . . . Entscheidungen," *Klio* 59 (1977): 45–81, who argues for elite domination. Cf. Gomme, "Working," 12; Finley, "Athenian Demagogues," 10–11; Rhodes, *Boule*, 79.

[79] For example, Jones, *AD*, 35–36; Perlman, "Political Leadership," 163.

show that an average family of four could be maintained on rather less than three obols a day.[80] Markle's figures for the overall cost of living may be somewhat low, but we need not demonstrate that an entire family could be supported from ecclesiastic pay in order to disprove the notion that the poor could not afford to attend the Assembly. First, it is not necessary to assume that the male "head of household" was the only member of the laboring class family who was able to generate income. Much evidence suggests that Athenian women who were not of the leisure class performed productive labor, and there is no reason to assume that their partly grown children were idle.[81] Thus, we do not need to prove that the *triōbolon* was enough to support a family for a day in and of itself. Next, since meetings apparently lasted only half a day, the remainder of the day was left free for wage-earning activities. Urban residents, at least, could attend the Assembly in the morning and plan on working at their regular employments for the rest of the day.

The equation of payment for attendance at the Assembly with wage earning is somewhat misleading. The Athenians were ambivalent

[80] Markle, "Jury Pay," esp. 277–81. He appears to me to underestimate living costs over and above the cost of grain. On grain his figures seem to me very reasonable; see above, III.n.68. For a close analysis of the various factors which made up the cost of living in late eighteenth-century Philadelphia, see Smith, "Material Lives."

[81] The mother of the litigant in Dem. 57 sold ribbons in the agora; the same litigant notes that in times of economic difficulty even upper-class women might serve as wetnurses; cf. discussion of this passage below, VI.D.2. "Socrates" recommended that a friend who had lost his fortune put the women in his house to work as weavers (Xen. *Mem.* 2.7); and Aristotle (*Pol.* 1300a4–8, 1322b37–1323a6) implicitly links women's labor (or at least the need to leave the home) with *aporia*. Cf. Lacey, *Family*, 170–71; Keuls, *Reign of the Phallus*, 229–64, esp. 231–32. Comparisons from other pre-industrial societies suggest that women's labor is important to lower-class households. For urban women see Smith, "Material Lives," esp. 201, who demonstrates that among the unskilled laborers of late eighteenth-century Philadelphia, "women and children rarely could earn their keep, but as a supplement to the wages of the household head, their income was essential to the maintenance of the family." For rural women, see R. O. and P. Whyte, *The Women of Rural Asia* (Boulder, Colorado, 1982), 159–77, esp. 159: "The lower the socio-economic level of the family, the greater the proportion of total income contributed by women. . . . The contribution of Asian women is often in the form of unpaid labour—work on subsistence plots which would otherwise be beyond the capacity of the husband alone"; ibid., 160: women also contribute cash to the family budget "either from the sale of grain received as payment for labour on large landholdings . . . or small sums derived from a multiplicity of secondary pursuits such as weaving, sewing, matmaking. . . ." I am indebted to Michelle Maskiell for this reference and for her comments on the economic role of women in pre-industrial societies.

about the propriety of a citizen working for wages paid by another individual—the procedure smacked of the relationship between a slave and his owner. Given a choice, the citizen might well choose a lower stipend from the state for performing the duties proper to a citizen over higher wages offered by an individual, even assuming he could always find work when he wanted it. And this last is not a necessary assumption.[82] The poorest of the citizens—the old, handicapped, unlucky, and unskilled—might well attend the Assembly regularly to collect money not otherwise available to them. This is the point of Demosthenes' comment (24.123) that the Athenians were high-minded, since they retained laws prescribing harsh penalties for disenfranchised citizens who attended the Assembly or sat as jurors, although "you [jurors] know that someone may do this only because of want (*penia*)."

Arguments that treat state pay as the equivalent of wages do not translate well to a rural setting. Because agriculture is a seasonal activity, there were some periods of the year (especially the summer, between harvest and sowing) when the rural citizen's farm work would allow him to travel to town as he wished. Even during the more active times of the agricultural year, he might well be able to afford to leave for a couple of days at a time; indeed, he would probably have to do so in order to transact his affairs in town (these might include selling seasonal produce in order to finance purchases of items he could not obtain locally). And, since he could plan on a half-day free after the Assembly meeting, he could combine the business of a citizen with his private business; attending the Assembly would help to subsidize a trip he might make anyway. The subsistence farmer was not dependent on wages to support his family; he would require only enough of a stipend to feed himself while in the city and to pay for lodgings if he stayed overnight and had no relatives or friends in town to put him up.[83] The members of his family who had stayed behind were provided for out of the farm's produce.

Although we obviously cannot determine what percentage of the citizens at any given Assembly meeting were rural residents, it seems likely that the farmers were a noticeable presence. In the *Ecclesiazusae* (280–81) Aristophanes refers to the "Assemblywomen" (in the guise of their husbands) coming to the Pnyx from the countryside (*ek tōn*

---

[82] Preference for community work (e.g., serving as a magistrate) over labor for an individual: Raaflaub, "Democracy, Oligarchy," 531–32; cf. below, VI.D. Markle, "Jury Pay," 296–97, points out that even skilled laborers would not work every day.

[83] A wealthy citizen might lease a room in a private home as a *pied à terre* for his visits to town: Ant. 1.14.

agrōn) in numbers large enough to threaten the townspeople's chance of collecting their own ecclesiastic pay.[84] Even if we suppose that the average Attic farmer attended no more than one Assembly in four (which would require only ten annual trips to town, or about twenty days away from home for residents of more distant demes), we may still guess that rural residents would be present at meetings in very significant numbers. Their geographic "disadvantage" was, at least to some degree, balanced by the lack of competition for their time in the form of regular urban employment.[85]

The demographic mix at each individual meeting of the Assembly would no doubt differ, depending on a variety of factors presumably including, but not limited to, the published agenda, the season of the year, and the state of the economy. On the whole, many more working than leisure-class citizens would be in attendance. Perhaps the rural population was underrepresented at some meetings, but significant rural underrepresentation cannot be demonstrated to have been the norm and need not be assumed *a priori*. The very rich, due to their greater leisure, and the very poor, due to their need, may have been somewhat overrepresented. But no evidence suggests that the Assembly was grossly unrepresentative of the social composition of the Athenian citizen body as a whole. The decisions made in Assembly affected all Athenians directly; there is no reason to suppose that the members of any identifiable social sub-group would systematically avoid the meetings. Indeed, both the importance of the decisions made in Assembly and the general scorn of the elitist writers for the Assembly and its decision-making methods suggest that the demos which sat at the Pnyx was demographically quite similar to the "imagined" demos, the demos that no one had ever seen assembled but which existed at

[84] As always with Aristophanes, one must allow for comic exaggeration and distortion; cf. Dover, *GPM*, 20–22. But in this case surely the humor of the reversal of sexual roles would be blunted by the introduction of a second level of improbability. The "turnabout" of Assemblywomen would become absurd if rural Assemblymen were already regarded as oddities.

[85] On the question of rural residents and political participation, see also Strauss, *AAPW*, 59–60, 69 n. 97, with literature cited; Carter, *Quiet Athenian*, 76–98; Osborne, *Demos*, esp. 184–85; Hansen, "Political Activity," 233–38. Wood, "Agricultural Slavery," 13–15, argues (against Jameson, "Agriculture and Slavery") that peasants who are not in debt to landlords have considerable nonproductive time that is available for civic pursuits. I do not think that Aristotle's (*Pol.* 1319a4–19) discussion of the "farmer's democracy," which he considered better than the extreme Athenian-type democracy—in part because farmers would tend to come to the city less frequently—is apropos, since Aristotle was discussing a hypothetical idealized state which is specifically contrasted to the existing Athenian order.

the level of popular ideology and elite political theory: the entire citizen body.[86]

⌈ Undertaking to address the Athenian Assembly must have been a daunting prospect, even to the trained orator. The audience was huge, so a strong voice was essential (Aristot. *Rhet.* 1414a16–17). In the *Rhetoric* (1358b6–10), Aristotle treats deliberative oratory (*to sumbouleutikon*), which included oratory in the Assembly and Council, as one of the three main branches of the art. He notes (1418a21–29) that deliberative oratory is much more difficult than forensic because deliberative oratory deals with the future, rather than with the past, and because it allows fewer chances for digression or making comments about oneself or one's opponent. The demos, as Demosthenes had discovered, felt no hesitation about shouting down any speaker who irritated them or who was wasting their time (cf. Aristot. *Rhet.* 1355a2–3). A politician's opponents would be quick to jump in if they perceived that the audience was becoming bored. Demosthenes (19.23–24, 46) recalls with some bitterness how, during a key meeting in 346, Aeschines and Philocrates stationed themselves at his side in order to mock him. Worse yet, the Assemblymen had found their quips amusing. This sort of behavior may have led to the "orderliness" *nomos* of 346/5 (above, III.B.2), but Hyperides (5.12), speaking in 323, claimed that it was still possible to purchase the services of "lesser rhetores" who were specialists at causing a ruckus to disturb the speaker. There are only seventeen preserved fourth-century speeches that were delivered to the Assembly, all but three from the period 355–338; deliberative speeches were apparently less frequently published than forensic speeches (above, I.E).[87]

E.3 COUNCIL (*Boulē*) AND AREOPAGUS

Speeches to the Council of 500 constituted the second major branch of Athenian deliberative oratory. Despite the importance of the Council as an empowering institution for the Assembly (see II.E.2), only five Council speeches are preserved, and in each case the speech is in the form of a legal plea, rather than advocating a policy. Apparently, like Assembly speeches, Council speeches on policy were seldom (if ever) published. We know, however, that the *bouleutai* could invite individ-

---

[86] Scorn for the Assembly and its methods; above, III.D.2. "Imagined society": above, I.C.6; cf. Loraux, *Invention*, esp. 336–38.

[87] Laughing and shouting down speakers: Plato *Euthyphro* 3b–c; Plut. *Demosthenes* 6.3; Aesch. 2.4. On symbouleutic oratory generally: Kennedy, "Focusing of Arguments," *Art of Persuasion*, 203–206; discussion of Demosthenes symbouleutic speeches: Montgomery, *Way to Chaeronea*, 39–63.

uals to speak before them when they were preparing *probouleumata*, and we know that expert politicians who were prominent in the Assembly and in public trials served terms on the Council.[88] Skill in oratory was presumably an advantage for a Councilman who wished to influence the decisions of the Council on agenda and *probouleumata*; late in 343/2 the Council invited the demos to join in honoring its best speaker of the year.[89]

The Council met in a special building (*bouleutērion*) in the agora each day of the year except for the sixty public holidays and an unspecified number of days of ill omen. By the 320s a Councilman received five obols for each day he attended, except for the tenth of the year his tribe was in prytany, when he received a drachma. We do not know how long an average meeting lasted, nor what percentage of the *bouleutai* attended regularly. Only citizens over age thirty were eligible to serve.[90]

Aristotle (*Pol.* 1299b30–38) notes the practical need for a probouleutic body to prepare an agenda for the Assembly, and he states that its composition can have a large effect on the character of the constitution. There has been a good deal of debate on the social composition of the Athenian Council. In 1906 J. Sundwall argued, on the basis of a prosopographical analysis of known *bouleutai*, that wealthy citizens predominated, but Davies has demonstrated that Sundwall's criteria for determining wealth status were faulty and his conclusions therefore dubious.[91] Yet, despite the absence of positive evidence, the domination of the Council by the rich is still sometimes assumed.[92] This

---

[88] See Rhodes, *Boule*, 3–4; de Laix, *Probouleusis*, 147; and above, II.n.77. Aeschines (3.3–4) inveighed against the evil men who insinuated themselves into the Council and secured for themselves the right of *proedria*; cf. Dem. 22.39.

[89] *IG* II² 233. Cf. Rhodes, *Boule*, 14 n. 9. Perlman, "Politicians," 344, suggests this decree, which honored Phanodemos, author of an *Atthis*, represented a vote in favor of a political group, but there is no evidence for this.

[90] *Bouleutērion* and associated buildings: Thompson and Wycherley, *Agora*, XIV.29–47. Meeting days and pay: *AP* 62.2; Rhodes, *Boule*, 13–14, 30. Hansen, "Political Activity," 229, cites Dem. 22.36, to argue that "quite a number" of *bouleutai* did not attend meetings.

[91] J. Sundwall, *Epigraphische Beiträge zur sozial-politische Geschichte Athens*. Klio Beiheft 4 (Leipzig, 1906); Davies, *APF*, xix–xx, *WPW*, 3–6.

[92] E.g., de Laix, *Probouleusis*, 149–53; Daviero-Rocchi, "Transformations," 39, 44. The attempt to demonstrate by quantitative analysis that "activity in the *boule* came to rest with well-known and generally wealthy men" by Osborne, *Demos*, 66–72, 81 (quote: 68–69), is not convincing. His sample is much too small to yield a statistically significant number. The tendency to use statistical analysis improperly causes flaws in several of the arguments in this otherwise stimulating study; cf. Ober, "Review of Whitehead, *Demes* and Osborne, *Demos*," 73–75.

seems unlikely on demographic grounds alone. Citizens could legally serve only twice, and there is little reason to believe that many citizens served more than one term. Since 500 Councilmen were needed each year, a large percentage of the citizen population *must* have served a term: estimates range from that of Gomme, who suggested that at least a quarter to a third of the citizenry served; to Woodhead, who claims less than half; to Osborne, who guesses about 70 percent; to Ruschenbusch and Hansen, who have suggested that almost all citizens would have had to serve.[93] If the higher estimates are correct, the question of the numerical domination of the wealth elite is moot, unless we assume massive dereliction of duty by all but the wealthy Councilmen. But even if only a third of the citizens served, working citizens must have predominated. It is certainly possible that some farmers and some urban residents—those who were able to make a better income and were unencumbered by civic spirit—avoided Council service or failed to show up regularly for meetings when chosen in the lottery. But on the other hand, we might guess that the indigent citizen would be eager to serve, since the office would provide a year of regular employment otherwise unavailable to him. While farmers and "middling" citizens may have been somewhat underrepresented at a typical meeting, P. J. Rhodes must be correct to suggest that the Council was "fairly representative of the citizens who were politically minded"; and I believe that the great majority of the total citizen population must fall into this category.[94]

When a citizen spoke in the Council, he was addressing a much smaller audience than he would in the Assembly. But, except for the absence of those between ages eighteen and thirty, the social compo-

---

[93] Limited evidence for two-term *bouleutai*: Rhodes, "Ephebi," 192 n. 7; Osborne, *Demos*, 45. Percentages of citizens who served: Gomme, "Working," 20; Woodhead, "ΙΣΗΓΟΡΙΑ," 133; Osborne, *Demos*, 91 ("most citizens" must have served at least once), 237 n. 56 (ca. 70 percent of citizens served); E. Ruschenbusch, "Die soziale Zusammensetzung des Rates der 500 in Athen im 4. Jh.," *ZPE* 35 (1979): 177–80, "Epheben, Bouleuten und die Bürgerzahl von Athen um 330 v. Chr.," *ZPE* 41 (1981): 103–105, "Noch einmal die Bürgerzahl Athens um 330 v. Chr.," *ZPE* 44 (1981): 110–112; followed by Hansen, "Political Activity," 229–30. Rhodes, "Ephebi," argues against Ruschenbusch's assertion that due to demographic factors all qualified citizens over thirty were automatically candidates and their names put into the lottery. Rhodes (ibid., 193) agrees with Ruschenbusch that the boule was de facto open to all citizens over thirty, but he still believes that there was some choice involved and that "it seems likely that there was a somewhat higher proportion of rich men in the boule than in the citizen body as a whole." Note that Rhodes' position is far from the outright dominance by the rich that others have assumed must have pertained.

[94] Rhodes, *Boule*, 3–6, quote: 215.

sition of the smaller group would probably not have been markedly different from that of the larger. Furthermore, as both *bouleutai* and orators knew, the Council existed to serve the Assembly and was watched over by the demos. Lysias' client (26.12–14) made this very clear when he asked the Councilmen, "What do you think will be the attitude of the mass of citizens (*to plēthos*) if you acquit this oligarch? Remember, you [*bouleutai*] are on trial before the whole polis here."

The Areopagus council tried certain classes of homicide cases and investigated other activities, including (after 344/3) some political matters. But we have only three speeches preserved that were delivered before the council of the Areopagus, all from the early fourth century. Technically, only citizens of zeugite status and above were permitted to serve on the Areopagus, but this stipulation was apparently widely ignored. In general, the sociopolitical conditions of speeches delivered before the Areopagus would probably not have been radically different than in other Athenian courts, which we may now consider in more detail.[95]

E.4 PEOPLE'S COURTS (*Dikasteria*)

The people's courts, which probably met as often as 150–200 days each year, provided an extremely important public forum for elite private citizen and politician alike.[96] As a defendant, the citizen might be called upon to defend his behavior generally; a politician might be expected to justify his policies and the proposals he had supported in the Assembly. As a prosecutor, the citizen could attack the personality and behavior of his enemies; if they were political enemies their policies could be undercut. As detailed above (III.B.2), court cases may be divided into public actions (*graphai, eisangeliai*, and certain other special actions) and private actions (*dikai*). The former frequently featured expert politicians or generals as protagonists, involved serious financial risks for prosecutors, and generally took an entire day to try. The latter sort of trial, which usually lasted only a few hours, generally concerned the affairs of *idiōtai*. We may suppose that expert politicians

[95] Types of legal trials and investigations that fell under the purview of the Areopagus: Wallace, *Areopagos*, chapter 4.ii; size and composition of the Areopagus in the fourth century: ibid., chapter 4.i, iv (an average of perhaps two hundred or fewer men, with an average age of perhaps ca. 47.5 years, who were not paid for their service); social status of Areopagites: ibid. chapter 4.iv. Comments by litigants being tried by the Areopagites, to the effect that they were more just, more worthy (and so on) than other judges (e.g., Lys. 3.2, [6].14), are not of much evidential value.

[96] Number of days: M. H. Hansen, "How Often Did the Athenian Dicasteria Meet?" *GRBS* 20 (1979): 243–46.

involved in public actions often wrote their own speeches; a wealthy litigant involved in a private case would, however, typically call upon the services of a logographer. In all actions, however, prosecutor and defendant argued their cases personally before a mass jury by means of prepared speeches which were strictly limited in length, though not in subject matter.[97]

Any citizen over age thirty who so desired could enter himself on the annual list of potential jurors; the fifth-century list normally had about six thousand names, and the fourth-century list was apparently similar in length. The jurors for the cases to be heard on a given day were chosen from those on the list who had appeared in person that morning. A complicated selection process assured that all potential jurors had an equal chance of being assigned to a court and that individuals from all ten tribes were represented on each jury. Jurors received a three-obol stipend for their day's service, a figure that remained constant from the late fifth century to the latter part of the fourth century. A typical jury might consist of two hundred men for a private trial or five hundred for a public trial, although much larger juries were occasionally empaneled for especially important cases. After the arguments on both sides had been heard, the jurors voted by secret ballot to acquit or convict the defendant. There was no formal consultation among jurors, and a simple majority determined the judgment of the court.[98]

There has been some debate over the social composition of Athenian juries.[99] Scholars who argue that juries were primarily made up of the well-to-do have pointed out that in some speeches litigants make comments that seem to imply that they were addressing an audience

[97] Differences between public and private cases: Hansen, "*Rhetores* and *Strategoi*," 152–55; Sealey, *Athenian Republic*, 54–55; Osborne, "Law in Action," 48–52. Length of trials: Harrison, *Law*, II.47, 161–63.

[98] Number of *dikastai*: Aristoph. *Wasps* 662; *AP* 24.3; *IG* I² 84 line 20; cf. Rhodes, *CommAP*, 302–303, 702–703. Jury selection: *AP* 63–69, cf. Harrison, *Law*, II.44; Maio, "*Politeia*," 29, 44; Rhodes, *CommAP*, 697–735. Hansen, "Initiative and Decision," 367, calculates that on an average "court day" some 1,500 to 2,000 jurors would be selected. Pay for jurymen: *AP* 27.2–5, 62.2; Aristot. *Pol.* 1274a8; cf. Harrison, *Law*, II.48–49, 156; Rhodes, *CommAP*, 339–40. Jury size: Harrison, *Law*, II.47; MacDowell, *Law*, 36; Hansen, "*Rhetores* and *Strategoi*," 154, *Eisangelia*, 10 n. 14. For a summary of the limited archaeological evidence for law courts in the Agora area and interpretation of the artifacts identified as courtroom equipment, see J. Travlos "The Lawcourt ἘΠΙ ΠΑΛΛΑΔΙΩΙ," *Hesperia* 43 (1974): 500–11; A. L. Boegehold "Philokleon's Court," *Hesperia* 36 (1967): 111–20; Thompson and Wycherley, *Agora*, XIV.52–72; Garner, *Law and Society*, 39–41.

[99] Jurors mostly well-to-do: Jones, *AD*, 36–37; Dover, *GPM*, 34–35; *contra*: Adkins, "Problems," 156–57 with n. 7; Markle, "Jury Pay."

of men of means (see below, v.d.2), but rhetorical statements about economic status cannot always be taken at face value. On the question of the adequacy of jury pay, the basic daily barley ration for an average family would have cost under two obols, and the other family members of poorer households could be expected to contribute to the family's total income (see III.E.1, 2). In light of these factors, three obols was never a starvation wage. It was admittedly, by the 320s, only half the normal Assembly pay, and a public court case might last longer than an average Assembly meeting. But this discrepancy in the size of stipends only appears problematic if we equate jury and Assembly pay with wages. If we assume rather that state pay was meant to provide participants with a subsistence ration, the three obols no doubt still fulfilled its intended function in the 320s, given the stability of the price of grain. The rise in Assembly pay by the 320s may have been neither an adjustment for inflation nor a way to lure recalcitrant citizens to the performance of their duty, but rather a way of redistributing surplus state revenue. Athenian revenues were relatively high by the 330s, and the rise in the rate of the *ekklēsiastikon* (which cannot be precisely dated) was perhaps seen as the most equitable way of allowing those Athenians who spent time making state policy to benefit directly from the state's prosperity.[100]

The little direct evidence that can be brought to bear on the problem of the social composition of juries suggests that poor citizens did sit on them and that the pay they received for jury duty was important to them. Early in the fourth century, Lysias (27.1–2; cf. Isoc. 20.15) urged a jury to remember the arguments that the defendant Epicrates had previously used as prosecutor: that the jurors would not get their three-obol pay unless they convicted the rich defendant. Lysias notes that there was presently a scarcity of funds in the treasury and suggests that this fact proved that Epicrates had embezzled the money that the state should have received from the convictions obtained by his use of this argument. Whether or not Athenian juries really could be persuaded to vote for conviction in hopes of filling the state coffers (cf. below, v.a.3), Lysias' statement would have no point if most jurors were unconcerned over the question of whether or not their pay would be forthcoming. Demosthenes' comment (23.123, cited above

[100] *AP* 41.3 associates only the introduction of the *ekklēsiastikon*, not the rise in the rate above three obols, to a need to attract citizens to meetings of the Assembly; cf. Aristoph. *Ecclesiazusae* 185–89. High revenues: Humphreys, "Lycurgus," 204–205; Burke, "Lycurgan Finances." The theoric distributions for festivals provided another way of distributing surplus: Din. 1.56; Hyp. 3.26; cf. Markle, "Jury Pay," 290; and below, III.n.116.

III.E.2; cf. 21.182), to the effect that some disenfranchised citizens served on juries for pay because of their poverty, suggests that at mid-century poor citizens did serve on juries. In 348 Demosthenes (3.34–35) proposed a state-paid national service to prevent citizens from falling into shameful (*aischron*) conditions because of need (*endeia*). He explained his proposal in terms of the existing system of dicastic pay; each citizen was to receive a standard stipend so that he could serve in the army, in the courts, or wherever else there was a need suitable to his age. Demosthenes' proposal may suggest that older citizens were particularly likely to serve as *dikastai*, but it also shows that pay was deemed to be economically necessary to the jurors.

In sum, there is little reason to suppose that a given Athenian jury was likely to be startlingly different in social composition than the average Assembly or Council. Probably the elderly tended to be over-represented, as Aristophanes' *Wasps* suggests they were in the late fifth century. Farmers might prefer to spend their limited "city" time in the Assembly, because Assembly decisions were more important to them or because the pay was better. But the large number of days in the year when the courts were in session would give the farmer a greater flexibility in planning his trips to town if he sometimes served as a juror rather than, or in addition to, attending the Assembly. Skilled craftsmen, able to find more remunerative employment, might prefer to spend their available "citizen-duty" time in the Assembly rather than on a jury, where they might be stuck sitting on a public trial for the whole day. On the other hand, as Markle points out, the court-room was often more exciting than the Assembly.[101] For a connoisseur of rhetoric—which many Athenian citizens certainly were (cf. below, IV.D)—a chance to judge an oratorical bout between the likes of Demosthenes and Aeschines might well be worth the loss in income.

We should also look briefly at the question of the "sovereignty" of the Athenian courts and their relationship to the Assembly (cf. below, VII.C). The judgment of an Athenian jury was, in principal, final, and there was no higher authority to which a convicted defendant could appeal (e.g., Dem. 42.31). In this sense the *dikastērion* may be regarded as sovereign. But, as Osborne has pointed out, most Athenian juries' decisions were not actually final until both parties agreed to call a halt to the proceedings, because of the great variety of legal actions to which an initially unsuccessful litigant could resort. The prosecutor in one action, dissatisfied with a jury's acquittal, might indict the same person, for the same crime, in front of a different jury by use of a

---

[101] Markle, "Jury Pay," 285.

different class of action. Similarly, a convicted defendant could pro-
long proceedings by turning prosecutor. Osborne suggested that multiple retrying of cases with the same cast of litigants made Athenian
legal proceedings into a sort of "social drama," aimed ultimately at
public display and at redressing social imbalance.[102]

Osborne's argument on the "open texture" of Athenian law becomes particularly important when viewed in terms of mass-elite relations. Only elite litigants could likely afford the time that multiple re-
tryings required. But since the elites threatened the social balance to
the greatest degree, the public airing of their difficulties before a series of mass juries was particularly salutary. The more often a case was
reheard and the more Athenian citizens there were who had the
chance to act as judges, the greater was the extent and complexity of
communication between mass and elite. Athenian law, according to
this analysis, was not only intended to solve conflicts between individual citizens by resort to a formal legal standard, but also, and perhaps
more importantly, legal action ensured ongoing communication between Athenians in a context that made explicit the power of the
masses to judge the actions and behavior of elite individuals.

When viewed from the context of "law as discourse" (to use S. C.
Humphreys' formulation), the problem of determining the comparative "sovereignty" of the people's court and the Assembly seems less
pressing. In arguing that the courts and laws were the "ultimate" sov-
ereigns against the lesser, "immediate" sovereignty of the Assembly,
Hansen quite rightly points out that the term demos, while frequently
used of the Assembly, is seldom used for juries.[103] But the juries *did*
act in place of and on behalf of all the citizens. Dinarchus, who recognized the legal distinction between demos and *dikastērion* (e.g.,
1.105, 3.16), describes (1.84) the jurors as those "who have been assembled on behalf of the people (*huper tou dēmou suneilegmenōn*) and
who had sworn to obey both the *nomoi* and the *psēphismata* of the demos."[104] Furthermore, the jurors could in fact be held to represent the
Assemblymen themselves, at least indirectly. Thus Demosthenes (e.g.,

[102] Osborne, "Law in Action," esp. 52–53.

[103] Hansen, "Demos, Ecclesia," 131–35. For the traditional view that the jury in
essence *was* the demos see, e.g., Larsen, "Judgment," 3; Finley, *DAM*, 80; Mac-
Dowell, *Law*, 40. The "locus of sovereignty" problem assumes a narrow definition
of political power as unitary state power. For a cogent critique of this conception
and a discussion of the historical origins (in the sixteenth to eighteenth centuries)
of the notions of unitary sovereignty and the separation of powers, see Bowles and
Gintis, *Democracy and Capitalism*, esp. 22–24, 167 with n. 27.

[104] For an analysis of the problem of relating Dinarchus' comment to the heliastic
oath, see Harrison, *Law*, II.48.

19.224) could blame the jurors for errors in state policy, and Hyperides (1.17) and Lysias (19.14) could discuss how "you jurors" had elected persons to be phylarch, hipparch, and general; the actual elections were, of course, held in the Assembly. In the speech *Against Meidias* (21.214–16) Demosthenes reminds the jurors that the demos had indicted Meidias at a preliminary hearing (*probolē*) in the Assembly and argues that it would be an awful thing if "when [in the Assembly] the offenses were clear in your memory . . . you shouted at me not to let him off . . . yet after all you acquit him" in court. Aeschines (2.84) was certain that all his jurors would remember the Assembly at which Demosthenes (as *proedros*: one of the nine *bouleutai* chosen by lot to preside over each meeting of the Assembly) had tried to block voting on a resolution, but "you shouted out (*boōntōn de humōn*) and called the *proedroi* to the bema," and so forced a vote on the resolution. Dinarchus (1.86) tells the members of a jury that "in the Assembly" Demosthenes made "you" his witnesses. Elsewhere (3.19), Dinarchus comments that by voting for a conviction, the jury would demonstrate that "the mass of the people" (*to tou dēmou plēthos*) had not been corrupted. Isaeus' client (5.38) says to the jury that the prosecutor was not so clever that he had been able to fool "you all when you were united in the Assembly." These statements cannot be explained simply by the fact that there was a good deal of personnel overlap between courts and Assembly (although indeed there was: Dem. 21.193–94, 22.10; Din. 3.1), but they suggest rather that the citizens empaneled on a jury were regarded as standing in for the demos and as representing the demos' interests.

Litigants frequently reminded the jurors of their responsibilities to the mass of citizens in whose interests they acted. Demosthenes (21.2) pointed out to his jury that the entire Assembly voted unanimously against Meidias at the *probolē*, and later in the speech (21.227) he urged the jurors to do "what is pleasing to the demos." Dinarchus (1.106) asked his jury if they, who were masters of all affairs (*kurioi pantōn*), would take it upon themselves to ignore the things that had seemed just to the demos. Jurors might be warned to remember that their actions were of great concern to their fellow citizens who would inquire as to what their judgment had been (e.g., Lys. 12.91, 22.19). Dinarchus (1.3; cf. 2.19) claimed that the jurors themselves were standing trial before the other citizens who would judge them according to whether they decided rightly or not. Perhaps less intimidating, but not necessarily less effective, were reminders that the jurors had been given a sacred trust by the citizens and were responsible for the safety of the polis as a whole.[105] The courts may indeed be regarded as "sovereign" in abstract legal terms. But the Athenians did not typically think in abstract legal terms and apparently regarded the authority of the courts as deriving from the will of demos *as well as* from their role in interpreting the laws. In literary terms, demos and *dikastērion* stood in a synecdochical relationship: the part (*dikastērion*) stood for the whole (demos), and, in the rare instances in which the Assembly served as a jury, the whole took the role of the part. When a speaker addressed the Assembly or the court, his audience represented the interests of the Athenian people. In each instance, a mass audience, broadly representative of the social composition of the demos at large, served as his judge.[106]

Significant similarities and differences existed between deliberative and forensic oratory. The most important similarity is in form: in both cases an individual addressed and was judged by a mass audience. Furthermore, the litigant, like the speaker in the Assembly, had to put on a good performance if he hoped to keep his audience's attention. If he irritated the jury, he faced heckling from the jurymen.[107] But while his water clock was running he did not have to worry about direct competition from his opponents for the jury's attention. Perhaps the most salient difference is that the courtroom gave the speaker a greater opportunity to discuss himself and his opponent, and so arguments based on personal character (*ēthos*) could be developed in much greater detail. Aristotle (*Rhet.* 1377b20–1391b6, 1416a4–37) emphasizes the importance of establishing one's own character and of attacking that of one's opponent as a factor in successful forensic rhetoric. In the case of an *idiōtēs*, the jury's impression of the litigant might be formed solely through his own and his opponent's ethical discussion; no matter what the facts of the case, he had to prove that he was the sort of person deserving the jury's respect and that his opponent was not. If his legal case were weak, his only hope might be to sway the jury through argument based on *ēthos*.

[105] E.g., Lys. 12.94; Aesch. 3.8; Din. 1.107, 3.16; Lyc. 1.4.

[106] On the question of representationality, cf. the comments of Rhodes, *CommAP*, 318, 545, with reply by Hansen, *AECA*, 159–60; above all, Maio, "*Politeia*," esp. 24: adjudication was in general the "creature and servant" of the *politeia* because courts were composed of citizens who acted according to the norms of the general political culture, and 30: the people's courts were "bodies of citizens that represent the *polis* in both appearance and substance and thus legitimately exercise its sovereign power."

[107] On the tendency of jurors to demand good speeches and to interrupt the speaker, see, for example, Lyc. 1.52; Plato *Euthyphro* 9b–c; cf. V. Bers, "Dikastic Thorubos," in Cartledge and Harvey, edd., *Crux: Essays Presented to Ste. Croix*, 1–15.

For the politician as litigant, the situation was somewhat different. Many jurors would already have formed an opinion of him and of his opponent, an opinion that might have a considerable bearing on the outcome of the case and which each side would variously attempt to strengthen or undermine. Furthermore, courtroom appearances had long-term effects on a politician's career. The significance of the court-room drama was not only a matter of whether he won or lost a partic-ular round in an ongoing series of legal contests. Each courtroom ap-pearance was also a chance to enhance his image. Even if he lost the round on the weakness of his factual or legal case, he might have scored some political points. The juror who had been favorably im-pressed by his character might be expected to listen attentively to his policy speeches in the Assembly. If very impressed, that juror might tell his friends and they their friends. Hence, for the politician every appearance before a jury had the nature not only of a legal dispute but of an ongoing quest for the respect and approval of the citizenry as a whole.

E.5 RUMOR (*Phēmē*)

The politician's statements in court were part of his ongoing campaign to create a positive image of himself in the minds of his fellow citizens; that positive image would help him in future legal disputes and in the Assembly. But "official" public appearances only formed part of the overall picture of a prominent citizen held by the populace. Much de-pended on rumor and gossip, which were particularly important in a society that lacked organized news media. It is impossible to determine just how rumors were spread in Athens, but we know they did spread rapidly and crossed class lines easily. News of the Sicilian disaster, for example, was disseminated very quickly throughout the city from the barber shop in which the story was first related (Plut. *Nicias* 30.1). The agora and the shops in the area around it were natural news centers where the elite and non-elite could mix freely. Lysias' client (24.19–20) notes that "each of you" Athenians is in the habit of spending some time at one shop or another, "a perfumer's, a barber's, a shoe-maker's, or whatever." Isocrates (7.15) mentions that the Athenians tended to sit around in the shops (*ergastēria*) complaining about the existing political order. The complaints may have been particularly prevalent in his elite circle, but political discussion was no doubt com-mon in all levels of society. The comic poet Eupolis (F 180 [Kock, *CAF* 1, 308]) has the late fifth-century politician Hyperbolus claim that he had learned a lot from hanging around in barber shops "sitting there unsuspected and pretending not to understand."[108]

Presumably, more intimate and private forms of social intercourse also helped to spread news across class lines. A client of Lysias' (24.11), who was on the state rolls as a handicapped indigent, occasionally borrowed a riding horse from wealthy friends. He may not have been as poor as he claimed (see v.D.2), but he expected the jury to believe that a poor citizen could have rich friends. Prostitutes and entertainers may have been conduits of gossip between classes. The anonymous author of a lengthy curse tablet from the late fourth century includes both liturgical-class politicians and common prostitutes (male and female) in the list of individuals to be cursed; presumably, his circle of personal acquaintances included members of both groups.[109] A client of Isaeus (6.19) stated that all the jurors would know the prostitute Alke; Apollodorus ([Dem.] 59.108–11) assumed the Athenians and their wives were familiar with the notorious Neaera, and several prominent politicians spoke on her behalf. Flute players and other professional entertainers, as well as prostitutes, were commonly featured at elite drinking parties and presumably picked up some of the dinner chat in the process.[110]

Athenian speakers often said to their audience "you all know" the character or actions of a litigant, either that he was a good man who lived an upright life or an evil one who did evil things.[111] The statement that everyone knew something could be used in an attempt to manipulate the audience. Aristotle (Rhet. 1408a32–36) says that speechwriters used the tactic of saying everyone knows something to secure the agreement of even those who did not know it, because the latter would be ashamed at their ignorance of what was common knowledge. Hyperides' (4.22) statement that even the schoolchildren of Athens know which of the orators had been bribed might be interpreted in this light.

---

[108] Cited and translated by Ehrenberg, *People of Aristophanes*, 354.

[109] D. R. Jordan, "A Survey of Greek Defixiones Not Included in the Special Corpora," *GRBS* 26 (1985): 164 no. 48 (ca. 323 B.C.). The wealthy politicians are Xenocles (Davies, *APF* 11234) and Deinomenes (Davies, *APF* 3188). I am indebted to David Jordan, who alerted me to the existence of this document and offered a copy of his (unpublished) improved reading of it.

[110] On prostitutes at symposia, see Keuls, *Reign of the Phallus*, 160–68. Flute girls: C. G. Starr, "An Evening with the Flute Girls, *Parolo del Passato* 183 (1978): 401–410.

[111] Good: e.g., Lys. 21.19; Dem. 18.10; evil: Is. 3.40; Dem. 19.199–200, 226; Din. 2.8; cf. also Lys. 29.6; Is. 3.19; Dem. 21.149.

In democratic Athens, however, the "everyone knows" topos had more to it than merely shaming the uninformed into acquiescence. The topos created the fiction that the entire polis was the sort of face-to-face community that in reality existed only at the level of the demes, and the topos may have its roots in village-level judicial decision making.[112] But the statement that everyone knew something was also directly linked to egalitarian ideology. When Hyperides (1.14) argued that a legal defense should be based on a man's whole life, as no individual in the polis could hope to deceive "the mass of you" (*to plēthos to humeteron*), he implied that arguments based upon common report were just and democratic. Hyperides bases his argument on the assumption that, although a clever speaker might fool the members of a jury, he could not hope to fool "all of the people all of the time." Because the jury's decision stood for the decision of the society as a whole, it was regarded as right that society's opinion be taken into consideration by a jury. This helps to explain why Aeschines (2.145), who praised the divinity of *phēmē*, said that it was at work "when the mass of citizens of their own will . . . say that something is the case." Taken to extremes, this line of reasoning implied that common report should be given greater weight than the verbal arguments made in court. Aeschines urged this interpretation when he said that the jurors not only should be (1.179) but were (2.150) more concerned with the orator's lives as a whole than with their speeches (*logoi*). Hyperides (4.40) urged the jurors to ignore all arguments made in court when it came time to vote and to cast their ballots as seemed most just to themselves.[113]

The perceived democratic nature of common report made it particularly difficult to defend oneself in court against rumors. One possible

[112] Cf. above, I.n.76. Haussoullier, *Vie municipale*, 179–80, takes the topos literally and hence makes an overly direct equation between the experience of deme and polis.

[113] Cf. below, IV.B.4. On the importance of gossip and scandal in preserving and enforcing adherence to group values and in promoting group cohesion, see Max Gluckman, "Gossip and Scandal," *Current Anthropology* 4 (1963): 307–16. Starr, *Individual and Community*, 53, notes that a high level of concern with conformity typified the early polis and cites the lyric poets for the pitiless censure by the citizens of behavior deviating from the norm. He also (113 n. 1) cites J. Du Boulay, *Portrait of a Greek Mountain Village* (Oxford, 1974), 181–82, 200–211, on the role of gossip as a means of enforcing conformity in modern Greek communities. Cf. also Garner, *Law and Society*, 16–18; Ostwald, *From Popular Sovereignty*, esp. 133 (speaking of the late fifth century): ". . . the laws established by the sovereign people contributed to setting a moral standard for society. . . . The sovereign people sets the norm not only for political but also for moral conduct."

defense was based on contrasting common report, which was acknowledged to be valid, with slander, which, as Aeschines (2.145) said, was
"the brother of sycophancy" and (2.149) went "no further than the
ears." Aristotle (*Rhet.* 1416a36–38) suggests a similar approach, that
litigants try attacking slander as an evil that corrupts judgments. He
also (*Rhet.* 1400a23–29) suggests that one may fight against slander by
showing the origin of the false opinion. The plaintiff in a speech in
the Demosthenic corpus (37.55–56) attempts to explain that his habit
of "fast walking and loud talking," which his opponents used to show
his bad character, was an uncontrollable natural trait, to be contrasted
with his general reputation, since "none of you, though you are many,
know of any evil in me." And the best defense was always a good offense. Aristotle (*Rhet.* 1416a26–28) encourages the litigant concerned
with removing the stain of open or hidden prejudice from himself to
counterattack by attempting to blacken the reputation of the accuser,
since no one will believe the speech of a man who is himself untrustworthy (*apistos*). This technique was a favorite of the political orators.

Compared to modern polities, the Athenians drew relatively few
distinctions and imposed few effective buffers between public opinion
and decision making—either at the level of state policy formation or
legal judgment. Objectivity was not considered possible or even particularly desirable. That there was a relatively direct and causal relationship between the opinion of the majority, and state policy and legal
decisions is a fundamental difference between Athenian democracy
and modern governmental systems.[114] This direct and causal relationship must be a key factor in our assessment of the social function of
Athenian political oratory. When speaking in public, the Athenian had
a doubly difficult task. He won the vote only if the opinion of the majority was favorable to him, or at least more favorable than toward his
opponent. He could attempt to influence that opinion by the power of
his rhetoric, but his speaking time was always limited, and some opinions, based on ideological presuppositions, were not easily changed.
Thus, the astute speaker attempted to use ideology to his advantage
by persuading his audience that a vote in his favor was consistent with
their existing values. This technique required that the speechwriter be
closely attuned to the political attitudes common to the mass of the
citizens.

[114] On the tendency of modern governments to establish buffers between public
opinion and the decision-making process, see G. E and K. Lang, *The Battle for Public
Opinion: The President, the Press, and the Polls During Watergate* (New York, 1983), 10–
25.

E.6 THEATER

The final "political forum" to be considered is the theater. The citizens of Athens were connoisseurs not only of oratory but also of drama and other forms of theatrical performance. Since the late sixth century, the festival of Dionysus, celebrated annually in the city over the course of a week, had featured performances of dithyrambic choruses, tragedies, satyr plays, and comedies. By the mid-fourth century, traveling troupes of actors were performing plays in smaller theaters in the demes.[115] Drama was very popular in Athens, and by the mid-fourth century the state underwrote the price of dramatic festival admissions through the theoric fund.[116] Theater was not, therefore, an art form limited to the elite but was a public and political event, experienced by the citizenry at large. The theater of Dionysus (as remodeled in the 330s) could accommodate an audience of about 17,000, and most of the seats were apparently reserved for the Athenians themselves.[117] A large percentage of the citizens attended annually. Hence, the audiences in the Assembly and in juries would include very significant numbers—probably clear majorities—of regular "theater-goers."

Athenian theatrical performance was closely bound up in the attempt to resolve the contradictory social values of intense competition and political unity.[118] These values were also of great concern to the orators, and thus the experience of the Athenian demos in the theater had much to do with its experience as an audience of oratory. The responses of average Athenians to litigants in civil suits and to politicians in public trials and in the Assembly were, consequently, influenced by their experiences as members of theatrical audiences and vice versa. Notably, although perhaps inevitably, the physical settings for mass meetings of the people, namely, the Pnyx and the theater of Dionysus, were very similar in spatial organization. The seating in the theater was egalitarian, as it was in the Assembly and in court. In each case, the mass audience faced, listened to, and actively responded to individual speakers. In all cases, cooperation, both between individual

[115] On the Dionysia, see, in general, Pickard-Cambridge, *Dramatic Festivals*, 57–125. On traveling troupes in the demes, see ibid., 52; Ghiron-Bistagne, *Recherches*, 193–94.

[116] See Buchanan, *Theorika*, 28–93, with the review by Ste. Croix in *CR* 14 (1964): 190–92. On the date of introduction, cf. Rhodes, *Boule*, 105 with n. 6, *CommAP*, 492, 514.

[117] A. W. Pickard-Cambridge, *The Theatre of Dionysus in Athens* (Oxford, 1946), esp. 140–41 (capacity); Travlos, *Pictorial Dictionary*, 537–52. On the seating arrangements: Pickard-Cambridge, *Dramatic Festivals*, 269–72.

[118] Winkler, "Ephebes' Song."

and mass audience and between the members of the audience, was necessary. But each situation involved competition at various levels as well. The contests between *chorēgoi*, playwrights, and actors have some similarities to those between litigants and political orators. In each case, the outcome was decided by a mass audience sitting in judgment (directly or indirectly) over competing elites.[119]

Athenian dramas were composed by an elite author specifically for presentation to a demotic mass audience and allowed the Athenians to consider the nature of their own society at a remove. The images of human society in tragedy and comedy could be idealized, amusing, or horrific.[120] In the case of tragedy, the action typically involved the problems of individuals who were clearly identified as elites but who were in terrible straits. The process of identification with tragic characters provided the Athenians with symbolic paradigms and may have tended to humanize the elite litigant for the members of mass juries.[121]

The Athenian theater-goer was a self-conscious witness of a self-conscious acting performance. Actors were an important part of the dramatic scene, and prizes for acting were being awarded by the mid-fifth century. By the end of the fifth century, actors were well on the way to becoming professionals. The fourth-century Athenian citizen knew that the man behind the mask was an actor, but that knowledge did not interfere with his enjoyment of the performance or with the power of the performance to affect him. Rather, the recognition of the actor behind the mask doubled and enriched the dramatic experience and made it consequently more meaningful.[122] This suggests a symbolic context in which we can understand some rhetorical strategies that have confused historians who assume that forensic rhetoric provides a straightforward description of Athenian society. Theater-

---

[119] On the sociopolitical significance of theater seating, see Webster, *Theatre Production*, 2; Winkler, "Ephebes' Song," 30–32; Small, "Social Correlations"; I am indebted to David Small for discussion of this problem. Competitions and judging: Pickard-Cambridge, *Dramatic Festivals*, esp. 95–99; Maurice Pope, "Athenian Festival Judges—Seven, Five, or However Many," *CQ* 36 (1986): 322–26.

[120] For the complexities involved with representation of society in drama see, for example, Vernant, "Tensions"; Segal, "Greek Tragedy"; Zeitlin, "Thebes"; H. P. Foley, "The 'Female Intruder' Reconsidered: Women in Aristophanes' *Lysistrata* and *Ecclesiazusae*," *CPh* 77 (1982): 1–21.

[121] See Aristot. *Poetics* 1452a, 1453a, 1455a: tragedy is based on a shocking and terrible misfortune suffered by some apparently fortunate person. Cf. Segal, "Greek Tragedy," 66–67; Salkever, "Tragedy," 297, 300.

[122] Prizes: Pickard-Cambridge, *Dramatic Festivals*, 90. Professionalization: Niall W. Slater, "Vanished Players: Two Classical Reliefs and Theatre History," *GRBS* 26 (1985): 333–44; relationship of the citizens' experience to the recognition of the actor: Ghiron-Bistagne, *Recherches*, 160.

going citizens "learned" to suspend disbelief. The theatrical audience entered into a conspiracy with the playwright and actors which allowed the theatrical experience to take place. This "training" helped jurors to accept elite litigants' fictional representations of their own circumstances and their relationship to the Athenian masses. The complicity of speaker and audience to create and accept dramatic fictions regarding social status was an important factor in the maintenance of Athens' social equilibrium.

As we have seen, by the fourth century the political orators, like actors, had become experts. The Athenian politicians were, undoubtedly, acutely aware of the continuum between politics and theater, and they exploited it in the highly charged and competitive arenas of the Assembly and the popular courts.[123] The physical relations of actor in the orchestra of the theater and orator at the bema of the Pnyx to their respective audiences were similar. In at least one case, actor and orator were identical. Before he embarked upon his political career (it would be interesting to know how long before) Aeschines had been a professional actor. Demosthenes characterizes him as a *tritagōnistēs*, a bit player, but that may have been mere slander; Aeschines may have been among the better known actors of his generation.[124] As we have seen (III.C), Demosthenes himself took a lesson in public speaking from the professional actor Satyrus. When the audience in Assembly or the jury of a political trial listened to either Aeschines or Demosthenes, they were therefore hearing an indirect reflection of the cadences and gestures of the dramatic actor. The cases of Aeschines and Demosthenes were probably not unique; the two best-known politicians of the fourth century could hardly have been also the only ones

---

[123] The continuity of the experience of the political arenas and the theater is emphasized by Dem. 21.226–27. Cf. Rowe, "Portrait," esp. 404–406; Buxton, *Persuasion*, esp. 17–18; Garner, *Law and Society*, 82–83, 95–130. Sattler, "Conceptions of *Ethos*," 59, notes that the discussion of *ēthos* in Aristotle's *Rhetoric*, with its concentration on ways in which the orator reveals his character through his speech, is closely related not only to his general ethical doctrine (e.g., *Nicomachean Ethics* 1113b) but to the discussion in the *Poetics* (1450a29–33) of the ways in which a dramatic character reveals his *ēthos* through his argument (*dianoia*). North, "Use of Poetry," 6–7, also notes the frequency of cross-references between the *Poetics* and the *Rhetoric*, especially on the subject of metaphor, and points out the commonness of quotes from Euripides in the Aristotelian *Rhetoric to Alexander*. She also notes that in the *Rhetoric*, Aristotle uses many quotations from tragedy and that he assumes that knowledge of poetry is "indispensable" to the orator. Salkever, "Tragedy," 293–94, goes so far as to suggest that Aristotle considered tragedy to be a branch of rhetoric. Cf also below, IV.D, VI.D.3.

[124] Cf. Dorjahn, "Remarks"; Ghiron-Bistagne, *Recherches*, 158–61. On the term *tritagōnistēs*, see Kindstrand, *Stylistic Evaluation*, 20 with n. 15.

with overt theatrical connections.[125] Both by space and by behavior of the protagonists, the congruity between the theater and the Assembly was reinforced.[126]

The political orator had much to gain from being seen in "dramatic" guise. The actor-orator could call upon the audience's experience in listening attentively to long and complex speeches by elite characters engaged in fierce competition on the stage. Furthermore, in tragedy and comedy the protagonists interacted with and sometimes actively opposed the group, here represented by the chorus. In Old Comedy, actors occasionally even castigated and made fun of the audience. The Athenian theater-going citizen thus had some experience with individuals who legitimately confronted and opposed the group.

The political orator, like the private litigant, depended on his audience's willingness to suspend disbelief. But here again, the politician's task was more demanding. To be successful the political orator had to persuade the citizens that he was both an average citizen—*idiōtēs* and *metrios*—and, simultaneously, that he possessed abilities and attributes that legitimized his assumption of political privileges, especially the privilege to stand before and even against the masses. The politician had to play a complicated double role and maintain credibility in both roles over a long period of time, all the while in the face of acute public scrutiny and the jibes of his political opponents. The theatrical "training" of the masses helped to condition the Athenians to accept the strange double-role playing that their own value system imposed upon those who would be political leaders. The theater provides a useful metaphor for the orator's role in society, one that will help us to explore some of the complexities of the communication between elite public speakers and their mass audiences.

[125] The actors Aristodemos and Neoptolemos, for example, had important diplomatic careers: Dorjahn, "Remarks," 228; Ghiron-Bistagne, *Recherches*, 156–57. A modern parallel might be sought in the careers of Indian politician-film actors; see C. D. Gupta and J. Hoberman, *Film Comment* 23.3 (May-June 1987): 20–24.

[126] Aristotle (*Rhet.* 1403b24–26, 1413b8–14) recognized that there was a certain similarity between poetic and rhetorical delivery; cf. Pickard-Cambridge, *Dramatic Festivals*, 168. The connection between rhetoric and tragedy was later incorporated into Hellenistic rhetorical theory: Cicero *de Oratore* 1.128 suggested that the orator should possess the *vox tragoedorum* and was reputed to have studied with two actors (Plut. *Cicero* 5); cf. North, "Use of Poetry," 11 with n. 34.

CHAPTER IV

ABILITY AND EDUCATION:
THE POWER OF PERSUASION

Oratorical ability, as Michels points out, is a prerequisite for political leadership in a democracy.[1] Athenian politicians invariably possessed great public speaking ability, and their natural rhetorical skills had often been refined through formal education in schools of rhetoric (above, III.C).

A. Educated Elites

The political orators were, collectively, the most visible sector of the Athenian "educated elite," but, as argued above (I.B, III.D.1) they never became a ruling elite. Analyzing how the topics of ability and education are treated in public discourse reveals both continuities and discontinuities between Athenian political experience and the functioning of modern democracy. How did the Athenians regard those who possessed superior ability to communicate ideas to large audiences, and who had been educated in the arts of persuasion? How did the masses control the ambitions of the educated elite and so combat the drift toward oligarchy, which Michels considered the inevitable fate of democratic organizations?

B. Group Decisions and Collective Wisdom

Athenian procedures for making important political decisions, both at the level of legislation (in the Assembly and by boards of *nomothetai*) and at the level of the judiciary, always involved public discussion before a large group of citizens, followed by a group vote. The decision reached was typically binding on the society as a whole. Thus, Athenian decision making was explicitly predicated on the belief that group decisions were likely to be right decisions. The political implications of that conclusion, and of the assumptions that underpinned it, were far-reaching.

[1] See, for example, Michels, *Political Parties*, 67, 98–100; Marger, *Elites and Masses*, 196–98.

B.1 NATURAL ABILITY AND FORMAL EDUCATION
OF ORDINARY ATHENIANS

Part of the Athenians' faith in the wisdom of collective decisions made
by the masses rested upon their conviction that Athenians were by nature more intelligent than other people. Aeschines (1.178), for example, avowed that in his opinion Athenians were naturally more clever
(*epidexioi*) than other people and so naturally made better laws. Demosthenes (3.15) noted that the Athenians were quicker (*oxutatoi*) than
other men to grasp the meaning of speeches. Isaeus' client (11.19)
stated that he need say no more concerning the subject at hand, since
the jurors were intelligent men (*eu phronousi humin*), able to judge well
for themselves the rights and wrongs of the matter (cf. Euripides *Me-
dea* 826–27, 844–45).

The Athenians' image of themselves as a shrewd lot was sometimes
exploited by a public speaker in an attempt to shame the audience into
voting in his favor. Demosthenes (23.109) notes that the Olynthians
had demonstrated that they were able to plan ahead against Philip,
and he claimed that it would surely be shameful (*aischron*) if the Athenians, "who have a reputation for having superior ability in political
deliberations," should prove inferior to mere Olynthians. Elsewhere
(18.149), Demosthenes remarks that Aeschines had been able to fool
the non-Athenian members of the Amphictionic council, since they
were "men unused to speeches"; Demosthenes implies that his current
audience of experienced Athenians will not be misled so easily. Dinarchus (1.93) wondered which of the jurors was so blindly hopeful, so
ignorant (*alogistos*), or so unaware of affairs (*apeiros*) as to vote for Demosthenes, and he suggested (1.104) that Demosthenes himself had
too much faith in his power of speech and in the jurors' simplemind-
edness (*euētheias*). Hyperides (3.23) claimed that his opponent regarded the jurors as fools (*ēlithious*) who would not recognize his effrontery.

The native intelligence of the common Athenian may have been
reinforced by at least some formal schooling. The excellence of Athenian education was a topos of funeral orations.[2] But in fact we know
regrettably little about primary education in the Greek poleis before
the Hellenistic period and virtually nothing about the education of the
non-elite.[3] Basic literacy—the ability to read and to write some

[2] Thuc. 2.40–41; Lys. 2.69; Dem. 60.16; Hyp. 6.8; contrast Loraux, *Invention*,
151.
[3] See esp. Plato *Protagoras* 325e–26a; cf. Marrou, *Education*, 63–146, esp. 65; Pélékidis, *Éphébie*, 31–32, 62.

words—seems to have been general among the citizen population of Athens, at least by the fourth century and perhaps well before.[4] In order to function as a citizen, and certainly in order to carry out the responsibilities of many of the magistracies, the Athenian citizen needed a basic command of letters. On the other hand, it seems unlikely that many Athenians were fully literate in the sense that they read easily and frequently, for pleasure and instruction. Books were, relatively speaking, rare and expensive. Although books were no longer exotic by the later fifth century, they were probably still, for the most part, the possessions of the educated elite, and Athenian political culture remained at its heart an oral culture.[5] Thus, in the Funeral Oration (Thuc. 2.40.2) Pericles emphasized that the Athenians made good political decisions because they believed that speeches (*logoi*) were not a hindrance to action, but rather they regarded it as a disgrace not to be well instructed by public debate before engaging in action.[6]

Even if the common Athenian citizen was not fully literate, he was widely exposed to the products of literary culture. The state-subsidized performances at the Panathenaic festival and the festival of Dionysus exposed the average citizen to poetry, music, and dance (above, III.E.6). He might also attend various public readings, such as the ones Herodotus reputedly gave of his *Histories*.[7] The average Athenian had no doubt gained at least a passing acquaintance with the stories of Homer and the myths and legends associated with Athenian antiquity. Much would have been learned from his parents and relatives, much picked up casually in the course of listening to others, perhaps especially to the elders of his deme.

Attendance at Assemblies and participation in the law courts as a

---

[4] See esp. Harvey, "Literacy"; Burns, "Athenian Literacy." Cf. Davison, "Literature"; Woodbury, "Aristophanes' *Frogs*," esp. 355–57. For the even more difficult question of female literacy, see S. G. Cole, "Could Greek Women Read and Write?" in H. P. Foley, ed., *Reflections of Women in Antiquity* (New York, 1981), 219–45.

[5] On the interrelations among literacy, citizenship, and literature, see Harvey, "Literacy"; Burns, "Athenian Literacy," esp. 384–85; Whitehead, *Demes*, 139 (literate demarchs); Finley, *Authority and Legitimacy*, 9–10; Davison, "Literature," 219–21.

[6] Cf. similar sentiments in Lys. 2.19. Contrast Thucydides' discussion (3.83) of the atmosphere of distrust of speeches and cleverness generally in the Corcyraean civil war, where he contrasts those who think ahead with those who act immediately; see also Connor, *Thucydides*, 14–15, on this passage.

[7] For a critical review of the evidence for Herodotus' public readings at Athens, see A. J. Podlecki, "Herodotus in Athens?" in K. H. Kinzl, ed., *Greece and the Eastern Mediterranean in Ancient History and Prehistory. Studies . . . to F. Schachermeyr* (Berlin, 1977), 247; cf. Starr, *Awakening*, 132–33.

juror gave the citizen considerable experience with highly sophisticated rhetoric, and he considered himself competent to judge both the merits of an argument and the style in which it was delivered. In the Mytilenean debate (Thuc. 3.38.2–7) Cleon berates the Assemblymen for regarding themselves as connoisseurs of rhetoric and acting as if they were listening to the haggling of sophists, rather than acting like men involved in making serious decisions that would affect the fate of the polis. This taste for fine rhetoric certainly continued into the fourth century. Although few public speakers attained Demosthenes' level of skill, the corpus of Attic orators is testimony both to the high standard that deliberative and forensic rhetoric achieved in the period and to the Athenian public's appreciation for fine speaking.[8] In general, we may assume that the common citizen could appreciate many of the fine points of poetry, performing arts, history, and rhetoric, although he would probably not have made the distinctions between these fields that his more highly and formally educated elite fellow citizen might have been taught to do.

B.2 PRACTICAL EDUCATION IN POLITICS

In a famous passage in the Funeral Oration (Thuc. 2.41.1) Pericles praised the city of Athens as an education to her citizens and to all of Hellas. The education provided by the polis was not, by any means, limited to literary culture and its popular by-products. A major part of the citizen's education came through performance of his political role.[9] The citizen's first formal experience with democratic government was in his deme, when he was presented to the demesmen and they voted to grant him citizenship. The political organization of the deme was modeled, both in theory and practice, on the polis government. The deme assemblies were training grounds for citizens in what Whitehead has called the "cardinal principles" of "communal decision making and responsibility."[10] As was suggested above (II.F.1), members of different demes learned how to cooperate with residents from elsewhere in Attica in the tribal assemblies and, especially, on the Council, which gave the citizen an extended and intimate look at many aspects

[8] This is not to say that public rhetoric was ornate to the exclusion of meaning; cf. above, III.D.2. Aristotle (*Rhet.* 1404a25–28) notes with scorn that most uneducated people still think the poetic style of rhetoric developed by Gorgias to be the finest, but this is surely a reference to epideictic rhetoric.

[9] See, for example, Finley, *DAM*, 29–31, *PAW*, 27–29; Loraux, *Invention*, 144–45.

[10] *Demes*, 120, cf. ibid., 92–96, 313–15; Raaflaub, "Freien Bürgers Recht," 41–43. Hopper, *Basis*, 13–19, overstates the case, as Whitehead, *Demes*, 315–24, demonstrates.

of the government.[11] Service in other magistracies—in addition to the five hundred *bouleutai*, some seven hundred other offices were filled each year—might give the citizen further experience in dealing with different elements in his state and society.[12] Military service, too, offered valuable education, by helping to instill a sense of common purpose and the necessity of cooperation in those who marched in the phalanx or rowed the triremes.[13] At least in the last third of the fourth century, and perhaps earlier, the state provided the ephebes, citizens aged eighteen and nineteen, with two years of moral, religious, and formal military training.[14] Finally, as noted above, the experience of service as a juror and as an Assemblyman was of primary importance in the practical political education of the citizen.

B.3 NORMATIVE FUNCTION OF STATE INSTITUTIONS

The educational function of the polis was not limited to the "practical" training in the political process offered to the individual citizen. Perhaps more telling, in both popular ideology and elite political theory, was the normative role of the ethos of the polis, expressed through the organization and actions of governmental institutions. The convictions that a good life can only be lived in a good polis, that therefore the moral duty of the citizen is to improve the ethos of the polis, and that the ethos of a good state will be exemplified and maintained by its institutions are central to the political thought of Plato and Aristotle.[15] Isocrates completely agreed; his ideal *paideia* stressed not only the formal education of children but the moral education which good institutions would inculcate in the mature citizens.[16] The differences of opinion between Isocrates and Plato, as between the elite political

---

[11] Tribal assemblies: Hopper, *Basis*, 14–16. Council: Gomme, "Working"; Woodhead, "ΙΣΗΓΟΡΙΑ," 133–35; Finley, *PAW*, 71–74. For the numbers of citizens who served on the Council, see above, III.E.3.

[12] Number of officeholders: Hansen, "Seven Hundred *Archai*."

[13] See Ridley, "Hoplite"; cf. above, II.F.2.

[14] There is a voluminous literature on the ephebia, but Pélékidis, *Éphébie*, is still the most useful summary. I argued in *FA*, 90–95, that specialized military training for the ephebes dates back to the second quarter of the fourth century, but the specifically educational aspects of the institution may be late fourth-century developments. E. Ruschenbusch, "Die soziale Herkunft der Epheben um 330," *ZPE* 35 (1979), 173–76, argued that all eighteen- and nineteen-year-olds—not only those of the hoplite class—were ephebes, which I believe is quite likely. For the debate on this issue, cf. above III.n.93.

[15] Esp. Plato *Apology, Crito*; Aristot. *Pol.*, Books 3 and 6. Cf. Jaeger, *Paideia*, II.150, III.67.

[16] Esp. Isoc. 7.37, 48–50; cf. Jaeger, *Paideia*, III.119–22.

theory and mass ideology, were not over whether the state and its institutions should be a reflection of moral good.[17] The disputes rather concerned how the good should be defined, who was capable of achieving goodness, and whether goodness could be taught.

The Athenian masses, unlike the elite theorists, tended to assume that the existing state was good and, if imperfect, capable of improvement. The institutions of the state were therefore also essentially good and could justly be expected to perform a major educational and normative role in improving the citizens (cf. Plato *Apology* 24d–25a). Given the directness of the democracy—the lack of a government interposed between people and state—this meant not only that the laws must be as just and democratic as possible, but that the decisions reached in the Assembly and in the courts had an important didactic role. Good decisions would improve the citizenry; poor decisions might worsen it. Thus Demosthenes, for example, could argue (19.343) that a failure to convict Aeschines and his cronies would result in the worsening of every citizen, since all would see that traitors received wealth and honors, while just persons who spent their personal fortunes for the public good were ill treated. Citizens who performed significant political functions were an important focus of normative decision making. Demosthenes (22.37) urged that if the present *bouleutai* lost their honorific crown as punishment for having been misled by a rhetor, future Councilmen would be encouraged to perform diligently and to reject attempts by political experts to dominate the proceedings. The didactic example of judicial decisions was not, however, limited to the political behavior of male citizens. Apollodorus ([Dem.] 59.113) argued that acquittal of the prostitute Neaera would encourage poorer female citizens to become prostitutes in order to earn money for their dowries.

Of vital importance was the education of the youth of the city in the political values and ideological precepts that enabled the democracy to function. Aeschines (3.246) argued that the wrestling grounds (*palaistrai*), formal educational institutions (*didaskaleia*), and lyric poetry (*mousikē*) do not, by themselves, educate (*paideuei*) the youth of the city; more important were the decisions of the demos (*ta dēmosia kērugmata*). Lycurgus (1.10) claimed that the jurors knew perfectly well that their votes must be an incentive to the young, since the education of the

---

[17] It is often assumed (for example by Adkins, "Problems," 145–47) that the similarities between ideas in "popular" literature and elite literature may be traced to a "trickle-down" of the ideas of elite thinkers to mass culture. But one might rather choose to regard some of the ideas of elite writers as formalizations and elaborations of the popular ideology of the society in which they lived. See below, VII.G.2.

youth consisted of the punishment of wrong and the rewarding of the virtuous by the state. Isocrates (20.21) urged the jurors not to wrong themselves collectively, nor to teach the youth to despise the mass of the citizens (*kataphronein tou plēthous tōn politōn*), by acquittal of a rich man accused of hubris.

Isocrates' comment on the youth and the hubristic rich and Demosthenes' comments on the *bouleutai* and the political experts suggest that the normative function of mass decisions was especially important in light of existing sociopolitical inequities. Lysias' client (30.24) noted that the punishment of those unable to speak well was not useful as an example but that meting out justice to powerful speakers (*dunamenoi legein*, cf. above III.B.1) was a fine example (*paradeigma*) to others.[18] And Demosthenes (21.183) exhorted the jurors in the trial of Meidias not to create an example (*deigma*) of forgiveness of the rich man, when they had formerly convicted without pity a man who was moderate (*metrios*) and who conformed to democratic values (*dēmotikos*; cf. below, V.F). The decisions of juries could, furthermore, be regarded as a means of forcing elite citizens to conform to the norms established by the masses. Lysias (14.45) urged that the conviction of Alcibiades the Younger would be a good example to his friends (*philoi*) who were planning on becoming demagogues themselves. Demosthenes (51.22) urged the jurors not to allow the honorable ambitiousness (*philotimia*) of those who were willing to contribute materially to the state depend on the persuasion of expert speakers, lest the Athenians teach the rich to pay as little as possible to the state and to hire many rhetores to defend them in court. On a more positive note, Aeschines (2.183) states that if the jury saves him from Demosthenes, they will find that many others will be ready to work for the collective good of the polis.

Ecclesiastic decrees and dicastic judgments had for the Athenians a significance that transcended the particular case at issue and went beyond the establishment of formal constitutional or legal precedents. The democracy depended upon the maintenance of an ideological consensus among the citizen population. Lacking a formal state-run system of formal education, the demos itself, through the Assembly and the courts, took on a large part of the task of instilling social values in the citizens. The young who were not yet fully socialized and the elites who might be influenced by value systems antithetical to democratic government were the particular groups at which much of the normative education through legislation and legal judgment was aimed. But all citizens were educated, for good or ill, by the right and

---

[18] Cf. Lys. 14.12, 27.5.

wrong decisions of the Assembly and juries, as well as by the laws of the state (cf. Aesch. 1.192–95).

B.4 WISDOM OF THE MASSES

The educational function of the Assembly and courts made reaching right decisions all the more important. The various decision-making bodies were composed of citizens who possessed high native intelligence (or so the Athenians liked to believe), were at least basically literate, had collectively a good grasp of literary culture, and had a high degree of practical experience in the mechanics of government and in cooperation toward a common end. But these factors do not adequately account for the strength of Athenian faith in group decision making. Rather, that faith was grounded in the assumption that the collective wisdom of a large group was inherently greater than the wisdom of any of its parts. This conviction is one of the central egalitarian tenets of Athenian political ideology. It is implicit in both the structure of the decision-making process and the emphasis the Athenians were willing to place upon "common report" as an index of an individual's character and behavior, since what "everybody knows"—or everybody believed—was deemed likely to be right (above, III.E.5).

The assumption that groups composed of individuals lacking specialized skills or education tended to produce wise decisions was explicitly, emphatically, and repeatedly rejected by Plato and sometimes by other authors of elite texts as well.[19] But some elite writers were willing to consider the concept of collective wisdom seriously. In his essay attacking the "sophists," Isocrates (13.8) notes that those who rely on opinions (*doxai*) tend to agree with one another more (*mallon homonoountas*) and are more often correct than those who profess to have exact knowledge (*epistēmē*) and that, therefore, *idiōtai* have good reason to despise specialized studies. This passage was written in the context of an intra-elite debate over higher education and is not necessarily representative of Isocrates' general beliefs, but it shows that he was willing and able to use the topoi of popular ideology for polemical purposes.[20] More striking, perhaps, is Aristotle's (*Pol.* 1281a39–b9) treatment of the issue. In the context of his discussion of the merits of democracy, he raises the possibility that the mass (*plēthos*), rather than the excellent few, should be master (*kurios*) of the good state. He argued that although the individuals who compose the mass are not wor-

---

[19] E.g., Plato *Crito* 47a–48a, *Protagoras* 317a; [Xen.] *Const. Ath.* 1.5–10; Euripides *Andromache* 470–85.

[20] Cf. Jaeger, *Paideia*, III.58–59.

thy gentlemen (*spoudaioi andres*), they may be better collectively than
the few persons who were. Hence, he points out, the mass, by common
consent, was the best judge of music, of poetry, and other fields: with
its many senses, it becomes like a single human being with respect to
its characteristics (*ta ēthē*) and decision-making ability (*dianoia*). While
noting that there were some objections to this point of view, Aristotle
continues (1281b9–1282a41) by pointing out that the sum of individually inferior parts is indeed very great, and so the courts, Council,
and Assembly should be left in charge of important affairs.[21]

If Isocrates and Aristotle were willing at least to consider the idea of
collective wisdom, it is hardly surprising that the political orators typically took it for granted. The elitist attack on mass decision making
was specifically refuted in the Thucydidean speech of Athenagoras of
Syracuse (Thuc. 6.39.1). He attacked the argument that democracy
was neither wise nor truly egalitarian by asserting that the many (*hoi
polloi*), having listened to the deliberations of wise men (*xunetous*,
meaning popular speakers like himself), were the best judges of what
was right and productive of equality.[22] Demosthenes (*Ex.* 44.1) stated
that he would not have come before the Assembly if the Athenians all
held the same opinions on the matter at hand, even if his own opinion
were different, since "I, being one, would be more likely to be mistaken than all of you." And again (*Ex.* 45), when arguing that making
a good speech and choosing sound policies were not the same, he
stated that the former was the work of the rhetor, the second of a man
possessing intelligence (*nous*). Therefore, he continued, "you, the
many" are not expected to speak as well as the orators, but "you, especially the older ones of you, are expected to have intelligence equal
or better than that of the speakers, since it is experiences and having
seen much that makes for intelligence." The appeal to the older citizen

---

[21] Cf. *Pol.* 1284a30–34, 1286a25–35. Ultimately, in the discussion of the ideal
state in Books 7 and 8 of the *Politics*, Aristotle rejects the wisdom of the masses in
favor of a narrowly elitist aristocracy, due at least in part to his inability to solve the
problem of how to create a just form of proportional equality; see below, VII.A.
Aristotle's willingness to consider the possibility of mass wisdom may also be exemplified by the assumption in the *Rhetoric* that common opinions manifest at least
a partial grasp of truth and so can be used in the formulation of enthymemes which
are legitimately part of rational political discourse; for the rationality of enthymemes and the reasonableness of arguing from common opinions, see Arnhart,
Aristotle, esp. 5–7, 28–32, 183–88.

[22] Jones, *AD*, 43, notes that the "Sicilian" speeches, which refer to democratic
principles, are probably modeled on Athenian prototypes. The same general idea—
that simple people deciding together are wiser than clever individuals—crops up in
an extreme form in Cleon's Mytilene speech (Thuc. 3.37.3–5).

is obvious, but the passage also affirms the conviction that collective judgment by the many was superior to individual perception and more important than mere speech. Even when berating the jurors for their inconsistency, Demosthenes (23.145–46) emphasized their good judgment and claimed that everyone (*hapantes*) quite correctly agreed that bribe-taking politicians were the worst men in the state.

The rhetor's appeal to the mass wisdom of the particular group he was addressing was based on the generalized faith the Athenians had in the collective knowledge, experiences, and judgment of the citizen body as a whole. Hyperides (1.14, cited above, III.E.5) supported an argument for the validity of a legal defense that was based on a man's whole life by reference to the assumption that no one in the polis can deceive "the mass of you." Dinarchus (1.33; cf. 2.2) notes that "you [jurors] see and know" the facts of Demosthenes' life "much better than I do." Since Dinarchus proceeded to relate Demosthenes' crimes in considerable detail, he cannot have expected his audience to believe that all the jurors or even any individual juror *actually* knew more about Demosthenes' life than he himself did. Rather, he was expressing his solidarity with an ideology that stressed group over individual knowledge. Athenagoras, Demosthenes, Hyperides, and Dinarchus all leave a place in the decision-making process for the expert politician, but each affirms that the collective wisdom of the masses must be the final arbiter.[23]

The Athenians' belief in their collective wisdom as a group need not be seen as contravening their faith in the wisdom of their laws. The laws were a highly esteemed expression and "concretization" *of* mass wisdom. Laws had been, in some cases at least, affirmed by several generations of Athenians and thus represented the epitome of the masses' collective wisdom over time (see also below, VII.C). The laws need not be seen as external to, or as a check upon, the judgment of the demos, but rather as a partial expression of some of its most cherished and time-tested ideals.

C. Dangers of Rhetoric

The Athenian emphasis upon group decisions is the context in which we must view the forensic orator's strategy of attempting to persuade the jurors that their collective wisdom, knowledge, and experience

---

[23] Humphreys, "Discourse of Athenian Law," notes that in speech 23, Demosthenes uses non-technical language and a sense of "what you all know" in reference to homicide law, and she contrasts this with the practice of Lysias. Cf. Dem. 24.123; Ant. 2.4.1.

were being challenged by the duplicitous arguments of his opponent. The jury was cast in the role of a unified body of citizens confronted by an individual (the opponent) who was perversely attempting to oppose the group's will. The orator who succeeded in generating in his audience a group-versus-individual state of mind had won the day, since by definition the group must prevail over the individual in a direct democracy of the Athenian model. This is Demosthenes' strategy (19.297) when he reminds the jurors that in the courts "no one has ever been greater than you, or the laws, or your oaths" and urges the jurors not to let Aeschines become greater than themselves. Of course, the elite of trained and able speakers were the most likely to try to oppose the will of the jury; Demosthenes' client (39.14) asserts that "you jurors" know how to keep control over even the most clever folk (*tous panu deinous*) when they overreach themselves. Lycurgus (1.20) confidently asserts that "you jurors" are not ignorant of the advance preparations (*paraskeuas*) used by the defendants.

C.1 RHETORIC VERSUS MASS WISDOM

Yet, despite the general Athenian faith in mass wisdom, doubts persisted. The adversarial nature of public trials and of many Assembly debates forced the voters to choose between two speakers (or potentially more, in the Assembly), only one of whom could be urging the best decision. There was a very real possibility that the jurors or Assemblymen would be taken in by the more clever speaker and would reject the less clever, even if the latter was in the right. This was potentially a serious political problem, especially in light of the normative role the Athenians attributed to the decisions of the Assembly and courts. Consequently, Athenian jurors were often warned by orator A to beware of orator B's eloquence. Aeschines urged the jurors to watch out for Demosthenes' rhetorical tricks: "Just as in gymnastic contests you see boxers contending with one another for position, so, for the sake of the polis, you [jurors] must do battle with him all day long for position in regard to his speech" and watch out for his evasive tactics (3.206).

The perception that rhetorical skill represented a potential threat to the validity of the democratic decision-making process put the expert speaker in a difficult position. An orator who attempted to use his power of speech to deceive a mass audience into voting against its collective interests was obviously setting himself up as superior to the masses, a situation the demos must regard as anathema. Why then, if rhetoric involved deception, should expert rhetores be allowed to speak to the demos in the first place? In *On the Crown* (18.280) Demosthenes lays out what, according to his considered opinion, comprised the worth of the rhetor. After accusing Aeschines of beginning a prosecution merely to make a public display of his fine voice and rhetorical ability, Demosthenes proclaims, "But it is not the speech (*logos*) of a rhetor, Aeschines, or the power of his voice which are his worth, but it lies rather in his preference for the same things as the many and in his hating and loving the same things as his homeland. Having such a disposition (*psuchē*), everything a man says will be patriotic (*ep' eunoiai*)." This passage, taken literally, leaves no room for legitimate political or legal debate. The worthy orator prefers the same things as the many, and therefore, when speaking in public, he simply vocalizes the desires of the majority of his listeners. Because the wisdom of the group is superior to that of the individual, the desires of the majority are right desires, and the orator who voices these desires is therefore advocating the right decision. Since his opponent urges a different decision, his opponent must be wrong and consciously opposing the preferences of the people.

Demosthenes' dictum, by eliminating legitimate difference of opinion as a basis of political debate, allows—even requires—the orator to ascribe the worst possible motives to any speaker who advocated a position significantly different from his own. Since there was no legitimate reason for adopting a viewpoint at variance with the wishes of the majority, anyone who persisted in doing so must have been motivated by illegitimate and selfish personal interests. Thus a common ploy for the orator was to suggest that his opponent and his opponent's supporters were bribed or hired to say the things they did, and in either case they clearly preferred making money to speaking the truth. The bribe-taker who decided that his personal enrichment was of greater value than agreeing with the masses obviously had no love for the democracy (cf. below, VII.F.2). Indeed, one might safely suggest that he hated the democracy and was probably willing to support a revolution that would destroy the power of the people (e.g., Lys. 25.26–27). The presumption that to agree with the masses was to be in the right easily led to the implication that one's opponent must be regarded as a traitor. The savage tenor of Athenian political invective must be seen in the light of this progression.

Demosthenes' dictum on agreeing with the masses was an extreme position, and, as we will see (IV.E), he suggests a very different interpretation of the orator's role later in *On the Crown*. His dictum assumes that the speaker is precisely aware of the preferences of the people. On some issues, and in broad terms, no doubt the orator did know what the majority was likely to prefer. But if the will of the masses had actually been as self-evident as Demosthenes implied, there would be no need for *isēgoria*, and the Athenians would not have had to bother listening to lengthy arguments or even with voting; all decisions would be by consensus and could be announced by acclamation. The structure of Assembly meetings and jury trials was, however, predicated on the assumption that there were issues upon which debate was both legitimate and necessary. Demosthenes' dictum helps to define one end of the ideological spectrum on the subject of the relations between speaker and audience. It represents an ideal of decision making by universal consensus which could seldom be achieved in practice. However, the ideal of a polity based on consensus survived into the fourth century (for its origins, see above, II.E) and buttressed the notion that the orator should be simply the mouthpiece of unspoken mass will. This constellation of ideas was an important aspect of Athenian political ideology and provided the rationale for very extreme statements by the orators regarding one another's ulterior motives.

In the normal course of events, the preference of the people remained at least formally latent, and debate could therefore be regarded as legitimate, until the vote was taken. The vote of the Assembly or jury was, however, an unambiguous statement of the people's will. After any vote that had been preceded by debate, the demos knew that at least one speaker had been arguing against the position that later turned out to be the correct one, the one that expressed the will of the majority. No rhetor could hope to win every vote. The expert politician who, by definition, engaged frequently in public trials and spoke often in the Assembly must lose occasionally, and when he lost he was in the uncomfortable position of having publicly opposed the group. How was the orator to explain his failure and justify his willingness to continue advocating a policy that the masses had rejected? Demosthenes (9.54) tried suggesting that some evil demon was driving the Athenians to prefer the purchased minions of Philip to himself, but this is not an argument one wanted to use very often.[24] Much more common was the suggestion that despite their collective wisdom, the people had been (or might be) misled by the clever and superficially convincing, but evil and deceptive, speeches of one's opponent.

---

[24] Cf. Aesch. 3.117: something demonic perhaps led a rude fellow to interrupt his speech to the Amphictionic council; And. 1.130–31. Mikalson, *Athenian Popular Religion*, 19, 59–60, notes that the attribution of an event's outcome to a god, demon, or Fortune seems to depend on how the speaker is affected by the event. K. J. Dover, in his review of Mikalson (*Phoenix* 38 [1984]: 197–98), stresses the importance of this conclusion, while noting that there are some apparent exceptions.

Therefore, at least in part in order to create a justification for their own failures to convince the demos and for the successes of their opponents, the orators acknowledged the power of rhetoric to lead the Assembly, the jury, and the state as a whole into error. Demosthenes (51.20), for example, stated that because of the speeches (*dēmēgoriai*) of the rhetores, many matters in the state were going from bad to worse.[25] This tendency might be exacerbated in periods of financial difficulty. Lysias (30.22) noted that in such times the Council was led to accept *eisangeliai* and to make public the property of citizens, being persuaded by the rascally advice of the rhetores. But the citizens themselves, as *idiōtai* and collectively as the demos, suffered in the end. Aeschines (3.233) claimed that the juror who voted for Demosthenes would make himself weak and the rhetor strong, while the correct situation in the democratic polis was for the *idiōtēs* to rule (*basileuei*) through the law and the vote.[26]

The orator who could deceive the people into voting wrongly was a manifest danger to all other citizens.[27] Hyperides (5.25–26, cf. 4.27) noted that if *they* were defendants, the members of the jury, being *idiōtai* and inexperienced, would be overwhelmed in the courts by the rhetorical ability (*k[atarhē]toreutheis*) of those who were currently under indictment and subsequently *they*, though innocent, would be convicted and either executed or banished. The orator who put great store by his speaking ability was not merely unseemingly vain but threatened the whole state.[28] He set himself above the decrees of the Assembly (e.g., Dem. 51.22) and believed that his ability to speak well gave him immunity from prosecution (Aristot. *Rhet.* 1372a11–17). According to Aeschines (3.253), Demosthenes' eloquence allowed him to sail on a ship of words over the *politeia*. While taking for himself the name of protector of the democracy, which should be common to all, Demosthenes was in fact the furthest from being a true democrat (Aesch. 3.248). Demosthenes (19.120), on the other hand, claimed that Aeschines took up a prosecution as easily as a dramatic role and that his ability to convict his opponents within the time limit and without the use of witnesses was evidence for his cleverness at speaking.

There can be little doubt that, although the Athenians delighted in rhetorical displays, they remained suspicious of the expert orators and their verbal skills. The orator involved in a political fight might exploit

[25] Cf. Lys. 18.16, 27.4–6, 28.11; Aesch. 3.168, 228; Hyp. 4.36.

[26] Cf. Lys. 28.9, 29.6; Dem. 23.184, 201, 51.1–2; Aesch. 3.220; Lyc. 1.138.

[27] This concern provides at least a partial context for the attacks upon rhetores in Attic comedy, for which see Ehrenberg, *People of Aristophanes*, 350–53.

[28] E.g., Isoc. 18.21; Aesch. 2.22, 3.228; Din. 1.113.

the popular distrust of the rhetores against an opponent, despite the
obvious danger of being tarred with his own brush. Dinarchus (1.98)
reminded the jurors of oracles that he suggested warned the Athenians against rhetores. Hyperides (F 80 [Jensen] = B.19.5 [Burtt])
claimed that all rhetores were like snakes and therefore hateful. Some,
he says, were adders who were harmful to men, while others took the
role of the adder-eating brown snake. Presumably, Hyperides hoped
his audience would think of his opponents in the former category and
of himself in the latter. His listeners might, however, legitimately ask
themselves why snakes should be tolerated at all. The orators used the
demos' fear of being misled by rhetoric to discredit their opponents,
and the power of rhetoric provided a convenient excuse for a politician to explain why his policies were sometimes rejected by the people.
The central question of why expert politicians should have been allowed to practice in Athens' political arenas remains to be answered.
Indeed, the arguments of the orators cited above might seem to provide material for a strong case in favor of excluding experts in rhetoric
from the democratic decision-making process.

C.2 EVILS OF RHETORICAL EDUCATION: SOPHISTS AND SYCOPHANTS

The orator's power to deceive his audience into voting wrongly lay in
his speaking ability, which was typically at least partially the product
of a specialized education. Education in rhetoric was a potential focus
of popular suspicion; at worst it could be characterized as a corrupting
and destructive influence in the state. In the speech *Against Lacritus*
(35.40–43) Demosthenes' client played upon the jurors' distrust of
rhetorical training. He asserted that, while he did not himself hold a
grudge against anyone who desired to become a sophist and so paid
Isocrates a stiff fee to that end, he did not think that such people had
the right to look down upon others (*kataphronountas*) or, thinking
themselves clever (*deinous*) and trusting in their speeches (*tōi logōi pis-
teuontas*), to cheat other citizens. These, he said, were the attitudes and
actions of the perfidious (*ponēros*) sophist who believed he could lead
jurors astray with his tricky harangues. The defendant, Lacritus, considered himself a master at deceiving juries and collected money from
others for teaching them to do likewise. The prosecutor acknowledged, however, that he would have to admit that his opponent was
indeed the greatest of sophists (*sophōtatos*) if Lacritus, who put his faith
in his eloquence and in the 1,000 drachmas he had paid Isocrates, was
able to fool the present jury.

The passage is very neatly constructed. Beginning with a claim of

neutrality on the topic of rhetorical education, the prosecutor shows
how the defendant's training in rhetoric had made him both arrogant
and dangerous. This leads inevitably to the conclusion that if the jurors acquitted the defendant, they would acquiesce in the methods of
vicious sophists who thought themselves superior to the masses and
safe from conviction by virtue of their special training. Since Lacritus
was not only a student of Isocrates but also a teacher of rhetoric in his
own right, his acquittal would presumably encourage others to study
his methods of jury subversion. Seen in this light, a school of rhetoric
was, to borrow Hyperides' imagery, a nest of vipers which poisoned
the entire state. The jury's didactic function of establishing and enforcing models of correct social behavior was perverted into one of
helping the sophist prove to potential students the persuasive power
of his rhetoric.[29]

Isocrates himself discovered that he was much less popular among
the Athenians than he had imagined, when his enemies succeeded in
having him saddled with a liturgy. According to Isocrates' account of
the matter (15.4–5), his opponents at his property-exchange trial
played upon the jury's distrust of his power of speech (*tēn tōn logōn tōn
emōn dunamin*) and emphasized the large number of his students. Furthermore (15.30), they stressed that among these students were not
only *idiōtai* but rhetores and generals, as well as kings and tyrants.[30]

The execution of Socrates was an exceptional case, carried out in
exceptional historical circumstances, but to be labeled a sophist and
teacher of dangerous men was never good in Athens.[31] In the speech
Against Timarchus (1.173) Aeschines uses the cudgel of popular mistrust of higher education against Demosthenes: "Oh Athenians, did

[29] For a close parallel, see Ant. 5.80: you jurors must help me by refusing to teach
the evil sycophant to be greater than yourselves (*meizon humōn autōn dunasthai*), because if they succeed in this trial it will be a lesson to their victims, who will be more
likely to knuckle under and pay them. But if the sycophants are shown in court to
be evil men, "you" will enjoy the honor and the power (*dunamis*) that is your right.

[30] On the unpopularity of "sophists" of various stripes, cf. Thuc. 8.68.1; Isoc.
13.1, with Jaeger, *Paideia*, III.56; Aristot. *Rhet.* 1399a11–18. For scorn for the
profession of logographer, cf. below, VI.D.1.

[31] For the political background to the trial of Socrates, see M. I. Finley, *Aspects of
Antiquity*[2] (New York, 1977), 60–73; G. Vlastos, "The Historical Socrates and Athenian Democracy," *Political Theory* 11 (1983): 495–516, with discussion (at 495–96)
of Aesch. 1.173. For Socrates' views on democracy, the lively and polemical account
of Stone, *Trial of Socrates*, may be balanced by the more philosophically nuanced
discussion of Kraut, *Socrates*, esp. 194–244. Finley, *DAM*, 96, notes that after the
trial of Socrates the "baleful atmosphere" of anti-intellectualism thinned markedly
and that indeed orators (e.g., Aesch. 3.257) could use the term *philosophos* in reference to such revered figures as Solon. See also Dover, "Freedom."

you not execute Socrates the sophist for being the teacher of Critias, one of the Thirty who put down the democracy? . . . then shall Demosthenes snatch his cronies (*hetairoi*) from your hands? He who takes vengeance upon *idiōtai* and friends of the people (*dēmotikoi*) for their *isēgoria?*" Aeschines then mentions (1.173) that some of Demosthenes' students were at the trial, having come for a lesson in clever speaking. He urges (1.175) the jurors not to furnish "Demosthenes the sophist" with a source of laughter and a teaching example (*diatribē*) at their own expense. "Imagine," Aeschines (1.175) goes on to say, "when he is at home with his pupils how he will brag that he stole the case away from the jurors" by his cunning speech.

This passage strikes a number of themes, each one calculated to arouse the jurymen's ire. Demosthenes is a sophist, like Socrates. The Athenians had justly executed Socrates for his role in teaching the arts of subversion to Critias, one of the Thirty Tyrants. Since Demosthenes himself teaches students, the jury could presume that he is teaching his students the same sort of thing Socrates had taught Critias, and Demosthenes therefore deserves a similar fate. Inversely, if Demosthenes is innocent, though a sophistic teacher, then Socrates had been innocent, and the current jury would be implicated in an unjust execution. This had occurred over fifty years previously, but we may note Aeschines' use of the second person plural for those who had executed Socrates. Worse yet, Demosthenes' power of speech limits the *isēgoria* of common citizens; his oratorical skill therefore undercuts a basic principle of the democracy. If the jurors acquit the defendant, they, like the jurors in the trial of Lacritus, acquiesce in helping to teach rhetoric. Aeschines makes the insidiousness of this acquiescence explicit by claiming that the trial was being used as a lesson by Demosthenes. Furthermore, adding insult to injury, Demosthenes' students will laugh at the jurors' gullibility in the privacy of his house—obviously *they* do not view the Athenians as naturally astute—and Demosthenes will become even more vain and dangerous than before.[32]

Demosthenes could hardly let this sort of abuse go unanswered, and in *On the False Embassy* he turns the tables on his opponent. Aeschines, he says (19.246–48), calls other men logographers and sophists as an insult but is himself open to the same reproach. Demosthenes sets about proving this by pointing out that in the course of his speech Aeschines quoted from Euripides' *Phoenix*, which he had never performed on stage himself. Yet Aeschines never quoted from Sophocles' *Antigone* which he had acted many times. So, "Oh Aeschines, are you

---

[32] Cf. Aesch. 2.148, with Dover, "Freedom," 50–51.

not a sophist . . . are you not a logographer . . . since you hunted up (*zētēsas*) a verse which you never spoke on stage to use to trick the citizens?" (19.250). The argument that underlies Demosthenes' rejoinder says a good deal about Athenian attitudes toward specialized education. According to Demosthenes, Aeschines is a sophist because he "hunts up" quotes from a play with which he had no reason to be familiar in order to strengthen his argument. Clearly the average Athenian would not be in a position to search out quotes when he wanted them; if the ordinary citizen ever wanted to quote poetry he would rely on verses he had memorized, perhaps from plays he had seen performed in the theater. Demosthenes implies that the contents of an individual's memory and his general knowledge learned from experience were perfectly democratic and egalitarian; specialized research undertaken to support an argument in court, on the other hand, was sophistic and elitist. What Aeschines should have done (and, as Demosthenes implies, *would* have done were he not a sophist) was to quote the plays that he had memorized. Since he ignored the play he knew and quoted poetry from a play he did not know, he was proved to possess a sophist's training which he used to trick the average citizens on the jury. The orator who displayed evidence of special knowledge left himself open to the charge of using his elite education to deceive the audience.[33]

Popular mistrust of rhetorical ability and the skilled speakers who misused it is demonstrated by the eagerness of private trial litigants to portray their opponents as slick speakers who were using their rhetorical ability to evil ends. One of Isaeus' clients (10.1) said that he was unequal to his opponents, who were powerful speakers (*legein deinoi*) and well prepared (*paraskeuasasthai hikanoi*); the plaintiff himself claimed to have had no practice in speaking in court, while his opponents were experienced litigants. Another of Isaeus' clients (9.35) cried, "Help me, jurors. If [my opponent] Cleon is a better speaker than I (*legein emou dunatai . . . mallon*), do not allow this fact to be stronger than law and justice."

The notion of the wrongfulness of advance preparation, which Demosthenes used against Aeschines in regard to poetic quotation, was used by other litigants whose opponents were castigated for having "prepared their rhetores" against an innocent *idiōtēs*.[34] Those who used their rhetorical skills to destroy other citizens in court were often

---

[33] For other passages emphasizing the wrongfulness of orators' use of formal training, practice, and advance preparation, see Dover, *GPM*, 25–28; Kindstrand, *Stylistic Evaluation*, 18–19; cf. Ostwald, *From Popular Sovereignty*, 256–57, 273.

[34] E.g., Is. 1.7, F 1.1 (Forster); Dem. 44.15.

identified by their opponents as sycophants, trained speakers and experienced litigants who engaged in prosecutions solely for pecuniary gain. The sycophant was similar to the bribed politician. Both used the political apparatus of the state for illegitimate personal advantage, but, while the bribed politician sold his convictions for pay, the sycophant had no convictions in the first place. The sycophant was consequently regarded as a leech on society, who had no regard for truth or the rights of a case but was a master of slander (e.g., Dem. 57.34).

Worst of all, the sycophants were an uncontrolled element in the democracy. They grew rich from perverting the state's legal machinery to their private ends, but they had no personal stake in their prosecutions. The sycophant made his living primarily by extorting money from victims who preferred to pay up rather than to face the uncertainties of a jury trial, at which they would be outmatched rhetorically. Thus, unlike the politician who, even if bribed, sincerely desired the jury to vote in his favor, the sycophant did not necessarily care personally about getting a conviction when he was forced by his victim's intransigence to go to trial.[35] For this reason, sycophants did not feel a proper sense of gratitude to the Athenian demos when they won their cases (e.g., Dem. 58.63). The sycophants hence represented the least attractive element of the educated elite. The expert politician, who spent much of his life giving speeches, ran the risk of being branded a mere sycophant, motivated by lust for personal gain rather than by a patriotic desire to serve the polis. The line between the sycophant and the politician was somewhat vague; Lycurgus (1.31) anticipated that Leocrates would attempt to portray himself as an *idiōtēs* who had fallen prey to "a rhetor and a most terrible sycophant."[36]

C.3 INNOCENCE, IGNORANCE, AND DRAMATIC FICTIONS

The logical corollary to the topos of "my opponent is a skilled speaker" was the claim by the speaker to be unskilled and inexperienced in public speech. A client of Lysias (19.2), for example, assured the court that everyone who knew him was aware of his inability to speak well (*apeiria*). Another of Lysias' clients (17.1) was concerned that some of the

[35] See, for example, Ant. 5.80; Isoc. 21.8; Dem. 55.33, 58.33; Hyp. 1.2. For sycophancy in comedy, see Ehrenberg, *People of Aristophanes*, 343–47.

[36] Cf. Aesch. 2.145, who defines sycophantism as when one man insinuates a false impression of another into the minds of the people by calumniating him in all the Assemblies and in the Council; Hyp. 1.19, 4.13. Osborne, "Law in Action," 44–48, points out that the existence of potentially remunerative public actions did not actually lead directly to sycophantism.

jurors might have the idea that because he was ambitious, he could also speak better than other people (*epein . . . mallon heterou dunasthai*). This, he assured them, was not true. Indeed, he was unable to speak well on his own behalf, much less in regard to the affairs of others.[37]

Some fairly obvious hypocrisy is involved with these professions of lack of ability, and Demosthenes (21.141–42) trusted that his jury would be aware that the claim that one could not speak properly (*mē dunasthai legein*) was among the myriad excuses by which individuals rationalized their failure to defend themselves in court. The extant speeches were preserved because of their quality as rhetorical literature. Some speeches are better examples of the orator's art than others. Some are artfully composed to give an impression of artlessness. But no speech in the corpus could possibly be construed to be the spontaneous creation of a semi-educated man "unfamiliar with speaking" (cf. above, I.E). Hence, even if the actual litigant who delivered the speech in question was *not* an experienced speaker, in the case of the preserved speeches, at least, the "I am ignorant of rhetorical ability or training" topos describes a fiction. As we have seen, however, the Athenian citizens had some pretensions to connoisseurship in rhetoric, and many of the jurors no doubt recognized the product of the logographer's pen when they heard it. But, since logography apparently continued to flourish through the fourth century, we must conclude that the topos passed muster with the jurors, and so we may suppose that the fiction it depended upon was agreeable to them.[38] The very transparency of the fiction is indicative of its importance to the participants and reveals the deep distrust of rhetoric which coexisted with the aesthetic appreciation the jurors felt for a well-composed oration. The courts, like the Assembly, ran on a fuel of sophisticated rhetoric which the Athenians recognized was potentially

[37] Cf. Lys. 31.2, 4, F 24.1.4 (Gernet-Bizos); Dem. 55.2, 7; Hyp. 1.19–20, 4.11; Aesch. 3.229; Plato *Apology* 17a–d. On the related topos of the *apragmōn* citizen who does not get much involved in public affairs, see Hansen, " 'Politicians'," 43–44; D. Lateiner, " 'The Man Who Does Not Meddle in Politics': A *Topos* in Lysias," *Classical World* 76 (1982–83): 1–12; and esp. Carter, *Quiet Athenian*, 105–10. The *apragmōn* topos must to be read in the contexts of related topoi, the distinction between rhetor and *idiōtēs* and the general distrust of the wealthy. It does not, in my opinion, constitute clear evidence of the rejection of the "world of the citizen" by either Athenians in general or the elite in particular.

[38] On the concept of accepted fictions and social order, cf. the discussions of C. Wright Mills, *White Collar: The American Middle Classes* (New York, 1951), 33–59; Edmund S. Morgan, *Inventing the People: The Rise of Popular Sovereignty in England and America* (New York, 1988), esp. 152–73.

corrosive to the machinery of the state. Thus the illusion was maintained of the simple man relating the unvarnished truth to the representatives of the demos, who would apply their collective intelligence
in arriving at a just verdict. The whole process had much in common
with a theatrical performance, and it may best be understood in light
of the jurors' willingness to suspend their disbelief when to do so
would benefit themselves and the state (see above, III.E.6).

The interplay between the jurors' tendency to be swept away by rhetorical skill and their mistrust of rhetoric is particularly well elaborated
in two speeches in the Demosthenic corpus. In *Against Theocrines*
(Dem. 58) Epichares urges the jurors to

> aid me, caring nothing for the fact that it is not Demosthenes who
> is the prosecutor, but a mere boy. Nor should you consider the
> laws more binding when someone presents them to you carefully
> in rhetorical language (*eu tis tois onomasi sumplexas*) than when they
> are recited in the speech of everday (*tōn hopōs etuchen legontōn*). . . .
> You should all the more readily give aid to the inexperienced and
> the young, since they are less likely to lead you astray. (58.41)

And again, in the peroration:

> Since we are engaged in so unequal a contest, we beg you to come
> to our aid and to make it clear to all men that whether a boy or
> an old man, or one of any age, comes before you in accordance
> with the laws he will obtain complete justice. The honorable
> course for you, men of the jury, is not to put the laws or your own
> selves in the power of the expert speakers (*epi tois legousi*) but to
> keep the speakers in your own power and to make a distinction
> between those who speak well and lucidly (*eu kai saphōs*) and those
> who speak what is just; for it is concerning justice that you have
> sworn to cast your votes. (58.61)

In Demosthenes' masterful speech *Against Aristocrates* (23.4–5) the
prosecutor Euthycles begs for the attention of the jury by saying that
"I am neither one of the orators who annoy you (*tōn enochlountōn*) nor
am I one of the politicians who are trusted by you (*tōn politeuomenōn
kai pisteuomenōn*)." But if the jurymen will listen with goodwill, they will
help to overcome the natural reluctance of "one of those of us" who
desires to do the state a good turn, but who fears that it is a difficult
thing to present a speech in public. As it is, he continues, many citizens
who are poorer speakers, but better men than the eloquent ones, live
in such terror of court proceedings that they never take part in public
trials.

In each of the three passages cited above, the speaker contrasts himself, young/inexperienced/fearful, with his experienced and silver-tongued opponents who were used to misleading juries. The speaker professes to be genuinely apprehensive that the jurors will prefer the polished and misleading rhetoric of his opponents to his own clumsy but true account.[39] The speaker puts himself in the position of attempting to break the seductive hold that rhetoric currently exerts upon the jurors in order to win them back to the side of the average citizen and the law. This is supposed to be for the good not only of the speaker but of the jurymen themselves and of the state as a whole.[40] The speaker's acknowledgment of the jury's tendency to be seduced by rhetorical display may seem a dangerous tactic, but it actually strengthens his case. By magnifying the persuasive power of his opponent and stressing his own inarticulateness, the speaker predisposes his jury to distrust any argument made against him, no matter how convincing, and to believe his own arguments, no matter how incoherent. Of course, in each case the author of the "inexperienced" speaker's oration was a master rhetorician. The ploy could succeed only if the jurymen, who were aware of and worried about the danger of allowing rhetoric to pervert justice, were also willing to maintain the fiction that those who warned them of the danger were as innocent of rhetorical skill and preparation as they claimed to be.

D. Rhetores' Use of Poetry and History

The highly ambivalent attitude of the demos toward the entire subject of rhetoric, rhetorical ability, and rhetorical education made the role of the rhetores more complex and problematic. When a well-known

[39] Cf. Aesch 1.30–31: the lawmaker who established the procedure of *dokimasia rhētorōn* thought that a speech by a good man, even if it were said clumsily and simply, was likely to be useful to listeners and that the words of evil men, even if spoken well, would be of no benefit. Ant. 3.2.1–2 is a sophisticated play on the "unskilled speaker" topos. In Ant., 5.1–7, the defendant emphasizes his youth and lack of skill in speaking; he notes that many inarticulate litigants have formerly been unjustly convicted, while glib ones get off; he begs the jurors to forgive his errors in speaking and hopes they will not consider it to be cleverness if he should happen to speak well.

[40] The topos of the innocent individual saving the decision maker from being fooled by the clever speech of a third party precedes the fourth century; e.g., Herodotus' story (5.51) of Cleomenes' daughter and the Milesian envoys. Perhaps the speech of Sthenelaides at Sparta in 432 (Thuc. 1.86) might be seen in the same light. Cf. Cleon's comments in the Mytilenean Debate (Thuc. 3.38.2–7). Aristotle's comment (*Rhet.* 1395b20–1396a4) to the effect that the uneducated (*apaideutoi*) speak more pleasingly to the masses because they tend to speak more directly of what they know (the specific) and what concerns the audience (the general) seems inadequate to fully explain the "unskilled speaker" topos.

political orator stood up to speak in the Assembly or in a law court, his audience was aware of his reputation for skill at public speaking. They were both fearful of his power to sway them and eager to be entertained and instructed by a master of a highly competitive and refined art. They might distrust him if he revealed too obviously the extent of his skill, but they would be disappointed if the show was not up to their expectations. For his part, the expert speaker knew that his political career depended upon neither alienating nor disappointing his listeners. The Athenian orator who hoped to capture and hold the attention of his audience might have spent hours or days composing his speech so that the argument would be tight, the style engaging, and the delivery smooth.[41] But he was expected to maintain the fiction that his eloquence was born of conviction and the passion of righteous indignation, rather than preparation. Demosthenes' opponents mocked his speeches for having the "stink of midnight oil" (Plut. *Dem.* 7.3, 8, 11), and Demosthenes, who had the reputation (rightly or wrongly) of being poor at extemporaneous speaking, had to overcome the opprobrium of working too hard at his speech writing.[42] The Athenians demanded a very high standard of oratory from their politicians, but they did not necessarily like to be frequently reminded that the orator was an educated expert who possessed abilities and training that set him above the average citizens.

The difficulties faced by the orator who had to put on a good show, but avoid giving offense, are well illustrated by politicians' use of poetry and historical examples. Quotations of poetry and citations of historical precedent could enliven a speech and help to buttress the argument by the inspired wisdom of the poet and the authority of past practice. The technique held a certain risk for the speaker, however. As we have seen (above, IV.c.2), Demosthenes attacked Aeschines for "hunting up" a quote which he had no good reason to have memorized. The orator also had to be very careful to avoid giving the impression that he disdained the educational level of his audience. The orator's role was, in its essence, a didactic one: he attempted to instruct his listeners in the facts of the matter under discussion and in

---

[41] Isocrates (4.14) claimed to have spent years perfecting his showpiece speeches.

[42] A. P. Dorjahn has argued in a series of articles that Demosthenes in fact did have the ability to speak off the cuff; see, for example, "A Third Study of Demosthenes' Ability to Speak Extemporaneously," *TAPA* 83 (1952): 164–71. Cf. Kennedy, *Art of Persuasion*, 210 with n. 113. For a detailed attack by a rhetorician on prepared speeches, see Alcidamas F 6 (Sauppe); cf. Jaeger, *Paideia*, III.60. Bryant, "Aspects I," 172, notes that "there has always been a certain fondness in the public and in speakers for the impression of spontaneous eloquence. . . ."

the correctness of his own interpretation of those facts. But when using poetic and historical examples, the orator must avoid taking on the appearance of a well-educated man giving lessons in culture to the ignorant masses.

A passage in Aeschines' speech *Against Timarchus* that precedes a series of poetic quotations makes clear the pitfalls the orator faced in citing poetry.

> But since you [my opponents] bring up Achilles and Patroclus, and Homer and the other poets as if the jurors are without education (*anēkoōn paideias*), and you, yourselves, on the other hand, are superior types (*euschēmones tines*) who far surpass (*periphronountes*) the demos in learning (*historia*)—in order to show you that we too (*kai hēmeis*) have listened carefully and have learned a little something, we shall say a few words about these matters. (1.141)

Aeschines justifies his intention to use poetic quotations by referring to his opponents' plan to cite poetry against him. He characterizes his opponents as educated snobs who imagine themselves to be in possession of a grasp of literary culture that is superior to that of the demos. Aeschines uses the first person plural to suggest that he is one with the demos whose knowledge of the poets has been impugned. He suggests that "we"—Aeschines and, at least by implication, the people—have listened to the poets, not that he himself has made a special study of literature. Thus Aeschines makes himself a spokesman for the demos, called upon to defend the jurors against the scurrilous implication that they are ill educated. The jurors are therefore prepared to listen sympathetically to the series of quotes that Aeschines will recite in order to disprove the elitist claims he has imputed to his opponents. Aeschines' elaborate justification appears worthwhile only if he believes the quotes will help to convince the jurors, but at the same time he is worried that they could construe his poetic excursus as exactly the sort of intellectual snobbery he accuses his opponents of indulging in.[43]

In another speech (3.231) Aeschines notes that if a tragedian represented Thersites as crowned by the Greeks, "no one of you [jurors] would allow it," since Homer says that Thersites was a coward and a sycophant. Here Aeschines grants his audience a fairly detailed knowledge of, and respect for, Homer's poem. His chosen example is particularly interesting, since Thersites was the commoner who dared speak up in the assembly of Achaean warriors and was trounced by

---

[43] Cf. North, "Use of Poetry," 27; Plato *Apology* 26d.

the aristocratic Odysseus for his effrontery (*Iliad* 2.211–78). Aeschines seems oddly unconcerned about the possibility that the unegalitarian nature of the Thersites story might undercut the sympathy his audience would feel for the poetic example.[44] Perhaps he trusted that his audience would remember that Thersites was labeled a coward and not pay much attention to the part social status played in the incident. But this would seem to be a considerable and unnecessary risk if Aeschines assumed that the ideology to which he was expected to conform was straightforward egalitarianism. We will have reason to return to this passage below (IV.F).

Demosthenes also used quotations from poetry in his speeches against Aeschines, although he employed poetic quotations more rarely, and he invariably justified himself by Aeschines' prior citations. Typically, he simply throws back at Aeschines the passages his opponent had previously quoted and so carefully avoids suggesting that his own knowledge of poetry is superior to that of his audience.[45] Demosthenes (19.247) assumes that his audience is composed of theatergoers. When mocking Aeschines' career as a tragic actor (19.247), he says that "you [jurors] know perfectly well" that it is the privilege of bit-players (*tritagōnistai*—see VI.D.1) like Aeschines to play the role of the tyrant. The orator thus uses the "everyone knows" topos (see above, III.E.5) to avoid the impression of having a greater knowledge of theatrical performance than that of his audience.

Lycurgus made extensive use of poetic quotations in his only preserved oration. He introduced a passage from Tyrtaeus by asking hypothetically, "Who does not know" that the Spartans took Tyrtaeus from Athens to train their youths in virtue (1.106). And, after a long quote from Euripides, he states (1.101–102) that "these verses, gentlemen, educated (*epaideue*) your ancestors" (*pateras*). He also (1.102) recommended Homer to the jurors, whom "your ancestors" thought alone of the poets worthy of recitation at the Panathenaic Festival. The potentially elitist thrust of Lycurgus' hortatory comments is deflected by the speaker's emphasis on the traditional Athenian respect for the

---

[44] Notably, Xenophon (*Mem.* 1.2.58) states that one of Socrates' "accusers" (presumably Polycrates, in a pamphlet) cited the philosopher's partiality for this section of the *Iliad* as evidence for his anti-democratic attitudes; cf. the comments of Stone, *Trial of Socrates*, 28–38. For a succinct discussion of the unequal social relationships implied by the scene, see Raaflaub, "Freien Bürgers Recht," 25; cf. Donlon, *Aristocratic Ideal*, 21–22.

[45] E.g., Dem. 19.243, 245. Cf. North, "Use of Poetry," 24–25; Perlman, "Quotations," esp. 156–57, 172.

poets and his reference to the value of poetry being proved by its inclusion in the public festival.

The orators used a similar approach in citing examples from history
or myth. Demosthenes usually introduced his historical excurses with
a prefatory "I am sure you all know . . . ," thereby avoiding giving the
impression that he knew more about the past than the average citizen.[46] In a similar vein, his client (Dem. 40.24–25) discussed the career
of the demagogue Cleon whom "they say" captured many Lacedae-
monians and had great repute in the polis. Aeschines (2.76) cited the
example of Cleophon "The Lyremaker" whom "many remember" as
a slave in fetters. One did not want to claim a specialized knowledge
of history, but an appeal to the memories of the Athenian elders was
acceptable. In discussing exiles during the Corinthian war, for example, Demosthenes (20.52, cf. 19.249) mentioned events he had heard
about from "the older citizens among you." Aeschines suggested
(2.150) that the older demesmen of Paiania would be able to confirm
that his father-in-law had helped to get young Demosthenes enrolled
as a citizen. He also (2.77–78, 3.191–92) recounted how his own father, who lived to be ninety five and had shared in the great struggles
that followed the Peloponnesian War, had many times told his son the
story of the disasters of the war and of the virtuous conduct and strict
standards of jurors in the postwar years.[47] Allusions to the memory of
the older citizens or of one's own ancestors allowed the orator to avoid
assuming the role of an educated man instructing his inferiors. There
was clearly an appeal to authority involved in the references to elders,
but notably the elders were the only subset of the demos to possess
clearly defined legal and political privileges (see above, I.B).

The Athenians' demonstrated concern with native intelligence, their
distrust of elite education, and their respect for the authority of the
elders are parodied by Aristophanes, who mimics rhetorical topoi in
the speech of Lysistrata, the female demagogue.

[46] See Pearson, "Historical Allusions," 217–19, for a list of examples. On the orators' use of history generally, cf. Perlman, "Historical Example"; Michel Nouhaud,
L'utilisation de l'histoire par les orateurs attiques (Paris, 1982), noting in passing that the
orators normally assume their audiences have no formal knowledge of history apart
from what they tell them (354) and that it took about twenty years for an event to
pass from current politics to the realm of history (369).

[47] Cf. Ant. 5.70–71: the defendant discusses the wrongful execution of nine hel-
lēnotamiai and concludes that the older ones of "you" will, I suppose, remember it
and the younger ones will have learned of it "just as I have"; Lys. 19.45: I was told
by my father and by other older men that "you" had previously misestimated the
size of rich men's fortunes.

Listen to my words
I am a woman, but I'm smart enough
Indeed, my mind's not bad at all.
Having listened to my father's discourses
And those of the older men, I'm not ill educated.

(Lysistrata 1123–27)

E. Rhetores on the Advantages
of Elite Education

The average citizen's belief in the potential power of rhetoric to corrupt the democratic processes of the state helps to explain why both private litigants and expert political orators depict their opponents as clever speakers, wily sophists, and unscrupulous sycophants, whose persuasiveness was matched only by their venality and traitorous willingness to subvert the people's will. It also explains why *idiōtai* depicted themselves as innocent of rhetorical ability or training. The private litigant was seldom eager to complicate the basic scenario: he, an average citizen without experience or skill in public speaking, was opposed by a trained and experienced speaker who threatened both the individual and the state.

The Athenian politician's portrayal of his own and his opponent's relationship to rhetoric and education was considerably more complex. In a searing passage from *On the Crown*, Demosthenes questions Aeschines' right to appeal to virtue, intelligence, and education.

> You filth, what have you or your family to do with virtue? How do you distinguish between good common report and slander? Where and how do you qualify as a moralist? Where do you get your right to talk about education? No truly educated man would use such language about himself, but would blush to hear it from others. But people like you, who make stupid pretensions to a culture of which they are utterly destitute, succeed in disgusting everybody whenever they open their lips, but never in making the sort of impression they desire. (18.128)

This passage is the very antithesis of the topos of depicting one's opponent as an articulate, well-trained orator. Aeschines is characterized as a lout so ill-educated that he is completely unable to impress his audience. How, then, could he be a dangerous rhetor whose eloquence was likely to trick the jurors into voting against justice and their own interests?

Demosthenes' attack on Aeschines' lack of education is no isolated instance; in fact, political orators quite commonly claimed that their opponents were stupid, ignorant, and boorish. Demosthenes (22.75) calls the politician Androtion so dull-witted (*skaios*) as to be unable to tell the difference between symbols of virtue and mere wealth. In describing an Amphictionic meeting, Aeschines (3.117) notes how an Amphissan who attacked him was clearly without education (*oudemias paideias*). This might be explained as an example of contrasting the cultivated Athenians with the rest of the Greeks, but Aeschines elsewhere (1.166) claims that, in addition to his other undesirable traits, Demosthenes was uncouth (*amousos*) and uneducated (*apaideutos*). By their arrogant self-praise, he argues (3.241), Demosthenes and his ally Ctesiphon show their lack of education (*apaideusia*). A client of Lysias (20.12) attempts to undercut the argument that his father was a childhood friend of the oligarch Phrynichus by claiming that the latter had spent his impoverished childhood in the country tending sheep, while the plaintiff's father was being properly educated in the city (*en tōi astei epaideueto*). The claim that one's political opponent was an undereducated knave could be directly associated with the seemingly incongruous claim that he was an adroit speaker. Lysias (20.12) goes on to suggest that after spending his childhood in the fields with the sheep, Phrynichus came to the city to be a sycophant, while his own father retired to the life of a gentleman farmer in the countryside. Among the insults he lavished on Aeschines, Demosthenes (18.242) calls him a "country bumpkin tragedy-king" (*arouraios Oinomaos*) and a counterfeit rhetor whose cleverness (*deinotēs*) is useless to the state. These passages are difficult to reconcile with the view that the Athenians regarded simplicity as an unalloyed virtue in a speaker.[48]

Perhaps even more surprisingly, the politician sometimes took it upon himself to praise his own upbringing and education. Demosthenes (18.257) makes a point of contrasting Aeschines' lack of education with his own impeccable upbringing: "In my boyhood, Aeschines, I had the advantage of attending respectable schools (*phoitan eis ta prosēkonta didaskaleia*), and my resources were such that I was not required to engage in shameful activities through need." This is in contrast to Aeschines who, we are told (Dem. 18.258), spent his boyhood as a servile ink-grinder and floor-sweeper in his father's disreputable schoolroom. The entire section of the speech in which Demosthenes praises himself and mocks Aeschines (18.256–67) is written in highly poetic language; the rhetorical structure of the passage as well

[48] Cf. Aristot. *Rhet.* 1418b23–25, on insult and envy.

as its content displays the speaker's pride in the quality of his upbringing and formal education.[49]

Demosthenes claims to be reticent about saying too much about the advantages "in which I take some pride" (18.258), and he prefaces his remarks (18.256) with a plea to his audience to forgive him for seeming immodest, but the appeal to an elitist sensibility is unmistakable. Here Demosthenes is at one with Isocrates who, in his pamphlet addressed to Philip of Macedon (5.81–82), says that "although someone will say it is boorish (*agroikoteron*) for me to say it, I do lay claim to judgment and fine education (*phronein eu pepaideusthai kalōs*), and in comparison with others I would count myself not among the last, but among the foremost." In an unassigned (possibly epideictic) fragment (F XV.5 [Conomis] = E.6 [Burtt], preserved only in Latin translation), Lycurgus says that it did not surprise him to find a man of great diligence who had risen so high, since a strong-willed individual is likely to be industrious. This quality would lead him to knowledge, from which comes the oratorical ability that results naturally in true renown. It is in the context of the pride an orator felt in his abilities and education that we must view Aeschines' peroration to his speech *Against Ctesiphon* (the passage to which Demosthenes objected so vigorously): "I, oh Earth and Sun and Virtue and Intelligence (*sunesis*) and Education (*paideia*) by which we make distinction between what is good and what is shameful, I have aided [the state] and I have spoken" (3.260).[50]

There is, of course, no reason that the skilled orator should not have harbored a personal pride in his education and speaking abilities. Aristotle (*Rhet.* 1378b35–1379a4) maintains that all men feel that they have the right to be esteemed by their inferiors according to whatever respect in which they excel. He includes among his illustrative examples the rhetorician (*ho rhētorikos*) who naturally feels superior to the man who is unable to speak well (*adunatos legein*). If, however, we are correct in supposing that an orator's public remarks were circumscribed by a close and generally accurate reading of popular ideology (above, I.E), we must assume that in certain instances, at least, the rhetores felt that the Athenian public would willingly countenance their

[49] Cf. Perlman, "Quotations," 171–72. For further discussion of this key passage, see below, V.F.2, VI.E.1.

[50] Kennedy, *Art of Persuasion*, 239, suggests that Aeschines "has about him some of the self-satisfaction of Cicero or other self-made men. They are inordinately fond of quoting themselves and proud of their education." No doubt, but in light of Demosthenes' similar pride in *his* education, this comment seems to miss the more general point.

praise of their own education as well as their sneers at their opponent's lack of educational attainments.

How are we to reconcile the egalitarian attack on the dangers of oratory and appeals to the virtue innate in simplicity with the elitist attacks on ill-educated politicians and praise for elite education? Certainly *paideia*, construed broadly, could mean much more than formal rhetorical training.[51] *Paideia* was associated with the virtuous leaders of Athens' past. Isocrates, in the *Panathenaicus* (12.198), praised the leadership of the "well born, well-raised, well-educated" Athenians of the Persian War generation. These comments might be attributed to Isocrates' elitist point of view, but Aeschines (3.208) remarks that, more recently, the "men from Phyle," who put down the dictatorship of the Thirty Tyrants, were led by their *paideia* to promote the amnesty of 403 as the best policy for the polis.

There was, however, more to the orator's self-praise than a general notion that *paideia* was a good thing when viewed abstractly or in a historical context. The Athenians, despite their distrust of the power of rhetoric did, after all, continue to listen willingly, even eagerly, to the speeches of trained orators both in the Assembly and in the courts. Had they so desired, the Athenians could have passed laws against training in rhetoric, or they could simply have refused to listen to anyone whose speeches smacked of rhetorical sophistication. As noted above (IV.C.1), the orators' own attacks on the potential evils of rhetoric might have been taken as providing the basis for excluding expert speakers from the decision-making process.

Yet the Athenians did not banish the rhetores. On the contrary, they often granted them public honors and respect. Two of the greatest speeches in the corpus (Aesch. 3, Dem. 18) concern whether or not Demosthenes had legitimately been granted the honor of a public crown. And Lysias' ambitious young client Mantitheus (16.20–21) was eager to speak to the people in the Assembly (*legein en tōi dēmōi*), because he saw that the only men the Athenians considered truly worthy (*axioi*) were those who participated actively in politics. Since the Athenians held this opinion (*gnōmē*), he asks, who would not be stimulated to act and speak out for the good of the polis? How, he wonders, could the Athenians ever be annoyed at the politicians, since they themselves were their judges? More experienced speakers made even bolder statements. Lycurgus (1.3) suggested that it was a privilege (*ōphelimon*)

---

[51] Cf. esp. Jaeger, *Paideia*, a brilliant and voluminous, if not always convincing, attempt to "examine the whole development of Greek paideia and to study the complexities and antagonisms inherent in its problems and its meaning" (III.47).

for the polis to have at hand persons willing to engage in public trials. He felt that "the many" should feel a suitable sense of *philanthrōpia* toward the prosecutor, rather than be irritated at him and regard him as a busybody (*philopragmōn*). When Dinarchus (1.102) attacked Demosthenes for his failure to indict his former associate Demades on charges of treason, he asked, "Wherein do we see [in Demosthenes] evidence of the orator's protective power?" The implication seems to be that the orator's speaking ability could and should serve as a positive benefit to the state (cf. below, VII.E.2–4).

The orators were occasionally willing to make explicit the didactic role which was always latent in their speech making. Hyperides (5.21–22) hints at this when he says that the younger orators should be educated by (*paideuesthai*) Demosthenes and the older generation of speakers, but as it turned out the young served as trainers (*sōphronizousin*) for their elders. Again, Lycurgus (1.124) is more daring when he says that he will describe to the jury the stele in the *bouleutērion* inscribed with a law concerning traitors "for my instruction (*didaskein*) backed up by many examples (*paradeigmata*), makes your decision an easy one" (cf. Dem. 21.143).

In a passage cited above (IV.C.1) from *On the Crown* (18.280), Demosthenes defined the orator's worth as consisting of his preference for the same things as the majority of the people. Clearly, however, Demosthenes' dictum was an inadequate justification for the political role of the rhetor and represented an ideological extreme. Later in the same speech, Demosthenes suggests a very different interpretation of his own role in the state: "When the polis was free to choose the best policy, when there was a competition for patriotic behavior which was open to all, I revealed myself to be the best speaker (*egō kratista legōn ephainomēn*), and all business was conducted according to my decrees, my laws, and my diplomatic delegations. . . ." (18.320). Albeit Demosthenes is contrasting himself with his do-nothing political opponents, and he mentions that his superiority coincided with the polis' freedom to choose between different policies, the extreme egotism and vainglory that his words imply cannot be fitted into the context of a purely egalitarian ideology. Demosthenes comes close to advertising himself as the man who ran the state, and he makes no attempt to hide the fact that his ascendency depended upon his superior speaking ability. In another important passage earlier in the speech, Demosthenes (18.172) discusses his unique qualifications to advise the people at the moment of crisis in autumn of 339 B.C. when Philip arrived at Elatea. At that time, the "voice of the country" had called for someone who was not merely wealthy and patriotic but who had "closely studied events from the beginning" and "had rightly fathomed Philip's intentions and decisions." Among all the Athenians, only Demosthenes fitted the bill, because only he had conducted adequate personal research on Philip and his motives. This research might be seen as comparable to the literary researches he attacks Aeschines for having undertaken (above, IV.c.2).[52] But Demosthenes is evidently unconcerned about that; he advertises himself as having been the man of the hour, *because of* his preparation and his speaking ability. In sharp contrast to his suggestion that the orator should be the mouthpiece of the people, in these two passages Demosthenes indicates that the orator must be an expert, an adviser, and even a leader of the state.

The political orators' suggestions that the Athenians should be grateful to them for their services, as well as their willingness to praise their own educational attainments while denigrating the education of opponents, imply that they believed that they should be granted a special position in the state. Furthermore, they felt that this special position was justified in part by their special abilities and elite education. The orators saw themselves, and expected their audience to regard them, as defenders, advisers, and leaders of the polis. Speaking ability and education in rhetoric were basic to their ability to perform these various roles. Hence, rhetorical education might be viewed as useful to the democratic government at least as long as educated speakers were patriotic citizens who kept the best interests of the state in mind when they addressed mass audiences. Throughout the period of the democracy, the Athenians continued to listen to, and often followed the advice of, the expert speakers, which suggests that the demos was in fact willing to grant the elite of ability and education certain tacit privileges within the framework of the democratic government. The masses seem to have accepted the propositions that individual Athenians could be granted political privileges and that these privileges were legitimated by those individuals' personal attainments.

F. Ambivalence and Balance

The expert speaker's privileged position was always a tenuous one, however, because of the strong undercurrent of distrust for rhetoric with which he had to contend. In *Against Ctesiphon* Aeschines under-

[52] Given that information on which major decisions were made was generally public property in Athens, the ancient orator could not often support his position by reference to secret sources of information, a common tactic of modern politicians who in fact have access to much information that is not available to their constituencies. I owe this point to John Jacob.

lines the political orator's special place in the state, but the speech also demonstrates that he is aware of the suspicion under which politicians operated.

> If you jurors pay attention to the pleasing sound of his [Demos-thenes'] speech, you will be deceived, just as you have been in the past; but if you pay attention to his character (*phusis*) and to the truth, you will not be deceived. . . . With your help I will reckon up the necessary characteristics of the friend of the people (*dē-motikos*) and the orderly individual. (3.168)

Aeschines suggests that the *dēmotikos* must be freeborn, must inherit a love of democracy from his ancestors (cf. below, VI.C.1), must live a moderate sort of life, and

> fourthly, he should be a man of good judgment (*eugnōmōn*) and a good speaker (*dunatos eipein*), for it is well that his discernment (*dianoia*) should prefer the best things and also that his training in rhetoric and eloquence (*tēn de paideian tēn tou rhētoros kai ton logon*) should persuade his listeners. But if he cannot have both, good judgment is always to be preferred over eloquence. (3.170)

Aeschines concludes that the good politician should be brave so that he will not desert the demos (3.170).

Aeschines then proceeds to test Demosthenes against the criteria he has just established and, not surprisingly, finds his opponent sadly wanting. He first relates a highly colored story of Demosthenes' du-bious antecedents and his family's willingness to intermarry with bar-barian stock for the sake of gain (see below, VI.C.1). Then, as for De-mosthenes himself, "From the trierarch there suddenly appeared the logographer . . . but he earned a reputation of being untrustworthy even at this job, for he showed his speeches to his clients' oppo-nents. . . ." But what about good judgment and power of speech? "A skillful speaker, but one who has lived an evil life. . . . His words are pretty sounding (*logoi kaloi*) but his actions worthless." And he is a cow-ard to boot (3.173–75).

Aeschines begins this section of his speech with a warning to the jurors not to be misled, as they had been in the past, by Demosthenes' eloquence. Having invoked the aid of his listeners, he then lists the background and character proper to the *dēmotikos*; notably, the list in-cludes formal education in rhetoric. Rhetorical training and eloquence are praised as perfectly suitable to the *dēmotikos*, but the praise is qual-ified: eloquence must always be subsidiary to good judgment and is useless unless the individual in question has lived a good life. The passage is structured to put Demosthenes in the worst possible light, but Aeschines must have assumed that the individual elements of his definition of the good politician's attributes would be unexceptionable to the majority of his audience. Both the positive aspects of rhetorical education and eloquence as a benefit for the demos and the need to limit the power of eloquence—by permitting it to be used only by the discerning and the moderate citizen—are implicit in Aeschines' definition.[53]

Aeschines' discussion of the *dēmotikos* provides a basis for analyzing the relationship between the two seemingly antithetical attitudes toward rhetoric and rhetorical education that are evident in many speeches in the corpus. On the one hand, education in the arts of persuasion is dangerous to the state, since it threatens to undermine the validity of democratic institutions by destroying the ability of mass Assemblies and juries to come to the right decisions. This in turn threatens the fabric of society, since the decisions of the Assembly and courts, along with the laws, served a normative function and were especially important in educating the young and restraining the elite. On the other hand, the Athenians recognized that skilled orators could be useful. Expert speakers participated in many facets of Athenian decision making; notably, they proposed decrees and initiated public trials. The nature of democratic decision making and the constitutional organization of the Athenian state required a great deal of public debate and the rhetores were enjoyable, as well as instructive, to listen to.

The dissonance between the Athenian distrust for oratory and the recognition that the orators performed a useful function is inextricably bound up in an ideological conflict intrinsic to the structure and functioning of the democracy. Egalitarian ideology stressed the native intelligence of the average Athenian, the wisdom of group decisions, the need to ensure that individuals would abide by the decisions of the majority, and the evil potential of those who possessed special abilities and training. Elitist ideology emphasized that some men did possess extraordinary skills and that these skills, which could be refined by advanced education, were useful to the state. Therefore, the elite of ability and education deserved a privileged position in society and in the political organization of the state. The considerable space devoted

---

[53] Cf. Thuc. 3.42.5–6 (speech of Diodotus), discussed below, VII.E.4. On the term *dēmotikos*, especially in Aristotle, see Ste. Croix, "Character of the Athenian Empire," 22–26.

by public speakers to passages that refer to each of these ideologies suggests that the two ideologies coexisted within the democratic ethos.

In this context, the double thrust of Aeschines' reference to the impossibility of the Athenians allowing a tragedian to depict the crowning of Thersites (3.231, above, IV.D) becomes clear. The assumption that the Athenians were sufficiently cultured to disallow a scene that makes hash of Homer is a play to egalitarian sentiments. The choice of Thersites, the commoner whom Homer depicts as unworthy of speaking to the assembled Achaeans not only because of his "cowardice" but also because of his low status, makes a statement about the elite privileges that the current speaker considers his due and denies to his opponent. This impression is reinforced shortly thereafter when Aeschines (3.237) tells Ctesiphon that by crowing Demosthenes he deceives the ignorant (*agnoountas*) and commits violence (*hubris*) against the knowledgeable and well informed (*eidotas kai aisthanomenous*), and he gives to Demosthenes the credit that belongs to the polis, thinking that "we" do not recognize this. Again there is an elitist stratum (the deception of the ignorant contrasted to the offense to the knowledgeable) and an egalitarian stratum (the credit belongs to the polis, not to an individual). "We" may refer to Aeschines, to Aeschines and the "well-informed" people in the audience, or to "all we Athenians." The ambiguity must be intentional.

The coexistence of the contradictory ideologies created a tension between the elite claims of the educated speaker and the sensibilities of his mass audience. This tension was, to some degree, mediated by the elaborate "dramatic fictions" that orator and audience conspired to maintain: the private individual who delivered an ornate speech that he had purchased from a logographer presented himself in the guise of a simple man who begged the jury to forgive his lack of eloquence. The expert political orator, who had painstakingly prepared his speech down to the last nuance, was a concerned citizen who spoke spontaneously out of conviction and the passion of the moment. The orator who had spent considerable time and money acquiring rhetorical training professed to be no more familiar with poetry and history than the average citizens of his audience; like them, he learned poetry in the theater and history from his elders. These fictions are quite transparent to us, and we need not assume that the Athenians were "fooled" by them either. Rather, the members of the mass audience suspended their disbelief in order to smooth over the ideological dissonance.

The dramatic fictions created a modus vivendi between elite rhetor and mass audience. By helping to mediate the power inequities that differing levels of speaking ability inevitably introduced into a society politically dependent upon oral discourse, the fictions helped to maintain the ideological equilibrium necessary to the continued existence of direct democracy at Athens. When they addressed the demos, or a fraction of it, the members of the educated elite participated in a drama in which they were required to play the roles of common men and to voice their solidarity with egalitarian ideals. This drama served as a mechanism of social control over the political ambitions of the elite. Only if they played their demotic roles well were the elite political orators allowed to "step out of character" and assert their claims to special consideration. Thus the Athenians reaped the benefit of having educated men serve in advisory roles of the state. At the same time the Athenians kept their well-educated advisers on a tight leash and restrained the tendency of the educated elite to evolve into a ruling oligarchy.

CHAPTER V

CLASS: WEALTH, RESENTMENT,
AND GRATITUDE

The unequal distribution of wealth among citizens was perhaps the most politically problematic condition of social inequality pertaining in democratic Athens. Athenian society was clearly divided along class lines. Most citizens had to work for a living; a few did not. The Athenian leisure class consisted of only some 5 to 10 percent of the total citizen population, but the great majority, perhaps all, of the public speakers represented in the corpus of Attic orators, both private litigants and expert politicians, were members of this leisure class (above, III.c). The wealthy public speaker (at least one known by his audience to be wealthy) would stand to gain by his class position if the rich were collectively perceived as good.[1] If they were perceived as bad, he would have to deal rhetorically with the opprobrium that his class membership brought upon him. The Athenians' views of the wealth elite and of the propriety of the role the rich played in society and politics were complex. As was the case with the elite of ability and education, the wealthy politician was judged by somewhat different and more complicated criteria than was the wealthy *idiōtēs*. A separation is sometimes necessary, therefore, between Athenian ideas about the wealth elite as a class and Athenian views of the rich rhetores as a subgroup of that class.

A. Economic Inequality in
the Egalitarian State

In the *Politics* (1279b17–1280a4, cf. 1309b38–1310a2) Aristotle defines democracy as the "rule of the poor." Since, in the world of the

[1] Finley's descriptions of the ideology of wealth in *AE*, 35–42, and *PAW*, 1–23, are good general introductions to the subject, but Finley tended to oversimplify the issue by implying that wealth was always perceived by the Greeks (and Romans) as an unmitigated good; see, e.g., Finley, "Technical Innovation," 179: ". . . the ancient world was very unambiguous about wealth. Wealth was a good thing, a necessary condition for the good life, and that was all there was to it." Cf. the comments of R. Seager, review of Finley, *PAW*, *CR*, n.s. 35 (1985): 103–105, esp. 104.

Greek polis there were always many more poor than leisure-class individuals, the rule of the poor invariably meant majority rule. But Aristotle goes on to say that if the rich were the majority in a state and the poor the minority, that state should properly be called a democracy only if the poor minority had control of the government. Aristotle contrasts democracy with oligarchy which was, by his definition, the rule of the rich. The rich were typically the minority, but Aristotle does not flinch from stating that if the rich *were* a majority and ruled, that government must also be called an oligarchy. Hence, Aristotle, along with other elite writers of the fifth and fourth centuries, identified democracy directly with the domination of the political sphere by the poor. The rule of the poor was regarded by elite writers as unjust, since they saw this situation as giving an unfair advantage to mere numbers over quality and virtue. Democracy was, therefore, seen by them as a political extreme, the reverse side of tyranny.[2]

The Athenian demos obviously took a rather different view. At Athens the masses ruled, and the decisions of the majority were binding upon the minority. Common Athenians would not likely have agreed (had they bothered themselves with the question in the first place) with Aristotle's reasoning on the necessary correlation between democracy and the rule of the poor. Undeniably, however, the vast majority of Athenians were poorer than the minority represented by the leisure class. The Athenian democratic constitution ensured that the overt legal and political advantages enjoyed by the wealthy few in oligarchic states were minimized at Athens. The absence of property qualifications for the exercise of citizenship rights was a basic principle of the Athenian political order. Pay for officeholding and for political participation, selection of magistrates by lot, and the right of free speech in the Assembly—all of which were guaranteed by the binding nature of mass decisions upon the entire populace—made domination of the state's political apparatus by rich citizens more difficult.

[2] For elite views of democracy, cf. Jones, *AD*, 41–72. On Aristotle's "sociology of Greek politics," see Ste. Croix, *CSAGW*, 69–80, esp. 72, 77. Ste. Croix argues that class (not status) formed the basic structure of political struggle. Finley, *PAW*, 1–3, with 3 n. 5, agrees that the ancient political order was based on class, but does not use class in a strictly Marxist sense (10). See also Finley, *DAM*, 55–56: the interest-group structure of Greek political society (that is, the citizen body) was simple, rich versus poor; "Athenian Demagogues," 6–8: the demagogues were perceived by the elite as representing a limited, lower-class interest and were therefore seen as evil. For a discussion of the applicability of class, status, and order categories to Aristotle's political thought—and to Greek antiquity generally—see Ober, "Aristotle's Political Sociology"; cf. also below, VI.A.

The importance to the democratic form of government of the disjunction of property ownership from political participation was underlined by Pericles in the Funeral Oration (Thuc. 2.37.1). Pericles states that one of the reasons the Athenian form of government was imitated widely was because no citizen with something worthwhile to contribute was excluded by his poverty (*kata penian*) from participation in the decision-making process.[3] In his speech defending democracy at Syracuse, Athenagoras claims (Thuc. 6.39.1) that some say both that democracy is neither wise (*xuneton*) nor equal (*ison*) and that those who possess wealth are the most worthy of ruling. Athenagoras vigorously refutes this interpretation. The rich, he says, are indeed the best guardians of wealth, but the many are the best judges of what is right for the state (cited above, IV.B.4; cf. below, V.A.2). Lysias' pamphlet *Against the Subversion of the Democracy* (Lys. 34), which takes the form of a speech to the Assembly, is an extended discussion of the merits of a democracy free of property qualifications. Even Isocrates pays lip service to this ideal in the *Panegyricus* (4.105), praising Athens on the grounds that the Athenians judged it a terrible thing that the many should be ruled by the few and equally terrible that those who lacked property (*tous tais ousiais endeesterous*), but who were otherwise not bad men, should be barred by their poverty from state office.

A.1 DEFINITIONS AND TERMINOLOGY

Major differences in individual wealth were, of course, perfectly obvious to all Athenian citizens. Although by the later fifth century most of the rich men had given up the habit of wearing long linen chitons and pinning up their hair with golden "grasshoppers" (Thuc. 1.6.3), marks that distinguished them from their poorer neighbors, the wealthy could still easily be identified as a distinct social class. Both public speakers and writers who were addressing elite audiences tended to divide society into two classes: the "rich men," *plousioi*, who possessed much wealth (*ploutos*) and the "laboring men," *penētes*, who possessed much less.[4] Aristotle (*Rhet.* 1361a12–16) defines wealth (*ploutos*), for the purpose of oratory, as the quality of having a great deal (*plēthos*) of money or land, possessing real estate, furniture, livestock, and slaves in large quantity and of high quality. Poverty (*penia*), then, would be the quality of lacking many fine possessions. But Aris-

---

[3] On class in the Pericles' Funeral Oration, cf. Loraux, *Invention*, esp. 182, 188.

[4] On the vocabulary of wealth and poverty, cf. Gauthier, *Commentaire des 'Poroi'*, 38–39; Finley, *PAW*, 10; Strauss, *AAPW*, 42–43; Ober, "Aristotle's Political Sociology." Cf. *Belegstellenverzeichnis*, s.vv. πλούσιος, πένης, πτωχός.

totle does not tell us how much property was necessary before a man could legitimately be called rich. Obviously, neither the *plousioi* nor the *penētes* constituted an economically homogenous group, and it is impossible to draw a single line across any hypothetical Athenian wealth/population curve that would adequately explain all fourth-century rhetorical uses of the terms *plousios* and *penēs*. Certainly, the ca. three hundred to four hundred payers of liturgies, who controlled fortunes of some three to four talents or more, were wealthy by any Athenian standard. Some of the rhetorical references to the *plousioi* seem to refer specifically and exclusively to this wealthiest group of Athenians.[5] But the most common and most straightforward meaning of *plousioi* was "the leisure class," those who possessed family fortunes of about a talent or more and so were freed from the necessity of working.[6]

Anyone who was not a *plousios* was a *penēs*, and, depending on the definition of *plousios*, a man might be identified as a *penēs* because he owned less than a liturgical fortune or because he was not a member of the leisure class. An individual with a family fortune of about two talents (leisure class, but below liturgical class) could therefore be a *plousios* according to one definition, a *penēs* according to another. By either definition, however, the *penētes* were a clear and obvious majority of the citizen population. The vocabulary of wealth supports the notion that the Athenians viewed their society as divided into two major classes and that the key division was between those who had to work for their living and those who did not.[7]

Although the Greeks never developed a specialized vocabulary for economic analysis, most Athenians would not, I think, quarrel with defining the *plousios* generally as an individual who made his living by controlling the means of production, exploiting the labor of others, and extracting the surplus value of their labor. It is important to keep in mind, however, that the laboring force from which the upper-class

---

[5] Numbers and wealth of liturgists: see above, III.E.1. For an analysis of liturgists in rhetoric, see Davies, *WPW*, 9–14, 28–29, *DCG*, 35. Demosthenes (20.21) claimed that only about sixty individuals regularly performed non-trierarchic liturgies; but J. K. Davies, "Demosthenes on Liturgies: A Note," *JHS* 87 (1967): 33–40, shows that there must have been ca. 97–118 regular annual liturgies, in addition to the irregular trierarchic liturgies.

[6] For *plousioi* as the leisure class and identification of this group with the *eisphora*-payers, see Davies, *WPW*, 10–14; Ste. Croix, *CSAGW*, 114–17; Finley, *AE*, 41; Gabrielsen, *Remuneration*, 123–25 (with sources cited); Markle, "Jury Pay," 267–71. Cf. Plut. *Phocion*, 23.2.

[7] *Penēs* and *plousios* are used as class terms in, e.g., Dem. 22.53, 44.4, 45.80; Is. 11.37, 6.59; Lys. 24.9; Aristot. *Rhet.* 1379a1–2.

Athenian extracted the surplus that provided his leisure would often consist of slaves as well as working citizens. The means of production would generally include agricultural land, although rich Athenians were also deeply involved in mining, manufacturing, and financing overseas trade. The *penēs*, by way of contrast, was normally one who depended, in large measure, on his own labor and the labor of his family to produce his sustenance. He might work for a *plousios*, but often he was "self-employed"—perhaps as a small-scale manufacturer or tradesman but probably, most commonly, as a subsistence farmer.[8]

The foregoing definitions appear to explain most uses of *penēs* and *plousios* in the corpus of orators, but not all. Under certain circumstances, individuals who possessed liturgical fortunes, and would therefore fall into the class of *plousioi* according to either definition given above, could nevertheless describe themselves in speeches as *penētes*. They argued that although they possessed liturgical fortunes, they possessed less wealth than their (also liturgical) opponents, who are referred to as *plousioi*. The *plousios/penēs* terminology could, therefore, be used in two different senses: absolutely, as a class definition in which the speaker assumes the existence of measurable criteria for membership in one class or another; or relatively, in which case the speaker indicates that the *plousios* is richer than the *penēs* but not necessarily that *penēs* and *plousios* belong to different economic classes.[9] The first, absolute, sense seems to have dominated popular Athenian thought on the subject of wealth. By implication, Athenian society was divided into two interest groups based upon economic class; each Athenian citizen normally viewed himself as a *penēs* or a *plousios* and might be expected to see the interests of his class as his own. The second, relative, sense implies no such division, only a recognition that each individual citizen was either richer or poorer than any other given citizen. This latter sense was employed by wealthy litigants in their attempts to blur the class distinctions between themselves and the men who sat in judgment upon them (below, V.D.2). For our purposes, it is sufficient to note that *hoi penētes* could describe a class distinct from the class of *hoi plousioi*. The terminology of wealth, whether used in an absolute or relative sense, always implied inequality, regardless of whether that inequality was general and corporate, or particular and individual.

[8] Applicability of Marxist categories in ancient economic analysis: above, I.nn.12, 18. Slaves in Athenian production: above, I.c.4; sources of wealth: above, I.nn.59, 69, 71. Occupations of *penētes*: above, III.E.1.

[9] *Plousios*, *penēs*, and their cognates used to describe relative inequality between members of the wealth elite: e.g., Dem. 21.198; Isoc. 18.35.

A.2 FEARS OF CLASS REVOLUTION

Given the existence of a dominant ideology of egalitarianism, we might expect that the poorer Athenian majority would have considered equalizing the distribution of wealth among all citizens by legal fiat. Given that they lived in a community whose members were aware of the existence of unequal economic classes, in which all citizens were theoretically political equals, and in which the majority had the constitutional means of imposing its will upon the minority, the Athenians might well have conceived of putting into practice something akin to Marx's ideal of wealth distribution in a classless society.[10] Class conflict, leading to forced redistribution of wealth, was more than a theoretical issue for the ancient Greeks. The archaic period had seen considerable pressure on the rich for land reform, and some tyrants had probably carried it out. During the late fifth and fourth centuries, social revolutionaries in several poleis attempted to redistribute the wealth amassed by the rich among the poorer citizens.[11] Greek elites who wrote on political sociology expressed deep concerns that the resentment of class inequality among the poor would lead to social upheaval. According to Aristotle, Phaleas of Chalcedon suggested that the best way to avoid class revolution was for the wealth elite itself to initiate a program of property equalization. Aristotle (*Pol.* 1266a31–1267a1) argued that Phaleas went too far, but Aristotle himself argued that the state should provide the poor with a minimum amount of property (*Pol.* 1267a10–11, 1320a32–b13), and he suggested various other ways ruling elites might diffuse class tensions through ideological and legal means.[12] The Athenian wealth elite was particularly concerned with the possibility that the demos might use its political power to impose economic equalization, and elite writers used the specter of social leveling as an argument against the justice of the democratic form of government.[13] In his pamphlet *Against the Subversion of the Democracy*

[10] In both of his preserved early fourth-century plays (*Plutus, Ecclesiazusae*), Aristophanes created a society in which property was redistributed among the citizens. Sommerstein, "Aristophanes," argues persuasively that Aristophanes was being neither ironical nor fantastic in his evocation of a new economic order. Cf. David, *Aristophanes*; Ehrenberg, *People of Aristophanes*, 67–68, 358–59, who considers the *Ecclesiazusae* to be the only example of an Attic comedy that deals with a fundamental idea of political philosophy.

[11] For example, through lawsuits at Rhodes in ca. 390, which resulted in an oligarchic counter-revolution: Aristot. *Pol.* 1302b24–25; 1304b27–30; Diodorus Siculus 14.97. Cf. Ste. Croix, *CSAGW*, 295–98; above, I.nn.36, 37.

[12] Esp. *Pol.* 1309a23–26; cf. 1281a13–21, 1304b14–1305a7, 1318a23–26. See also Fuks, "Sharing of Property," esp. 53–56; Mossé, *Fin de la démocratie*, 239–47.

[13] Cf. Jones, *AD*, 54. Similar fears were expressed by seventeenth-century English

(34.5), written in 403, Lysias argued against the validity of these upper-class fears by stating that confiscations of property were most frequently carried out under oligarchies, not democracies. Lysias concluded that there was no reason for the wealthy Athenians to attempt to limit the franchise, since their possessions were not threatened by the democratic political order.

Lysias was quite right, as it turned out. The Athenian demos never made any move to deprive the rich as a class of their wealth. Despite their concern with preserving political and legal equality, the Athenians never came to believe in the wisdom of economic equality for the citizens. Athenian laws gave the poor man a degree of legal protection against the rich man, but the constitution itself, which retained the Solonian census classes de jure if not de facto, recognized that economic distinctions were deeply ingrained in Athenian society. Demosthenes (22.25–27) praised Solon for his wisdom in realizing the impossibility of true equality in either wealth or ability and for designing a form of legal arbitration by which a poor man could secure a legal decision against a rich man without having to put up the 1,000-drachma surety required for public actions.[14] Even in the speech *Against Meidias*, in the midst of a diatribe against the improper exercise of the power derived from wealth, Demosthenes (21.210) states that "they [the rich] have great wealth (*polla agatha*) which no one keeps them from enjoying; therefore they must not keep us [the demos] from enjoying the security (*adeia*) which is our common possession— the laws." Throughout the speech, Demosthenes attacks the accrual of special legal and political privileges by the rich, but he also specifically states that they had the right to keep their wealth. In his Assembly speech *On the Symmories* (14.25–28) Demosthenes argues that money should be left in the hands of private individuals until it is needed by the state for war at which time he believes the rich will give generously. Athenagoras, in the passage cited above (v.a: Thuc. 6.39.1), would seem to agree, since he notes that the rich are the best guardians (*phulakes*) of wealth. Despite the *tension* between upper- and lower-class citizens, there was remarkably little overt class *conflict* in fourth-century Athens.[15]

---

writers opposed to the "Levellers" movement: Bowles and Gintis, *Democracy and Capitalism*, 28–29. See ibid., 27–63, on the inevitability and consequences of the collision between developing citizen rights and property rights in modern liberal democracies; esp. 41: "Most nineteenth-century liberals . . . understood that a society dedicated to civil equality and economic inequality faced novel problems of social stability."

[14] Cf. Osborne, "Law in Action"; discussed above, III.E.4.

[15] On the notable absence of class consciousness or class struggle (in a Marxist

A.3 Modes of Redistribution:
Liturgies, Taxes, Fines

Class differences based upon economic inequalities were not regarded by the Athenians as innately undemocratic. Yet, the Athenians believed that part of the surplus wealth enjoyed by the members of the upper classes should be used to ensure the security of the state and for the general benefit of the citizenry. While never introducing the principle of enforced economic equality, the Athenian demos did find ways to encourage, and ultimately to coerce, rich individuals to expend a certain portion of their wealth upon the good of the society as a whole. The state taxed the rich by various means; the most important were liturgies (voluntary or assigned), war taxes (*eisphora*), and punitive fines levied by the popular courts.

Liturgies, the funds donated by an individual to support some state activity, included equipping a trireme (trierarchy) and underwriting a group of plays or some other form of performance at a state festival (*chorēgia*). Liturgies may once have been largely voluntary contributions and as such served as expressions of patriotism and personal goodwill toward the state. By the fourth century, although some citizens continued to perform liturgies voluntarily, the state normally assigned liturgies on a regular rotation. The legal action of *antidosis*, whereby a man saddled with a liturgy could challenge another to an exchange of property, ensured that the burden was more or less evenly distributed across the ranks of the very wealthy citizens (and metics) who were uniquely liable to liturgical service.[16]

The *eisphora* was levied upon leisure-class citizens on an occasional basis, usually at a time of military emergency. The *eisphora* was a regressive tax in that it was assessed as a simple percentage of capital, but the poorer citizens were exempt in any case.[17] The *eisphora* caused

---

sense) in fourth-century Athens, see Dover, *GPM*, 37–41; Rhodes, "On Labelling," 208; Ste. Croix, *CSAGW*, 281–87 (esp. 284), 292; Vernant, "Remarks," 73; Daviero-Rocchi, "Transformations," 35; Garner, *Law and Society*, 64–66, who (in my opinion) much underestimates the role of tension between rich and poor in Athenian courtrooms. Contrast David, *Aristophanes*, esp. 4, who argues that the long-term economic ramifications of the Peloponnesian War led to social conflicts that destroyed the city-state.

[16] Liturgies: Mossé, *Fin de la démocratie*, 305–309; Davies, *WPW*; Lauffer, "Liturgien"; Jordan, *Athenian Navy*, 61–93; Whitehead, "Competitive Outlay." *Antidosis*: Andreades, *History*, 293–94; MacDowell, *Law*, 162–64; Osborne, "Law in Action," 53.

[17] On the organization of the *eisphora*, see Ste. Croix, "Demosthenes' TIMHMA"; R. Thomsen, *Eisphora*, 57ff.; idem, "War Taxes in Classical Athens," in *Armées et fiscalité dans le monde antique* (Paris, 1977), 140–44; Rhodes, "Athenian Democracy,"

the rich to finance warfare, particularly by providing funds for military pay. Provision of pay allowed the poorer citizens, who could not otherwise afford to serve, to do their part in defending the state.[18]

The *eisphora* and liturgy systems can be viewed as instruments of economic redistribution, since both took money from the richer citizens and gave it (indirectly) to the poorer. This arrangement helped to guarantee the security of the state not only from outside forces but from the internal stresses caused by economic inequality. The redistributive function of taxation was well understood in fourth-century Athens. As Demosthenes (22.51) explained to his audience in a speech written for the trial of Androtion who, as magistrate in charge, had collected arrears in *eisphora* payments with greater than the usual vigor: "Do not misunderstand me; I too think the *eisphora* should be extracted from defaulters . . . as the law says, 'for the benefit of the other citizens' (*tōn allōn heneka*) for this is the democratic way (*dēmotikon*)." Elsewhere (1.28), Demosthenes states that in light of the great amounts that they are lucky enough to possess, the rich (*euporoi*) should willingly expend a small part of their fortune on the *eisphora* in order that they may be allowed to reap the benefit of their remaining wealth without disturbance (*ta loipa karpōntai adeōs*). There seems to be an implied threat here, that if the rich do not give willingly, they may have their property confiscated. The threat does not refer, however, to a class revolution leading to a general redistribution of property, but to the legal means of recourse by which the money could be extracted from the wealthy shirker.[19]

The harshest method of economic redistribution that the Athenian state resorted to was the confiscation of an individual's property for the payment of fines resulting from conviction in a legal action. Some fines were extremely high and clearly were designed to be punitive. Jurors who imposed high fines upon rich litigants might appear to be motivated by greed, and wealthy Athenians sometimes complained that the popular courts condemned rich men in order to get their property paid over to the state treasury, from whence it could be used to pay the poor for political participation.[20] The Athenian certainly saw fines levied upon the rich as potentially beneficial to the demos.

---

311 with n. 49; Brun, *Eisphora*, 26–73. The number of citizens who paid it: above, III.E.1.

[18] Cf. Finley, "Freedom of the Citizen," 16–17.

[19] On the role of taxation in Athenian class struggle, cf. Vernant, "Remarks," 75–76.

[20] List of examples: Jones, *AD*, 58–61. On the redistributive function of the courts, cf. Ste. Croix, *CSAGW*, 97; Osborne, "Law in Action," 53.

In his speech *Against Timocrates* (24.111) Demosthenes argues that Timocrates' new *eisphora* law, which Timocrates had claimed was drafted "for the good of the demos," would deprive the Athenians of the just repayment of fines, which would be lessened under the new law. Thus, the new law in fact attacked "the mass of you all" (*to plēthos to humeteron*).

No doubt the Athenian jurors were tempted, especially in times of economic hardship, to convict wealthy defendants in order to secure the solvency of the state treasury. Furthermore, some convictions possibly were due, at least in part, to self-interested behavior on the part of the jurors, whose dicastic pay came out of the state coffers. On the other hand, that litigants felt free to condemn this tendency in the popular courts suggests that the jurors themselves recognized the injustice of convicting on the basis of wealth alone. Hyperides (4.33–36) calls the Athenian demos the most great spirited (*megalopsuchoteron*) of all people because it refused to convict rich men attacked by sycophants. He cites the example of Euthycrates, whose sixty-talent estate was indicted, but the jurors on the case, "so far from approving the prosecution or desiring the goods of others," refused to give the prosecutor even one-fifth of the votes. Hyperides notes that since wealthy men no longer felt afraid to invest their wealth there had been a rise in the state revenues (acquired through normal taxation) that certain rhetores had formerly impaired by misleading the demos into voting for convictions of rich men in court. There is actually not much evidence to suggest that the imposition of legal fines was a major threat to the wealthy as a class or that fines caused widespread economic upset.[21] The most radical statement in the corpus on the subject of fines is probably Demosthenes' comment in *Against Meidias* (21.211) that Meidias would not suffer anything awful if he was made to possess the same amount as poorer citizens, whom he now had the effrontery to call beggars (*ptōchoi*). This almost sounds like an appeal to an ideology of economic equalization, but in the end it becomes clear that Demosthenes wants Meidias stripped of his wealth only to humble his terrible hubris (below, v.b.2).

In sum, the Athenian state did employ various legal means of economic redistribution. The rich were expected to contribute enough of their accumulated surplus wealth to allow the machinery of the democracy to function and the state to carry out its foreign policy. Even donations that provided for entertainment could be seen in terms of

[21] See Jones, *AD*, 54–61; Finley, "Freedom of the Citizen," 19–20; Ste. Croix, *CSAGW*, 297–98.

the duty of the rich toward the poor. Demosthenes' client (42.22) states that he did not begrudge (*ou phthonō*) the fact that Phaenippus' two fathers (natural and adoptive) were so rich that each was able to set up a choregic monument, because, he says, rich men (*euporoi*) must use their wealth for the benefit of the citizens. The poor were indirectly subsidized by the rich when they were paid to fight in the armed forces but also when they received state pay to serve as magistrates, to attend the Assembly, and to serve as jurors on the people's courts. That the democratic government provided certain economic benefits for its poorer members was recognized as just even by some elite Athenians. Isocrates (15.151–52) claimed that he himself had declined to accept the various forms of state pay (*lēmmata*) that the state offered its citizens, out of a consideration that one such as himself, able to live from his private resources, should not absorb funds that might more properly be expended upon those in need.

In the *Third Olynthiac* (3.34–35) of 348 B.C., Demosthenes proposed a more comprehensive state welfare system under which not only soldiers and jurors would be paid, but each and every Athenian citizen would receive a regular stipend that would enable him to perform whatever state duty most suited his age and situation, "free from the danger of falling into shameful conditions because of need." That Demosthenes could make such a proposal to the Assembly shows that the Athenians were willing to devote some attention to the question of the extent of the society's duty toward its poorer citizens. The proposal was never adopted, however, which suggests either that the existing system was deemed adequate or that the proposed one was considered unworkable. The redistributive function of the democratic government ameliorated the extent of citizen destitution and hence undercut the rise of a sentiment that might favor a more thoroughgoing attempt to enforce economic equality.[22]

A.4 Functional Consequences of Economic Inequality

The limited redistribution of wealth by the Athenian state helped to alleviate, but never eliminated, the tension between rich and poor which was endemic in ancient Greece and which, at Athens, was exacerbated by the dissonance between egalitarian political ideology and obvious inequalities in property-holding. The poor majority stopped well short of depriving the rich as a class of their wealth but continued

[22] Aristotle, *Pol.* 1320a35–b17, notes the importance of economic redistribution in the promotion of social stability in democracies. Cf. Finley, *PAW*, 32–35; Fuks, "Sharing of Property"; and above, I.n.37.

to worry about the implications for the democracy of glaring inequalities. The rich man appeared to live a generally happier life than the poor man, which was naturally a source of envy among the poorer citizens. Inequalities of wealth among the citizens also created problems for a legal system based on egalitarian principles. Was equality under the law really possible, or even just? Some laws seemed to benefit one class more than another. Isocrates' client (20.15) claimed, for example, that judgments against thieves were of no use to poor men who had no property to lose. Therefore, when the jurors convicted a thief, they benefited only the wealthy.

Was it sensible that a poor man who won a private lawsuit be granted the same recompense as a rich man in the same position? Isocrates' client (20.19) professed to fear that because he was poor and one of the mass (*tou plēthous*) the jury might see fit to reduce the amount the defendant would be forced to pay him. It was not just, he argued, that one of the "unknown folk" (*adoxoi*) should receive less by way of recompense than "people with double names," nor should poor people (*tous penomenous*) be thought inferior to those who possess much property. Indeed, he said, you jurors would be voting against your own interests if you should decide thusly in regard to the many. But if poor plaintiffs could secure huge settlements by successfully indicting rich men, an increase in sycophancy might result. On the other hand, was it just that the poor wrongdoer be judged by the same strict standard as the rich criminal? Lysias (31.11–12) argued that it was not. In attacking a wealthy individual, he claimed that it was a universal custom for men to be particularly angry at rich malefactors whose wealth allowed them to avoid wrongdoing, but to forgive poor and handicapped men who might be driven by need to do wrong involuntarily.

On the political side, even if the rich man's vote counted no more heavily than that of his poorer neighbor, he might be able to influence state policy by withholding his wealth. He could accomplish this by refusing to perform liturgies voluntarily or by hiding his wealth in such a way as to free him from paying forced liturgies and war taxes (cf. below, v.c.1). If many of the rich managed to avoid paying their taxes, the state's policy options might be severely restricted when, for example, the military budget proved insufficient to maintain a credible armed force. Was it not, furthermore, possible that the rich men would tend to be more concerned with the protection of their wealth than with the defense of the state? Was not the rich man more likely to turn traitor if he could get a promise from the enemy that his own property would be secure? Was he not more likely to desire peace, even a shameful peace, if it would free him from the requirement of paying oppressive war taxes? The possession of wealth, according to this general line of reasoning, made the upper classes into a "state within a state." Their interests were, at least potentially, antithetical to the interests of the poor majority, and their wealth gave them the power to promote their special interests against the wishes of the masses.

Although the rich helped to finance the poorer citizens' participation in the armed forces, the concentration of wealth in the hands of the few created inequities even on the battlefield. The phalanx method of fighting battles may have tended to strengthen an ideology of conformity and equality among the hoplites, who were armed with similar equipment and fought shoulder to shoulder as a unit, rather than as individuals.[23] Nonetheless the rich Athenian appeared to retain some advantages. Most notably, he might not serve in the phalanx at all, but in the cavalry. The Athenian horsemen were recruited from the ranks of the richest citizens, and the cavalry was, consequently, regarded as the military branch of the wealth elite. As Glenn Bugh has demonstrated, at least for some years after the Peloponnesian War there was a good deal of popular resentment of the wealthy cavalrymen, who had supported the oligarchic regimes of the late fifth century.[24] Cavalry service was viewed (rightly or wrongly) as safer than service in the hoplite ranks. Lysias' politically ambitious young client Mantitheus was on the cavalry list when the Athenians fought at Haliartus in 395, but he chose to serve in the infantry instead, "because I thought it shameful to make preparations to serve in safety if the masses (*to plēthos*) were to be in danger" (Lys. 16.13).

Soldiers who had to work for a living, especially those with urban occupations, might suffer from being separated from their sources of income for an extended period (e.g., Lys. 14.14). The rich man could afford to stay away from home for as long as necessary. If the rich man were taken prisoner of war, his relatives could normally buy his freedom. The laboring-class soldier risked being sold into slavery if

[23] The political significance of equality among hoplites in archaic Greek political history is emphasized by Andrewes, *Greek Tyrants*, esp. 31–38; but Pritchett, *Greek State*, iv.1–93 (with very thorough review of bibliography), has argued that mass formations were used in Homeric warfare, and therefore against the idea that phalanx warfare had any major social or political impact upon the development of the archaic polis. Cf. above, iv.b.2.

[24] See G. Bugh, "Introduction of the *Katalogeis* of the Athenian Cavalry," *TAPA* 112 (1982): 23–32, *Horsemen of Athens*.

his friends and relatives could not come up with the ransom money to pay his captors.[25]

In short, the poorer Athenian was not functionally the equal of his rich compatriot, despite constitutional limits on the political privileges of the rich. This functional inequity inevitably generated resentment of the wealth elite. Because the Athenians developed neither effective legal mechanisms to promote economic equality nor social mechanisms to promote economic mobility, the paradox of unequal wealth distribution in a society governed by an egalitarian political order was left to be resolved at the level of ideology.[26] The Athenians had to develop methods of social control that would limit the tendency toward the accumulation of political power by wealthier citizens and, conversely, would prevent the resentment of the poor at the advantages enjoyed by the rich from breaking out into open class warfare. The orators were well aware of the tension between rich and poor, and their speeches offer a good deal of material useful for analyzing the ideological compromises that enabled rich and poor citizens to live together and to engage in communal political action within the context of the democratic polity.

B. Envy, Resentment, and the Evils of Wealth

When an average Athenian citizen observed a rich man, his emotions were complicated, but prominent among them was a straightforward sense of envy (*phthonos*). The poor man would like to have possessed the rich man's wealth and the fine things wealth could provide. Aristotle (*Rhet.* 1387a6–15) suggests that men tend not to be made indignant and envious by attainable virtues, such as courage and justice, but rather by attributes that they cannot hope to acquire, especially wealth and power.[27] This was no doubt true in all periods of Athenian his-

---

[25] E.g., Dem. 19.169–71, 230.

[26] In modern capitalistic democracies, class resentment is diffused and mediated by the general acceptance of an ideology that emphasizes the possibilities and virtues of individual freedom, personal initiative, and economic mobility: Washburn, *Political Sociology*, 244–45; R. E. Lane, *Political Ideology* (New York, 1962). This ideology was not operative in Athens because of the general perception that the possibilities for economic mobility were limited; see, for example, Aristot. *Rhet.* 1387a6–15, cited below, v.B. Cf. below, vi.D.2.

[27] Cf. Lyc. F XV.1 (Conomis) = E.2 (Burtt), who states that the *ploutos* is enviable (*zēlōton*), but that *dikaiosunē* is honorable (*timion*) and *thaumaston*. Ranulf, *Jealousy*, 1.142–46, treated the problem of envy of wealth in the fifth century, arguing that there was a "causal interdependence between poverty, envy and the zeal for jus-

tory. When Alcibiades (Thuc. 6.16.2–3) boasted of his great wealth and of the magnificent display he had made of it both in the city and at Panhellenic festivals, he also admitted that his activities produced envy among the urban population, but he was able to justify his display in terms of the impression it made upon foreigners. Alcibiades argued that private expenditures were not useless if the polis as a whole benefited from them. A generation later, after the upset of the Decelean War (413–404 B.C.) and its aftermath, the Athenians felt less willing to put up with such open ostentation. The Athenian general Chabrias reportedly did not dare reside for long in Athens, because he feared that envy of his elegant style of living would lead to his undoing (Cornelius Nepos *Chabrias* 3). Of course, what Chabrias feared was that he would be indicted by political enemies and convicted by resentful jurors. Demosthenes (23.208) played upon the jurors' natural envy of the rich when he claimed that his opponents "own more land than all of you in this court put together."

B.1 OSTENTATION, LUXURIOUSNESS, AND DECADENCE

Most jurors would have had no personal experience with luxury, although they might know what the outside of a rich man's house looked like, and they could recognize famous rich men who appeared in public. Demosthenes (19.314) portrayed Aeschines as strutting about the agora in the long strides of a Pythocles (a very wealthy man: Davies, *APF* 12444), dressed in a cloak reaching his ankles and with his cheeks blown out. But the law courts probably provided the first intimate view of upper-class life for many Athenians. A litigant's portrayal of his rich opponents was often intended to inflame to the point of open resentment the envy of a poor man who had previously observed the life of the leisure classes only from a distance. Forensic orators, therefore, commonly emphasized the conspicuous nature of their opponents' wealth and way of living. Apollodorus (Dem. 45.81) said that if only he could haul Phormio down to the state prison and pile on him all of the money he had stolen—"if that were in any way possible"—Phormio would no longer be able to deny his thefts. The jurors were, no doubt, to be outraged at the effrontery of a former slave stealing from his former master, but their envy and resentment at Phormio's wealth were brought into play when they were asked to envision the defendant buried beneath a mountain of ill-gotten gain.

---

tice." Ranulf concluded that Athenian envy seems to lessen by the late fifth century due to the wealth generated by the empire. On envy in Greek culture generally, cf. Gouldner, *Enter Plato*, 55–58; Peter Walcot, *Envy and the Greeks: A Study of Human Behaviour* (Warminster, 1978).

The ostentatious lifestyles of the rich provided the forensic orator with an obvious body of material which could be used in exploiting his audience's envy of the wealthy. Demosthenes (18.320) describes Aeschines and his cronies as "each one a great and resplendent (*kai megas kai lampros*) raiser of horses." Demosthenes' attack on Apollodorus' lifestyle (36.45) was more elaborate: "You wear a fancy robe (*chlanis*) and you freed one *hetaira* and married off another . . . and you take three slaves about with you and live so licentiously that everyone knows about it." In *Letter* 3 (29–30), Demosthenes brings up the corrupt rhetor Pytheas, who had become so rich through political activity that he went about in public with two *hetairai* and spent five talents as easily as formerly he would have spent five drachmas. Demosthenes gave his most thorough denunciation of ostentation in *Against Meidias*, a speech that will figure prominently in this chapter:[28]

> He has built at Eleusis a mansion so huge that it overshadows every other one in the neighborhood; he drives his wife to the Mysteries and wherever else she wishes to go with a matched pair of white horses from Sicyon; he swaggers about the agora with three or four cronies, describing his cups and rhytons and libation bowls in a voice loud enough for the passersby to hear. (21.158)

Even when he is on campaign, Meidias makes a vulgar display of his riches: "You [Meidias] rode on a saddle with silver trappings imported from Euboea, taking with you your fine robes, your cups, and wine mugs . . ." (21.133). Meidias' fancy equipment was, of course, beyond the means of the rest of the Athenian fighting men, and his ostentation did not go unnoticed: "These things were reported to us hoplites" (*hoplitas hēmas*: 21.133). Demosthenes disassociated himself from Meidias and from the other rich cavalrymen by showing that he was just one of the hoplites who happened to hear the story that was, Demosthenes would have his audience believe, the scandal of the campaign. Hence, the speaker puts himself at one with his listeners, average citi-

---

[28] It is often assumed, on the basis of Aesch. 3.52, Plut. *Demosthenes* 12, and supposed incongruities in the argument, that the speech was never actually delivered: see, for example, Dover, *Lysias*, 172–74; Osborne "Law in Action," 50–51. But the arguments of H. Erbse, "Über die Midiana des Demosthenes," *Hermes* 84 (1956): 135–51, in support of the position that the speech was actually delivered have not been answered by those (e.g., Montgomery, *Way to Chaeronea*, 21) who are uncomfortable with the clear class consciousness expressed in the speech. See also Finley, "Freedom of the Citizen," 12, who agrees with Erbse. In any case, *Ag. Meidias* is indisputably a genuine product of Demosthenes' pen, and there is no reason to suppose that the final version would have been any less vigorous in its attack on wealth privilege.

zens jointly confronted by the egregious display of a rich man's personal wealth. Demosthenes' harping upon Meidias' excessive wealth is intended to put his opponent into the indefensible position of the individual whose opinions or way of life were at odds with the norms of the group.

Excessive wealth led the rich man not only to unseemly ostentation but also to offensive luxuriousness and decadence. One of Demosthenes' clients (42.24) sarcastically says that his opponent, the rich farmer Phaenippus, is eager to be honored by the Athenians since—being young, rich, and strong—he turned his hand to horse raising. "What is the great proof of this? That he gave up his war horse . . . and bought a chariot . . . in order not to have to walk on foot. Such is his luxuriousness (*truphēs*)." Luxurious habits of this kind led inevitably to waste and dissipation. Demosthenes (38.27) refers to the evil men who use up their goods by engaging in feasting and wine guzzling. Mantitheus (Dem. 40.50–51), attempting to discredit his step-brother Boeotus' argument that Mantitheus was raised in the lap of luxury while he had no share in any such advantages, pointed out that Boeotus' mother Plangon used up their father's money on slaves and luxurious living. Aeschines (1.195) advised the jurors to tell those of Demosthenes' supporters who had shamelessly squandered their patrimonies to go do some honest work (*ergazesthai*).[29]

B.2 ARROGANCE AND HUBRIS

Envy by the poorer citizens of the material advantages of the rich was real enough, but if the advantages enjoyed by the upper classes were exclusively material, the concentration of wealth in private hands would not directly threaten the democratic political order, and no complicated system of social control of the rich would necessarily have been needed. But great wealth could also generate violence and arrogance. Aristotle (*Rhet.* 1390b32–1391a19) states that the natural characteristics of the rich man (*ploutos*) are clear for all to see: he is full of hubris, he is arrogant (*hyperēphanos*), and hence he swaggers about in an ill-mannered way. Wealth, hubris (which may be defined as violent insult, either verbal or physical), and arrogance were intimately conjoined in Athenian perceptions of the rich.[30] Lysias (24.16) notes that poor men who possess little (*lian aporōs*) are not likely to commit hubris, but rather those men who possess much more than they need.

According to Aristotle (*Rhet.* 1378b28–29) rich men commit hubris

[29] Cf. Is. F 1.1 (Forster); see Dover, *GPM*, 179–80, for other references.
[30] Cf. Dover, *GPM*, 110–11; Jaeger, *Paideia*, III.108.

specifically in order to demonstrate their superiority. Thus, not only did wealth enable the upper classes to *live* better than the masses, it caused them to act as if they *were* superior to the common citizens. Attitudes of superiority were not easily tolerated by those who accepted the validity of egalitarian political principles. The very existence of wealth inequities raised some problems in light of the democratic ethos, but those problems might be dealt with on an ad hoc basis. If, however, the wealthier citizens went about insulting and attacking poorer citizens at will, believing this to be their right and privilege, the existence of the democracy was obviously at risk.

Demosthenes' speech *Against Meidias* was written for the prosecution of a rich rhetor whose excessive wealth had led him to such a degree of hubris that he had dared to strike Demosthenes, who was serving as *chorēgos* in the theater of Dionysus (Dem. 21.16–18). Meidias is singled out as a particularly evil example of the hubristic man, but throughout the speech Demosthenes plays upon the jurors' fears of the rich as a class (especially 21.212). The speech provides an excellent picture of one end of the spectrum of Athenian attitudes toward the wealth elite.[31] If the speech tends to near hysteria in some passages, it is indicative of the profundity of Athenian fears regarding the potential power of wealth to undermine the fundamental principles of the democracy.

Meidias' hubris is manifested in a variety of ways. He is verbally arrogant. He gets up at every Assembly meeting and, bragging of his benefactions to the state, says in his singularly unpleasant and unfeeling way: "We are the liturgy payers, we are the ones who pay the special war taxes (*proeisphora*) to you, we are the rich men" (21.153). Demosthenes has put into Meidias' mouth words sure to make the jurors' hackles rise. The reiterated "we, we, we" (the rich) is specifically contrasted with "you" (the demos), so that Meidias is seen as deliberately isolating himself and the liturgical class from the demos as a whole. By implication, the rich men's interests were different from those of the demos; a small minority, therefore, was opposing the overwhelming majority. Later in the speech, Demosthenes goes further. Meidias, it seems, had offended even the other rich men; his fellow cavalry officers can no longer stomach him (21.197–98). Even his closest supporters are beginning to turn against him because he claims to be the only

---

[31] Perlman, "Politicians," 336, suggested that the speech was directed only against Meidias as an egregiously extreme example and not at the rich in general. This is true in that Demosthenes did not want to make any basic change in the political position of the wealthy as a class, but the rhetoric of the speech depends upon and plays to a deep stratum of popular distrust and fear of the upper classes.

rich man (*ploutos monos*) in the city; he considers all other to be paupers (*ptōchoi*) and subhuman (*oud'anthrōpoi*). Perhaps Demosthenes inserted this passage to appeal to the sympathy of any wealthy citizens who might be sitting as jurors, although his violently anti-elitist statements earlier in the speech would presumably already have alienated them. The passage is best interpreted as an example of the familiar tactic of isolating the opponent completely from the citizen group by depicting him as a renegade whose interests are irreconcilably at odds with the interests of the rest of the citizen population.

Hubristic actions speak even louder than words; Demosthenes notes that no mere words are as hard for you masses (*tois pollois humōn*) to accept, as when an individual violently attacks anyone who comes across his path (21.183). The situation would be different if Meidias used his wealth to further his own interests while not hurting others, but his preference was for ruining other men, all the while calling himself lucky for his superabundance of wealth (21.109). Demosthenes asks his audience (21.83–97) to consider the case of Strato, an innocent public arbitrator who had formerly fallen afoul of Meidias' wrath by giving a judgment against him.

Demosthenes (21.83) introduces Strato as "a laboring man and one uninvolved in public affairs, but not a rascal" (*penēs men tis kai apragmōn, allōs d'ou ponēros*), a phrase that is repeated almost word for word a short while later in the speech (21.95). The comment that Strato was not a rascal (*ponēros*) though a *penēs* has been taken by some commentators as appealing to an upper-class bias in the jury; according to this line of reasoning, the jurors would normally assume a *penēs* was likely to be a *ponēros* if not assured of the opposite.[32] But this interpretation pays insufficient attention to an important part of the context: Meidias had destroyed Strato by having him legally stripped of his citizenship so that he is debarred from speaking in court (21.95). Meidias' legal action against Strato had been undertaken in a popular court whose jurors clearly had decided that Strato was a criminal, reason enough for Demosthenes to feel the need of reiterating his nonrascally nature. Strato's relative poverty needed to be emphasized as well but for different reasons. Demosthenes was particularly anxious to demonstrate that Strato was attacked *because* he was poor; this charge is implicit from the first "laborer but no rascal" (21.83), but it does not become explicit until the culmination of the story (21.96), when Demosthenes

---

[32] Jones, *AD*, 36, cf. 83; and Dover, *GPM*, 34 n. 1, cited this passage to demonstrate the upper-class sensibilities of the Athenian jurors. On the tenor of the speech and the context of the Strato passage, cf. also Markle, "Jury Pay," 286–88 with n. 40.

announces the moral: "All this he [Strato] suffered because of Meidias and because of the wealth and arrogance of Meidias, due to [Strato's] poverty, his lack of supporters, and because he is one of the many."

Strato, then, is the exemplar of the average working Athenian, just as Meidias is the exemplar of the rich, hubristic man. What is the result when the rich man attacks the working man? The latter loses his citizenship, the one attribute—his membership in the citizen group—that should have protected him from the violence of the uncontrolled elite individual. The implications were clear. If individual citizenship could be destroyed at the whim of a powerful rich man, not only was each citizen threatened, but the collective rights of citizenship, that is to say the democracy itself, were endangered by the excessive power of the wealthy few.

Demosthenes is quick to follow up upon the impact he hopes the story of Strato will have produced. There is no just reason for Meidias' behavior; certainly his wealth is no excuse for him because "that [wealth] is the main cause of his hubris." The only hope for the average citizens is to strip Meidias of the source of his hubris (viz., his wealth), since "to allow such a reckless beast to be master of great wealth is to provide him with a weapon against yourselves" (21.98). The trial of Meidias must furthermore be an example to all other citizens: if you pity Meidias and allow a *penēs* to be unjustly ruined, whose hubris will be reduced? Whose hubris-generating possessions (*chrē-mata*) will be removed? Obviously, no one's (21.100).

Given his premises, Demosthenes' conclusions seem inescapable, and he repeatedly harps upon the necessity of stripping Meidias of his wealth in order to secure the safety of the individual and of the state. If Meidias is deprived of his wealth, either his hubris will be eliminated or he will be seen by future jurors for what he is, "worthy of less than the least one (*mikrotatou*) among you." For any misdeeds he might commit he would pay the penalty, just like "the rest of us" (21.138). Demosthenes later brings up the example of the banishment of Alcibiades, a man Demosthenes describes as much superior to Meidias, because "I want you to perceive and to know, oh Athenians, that there is nothing and never will be anything, not birth, not wealth, not power, which is fitting to be tolerated by you, the masses, if it is associated with hubris" (21.143).

Demosthenes' comments in *Against Meidias* represent an ideological extreme, but he was not the only orator to attack the hubris of the wealthy. Isocrates' client (20.15) notes that punishing the crime of hubris benefits all Athenians, rich and poor, and he urges (20.18) the jurors to consider their own interests as working men and vote for conviction of his hubristic opponent. Lysias (24.17), having noted that the rich are much more likely to commit hubris than the poor (cf. Aristoph. *Plutus* 564), adds that this situation exists because the *plousioi* can buy off dangers (meaning legal threats) with their money, while the *penētes*, due to their lack of means (*aporia*), are forced to act moderately (*sōphronein*).

B.3 CORRUPTION OF SOCIAL RELATIONS

Violent outrage was a crime frequently committed against strangers or enemies, but the orators argued that excessive interest in wealth corrupted relationships between friends and relatives as well. Isaeus' client (5.35), for example, was eager to demonstrate that his opponent was a rich man and that he acted as the most rascally of persons (*ponērotatos*) both toward the state (to which he refused to pay his fair share) and toward his relatives (whom he attempted to cheat of their share in an inheritance). The conjunction of wrongdoing to state and family is quite natural. Since the polis could be regarded as a macrocosm of the extended family/kinship network (see VI.C.1), anyone who cheated his family could be seen as potentially dangerous to society as a whole. One of Demosthenes' clients (48.52–55) discusses his brother-in-law Olympiodorus' poor treatment of his own sister and niece, due to his preference for the company of a luxury-loving *hetaira*. Could anyone, the plaintiff wondered, deny that these two ladies (the sister and the niece) were wronged and suffered terrible things when they saw "this *hetaira*, in defiance of what is proper (*kalōs*), decked out in masses of jewelry and beautiful cloaks (*himatia*), travelling abroad in style, and committing hubris with what is rightfully ours, while they are themselves too poor to enjoy any such things." Here, the relatives are outraged by the ostentatious display of an unsuitable person. Clearly, the plaintiff expects the jurors to feel that the defendant's sister and niece had more right to the use of his wealth than did a *hetaira*. At least Olympiodorus had the excuse of having been driven mad by the *hetaira*, and the family's wealth was only the means, rather than the cause of the outrage. Even worse were people whose lust for wealth destroyed in them all feelings of family loyalty. Isaeus (5.39), for example, describes an evil man whose unwillingness to share his wealth had led his relatives to seek mercenary service abroad due to the extremity of their need. Dinarchus (2.8) lambasts the wealthy Aristogeiton, asking "who does not know" that he allowed his own father only the bare necessities of life and deprived him of a proper burial.

In the speech *Against Stephanus* (Dem. 45) Apollodorus plays heavily upon the theme of money as a destroyer of proper social relations.

The speech is directed against the freedman Phormio, who has taken over the operations of the bank belonging to Apollodorus' father Pasio. According to Apollodorus (45.80), if Phormio had been honest, he would have remained a *penēs*. As it was, Phormio was rich, a situation that, when combined with his marriage to Pasio's widow, had grotesquely inverted the proper social order. Phormio is characterized as a misanthrope who goes about with a sullen look so as to avoid being approached by deserving citizens for aid (45.68–69). The proof of his misanthropy is that, despite his great wealth, no Athenian had ever been helped by him; Phormio preferred instead to lend out money at interest and so reap a profit from the misfortunes of others. Phormio's mad lust for lucre had also destroyed his natural family feelings: he ejected his own uncle from his home, stole his mother-in-law's money, and duns his debtors mercilessly (45.69–70). Apollodorus weaves together Phormio's disrespect for his own relatives and his failure to act properly toward needy citizens, thus demonstrating how the corrupting power of ill-gotten wealth rotted the fabric of a society based on mutual aid between members of kinship and citizenship groups.

It is an easy transition to the unfairness of Phormio's treatment of Apollodorus' own family. Is it not outrageous that he should allow us "who made him a Greek instead of a barbarian, a notable instead of a slave, who made him master of such wealth, to live in the depths of poverty (*eschatais aporiais*) while he is so rich?" (45.73) Is it right that Phormio should marry Pasio's wife but allow Apollodorus' daughters to remain undowered due to their lack of means (*endeia*) and thus unwed? (45.74) Apollodorus (45.75) then asks the jury to consider a hypothetical scenario which illustrates the perversity of Phormio's behavior: if Phormio had been poor and Apollodorus rich, and if Apollodorus suddenly died, Phormio's sons, being uncles (by marriage) of Apollodorus' daughters, would be able to claim them as wives. "The sons of a slave take as wives the daughters of the master!" Yet back in the "real" world (actually an elaborate fiction: v.D.2) where Apollodorus is the poor relative, Phormio refused to help dower the daughters. Moreover, Phormio has the effrontery to reckon up the amount of property that Apollodorus himself owes (45.75). The corrupting influence of Phormio's wealth infects those who come into contact with him. His supporter Stephanus, despite being cousin to Apollodorus' wife, is assumed to be similarly unwilling to dower Apollodorus' children, since "he has made the wealth of Phormio more important than the demands of kinship" (*sungeneias anagkaia*: 45.54).

Apollodorus' story is based upon a transparent fiction, since he himself was one of the wealthiest men in Athens (Davies, *APF* 1411, cf.

11672), but his tale is well calculated to play upon the sympathies of the poorer jurors who might themselves be in a position of hoping for some aid from better-off relatives. As born citizens, the jurors would also be expected to shudder at the thought of their freeborn daughters marrying the sons of slaves (cf. below, VI.C). Phormio's and Stephanus' wanton neglect of the duties imposed by kinship ties, like Meidias' hubris, are specifically traced to the corrupting influence of too much wealth in the wrong hands.

C. Wealth and Power Inequality

Demosthenes (*Ex.* 2.3) claims that for the demos to have nothing and for those who oppose the demos to have a superabundance of wealth is an amazing and terrifying (*thaumaston kai phoberon*) state of affairs. Amazing, certainly in light of the egalitarian ethos, but why terrifying? Ostentatious behavior, hubris, and poor social relations were potentially serious problems, but they might have remained inconsequential for many Athenians, who were not themselves direct victims. To produce the desired effect, the speaker referring to these problems typically resorted to imagery, implication, and extrapolation. Such tactics helped to lay the groundwork for a case against a rich opponent but were not necessarily sufficient to clinch the matter. The specific problems associated with wealth as a factor in the political processes of the state were, however, concrete and genuinely frightening. All Athenians knew that a few very wealthy citizens had an influence in the polis that was out of proportion to their relative numbers. The question was how and in whose interest that influence was exerted: Positively, in the interests of the demos? Or negatively, in the interests of the elite? All too often it appeared to the Athenians that the latter was the case.

The corruption caused by wealth, as we have seen (V.B.3), began at home, and if we are to believe one of Demosthenes' clients (57.58) it could easily spread to the deme level. According to him, in the deme of Halimous the demesmen erased the names of old men who were without resources from the citizen register but kept their sons on the register. This was a clear case of political corruption, since the son of a noncitizen could not normally be a citizen. But, while wealthy demesmen certainly played a major role in the public life of the deme and perhaps of the tribe, much of their activity was apparently benevolent and appreciated by their poorer fellows.[33] Most of the speeches in the

[33] On the role of wealth in deme society, see Daviero-Rocchi, "Transformations," 36–38; Osborne, *Demos*, 88–91; Whitehead, *Demes*, 234–52, "Competitive Outlay"; cf. above, I.C.6 with n. 75.

corpus bear more directly, however, on the national scene. Wealth power presented the gravest danger to the democracy when it was deployed on the level of polis politics.

C.1 POLITICAL CLOUT THROUGH WITHHOLDING CONTRIBUTIONS

The most obvious way in which the rich man could undermine state policy was by withholding the money he normally would have paid to the state through taxation or voluntary contributions.[34] Litigants quite commonly claimed that an opponent either failed to share any of his great wealth with the state or made contributions that were small and miserly in comparison to his net worth.[35] If one's opponent did contribute money to the state, one could assert that he did so only to benefit himself (e.g., Lyc. 1.139; Lys. 19.57). Other rich men were accused of hiding personal wealth from the eyes of the state so as to avoid being asked to give their fair share to the common good.[36]

The simplest motive for liturgy avoidance was mere greed and selfishness (e.g., Dem. 38.25, 27), but selfishness and preference for one's individual good over the good of the state could verge on treason. Lysias (31.6) attacks those who are citizens by birth (*phusei*), but by choice (*gnōmēi*) consider any region in which they own property to be their homeland (*patris*). Such men are willing to abandon the common good (*koinon agathon*) for private gain (*idion kerdos*), so that they make not the polis, but their wealth (*tēn ousian*) itself into their *patris*. Demosthenes accuses Meidias of particularly egregious behavior in regard to state payments. According to Demosthenes (21.203), Meidias frequently said that if the people will not pay *eisphora* and will not march out on campaign, he would withhold his own payments. This kind of statement, Demosthenes points out (21.204), is evidence that Meidias harbors "a secret hatred of you, the masses." Demosthenes' comment hits home at the deep-rooted fear of the demos that withholding by the rich was actually evidence of hatred of the people which might be expected to result in antidemocratic, revolutionary activity (cf. Aristoph. *Plutus* 569–70). This sense of fear is implicit in much of the rhetoric on the subject of the rich and their contributions to the state. Demosthenes' description (19.295) of the Megarian politician Ptoeodorus, who was the richest man in his polis and had insti-

---

[34] On individual withholding of wealth as a method of influencing policy, see Davies, *WPW*, 89–91; Perlman, "Politicians," 345–48; Gabrielsen, "ΦANEPA." Cf. above, V.A.4.

[35] Paid nothing: [Lys.] 6.48; Dem. 42.21. Paid too little: Is. 5.36–38; Dem. 21.154–55, 157.

[36] E.g., Is. 5.43, 7.40, 11.47, 50; Dem. 28.24, 42.22–23; Din. 1.70.

tuted a revolutionary plot inspired by Philip of Macedon, played on Athenian distrust of their own wealthiest men.

Seen in the light of potential treason, the attempts by the rich to worm out of their state-imposed taxes appeared extremely sinister. Obviously there was good reason to design legislation to force the wealthy to pay their due. In *On the Crown* Demosthenes made political hay out of the upper-class opposition to his trierarchic reforms: Formerly (before his legislation), the *plousioi* had gotten off with small contributions, while those with only moderate wealth or who possessed only a little (*mikra kektēmenoi*) were losing what meager means they had. Demosthenes' *nomos* had halted the abuses, made the *plousioi* pay a fair share, and stopped them from doing wrong to the *penētes* (18.102). The rich were horrified at Demosthenes' reforms and tried to bribe him (18.103); this was only to be expected, because under the old system they had paid little money and had the chance to grind down the poor citizens (*tous aporous tōn politōn epitribousin*: 18.104). Of course, Demosthenes refused the bribe, and his law was a great aid to the *penētes* (18.107) who, under the old system, had to pay liturgies unfairly; now the obligations were transferred from the propertyless (*aporoi*) to the wealthy (*euporoi*: 18.108).[37]

Demosthenes' use of the terminology of wealth and poverty in this passage is an example of emphasizing the relative economic inequalities that existed within the leisure class (above, v.a.1). The greater part of his audience would not personally have had to contribute to a trierarchy under either the new law or the old one. But Demosthenes assumes that his listeners will be sympathetic to the idea that the richest should be forced to pay heavily and should not be allowed to "grind down the poor." Never mind that the "poor" in question were all members of the leisure class and thus much wealthier than the average Athenians on the jury; the sense of distrust the Athenians felt at the very rich and the power of the rich allowed Demosthenes to evoke the fiction that this was a case in which the arrogant, selfish rich men had been humbled in favor of the rights of the patriotic, but oppressed, poor.[38]

In his comments on the trierarchic reform, and in a more extreme

---

[37] In an earlier speech (20), Demosthenes attempted to show that a *nomos* proposed by Leptines, which would have made liturgy and *eisphora* payments more equitable, was not a good idea. He was forced to admit that taxation of the rich was surely desirable, but that Leptines' law would produce bad side effects: 20.18–19, 127.

[38] On the evolution of the naval symmories and their relationship to other liturgies and to the *eisphora*, cf. the studies cited above, III.nn.58, 59, v.n.17.

form in *Against Meidias*, Demosthenes invokes a world in which it is taken for granted that the rich will grab and keep all they can and have no care for the sufferings of their less fortunate compatriots. The average citizens' only protection against the power of wealth lay in the collective rights guaranteed by the democratic constitution (e.g., Dem. 45.67). This conviction reinforced the presumption that the most vicious of the rich felt they had an interest in limiting those rights and in destroying that constitution. Thus Demosthenes (21.124) is able to argue that Meidias was intent on attacking the *isēgoria* and the liberty (*eleutheria*) of all of "us."

C.2 LEGAL ADVANTAGES

The only way Meidias and rich men like him could be restrained was through the votes of the many (cf. Dem. 42.31). But what if the rich refused to pay attention to the opinion of the majority? After the vote against him at the preliminary inquiry (*probolē*) held in the Assembly, Meidias continued to act arrogantly (Dem. 21.199) and considered himself none the worse for the negative vote (21.200). Such behavior was completely unacceptable: "A man who thinks it shameful to show any fear of you [Athenians] and who regards it as dashing to ignore you, does not such a man deserve ten deaths? Because he believes you have no control over him" (21.201). Demosthenes and his audience knew that the uncontrolled individual was a great danger to the democratic order. Yet how could Meidias afford to scorn the vote of the demos in the Assembly? How did he dare to act with such arrogant confidence when facing what, if there were any justice in Athens, would be a certain conviction in court?

Since the people's courts were the primary tool by which the many could hope to restrain the power of the rich, it was of paramount importance that the laws and the juries did not favor the upper classes. Isocrates' client (20.20) states that it would be the most dreadful thing imaginable (*pantōn . . . deinotaton*) if, in a democratic polis, "we" (the common citizens) who are considered worthy to hold office and who share the risks of war should choose to deprive ourselves of justice in respect to the laws by showing favor in court to those who possess wealth. One of Demosthenes' clients (51.11; cf. 21.183) asked his audience a question with the same import: if you jurors decide that a *penēs*, driven by need (*endeia*) to commit some misdemeanor, is to be liable to the greatest punishments, while a *plousios*, driven by lust for personal gain (*aischrokerdeia*), does the same and wins a pardon, "where is the equality for all and the democratic way?" (*pou to pantas echein ison kai dēmokrateisthai phainetai*). Elsewhere (24.112), Demosthenes argues that no punishment is too severe for the individual who demands tenfold restitution when, at an audit, he catches out some minor magistrate, some *penēs*, or some *idiōtēs* selected by lot, but then tries to change the law to protect *plousioi* who have been caught embezzling state funds.

In *Against Meidias* (21.209) Demosthenes resorts to a counterfactual example to show the jurors just how perverse it would be to allow Meidias to go free for the sake of his money. Just imagine, says Demosthenes—"though may it never happen, indeed it never will"—that the rich became masters of the state and that "one of you, the many and demotic" were to offend slightly one of them and be tried by a jury of the rich. What sympathy would the poor man get? None, of course. Would not the words of the wealthy jurors be, "The slanderer! The pest! That he should be allowed to commit hubris and yet breathe! He should be only too happy if he is allowed to live."

Demosthenes clearly intends to demonstrate by this horrifying hypothetical example that the interests of the upper classes were antithetical to those of the poor and that the former harbored an intense hatred for the latter. Demosthenes is then in a position to state that the jurors are fully justified in treating the rich as the rich would treat them if given a chance. In no case must the rich be allowed to interfere with the laws, which are the common possession of all citizens (21.210) and which, by implication, protected them against the power of wealth. Obviously, in light of the importance of the role of the courts as a defense against the power of the rich, legal privileges for the wealthy were a travesty and posed a manifest danger to the democracy. Demosthenes is clear on this point: Meidias is so powerful that he can normally prevent individuals from getting satisfaction, but "now, since he is caught, let him be punished in common by all of you acting on behalf of everyone, because he is a common enemy (*koinos echthros*) to the *politeia*" (21.142).

But Meidias was still confident of aquittal; obviously, he thought his wealth *could* pervert the legal system. Unfortunately, according to Demosthenes (21.112), the rich in reality had many advantages in respect to the law, and "we the remainder" (all the citizens but the rich) "have no share in equality and commonality" (*ou metesti tōn isōn oude tōn homoiōn*) in comparison to the rich, "No! No share at all!" The wealthy pick their own times for their trials; the rest of the Athenians must face the court right away. The rich have witnesses prepared in advance, while some of Demosthenes' witnesses are not even willing to speak up. Meidias' wealth is a citadel (*teichos*) which protects him from legal attacks (21.138). He is therefore beyond the control of the legal system. Nor was Meidias a unique case. Aristotle (*Rhet.* 1372a11–17) notes that the rich are among the groups of men who think they are able to do wrong without being punished for it.

But exactly how were members of the upper classes able to pervert the legal process? The most obvious way was by bribing individuals involved: witnesses for the other side could be suborned (as Demosthenes implied his against Meidias had been) not to testify or to give false witness; the prosecutor might be bribed to drop the case; even the demos as a whole might be offered money to win their sympathy.[39] More insidious was the awe or even fear that poorer citizens sometimes felt when confronted with a member of the wealthy elite. Lysias' client (7.21) says his opponent slandered him by saying that no one was willing to witness against him because of his power and his money. Lysias' client does not deny that his power and money might dissuade potential witnesses, but he asks why the prosecutor did not bring the archons or Areopagites to witness the crime (digging up a sacred olive stump); these worthies were apparently less likely to be overawed.[40] Demosthenes (21.20, 137) comments that many people feared to speak out against Meidias, recognizing that his violence, litigiousness, powerful supporters, and wealth made him strong and fearsome.

D. Mediating Negative Impressions of Wealth

The passages cited above paint a dismal picture of the role played by wealth in the polis of Athens. Wealth leads the rich to overweening ostentation and luxuriousness, which are envied and resented by the poorer citizens. Excessive wealth undermines proper social relations, even between relatives. The upper classes are arrogant and prone to commit acts of violent outrage against common citizens. The wealthy withhold their money from the state, due to their selfishness and hatred of the poor, and at least some of them were suspected of harboring treasonous designs. The power of wealth threatens the freedom of the poorer citizen, and the rich man believes he can commit crimes without paying the penalty. Worse yet, he apparently sometimes can do just that by bribing or by overawing the prosecutors, witnesses, and jurors ranged against him. The struggle of the poor man

[39] Bribery of witnesses: Dem. 44.3; of prosecutor: Dem. 58.33; of jurors: Aesch. 1.87–88; of the entire demos or great numbers of citizens: Dem. 21.2; Lys. 28.9, 29.12–13. Cf. below, VII.F.2.

[40] Or at least so the defendant wished to imply, perhaps since the Areopagites were themselves the judges in the trial. On the Areopagus as a court, see Wallace, *Areopagos,* esp. chapter 4.ii; cf. above, III.E.3.

against the rich man, even in the people's courts, was therefore an unequal one because the members of the upper classes were functionally superior to the average citizens.[41] One might, consequently, conclude that the rich were much too powerful and that their power was both an affront to egalitarian ideals and a very real threat to the democratic government. As Demosthenes (21.205) said of Meidias and his wealthy supporters, "They have grown too powerful to suit the interests of each one of us."

Granted this negative view of wealth, poorer jurors had every reason to be suspicious of wealthy litigants; rich citizens, for their part, had cause to worry that their wealth might prejudice juries against them. Isocrates (15.142–43) claims he was warned by his friends not to speak truthfully in court about his life, since "there are some [jurors] who are so consumed by envy and poverty and so hostile that they go to war, not against wrongdoing, but against prosperity." Isocrates (15.159–60) goes on to say that, due to the hostility in Athens toward the rich, one must defend oneself against the charge of wealth as if it were a crime and worse than a crime, since anyone discovered to be a rich man would soon be utterly ruined.

D.1 MODERATION AND HARD WORK

In the *Areopagiticus* (especially 7.31–35) Isocrates harks back to a better time in Athens' past, when the poor did not envy the rich but honored them and gratefully accepted employment and political privileges from their hands. The fourth-century Athenian demos may have agreed with Isocrates in viewing the past as an age of better relations between the classes, but it was likely to locate the modern decline in the character and habits of the elite, not of the masses. In the fourth century, the demos associated ostentation, hubris, and undemocratic power with wealth; presumably, in the good old days, frugality and moderation had been the norm among the elite. According to Demosthenes, these last virtues were indeed possessed by the Athenians' ancestors. In the glorious days of yore, the state was wealthy in common (*eupora . . . dēmosiai*), and no one individual set himself up as greater than the many, even in private (23.206). The personal dwelling of a Miltiades or an Aristides was no more awe-inspiring (*ouden semnoteran*) than that of his neighbor (Dem. 3.26, cf. 23.207). Rich litigants in the fourth century found it expedient to claim a similar lack

---

[41] On the concept of power inequality, see Humphreys, "Discourse of Athenian Law." Cf. below, VII.C. Finley, "Freedom of the Citizen," 11–12, notes that the self-help aspect of Athenian law weighted the process in favor of the wealthy.

of pretension. Apollodorus (Dem. 45.77–78) noted that despite his loud voice and habit of walking fast, he was moderate (*metrios*) in all his expenses and lived a more orderly (*eutaktoteron*) life than his opponent, Phormio. When defending the *eisphora* payers who were in arrears, Demosthenes (22.65) asked who were worse, the vicious embezzlers who were collecting the tax, or the honest farmers, who lived frugally (*pheidomenoi*) and who, due to the expenses of raising their children properly and maintaining their households, fell a little behind on their taxes?

A wealthy litigant might also attempt to deflect the jurors' resentment by showing that he had come by his wealth through hard work. The defendant in Antiphon's *First Tetralogy* (2.2.12) stressed that his wealth did not derive from litigation but from labor (*ou dikazomenon all'ergazomenon*). One of Demosthenes' clients, concerned lest he be despised as a money-grubbing loan shark, claimed to dislike professional lenders himself (37.53). But, he asks, if a man who had sailed the seas and had taken risks loans a little money out of his small fortune (*euporēsas de mikrōn*) as a favor, surely he does not deserve to be hated by the people (37.54). Another of Demosthenes' clients (42.20) freely admits (*homologō*) that he used to make a lot of money from mining "by wearing out my own body and by toil." Now, he argues, he has lost most of his money, while his opponent, the wealthy farmer Phaenippus, is a rich man who sells from his farm 1,000 measures of barley and 800 of wine at shockingly inflated prices. Here, once again, is the attempt to pit the common interests of the group against the selfish interests of the individual. The plaintiff portrays himself as a laboring man who has lost most of what he had made from the sweat of his brow, and so he stands at the same level as the jurors. Phaenippus, on the other hand, exploits everyone who must buy farm produce by inflating his prices during a time of shortages. He is more concerned with his profits than with the common good and so is located outside the interest group composed of all average citizens, a group that includes the majority of the jurors and into which the plaintiff has, for the moment at least, insinuated himself.

D.2 DRAMATIC FICTIONS AND TENSIONS WITHIN THE IDEOLOGY OF WEALTH

If a wealthy litigant could gain an advantage by showing himself off as moderate and hardworking, he might be even better off by claiming actual poverty. The speeches in the corpus provide a number of examples of litigants attempting to portray themselves as relatively poor men, oppressed by wealthy opponents. One of Demosthenes' clients, for example, claimed that his family was poor and powerless (44.28). He tried (44.4) to prove that his father was an impecunious *idiōtēs* by stating that his father had been a herald in Piraeus: "This is not only a mark of human poverty (*aporias anthrōpinēs tekmērion*) but of lack of concern with public affairs," so (lacking wealth and powerful political supporters) we have only the justice of our case to rely upon.[42] Yet, as suggested above (III.C), it is quite unlikely that we possess a single speech delivered by a genuinely impoverished Athenian.

The question arises whether the speakers actually expected the jurors to believe they were poor men. The defendant in Lysias 24, who was in court to defend his right to a pauper's stipend, must have hoped the jury would be convinced of his lack of means (e.g., 24.9). Jurors were sometimes warned not to believe in the claims of poverty made by the speaker's opponents (e.g., Is. 5.35, 43). But surely, in many instances such warnings were hardly necessary since the jurors would recognize that the litigant was a rich political orator or had hired a logographer to write his speech. Many jurors were presumably able to make the connection between a man's ability to purchase a speech and the extent of his means.

In some speeches the profession of poverty by the speaker is completely incredible. Did Apollodorus, well known as one of the wealthiest and most generous trierarchs in the city, really imagine that his jury would believe that he lived in abject poverty (Dem. 45.73) or that his daughters would die old maids because he could not provide them with dowries (above, V.B.3)? Demosthenes himself (28.21) made a similar pronouncement in his second trial against his guardians: if we lose the case, my sister will be unable to make a suitable marriage because of our *aporia*. The speaker in Demosthenes 57 makes a point of his sad circumstances: his father was a *penēs* who was lotteried to various magistracies (57.25); his mother had made a living selling ribbons in the agora. Of course, he claims, "if we were *plousioi*, we would not sell ribbons or be without means" (*aporoi*: 57.35). He complains that his opponents used the fact that his mother worked for a living in an attempt to disenfranchise him, but the jury, he says, must not expel *penētes* from the citizenship rolls; "their poverty is hard enough" (57.36, cf. 45). Somewhat later in the speech (57.52), he objects to his opponents' claim that he is a rich man (*euporos*) and so had been able to pay witnesses against them; "at the same time they hold against me

---

[42] The father was apparently a private herald who could be hired as needed, rather than a public herald; see Vocke, "Heralds," 264. Cf. Isoc. 18.35; Is. 6.59; Dem. 28.21, 45.85, 48.52–58, 55.35, 57.25.

the shame of my poverty (*penias adoxias*) . . . and say that I am able to buy anything because of my wealth." Yet still later in the speech (57.64), the same speaker mentions that he had dedicated military equipment to Athena. For this service the demesmen honored him with a dedicatory inscription, clear evidence for his relative wealth.[43] Obviously, the profession of poverty earlier in the speech was an exaggeration, and he deliberately shatters the illusion by discussing his dedications.

The wealthy citizens who pretended in court to be poor men were resorting to a dramatic fiction, similar to the "unskilled speaker" fiction discussed above (IV.C.3). The "poor little rich man" fiction also required the collusion of the audience. Many jurors must have known from the beginning that they were listening to a purchased speech delivered by a man of means; others would be apprised of the true situation before the end of the speech. The jurors were not fooled, but they were apparently willing to suspend their disbelief, to grant the rich man the same sort of sympathetic hearing they might grant to a genuinely poor man, if in turn the rich man was willing to assume the role of the poor man threatened by rich opponents. The wealthy litigant who took on the role of the *penēs* brought himself down to the level of the average citizens on the jury. Having humbled himself, he could then claim to share in the communal interests of the masses, interests that were set against those of his wealthy opponents.

The laws of Athens gave the average citizens on the juries of the people's courts a great deal of power over the disposition of disputed property, and the laws of property exchange (*antidosis*) ensured that there would be frequent legal disputes between the richest citizens (cf. above, V.A.3). The upper-class litigant who was willing to take on the role of the poor man symbolically lessened the degree of the power inequity that his wealth produced. He also explicitly allied himself with the masses and demonstrated to the jury that he was sensitive to their concerns and so gave the impression that he was likely to use his wealth in the common interest. His opponent, stranded outside the commonality, is portrayed as a selfish elitist whose interests inhere in his wealth and in his class and whose power threatens the state. The "impoverished" speaker typically (as in Dem. 57) gives away the game before the end of his speech, taking off the mask of the *penēs*, revealing himself (to use the terminology of Dem. 18.320) as a man of means

---

[43] On the wealth status of those honored by deme inscriptions: Whitehead, *Demes*, 237–41. He had also been a demarch, which is not evidence for his upper-class status: ibid., 236.

to even the slower-witted members of the jury. The ideological dissonance implied by the willingness of rich litigants to shatter the fragile
and laboriously constructed illusion of poverty exposes the complex
and internally contradictory nature of Athenian attitudes toward
wealth and the wealthy.

The presence of a positive view of the wealthy in popular ideology
is suggested by a second dramatic fiction, which was based upon flat-
tering the members of the audience by treating them if they were all
quite well off and hence confronted by the problems associated with
meeting financial obligations to the state. Lysias (28.3), for example,
claimed in an Assembly speech that it would be outrageous to allow
those who steal and take bribes to get off at a time when you Athenians yourselves are being weighed down by *eisphora* payments. It
would be especially unjustifiable to be lenient now, since previously,
when both your private domiciles (*oikoi*) and the state revenues were
imposing (*megaloi*), you punished with death those who stole from you.
As suggested above (III.E.1), it is unlikely that more than 5 to 10 percent of the citizen population actually paid the *eisphora*, and most
Athenians certainly never lived in imposing domiciles. The majority
of Lysias' listeners, then, did not fit his description, but this apparently
did not disturb them. Similar comments in forensic speeches, which
impute to the jurors ample means, payment of war taxes, and in general the concerns and worries that wealth brought in its wake, were
fairly common.[44]

These comments must be analyzed in the context of the speaker's
attempt to demonstrate the existence of bonds of mutual interest between himself and his audience. Orators who spoke against the tax
collectors were eager to impress upon their listeners the feeling that
the taxes were used for a common purpose, namely war, and were
therefore a communal concern and responsibility. The people as a
whole, and not only the more limited class actually liable to the tax,
would be hurt by irregularities in collection. The orator attempts to
generate a sense of group solidarity among both richer and poorer
members of the audience vis-à-vis the tax collectors.

But we must also account for Lysias' "big houses" and similar comments which seem to imply that the audience is composed exclusively
of men of means. Since this was not the case (above, III.E.2, 4), the
speaker's treatment of the audience as wealthy can be seen in terms of

[44] E.g., Lys. 28.4, 7; Dem. 1.20, 7.35, 24.111, 160, 198, 28.20, 45.86. Passages of
this sort were taken by Jones, *AD*, 35–37, as evidence of the actual status of Assemblymen and jurors. Cf. the insightful comments of Markle, "Jury Pay," 281–83, 288.

a symbolic elevation in wealth status, the inversion of the "poor little rich man" topos, but with a similar intent. The jurors, who are being treated by the litigant as fellow members of the leisure class, are encouraged to feel sympathy for the genuinely wealthy citizen. Once again, the jurors suspended their disbelief in the interests of blurring the sharp distinction between classes and in the interest of promoting a highly desirable ideological consensus. This fiction could only be maintained if the jurors were, in certain circumstances, willing to look upon the rich in a positive light.

Athenian litigants sometimes implied that private wealth was not really such a bad thing after all. Demosthenes (20.24) argued that a man who owns a great deal (*polla*), but has never done wrong to the people, did not deserve to be slandered. Elsewhere (23.146), Demosthenes praises the collective good judgment of the Athenians who, if asked which group in the polis was most rascally would certainly *not* say the farmers, the rich men (*euporoi*), or mine lessors, but would name the logographers. Demosthenes (58.65) castigates sycophants for regarding both people who do not involve themselves in public affairs and the *plousioi* as their enemies. These somewhat cautious statements imply that jurors need not necessarily regard rich men as their own natural enemies. In certain instances wealth could be associated with public honors. One of Demosthenes' clients (40.24), for example, brings up his grandfather whom he says was "honored by you and [was] the owner of a large fortune."

The interplay between negative and positive aspects of wealth can be seen in two contrasting topoi regarding the influence of wealth on juries. Litigants in Athenian courts quite often castigated the other side in the case for bringing up their opponents' great wealth, arguing that this was an unfair attempt to prejudice the jury.[45] On the surface, this topos further demonstrates the existence of strong negative perceptions of wealth. But if the jurors were known to react in a consistently negative fashion to rich litigants, why would a litigant want to call attention to his own wealth by accusing his opponent of using it as a covert attempt to discredit him? At the very least, this topos shows that Athenian jurors were aware of their tendency to be influenced by negative depictions of individual wealth and were willing to be reminded that this was not a just argument.

We may contrast the topos of "my opponent is unfairly using my wealth to discredit me" with Athenian litigants' injunctions to jurors

---

[45] E.g., Isoc. 15.4–5, 31; Is. 6.59, 11.38; Hyp. 4.32 (a particularly good example of the topos); Dem. 22.42, 27.53, 57, 29.49, 37.52.

not to allow themselves to be unduly impressed by the wealth on the
opposing side. Ps-Lysias (6.48), for example, says that Andocides is
powerful because of his wealth and predicts that Andocides will boast
of it in court, since he knows the jurors' habits. Demosthenes (21.2,
159, 214–15) professes to fear that the jurors will be misled by their
innate respect for Meidias' huge fortune. Again, the topos cuts two
ways. On the one hand, it can be read as an egalitarian appeal not to
let wealth have an undue influence upon legal deliberations. On the
other hand, it implies that the jurors could be influenced into voting
in favor of an upper-class litigant on the basis of their positive perceptions of his wealth. Both topoi appeal to the jurors not to let wealth
influence them, and both therefore assume that jurors could be
swayed by arguments that played not only upon negative but also
upon positive feelings toward the rich. Both, therefore, imply a deep
tension within the Athenian ideology of wealth.

E. *Charis*: Private Generosity and Public Gratitude

The orators who call upon jurors not to be positively influenced by the
wealth of their opponents do not typically argue that it is wrong in
principle to be impressed by wealth, but rather that it is wrong to be
impressed in this particular instance, since their opponents' wealth
had not been used for the good of the state.[46] Implicit in this argument is the counter-assumption that jurors should be positively influenced by wealth that *was* used for the common advantage. The rich
man's ability and willingness to contribute to the state and the sense of
gratitude the recipients (viz., the demos) felt toward the donor were
primary sources of the positive impressions which interacted with the
negative impressions of wealth to produce a constant tension within
the ideology of wealth—and the rhetorical topoi to exploit and
thereby illuminate that tension.

Rich litigants commonly pointed to the material benefits they and
their ancestors had conferred upon the state. Some individuals used
up much of the water in their clocks reciting lengthy and detailed lists
of liturgies they had performed.[47] Others pointed out to juries that
their liturgies had entailed considerable personal sacrifice and that the
benefactions had been in excess of what would normally be expected

[46] E.g., Dem. 21.158–59, 38.25; Lyc. 1.139.
[47] E.g., Is. 5.41–42, 6.60; Lys. 21.1–10; Ant. 2.2.12; for other examples, see
Dover, *GPM*, 176–77; Markle, "Jury Pay," 285, 287. On the general question of
liturgies and aristocratic ostentation, see Adkins, *Moral Values*, 119–25.

from an estate of a certain size.[48] Litigants who spent part of their limited speaking time discussing their liturgies obviously expected to evoke a positive response from the jurors. The performance of liturgies was one way that the wealthy individual might hope to deflect the natural envy of the poor. Isaeus (6.61; cf. Lys. 21.15) states explicitly that since his clients had performed liturgies it is not proper that they should be envied (*phthoneisthai*); in addition, he suggests that if the judgment goes in their favor, they will be even more eager to pay up in the future.

Athenian juries judged the worth of a litigant's liturgies not only quantitatively but also on the basis of the spirit in which they had been performed. In order to elicit the desired positive response, benefactions had to be given in the interests of the demos. Demosthenes (28.19–20) pointed out that his father had performed many liturgies and that he himself planned to do the same if victorious in the trial against his guardians. Demosthenes begs the jurors to save him for the sake of justice, for his own sake, and "for your own sakes as well."[49] Demosthenes is eager to show his audience that his personal interest is identical to their collective interest and that he will be just as patriotic a member of the liturgical class as his father before him.

In describing his performance of a trierarchy, Apollodorus ([Dem.] 50.2, 7–23) makes much of the fact that he had provided his own equipment, rather than taking the state-provided equipment for the ship, and he emphasizes that he paid his crews a lavish salary. This was a splendid display of wealth, but was it in the best interests of the state? Apollodorus' opponent in the trial, who had taken over the ship from him, was, we are told, irritated at Apollodorus' largess, which he claimed made the crews of other ships unruly. He also implied that Apollodorus surpassed everyone else in wealth, since "he alone" is able to make such a display (50.34–35). It appears that Apollodorus' opponent was trying to employ the familiar tactic of excluding his opponent from the common ground of the group, and one might wonder why Apollodorus himself uses up precious time repeating this seemingly damning attack upon himself. But as it turns out, Apollodorus has set up a straw man which he demolishes by demonstrating that the liturgy had been in the common interest: if my opponent says my pay rate has corrupted the crews, let him get crewmen who are willing to row without pay (50.36). Clearly the jurors, some of whom had probably rowed the triremes themselves, are to be impressed with

---

[48] E.g., Lys. 7.31; Dem. 42.23; Hyp. 1.16; Isoc. 18.63.
[49] Cf. Lys. 18.20–21; Dem. 21.101, 185; Lyc. 1.139.

Apollodorus' spectacular performance of the liturgy and also by his generous treatment of the men who had served under him. His opponent is shown to have taken up the liturgy without eagerness and under duress (especially 50.24–33) and also is made out to be the sort of cold-hearted, tight-fisted elite who regards demands by rowers for fair wages as unruliness.

Wealthy donors who had given generously to the state were in turn entitled to a certain consideration from their fellows. Litigants, then, quite naturally asked jurors to take into consideration the good things they had done for the state in the past and would be likely to do in the future.[50] The performers of liturgies who mentioned their contributions in court hoped that the common people would feel a sense of gratitude (*charis*) for service rendered them. Indeed, the hope for gratitude from the demos and especially from jurors was the motive behind many liturgists' acts of public generosity to the state, and some of them were not reticent about admitting it. Lysias' client (25.12–13), for example, states plainly that he had undertaken liturgies so that he would be thought better of by "you jurors" if he were ever summoned to court (cf. Lys. 18.23, 20.31, 21.15). Notably, these assertions were not made apologetically and were evidently not taken as evidence that the individual in question had given in the wrong spirit. The litigant who emphasized that his past benefactions had been a conscious attempt to win the people's goodwill showed himself to be sensitive to popular attitudes and properly respectful of the masses' legal and ideological power over himself as an individual. The notion that jurors would naturally feel gratitude toward those who gave money to the state was never disputed or denounced in principle by any of the orators, although, as we have seen, they frequently argued that gratitude should be denied anyone who did not perform his proper duties to the state or who only gave reluctantly.

The Athenian concept of *charis*, the gratitude felt by the recipient of a benefaction, was complex and seems to have overtones of what in Roman culture was formalized into the relationship between patron and client.[51] Like the ties between patron and client in Rome, the

---

[50] E.g., Lys. 3.47, 21.11–14; cf. Dem. 22.62. Gabrielsen, "ΦΑΝΕΡΑ," 112, points out that due to the ease of hiding property, "liturgical expediture remained in a sense optional with corresponding rewards of honours as an important element to attract volunteers."

[51] Aristotle (*Rhet.* 1385a16–b10) offers a succinct discussion of *charis* and its uses in rhetoric. On the evolution of the meaning of *charis* and associated terms, from Homer to ca. 400 B.C., see J. W. Hewitt, "The Terminology of 'Gratitude' in Greek," *CPh* 22 (1927): 142–61; cf. J. T. Hooker, "Χάρις and ἀρετή in Thucydides," *Hermes*

Athenian *charis* relationship probably had its origins in arrangements between individuals or families. In the sixth and early fifth centuries, these private arrangements were part of a general pattern of deference by the common citizens to elites, and they appear to have constituted one of the bases of political influence (above, II.B–F.3). Even in the fourth century, litigants made note of their gifts to poorer citizens. The father of one of Lysias' clients (19.59) spent his money on state liturgies, for dowries of poor citizens' daughters, for ransoming of prisoners of war, and for funerals. He did this, his son's audience is told, because it was the right thing for a noble man (*anēr agathos*) to do.[52] Andocides (1.147) reminded the jurors that his family home had always been open (*koinotatē*) to those in need. Both Lysias' client and Andocides ask for the jurors' *charis* for both private and public benefactions. Gifts to the state in the form of liturgies and the sense of gratitude jurors would feel for the good done the state can therefore be seen as an elaboration at a national level of a giver/recipient relationship between individuals, a relationship that continued to function alongside the system of state liturgies.

In classical Athens, the interaction between giver and recipient never developed into a formal system of patronage on the Roman model, but the Athenian relationship based on *charis* was overt nonetheless. The individual who had received a gift owed his benefactor not mere thanks but a favor in return. The benefactor could legitimately demand that the return favor be rendered. With the institutionalization at a national level of the *charis* relationship into the system of liturgies there were some changes; especially important was the introduction of the idea that the corporate recipients had the right to judge the spirit in which the gift was given. Yet the essential concept of the recipient's duty to repay the donor was retained. Thus, litigants who had performed remarkable liturgies could not merely request but also demand the jurors' sympathy.[53] This demand was apparently re-

---

102 (1974): 164–69, esp. 167–68. For the religious background of *charis* and the association of the personified Charites with democracy, see J. H. Oliver, *Demokratia, the Gods, and the Free World* (Baltimore, 1960), 91–120. On Roman patron-client relations, see Saller, *Personal Patronage*, esp. 7–39, 69–78.

52 Cf. [Dem.] 59.72 (financial support of a poor man lotteried as *basileus*); Lys. 16.14, 31.15, 19 (hoplite equipment); Dem. 57.25 (from *sungeneis* to the father of the litigant); Dem. 18.311 (an attack on Aeschines for not giving to the poor). Cf. above, V.B.3. The continued importance of leasing and tenant/sharecropping in rural areas, demonstrated by Wood, "Agricultural Slavery," 21–31, would have helped to maintain the symbolic power of private benefaction.

53 E.g., Lys. 21.17, 25; Isoc. 18.66–67; Is. 7.41. On the implications of judicial *charis* in Athens, cf. esp. Whitehead, "Competitive Outlay"; and Davies, *WPW*, 92–

garded as perfectly just by both sides; even litigants who argue against a particular opponent's right to the *charis* of the jury admit the justice of the notion of judicial *charis* in general.[54]

The sense of *charis* the demos felt toward the wealthy performers of liturgies provided a counterweight to the negative responses to the symbols of wealth considered above. Rich litigants could use monetary donation to the state to "buy off" the resentment that their wealth, power, and privileges naturally aroused among the less well-to-do jurors. The *charis* relationship provided a way for the upper classes to purchase insurance against the threat of social revolution and so to preserve the greater part of their property. It also helped to maintain mass acceptance of the general validity of unequal wealth distribution.

F. Politicians and the Ideology of Wealth

For many upper-class *idiōtai*—those who were patriotic enough to do their duty to the state but interested in being left alone to enjoy their property when the state did not require their services—the gratitude of the jurors was quite sufficient. Fearing indictment arising from a property dispute, such men would perform enough liturgies to balance the negative perceptions their wealth had engendered, but judicial *charis* in private suits (or perhaps in a magisterial *dokimasia* [scrutiny] or *euthunai* [review]) was the most they expected their benefactions to gain for them.[55] For wealthy rhetores, however, judicial *charis* in private suits, though important, was not enough. The politically ambitious Athenian desired not only the jurors' gratitude when he was forced to go to court to defend his property but also the respect and honor of his fellow citizens in the major arenas of political debate and decision. The fourth-century Athenian political orator was certainly aware of the contradictory views of wealth that pertained among the demos. Appeal to the ideology of wealth was a powerful rhetorical tool, but the interplay of resentment and gratitude made its

---

95, who claims (92) that it was a "determining factor in assessing the part which property-power could play in public affairs." See also Gabrielsen, *Remuneration*, 127–28; Jones, *AD*, 56–57. I cannot agree with Carter, *Quiet Athenian*, 189–90, that wealthy jurors took a "conciliatory and pleading" tone or that they "adopted . . . an un-Athenian attitude" in supplicating the jury.

54 E.g., Dem. 21.160, 38.25, 42.25; Ant. 2.3.8.

55 Isocrates (15.150–52), for example, stresses his desire to be left alone to lead a quiet life. Lysias' client (7.31–32) notes that although he had performed more liturgies than necessary, even if he had done only what was required and without zeal, he would be no worse than any other citizen.

use dangerous; there was always the chance that the tool would turn in his hand.

F.1 LITURGIES AND *Charis*

Discussion of his personal benefactions to the state was perhaps the safest way for the politician to use the ideology of wealth in his own favor. The expert political orator of the fourth century tended to demonstrate his desire for public honor and respect (*philotimia*) rather more prosaically than Alcibiades had been wont to do.[56] The great displays of the previous century might now be considered ostentatious and even otiose. Fourth-century Athenians were in need of more practical gifts, as Lycurgus (1.140) noted when he stated that horse breeding, choral production, and similar displays of private wealth were unworthy of the demos' *charis*, since the donor alone was crowned. According to Lycurgus, only he who performed a spectacular trierarchy, built walls for the state, or gave money to secure the safety of the community should be granted the people's special respect.[57] Even if he did not have the incentive to imitate Alcibiades, though, the ambitious and wealthy aspirant to a political career had many opportunities to demonstrate his worthiness by public donations. Demosthenes, in particular, made much of his liturgies, voluntary contributions, and public-spirited gifts to needy individuals.[58]

Like the rich *idiōtēs*, the rhetor who gave generously to the state clearly expected a return for his largess. The politician involved in public trials was frequently in need of the citizens' *charis*. In defense of his acceptance of the honorary crown he had earned by serving as wall-builder, Demosthenes reminded his jury of the *charis* that had been rendered to other magistrates who had contributed military equipment. He stated that his gift of money for the rebuilding of the city walls was worthy of the Athenians' *charis* and their thanks (*epainos*); thus, he fully deserved his crown (18.113–15). Later in the speech, Demosthenes stated that although he did not feel that a benefactor should dwell on his generosity, the recipient should always remember it (18.268–69). The politician might also remind the demos

---

[56] Alcibiades: Thuc. 6.16.1–4; cf. Davies, *WPW*, 97–98.

[57] Lycurgus is deliberately extreme in his rejection of all non-military liturgies. Certainly fourth-century litigants expected *charis* for serving as *chorēgos* and in some cases felt that bringing up their horse raising and athletic victories would gain the jurors' respect. See, for example, Hyp. 1.16; Isoc. 16.33; Lys. 19.63.

[58] To the state: Dem. 18.99, 257, 19.343, 21.154–57; to private citizens: 18.268–69, 19.230. On the political nature of politicians' bragging about their liturgies, cf. Finley, *PAW*, 37.

of his donations when he spoke in the Assembly. Demosthenes (8.70–71) declined to speak at length of his "trierarchies, *chorēgiai, eisphora* contributions, ransoming of citizens captured in war, and other instances of philanthropy," but the point was made by the time he had finished listing the things he would not discuss. Meidias, according to Demosthenes (21.153), bored the demos by harping on his liturgies at every meeting of the Assembly, yet apparently the people had allowed Meidias to go on about them. Meidias in turn had felt that prefacing his remarks with a few choice comments regarding his liturgical services would be to his advantage.

The Athenian public seems to have expected politicians to perform significant liturgies. According to Lysias (27.10), it was the duty of the "good demagogue" to donate money to the state. Consequently, if one's political opponent did not voluntarily give money when the state had need of it, his failure to do so could be used against him. Demosthenes (18.312) claims that Aeschines, who had plenty of money, contributed nothing to the special levy after the defeat at Chaeronea in 338, although all the other rhetores had given.[59] If one's opponent did give money to the state, he could be accused of having done so only when compelled (e.g., Dem. 21.154, 156) or having given much less than he should have (e.g., Din. 1.21, 69). Such grudging contributions were not enough to gain judicial *charis* for an *idiōtēs*; clearly, they were unworthy of the respect and honor the politician hoped his fellow citizens would feel was his due.

In order to maximize the return (in terms of respect and *charis*) from his expenditures for the common good, the orator had to speak of his liturgical services in public and so demonstrate to the demos his membership in the class of the wealthiest Athenians. That membership was a double-edged sword; the political orator who overplayed his wealth risked arousing the resentment of the poorer members of his audience. His opponents were always ready to fan a spark of resentment into flame by exaggerating his wealth and attributing to him the irritating arrogance and luxuriousness of the most ostentatious rich men in the city. This was obviously Demosthenes' strategy in the speech *Against Meidias*, but Demosthenes himself was subject to the same sort of criticism. Aeschines (3.240) attacked Demosthenes by saying, "You are a rich man (*plouteis*), and you serve as *chorēgos* to your own hedonistic pleasures" (*hēdonais tais sautou chorēgeis*). The sarcastic use of the term *chorēgos* is surely intended to remind the jurors of Demosthenes' obnoxious boasting about liturgies. Hyperides (5.17)

---

[59] Cf. Dem. 19.282; Aesch. 3.240.

claimed Demosthenes used his ill-gotten gains to engage in usurious nautical loans and house buying. Dinarchus notes Demosthenes' huge fortune (1.21, 69) and paints a picture of his opponent's luxuriousness that is worthy of the master's own speech against Meidias. According to Dinarchus, Alexander's absence in India made possible an Athenian revolt against the Macedonians, but Demosthenes wasted the opportunity and lived in luxury at the time of the polis' misfortunes, traveling in a litter down the road from the city to Piraeus and reproaching the *penētes* for their poverty (1.36).

Athenian politicians recognized the danger of being made out to be arrogant, wealthy cads. Although the offense that sparked the action had occurred when he was serving as *chorēgos*, Demosthenes portrayed himself as a simple hoplite in the speech *Against Meidias* (21.133). He limited his description of his fine upbringing and career in *On the Crown* (18.258) in order, as he says, "to guard against giving offense." Aeschines (3.218) made a point of his own moderate style of life: "A little [money] is sufficient for me, and I do not shamefully lust for more." Thus, Aeschines claims, he was able to speak or remain silent according to his own deliberations and was not constrained to speak impulsively in order to gain pay (in the form of bribes) to satisfy his lusts.

F.2 POVERTY AS A REPROACH: THE EVILS OF SUDDEN WEALTH

The political orators claimed to be moderate in their personal needs and habits, but they never attempted to elaborate a fiction of personal poverty along the lines of the "poor little rich man" topos used by *idiōtai* in private cases. The politicians quite clearly did not want to be perceived as poor.[60] Despite his protestations of modesty and eagerness to avoid giving offense in *On the Crown*, Demosthenes (e.g., 18.257, 265) is at pains to show that he is a man of substance. He specifically contrasts his comfortable background with that of Aeschines, whom Demosthenes publicly castigated for his family's lack of means. Aeschines, Demosthenes' audience was told (18.258), had been

[60] Adkins, "Problems," 154–55, cites Aristophanes (*Knights* 185ff.) to show that lower-class origins were certainly not an advantage to an aspiring politician in the late fifth century. Andocides' (1.144) claim that he was once a man of wealth but through the city's disasters came to be completely impoverished (*eis penian pollēn kai aporian*) is not really an exception to the rule, since it can be seen as a demonstration that his interests are identical to those of the city. Cf. Isoc. 15.161, Aesch. 2.147, and Lys. 20.33 for other claims of having lost the family fortune due to the disasters of the Peloponnesian War.

raised in abject poverty (*meta pollēs endeias etraphēs*). As a child he had
worked as a cultic initiator, paid with a ration of buns and cakes
(18.259–60), and later, as an actor in the theater, he had eked out a
living by subsisting on food thrown at him by his audience (18.262, cf.
19.200). As an undersecretary (*hupogrammateus*) for the magistrates, he
earned a modest salary of two or three drachmas per day, "being a
rascal" (19.200).

As in the case of his enumeration of his own liturgies, Demosthenes
prefaces his most vicious attack upon Aeschines' poverty-stricken
youth with a disclaimer, praying that no one think him cold-hearted
and claiming that "I for my own part do not judge it wise for anyone
to speak abusively of poverty (*penian propēlakizei*), nor, if someone is
brought up free from want (*en aphthonois*) do I regard it as something
to be proud of" (*semnunetai*: 18.256). But just a few sentences later
(18.258), Demosthenes states that he *is* proud of his upbringing (*sem-
nunomai*). He clearly expected his audience, the majority of whom
were much closer to the standard of living with which he reproaches
Aeschines, to scorn his opponent's humble past and to respect Demosthenes himself for having grown up in comfortable circumstances. Demosthenes emphasizes the contrast by asking the jurors to decide for
themselves whose personal fortune (*tuchē*) they would prefer for themselves, Aeschines' or his own.

Despite his obvious nervousness about bringing down upon himself
the opprobrium due the insolent rich man, Demosthenes hoped that
the jurors would perceive him as a wealthy man and worthy because
of his wealth, and Aeschines as originally poor and hence unworthy.
Demosthenes' attack on Aeschines' poverty and praise of his own
wealth, like his comments on their respective educations (above, IV.E),
seems to challenge the view that Athenian political ideology was based
primarily on egalitarian ideals.[61] Demosthenes was not the only orator
to deride the impoverished past of a political adversary. Aeschines was
unable to deny Demosthenes his comfortable childhood, but he stated
that Demosthenes was forced to turn to speech writing in order to
make a living after having shamefully squandered his patrimony
(3.173). Dinarchus (1.111) makes a similar point. Athenian political
orators commonly claimed that their opponents had begun life as *pe-*

---

[61] Perlman, "Politicians," 335 with n. 40, notes that Demosthenes' attack on Aeschines shows that according to Athenian opinion, politicians ought to be economically independent. Dover, *GPM*, 34–35, used Dem. 18.265 (among other passages)
in arguing (albeit cautiously) that the majority of jurors were probably "fairly prosperous," but Adkins, "Problems," 156, points out the error of this reading.

nētes, or even as paupers (*ptōchoi*), and that they only recently had become *plousioi*.[62]

Several explanations may be advanced for the popularity of the "impoverished youth/sudden wealth" topos. Basic to the topos was the assumption that since they had started with nothing, the newly wealthy politicians must have accrued their wealth dishonestly. Some were accused of war profiteering (e.g., Lys. 28.2; Aesch. 2.79).[63] This was potentially a very serious charge against a politician, since it implied that he had spoken in favor of going to war—a condition which put the citizen-soldiers and the state as a whole in danger—merely in order to create an opportunity in which he could make a personal fortune. Advocating public policy for personal enrichment was obviously a perversion of the expert orator's political role.

Other newly rich individuals were accused of having made their fortunes by acting as sycophants in the courts (cf. above, iv.c.2). Isocrates (21.5, cf. 21.9) claims that "everyone knows" that sycophants are "those who are clever speakers but own nothing." Lysias (25.26, 30) accused the suddenly rich sycophants of 403 B.C. of imitating the methods of the recently deposed Thirty Tyrants. Demosthenes (58.63) also makes a point of the lower-class origins of the sycophants who were presently rich (*euporountes*). These men, he claims, felt no *charis* toward the Athenians, but they went around saying that the demos was hard-hearted and without *charis* toward themselves, "as if you [Athenians] became rich because of them, rather then they from the demos." Demosthenes obviously expected his audience to assume that since the sycophants made their living by depending on the good graces of the demos, they should certainly be willing to render the demos a proper degree of *charis*.

Rapid upward economic mobility furthermore led individuals to put on unsuitable airs. Aristotle (*Rhet.* 1387a21–26) notes that the *nouveaux riches* who hold public positions of responsibility (*archontes*) because of their wealth are more annoying than persons holding similar positions who are members of old wealthy families, since the latter seem to possess what naturally belongs to them, while the former do not. Demosthenes (19.314) mocked Aeschines not only for his long cloak but also for his pretensions to being a gentleman-farmer and a

[62] Examples of the *penēs* to *plousios* topos: Lys. 18.18, 25.26, 30, 28.1–2, 4, 7, 29.4, 30.28; Dem. 19.146, 147, 23.209, 24.124; Isoc. 8.125, 127; Din. 1.111. Cf. Harvey, "*Dona Ferentes*," 80.

[63] War profiteering: cf. Aristoph. *Peace* 441f. with Ehrenberg, *People of Aristophanes*, 119–20. Sommerstein, "Aristophanes," 315, points out the stress in the *Plutus* on the idea that the only way to become wealthy is through crime.

notable. Demosthenes claims in the same passage that before Aeschines' sudden accession of wealth (as a result of bribes from Philip), Aeschines had freely admitted that he had formerly served as a clerk. He had been willing to render *charis* to the people for his election to ambassadorships and had acted moderately. But now Aeschines claims that those who speak of "Aeschines the clerk" foully insulted him. In another public speech (24.124), Demosthenes told the jurors that the rhetores who had ascended to wealth from poverty at the public expense bad-mouthed the people at private gatherings. According to Demosthenes, just as in the case of manumitted slaves who never render proper *charis* to their former masters but hate more than anyone else those who remembered their former servitude, the rhetores berate the masses who remember the habits of their poverty-stricken youths. In both passages Demosthenes argues that the sudden accession of wealth has made the recipient politicians gratingly and unsuitably arrogant, which coincides with Aristotle's comment in the *Rhetoric* on the perception of the newly wealthy. In both 19.314 and 24.124 Demosthenes refers to *charis*. The implication is that Demosthenes' newly rich political opponents are particularly evil since they do not render the *charis* they owe to the masses. In the case of the rhetores referred to in speech 24, Demosthenes attributes this failure to the nature of the individuals in question who have the habits of "rascally, shame-filled slaves," rather than of free men who would be expected to recognize their *charis* obligations and to fulfill them. In Aeschines' case, Demosthenes claims that the *charis* his opponent had once quite properly felt for the demos had been obviated by Philip's bribes. Demosthenes makes the identical point in his other major speech against Aeschines (18.131), when he states that Aeschines is utterly lacking in *charis* and is a *ponēros* since, although he was made a free man from a slave and a rich man from a pauper "by these men here" (the demos), he still took money to work plots against the people.

F.3 BRIBERY

Bribery was perhaps the most obvious way a poor Athenian could become rich quickly, and Athenian politicians were continually accusing one another of having been bribed.[64] Bribery was naturally related to *charis*; the verb *charizō* could be used in a negative sense to mean "to offer a bribe" (e.g., Dem. 8.71). Bribery was functionally very similar to more legitimate gift giving. The rich man gave money to poorer

---

[64] E.g., Dem. 18.114, 19.343; Din. 1.42; Aesch. 3.259. Cf. Harvey, "*Dona Ferentes*"; IV.E and VII.F.2, with literature cited.

individuals and to the state to secure goodwill, which might ultimately mean a vote in his favor in court. So too the individual who gave money to a politician expected to secure his goodwill and good offices in public forums. The bribed politician owed *charis* to the man who gave him money, just as the soldier who was given military equipment by his wealthier demesman or the demos who received a liturgy owed *charis* to the individual who gave the gift. This situation was obviously pernicious if the bribes in question were accepted by politicians who frequently advised the Assembly on public policy. As Hyperides (5.24) noted, it was one thing if an *idiotes* took someone's money in order to guard it but quite another when a rhetor took money "with some policy in mind."

The rhetor's acceptance of a bribe from an individual or an interest group interfered with the special relationship between expert speaker and mass audience. At the very least, the bribed politician's independence in terms of public speech was limited by the *charis* he owed to his benefactor. In the worst case, the bribe-taker was completely alienated from the interests of his state. The politician who took bribes from the state's enemies benefited from the state's sufferings (e.g., Dem. 19.146–47). Ultimately the bribe-taker would become completely corrupted and would reject the democratic institutions he had betrayed and no longer needed. Demosthenes (19.314) says that Aeschines went about in his long cloak, displaying himself as one of Philip's special representatives (*xenoi*) and close friends (*philoi*), one of those who want to overthow the demos, who consider the democracy "a mere wave and a momentary madness." This, says Demosthenes in outrage, is the very man who was formally a servant in the public offices!

The origin of the politician's willingness to be bribed was his desire for money. Since few Athenians could conceive of a poor man who did not desire to become rich (e.g., Aristoph. *Plutus* 188–97), most naturally assumed that the poor politician would be tempted to take a bribe in order to enrich himself.[65] Demosthenes (29.22) confidently asserts that his audience must agree that poverty (*aporia*) is a primary motive of individuals who accept bribes in return for lying at trials. The rhetor easily made the leap from "if poor, then bribable" to "if suddenly rich, then bribed" to "if bribed, then traitor." The argument

[65] Cf. Aristot. *Pol.* 1270b9 (bribability of poor Spartans). Notably, the Athenians never developed a topos of the "unbribable poor man" which was a mainstay of the Roman ideology of wealth; cf. the story of Curius Dentatus, told by Plutarch (*Cato* 2). The notion that the poor were particularly susceptible to bribes was also common in colonial Massachusetts: Zuckerman, "Social Context," 532.

leads to the conclusion that "if a politician was once poor, *ergo* he is a traitor." This chain of reasoning helps to explain a good many of the instances of the "impoverished youth/sudden wealth" topos. It was based upon and also helped to reinforce the negative impression Athenians had of upward economic mobility, at least among politicians.

One possible way out of the "poor *ergo* traitor" trap was for the politician to show that he cared more for the good of the state than for his private enrichment. Perhaps some Athenian politicians really did hold this view, but incorruptibility by means of high principles was difficult to demonstrate and equally difficult for members of a society in which gifts and *charis* played such a large part to believe. The other way out was for the politician to demonstrate that he was well enough off so as not to need bribes. This is the import of Aeschines' comment (3.218, cited above v.f.1) that he had sufficient resources not to be constrained to take money in order to satisfy his needs. Of course, the possession of wealth did not ensure incorruptibility, but the Athenians felt that it *should* do so. Dinarchus (3.18) castigated Philocrates, who had much property and no male children and lacked nothing that a moderate man might require, yet nonetheless allowed himself to be bribed to speak in support of those who opposed the best interests of his homeland.

F.4 JUSTIFIABLE PRIDE IN WEALTH

The politician who possessed a sufficiency of personal wealth was at least theoretically freed from the need to take money from those whose interests were at variance with the interests of the demos. The notion that men without capital were likely to accept bribes helps to explain why Athenian politicians would be cautious about depicting themselves in public speeches as poor men. It also helps to explain some of the seemingly elitist attacks on the impoverished backgrounds of rival politicians. A proclivity toward bribe taking was, however, only one of the various constraints upon the poor man, each of which was deemed unsuitable for the politician.

Poverty limited the sphere of the citizen's legal and political action and made him susceptible to the awe that wealth could inspire in the poor.[66] The rich man enjoyed the practical legal and political advan-

[66] The constraints of poverty are mentioned by, for example, Lys. 7.14 (the accused cannot show I was driven by poverty to commit the crime), 31.12 (necessity of forgiving the poor who do wrong involuntarily); Dem. 21.141 (poverty is one of the stock excuses for failing to defend oneself in the courts); Isoc. 7.44–45 (Athenian ancestors turned the poor to farming and trade, because they realized that

tages that derived directly from his possession of wealth, and, whether they liked it or not, the Athenians recognized this fact. The rhetor, part of whose role in society was to serve as the protector of the demos (e.g., Aesch. 3.250–51; cf. IV.E, VII.E.2), could only fulfill this adequately if he were the functional equal of the most powerful, which meant the most wealthy, men in the polis. The perceived necessity of owning wealth for anyone who hoped to face the rich offender on equal terms is demonstrated by Demosthenes' comments in *Against Meidias*. Despite the savage attacks on the privileges of the rich in that speech, Demosthenes is at pains to point out (21.111; cf. [Dem.] 53.1–2) that he himself is "not among those who are without friends (*erēmotatōn*) nor among those without resources (*aporōn*)." Demosthenes also implies that while his interests are identical to those of the masses, his economic position gives him a certain protection against the hubristic rich man: "It was not I alone who was wronged, but all others, who may be supposed to be less able to get justice than I . . ." (21.219). The good politician is one who uses his relative immunity not only for his own protection but also to help the people to humble the wealthy man who has stepped out of line. "I myself, or someone else" may have escaped Meidias' attack, "but what will you the masses do if you [jurors] do not by public example make it dangerous for anyone to use his wealth for such purposes?" (21.124).

Two of the rhetor's primary roles—giving advice in the Assembly and prosecuting individuals who threatened the state at public trials—could therefore be properly fulfilled only if he were a man of considerable means. In order that he might have a chance to gain the public trust, the rhetor had to be allowed to display evidence of his wealth. The special place occupied by the rhetores in the democracy therefore required that their public behavior be judged by a modified standard. Just as the rhetor had to prove that he was a good speaker, while the *idiōtēs* might resort to the fiction of claiming that he was unable to speak well (IV.E), the rhetor had to satisfy his audience that he was a man of means, and he could not, as the *idiōtēs* might, hope for sympathy for his poverty.

The unique relationship between a politician's role in the state and his personal wealth explains an otherwise jarring aspect of Demosthenes' description of his great moment following Philip's capture of Elatea in 339. Demosthenes (18.170–72) says that when "the common voice of the homeland" called for some man to speak for his country's

poverty leads to idleness and evildoing). For other examples, see Dover, *GPM*, 109–10.

salvation, more than mere patriotism was needed. If patriotism alone had sufficed, every Athenian citizen would have come to the bema. If the call had been to the wealthy, he continues, the Three Hundred (liturgy payers) would have come forward. If the call had gone out to those who were both wealthy and patriotic, those who later gave great amounts to the special levy after the battle of Chaeronea would have come forward. But "the call was for a man who was not only patriotic and wealthy" (*ou monon eunoun kai plousion andr'ekalei*) but who also had studied Philip carefully (cf. IV.E). Demosthenes states that at that moment it had not been *enough* to be patriotic and wealthy, but he clearly implies that both patriotism and wealth were the preconditions that had to be fulfilled before the final condition (which he alone satisfied) could be imposed. Patriotism was an egalitarian virtue; Demosthenes specifically describes it as a common possession of the demos (cf. VI.C.1). Wealth, on the other hand, was the possession of an elite. The orator, in order to serve the needs of the state, must share the patriotic interests of the masses, but he must also have access to the privileges and immunities that were recognized by his audience as the unique prerogatives of the wealth elite.

G. Control of Economic Inequality by Political Equals

The existence of economic inequalities created considerable tension in Athens. The demos needed the rich men, since with the loss of the empire the democracy was able to function only by taxing their surplus wealth. The wealthy in turn knew that the state was run out of their pocketbooks; they expected to be, and indeed were, allowed to retain certain social privileges in compensation for their cash outlay. The recognition that the rich were privileged inevitably led to a sense of resentment among the masses, whose dominant ideology stressed political and legal equality. Clearly, if the advantages enjoyed by the rich got out of hand, democracy would end. The power of the majority, acting in concerted defense of their interests, had to limit the dangerous accretion of power to the rich citizens. Demosthenes stresses this necessity in *Against Meidias* when he states that

> all of this [evidence for Meidias' wealth and power] is terrifying to each of the rest of you depending on the extent of your own individual fortunes. This is why you band together (*sullegesth' humeis*, viz., as jurors in court), since while individually you are weaker [than the rich] in terms of supporters or wealth or any-

thing else, assembled together you are more powerful (*kreittous*) than any one of them and able to put a halt to their hubris. (21.140)

But the demos could not exercise its collective legal power fully, for fear of alienating the wealth elite completely. If every rich man who came before a popular jury was convicted, the upper classes would no longer have any commonality of interest (*homonoia*, cf. Hyp. 4.37; Lys. 25.30; below, vii.B) with the poor. The result of such polarization would be disastrous; both leisured and laboring citizens recognized that open class warfare would destroy the state. The tension between rich and poor in Athens was consequently mediated through various symbolic means, at the level of ideology. Among these means were mutually accepted fictions. The rich man who assumed the role of a poor man gained the sympathy of the jurors by his demonstration of humility and his recognition of the legitimacy of communal concerns. Alternatively, the rich litigant who cast his jury in the role of fellow elites might persuade them to see his problems and concerns in a new light.[67] Both fictions had the effect of leveling the inequalities between the citizens and allowing the poorer majority temporarily to regard their wealthy fellow citizens as equals whose interests were identical to those of the common citizens.

The processes of wealth redistribution through taxation of the rich lessened the threat of social revolution but also created a certain amount of friction between the upper and lower classes. The wealthy individual was interested in retaining his wealth; the demos was interested in having him contribute a substantial portion of it to the state. The tendency for liturgies to become state-mandated rather than remaining voluntary has sometimes been seen as evidence for the alienation of the rich from the masses.[68] The imposition of forced liturgies upon the rich might, however, be seen in another light, as a democratization of the donation system. As long as liturgies were voluntary, the state had little effective control over the donors, since all voluntary donors would expect *charis* from the demos when they gave money to

[67] This tactic has much in common with the remarkably effective technique of reversed role playing used by some professional mediators to get disputants to come to grips with the other side's position (e.g., an oil company executive might be asked by the mediator to give a speech outlining an environmentalist's concerns about a proposed oil field near a wilderness area): L. Susskind and J. Cruikshank, *Breaking the Impasse: Consensual Approaches to Resolving Public Disputes* (New York, 1988), 154–55.

[68] See, for example, Andreades, *History*, 131–33, 293; cf. the studies cited above, v.A.3.

the state. When liturgies were made regular and were legally required, however, the demos obtained effective control over at least part of every very rich man's property. The individual who gave only what was demanded by the state, and then grudgingly, was not deserving of the demos' *charis*. By making *charis* more difficult to obtain, forced liturgies shifted the balance of wealth-power in the favor of the masses.

The legal mechanisms, which had to be elaborated as more liturgies became required, were also to the benefit of the masses. The process of *antidosis* pitted rich man against rich man with a popular jury arbitrating the outcome. The *antidosis* procedure had the double effect of discouraging class solidarity within the ranks of the wealth elite and of making the demos the controller of the fate of major fortunes. The importance of the demos' control over disputed property is demonstrated by the inclusion of the topic of property claims, along with such topics as state defense and the grain supply, on the standing agenda of the ten annual principal meetings of the Assembly (*AP* 43.4). The victor in a property trial owed his right to retain his property (or to seize the property of an enemy) to the demos. He therefore owed *charis* to the demos and could be expected to pay back the favor shown him. Isaeus' client (5.37; cf. Dem. 28.24) states explicitly that one who got his fortune by having received a favorable verdict from a jury was thereby duty bound to act generously (*eu poiein*) to the polis. Of course, the successful litigant may have secured his victory in court because of the *charis* the jury felt for his past services, and so the interplay of *charis* between wealthy individual and demos was intertwined and reciprocal: the jurors' sense of *charis* for past gifts helped gain the wealthy benefactor the legal victory, which then caused him to render *charis* to the demos in the form of more benefactions which might win the *charis* of future juries, and so on. The ongoing drama may have been fraught with tension on several levels, but it ensured that the wealthy individual and the masses were kept closely in tune with one another's interests by constantly involving both sides in reciprocal bonds of obligation and gratitude.

The rich Athenian who willingly contributed money to the demos demonstrated his solidarity with the democratic constitution by the act of voluntarily turning over part of his wealth—the source (or at least one source) of his elite status—to the discretion of the masses who would decide democratically how the money should be used. The donation of money lessened the degree of the giver's financial inequality, and he was consequently reimbursed by the *charis* of the citizens who showed their gratitude by giving him preferential treatment in his legal contests against other rich men who were less demonstrably generous. The *antidosis* procedure encouraged the rich to attack one another in court, and their natural *philotimia*—their tendency to compete with one another for honors—was given a democratic focus as they competed for the *charis* of the masses. By their competition they legitimated the system that gave the demos the right to control the disposition of their private fortunes. In asserting his right to the property of Apollodorus, one of Isaeus' clients (7.35, 40) states that Apollodorus knew of his (the client's) *philotimia* and expected that he would continue to use the money as Apollodorus himself had used it in the past, spending moderate amounts on himself and the remainder of his fortune on the public good. The rich were thus participants in a legal system and an ideological framework that gave the demos privileges in respect to the rich man's property. This system, in a sense, balanced the various privileges the rich man gained from the private possession of that same property.

Many of the rich were tempted to keep on playing the game not only because of the threat of legal convictions or of a fatal outbreak of class warfare but also because they actively and sincerely desired the recognition of their fellows. Isocrates' client (18.63) stated that "I hold not only my own property, but my very life less important than to be well respected among you" (*tou par'humin eudokimein*). This may have been hyperbole, but it expressed an ideal many Athenians, rich and poor, believed. Demosthenes (22.75), speaking of the state crowns his opponent Androtion had melted down, said that Androtion failed to realize that even small crowns were marks of *philotimia*. Fine plate, says Demosthenes, was only a symbol of wealth that might give a man a certain reputation for riches. But anyone who would take pride in such things, rather than hoping to win true honor (*timē*) from them, should be regarded as vulgar (*apeirokalos*). Rich men who strove for public honor and *charis* were controlled by their own desire for recognition; such men would not become alienated from the common interests of the demos.[69]

Just as dramatic performances could serve as a metaphor for political activity (III.E.6), so the choregic monument served as a metaphor

---

[69] On the concept of *philotimia*, see Dem. 22.75, 42.24. Among modern studies, see esp. Whitehead, "Competitive Outlay" and *Demes*, 234–52 (esp. 242–43 with n. 94: list of exempla from orators). Contrast Carter, *Quiet Athenian*, esp. 49: a major stimulus to *apragmosunē* by the Athenian wealth elite (especially in the fifth century) was the contradictory position he held; expected to take an active role in leadership and in liturgies, he was answerable to a popular tribunal that "was short tempered, short-sighted and had a short memory."

for the ideal relationship among honor, wealth, and the state. Each year several members of the wealth elite either volunteered or were appointed as *chorēgoi* by the state. Each was required to pay for the production of a group of plays or of a dithyrambic chorus; the latter featured fifty skilled flutists and was a good deal more expensive (Dem. 21.156). The performance was held in the theater of Dionysus and was enjoyed by, and also helped to educate, the mass of Athenian citizens. The performance was then judged by a panel of citizens who had been selected by lot, just as the jurors who sat in judgment on the elite litigant had been selected at random from the demos. The *chorēgos* who had financed the chorus awarded the first prize was himself awarded a tripod and granted the right to set up (at his own expense) a monument incorporating his prize. The monument was a permanent record of his achievement and his generosity to the people, to which he could later refer with justifiable pride, in court and elsewhere.[70] The rich man thus competed with other rich men in giving to the demos; the *chorēgos* who had given the most to the demos was allowed to make a public display. The masses, even though they had had a deciding role in the authorization of the monument, were nonetheless impressed by the man who had built it, and they paid him due honor. The interaction between the elite's desire to compete and to impress and the masses' authorization of his displaying a symbol that indeed impressed them closely parallels the action of the courts. There, the wealthy litigant was allowed to display his wealth to the impressionable jurors, but only after having submitted to mass judgment and after having demonstrated that he was in sympathy with mass ideology.

Moreover, the institution of the *chorēgia* and the choregic monument served the same function as the complex play-acting of elite litigants in the courtroom: in both cases, the rich man was ultimately granted the privilege of demonstrating his superiority in public and of receiving applause and rewards as a result. But at the same time, the masses maintained close legal and ideological control of the wealthy. The benevolent complicity of mass and elite in perpetuating an ideological compromise that bound both more closely together helped to dampen social antagonism by mitigating the unequal power relationships that pertained in Athenian society. The individual power of the rich man was lessened by his generosity and willingness to sub-

[70] On the *chorēgia* and the rules governing it, see Lys. 21.1–2; Dem. 21.56, with Pickard-Cambridge, *Dramatic Festivals*, 85–90, 95–99, *Dithyramb, Tragedy, and Comedy*[2] (Oxford, 1962), 35–37.

mit to mass judgment; the collective and legal power of the mass was lessened by their willingness to acknowledge and to be impressed by the benefits they had received from the elite.

Rich rhetores were subject to some of the same ideological constraints as were rich *idiōtai*. The rhetor's wealth, however, served the state not only in terms of cash donations but also by allowing the possessor to fulfill his specialized political roles. Hence, the political orators were somewhat less closely controlled by the ideology of wealth than were other members of the upper classes. Relaxation of any aspect of mass control over a powerful minority was, however, a potential danger to the democratic government and needed to be counterbalanced. I would suggest that control of the wealthy political orators was reasserted in part by an inversion of the *charis* obligation. As we have seen, even judicial *charis* was a two-way street; not only did the demos feel gratitude toward the wealthy donor, but the litigant victorious in a trial at which his fortune was at stake owed *charis* to the people. The politician who was always dependent upon the demos' goodwill might, therefore, be expected to feel a perpetual sense of gratitude toward them. But *charis* typically consisted of gratitude for a material benefaction; indeed, most Athenian politicians, whether or not they had begun life wealthy, benefited materially (directly or indirectly) by their political activities. Some forms of making money from politics—war profiteering, sycophantic legal attacks, and acceptance of bribes from enemies of the demos—aroused the righteous ire of the people and provided a rationale for orators to attack the sudden acquisition of wealth by political opponents (V.F.2–3). In certain circumstances, however, making money from public activities might be regarded as the politician's legitimate privilege. Demosthenes (21.62–63) may be hinting at legitimate peculation when he states that Iphicrates possessed great wealth (*polla chrēmata*) and other advantages but willingly submitted to the laws and the judgment of the people because he realized that he was well off (*eudaimon*) due to "your *politeia*" (cf. the stories of Iphicrates' humble origins: VI.E.2). Hyperides is more explicit when he states that

> you [Athenians] allow expert speakers and generals to make a great deal of profit (*polla humeis . . . di[dote e]kontes tois stratēgois kai tois rhētorsin ōphelesthai*), and it is not the laws that permit this, but your tolerance and goodwill (*praotētos kai philanthrōpias*). But you insist on one thing—that the money be taken in your interest and not against your interest. (5.24–25)

In a passage with a similar theme, Demosthenes (*Ex.* 55.1) notes how the city has always had an overabundance of those who are eager to play political roles, since it gives them a chance to reap a private harvest from the public sphere (*ta koina karpousthai*). But, Demosthenes goes on, the demos formerly had used this tendency to make a worthy spectacle (*horama . . . kalon*) for itself, one that was profitable (*lusiteles*) for the polis.[71]

The willingness of the demos to allow politicians to enrich themselves through public service was likely due to the conviction that the politician who made money (or was allowed to take it) as a result of his special relationship with the demos would feel increased *charis* toward the demos. This assumption explains Demosthenes' comment to the effect that Aeschines was not only a *poneros* but one lacking in *charis* (*acharistos*: 18.131). He who had been made rich by the demos must be utterly without a sense of gratitude if he accepted money from others to work plots against the masses. Several passages cited above (Dem. 19.314, 24.124, 58.63) confirm that the Athenians felt that he who took from the state owed *charis* to the state. The demos' tolerance of a certain amount of political peculation by rhetores may therefore be regarded as a covert means of controlling wealthy politicians. The rhetor knew that he would be allowed to enrich himself "in the interests of the state" as long as he showed a proper sense of gratitude to the people for their generosity. The politician who took from the state had conjoined his personal financial interests with the interests of the demos. As the state prospered, so did he.[72] He could therefore be expected to propose legislation that would be of benefit to the state as a whole. If, on the other hand, the politician was caught accepting bribes from individuals against the state or proposing policies that would hurt the state in order to enrich himself, he could expect to be shown little mercy. The inversion of the *charis* relationship therefore channeled the politician's urge to enrich himself into activities that benefited Athenian political society.

The imposition of *charis* obligations upon politicians was no more infallible than any other means of social control, but it helped to resolve one of the paradoxes innate in the position of the political ora-

---

[71] Lysias (19.57) makes the same point when he claims that some people spend money on the city with the intention of getting back double their investment from *archein* "which you [Athenians] feel they have earned." Cf. Hyp. 5.22; Isoc. 8.124; Lys. 27.11; Dem. 19.238, 249. See also Strauss, "Bribery," 71–74; Hansen, "Politicians," 35–36; Harvey, "*Dona Ferentes*," 108–112.

[72] Cf. Dem. *Letter* 3.29–30; Hyp. 5.22. The good citizen also suffered when the state suffered: cf. Lys. 16.10; above, v.n.60.

tors in the democratic state. The demos, of necessity, granted privileges to the political subset of the wealth elite that were above and beyond the privileges allowed to the less politically active members of the upper classes. Popular tolerance for a display of wealth in public speeches and money making from political activities allowed and encouraged the rhetores to fulfill properly their political role, but in turn that tolerance bound them ever more closely to the masses.

CHAPTER VI

STATUS: NOBLE BIRTH AND
ARISTOCRATIC BEHAVIOR

As a category of sociopolitical analysis, status is somewhat difficult to define. M. I. Finley was a prominent proponent of the use of status categories in the analysis of ancient societies, but he never offered a precise definition of status, remarking that it is "an admirably vague word with a considerable psychological element."[1] What Finley meant by status is, however, clarified by the examples he cites, especially in *The Ancient Economy*: status is defined in part by wealth but also involves the privileges associated with other attributes, notably birth and occupation.[2] Status is a broader and more fluid category than class and is specifically linked to consciousness: a consensus regarding the place in the social hierarchy to be assigned to specific descent and occupational groups.

A. Status and Social Standing

The category of status might be used as a catchall: the "status elite" of Athens could be defined as including anyone whose social standing was notably higher than that of his fellow citizens, because of his possession of any attribute or constellation of attributes that raised him above the norm.[3] On the other hand, Ste. Croix has argued, against Finley, that class alone has operational significance in the organization of human society; status, according to Ste. Croix, is useless as an analytical, as opposed to a descriptive, category.[4] But perhaps Ste. Croix has overstated the case. The standing of an Athenian in the eyes of his fellows and his ability to influence their actions were certainly based in

[1] *AE*, esp. 35–61, quote: 51.

[2] Finley's preference for the term 'class' in *PAW* was not a repudiation of his preference for status categories, see ibid., 10 with n. 26, *Ancient History*, 90. Cf. Ober, "Aristotle's Political Sociology," and above, v.n.2.

[3] For the tendency to blur status and class considerations, see, for example, Aristot. *Pol.* 1293b34–39. Cf. above, I.B, on the overlapping nature of Greek elites and the terminology for them.

[4] Ste. Croix, *CSAGW*, esp. 45, 80–98; cf. Shaw, "Social Science," 31–36.

part upon the wealth he controlled. But there were very wealthy (and highly educated) persons living in Athens who were not citizens. Without citizenship, they were denied the right to participate in the political processes of the state. Since political rights were demonstrably important, those denied citizenship—metics, slaves, and women—could hardly be considered members of the highest status groups of Athenian society, even if they controlled a great deal of property.[5] Furthermore, in the *Politics* Aristotle makes clear distinctions between categories of status and of class; his description and analysis of oligarchy and aristocracy are based explicitly on the differences between states dominated politically by those who were merely wealthy, and by those who were, by birth and demonstrated excellence, most worthy to rule and be ruled in turn.[6]

Birth and behavior are the characteristics that distinguish the category of status from the narrower categories of class and ability. The standing of Athenian aristocrats was often based upon their wealth and education as well as upon their birth and behavior. However, the term 'high status' will refer here to those residents of Athenian territory who were regarded as elite specifically because of their birth, distinctive patterns of behavior, or both.

The attributes of birth and behavior were closely intertwined in Athenian thought. Aristotle (*Pol.* 1301b1–4) defines the "well born" (*eugeneis*) as those who are preeminent because of their birth (*genos*) and who thereby claim to merit special privileges; furthermore, the well born are regarded as those to whom the *aretē* and the wealth of their ancestors belong. In this passage Aristotle conflates good birth with wealth (and thus status with class) but also the "genetic" category of birthright with the moral category of *aretē*. The implication is that high birth often leads to moral excellence but also that the two attributes were distinct. An individual with good blood might not be regarded as truly well born if his behavior was incompatible with his

---

[5] See, for example, Whitehead, *Ideology*, esp. 69–72. On slaves, cf. below, VI.D.1. Adkins, "Problems," 155–56, argues against the notion that *kalos k'agathos* is a class term by suggesting that in the orators prestige, courage, honesty, and other virtues *as well as* wealth were part of its connotation. Cf. Starr, *Individual and Community*, 95; Washburn, *Political Sociology*, 23–24. For the purposes of this chapter I am assimilating the analytic category of "order" (legal definition of social position) within the category of status; cf. Finley, AE, 45–48; Ste. Croix, *CSAGW*, 42, 94; Ober, "Aristotle's Political Sociology."

[6] Cf. Ober, "Aristotle's Political Sociology." Key passages include *Pol.* 1291b14–30, 1293b1–20, 1316b3–5, 1317b39–41, 1319a19–28, 1321a5–6; cf. *Nicomachean Ethics* 1131a24–29.

ancestry. The Greek aristocrat must have the right bloodlines,[7] but he must also act the part.

Those who were well born according to the lights of Greek aristocratic society were expected to conform to a code of behavior that emphasized loyalty to friends (*philia*) and bravery in battle (*andreia, aristeia*). Starr's definition of the aristocratic ethos is concise: ". . . an obligatory pattern of life and values *consciously* conceived and shared by a limited group which inherited its belief that it was 'best' and whose claims were generally accepted, even cherished, by other groups of society."[8] When they were not engaged in public affairs, Greek aristocrats tended to spend their time in the presence of their fellow nobles, in pursuits that were regarded as particularly suitable to their standing: athletic training and contests, hunting, horse raising, involvement in homoerotic love affairs, and attendance at exclusive drinking parties (*sumposia*).[9] In all of these pastimes, competition was a vital element, and competitiveness was a central organizing principle within the aristocratic code of values. Greek aristocrats competed with one another frequently and actively, in public and in private. The goal was individual preeminence and general acclaim; potential and actual opponents included all those who might be equals, thus, all others with claims to aristocratic status. Competition was serious and led to much tension, since for every winner there had to be a loser. The success of one nobleman detracted from the standing of his fellows. Thus Greek aristocrats inhabited a world whose values were defined by the contest

[7] On the key concept of good birth, cf. Starr, *Individual and Community*, 59–63; Arnheim, *Aristocracy*, 180–81, who cites Aristotle F 94 (Rose). In that fragment Aristotle argues that good ancestors create good men; therefore it was not the rich and good who were well born but those who descended from ancestors who have long been rich and good. In the *Rhetoric* (1367b28–32) Aristotle notes that in encomia, praise of *eugeneia* and education should be secondary to praise of deeds, because it is likely that those born of *agathoi* will themselves be *agathoi* as well as properly brought up. Aristotle suggests a very different view of inherited virtues elsewhere, however: below, VI.B.2. See also Dover, *GPM*, 88–95, on the question of the Greek idea of the influence of heredity and environment on the formation of the individual; ibid., esp. 93–95, on the idea of "good birth."

[8] Starr, *Individual and Community*, 30. On the aristocratic code generally, cf. idem, *Economic and Social Growth*, 119–46; Jaeger, *Paideia*, I; Adkins, *Merit and Responsibility*; Davies, *DCG*, 41; Donlon, *Aristocratic Ideal*, 113–53. Arnheim, *Aristocracy*, 158, defines aristocratic ideology as the belief that some people are superior to others innately and by heredity, and he argues that aristocratic ideology is therefore innately anti-egalitarian; cf. below, VI.B.

[9] See, for example, Marrou, *Education*, 65–67; Donlon, *Aristocratic Ideal*, esp. 155–77; cf. Carter, *Quiet Athenian*, 21–23.

(*agōn*) and the *agōn* was, in A. W. Gouldner's classic formulation, a zero-sum system.[10]

B. Athenian Aristocrats

Many aristocratic values appear incompatible with the principle of political equality. In light of their egalitarian political ethos, we might suppose that the Athenians would have rejected the concept of the inheritability of superiority as overtly elitist. But before the establishment of the democratic constitution at Athens, aristocrats had played a dominant role in the state and formed both a social elite and a ruling political elite (above, II.B). In the course of the generations of aristocratic domination, the concept of ancestral worth was deeply embedded in Athenian social attitudes. The growth of democracy in the fifth century resulted in major changes in the political role aristocrats were able to play in Athens (II.C–F), but some of the key concepts underpinning the ideology of aristocracy—the belief in the inheritability of attributes, the association of inborn attributes with a distinctive pattern of behavior, and the conviction that some individuals deserved special privileges as their birthright—were extremely tenacious and survived into the fourth century and beyond. Consequently, there remained much that was identifiably "aristocratic" in the political ideology of democratic Athens. Whether this undeniable fact requires us to agree with M.T.W. Arnheim that "the principle of equality held little attraction for the ancient Greeks," or that "the idea that the Greeks were believers in equality must be buried forever," remains to be seen.[11]

The Athenian aristocrat was differentiated from, and might be perceived to be better than, the non-aristocrat because he was thought to have inherited from his ancestors certain desirable traits—especially the qualities of being noble and good (*agathos*) and physically beautiful (*kalos*)—and because he acted differently from ordinary men. Since Athenian aristocrats were believed to have a notable ancestry, shared a common value system, socialized with one another, and tended to intermarry, they were identified by their fellow citizens as a distinct status group. Contemporary writers used various terms to describe them (e.g., *chrēstoi, epieikeis, charientes*), but perhaps the most common

[10] Gouldner, *Enter Plato*, 13–15, 45–55; cf. Garner, *Law and Society*, 11, 14–19, 58–60. In a zero-sum system the gain of the winners equals the loss suffered by the losers.

[11] Arnheim, *Aristocracy*, 167 68, 181.

and the most descriptive was *hoi kaloi k'agathoi*: the beautiful and noble ones.[12]

B.1 *Gennētai* AND ARISTOCRATIC PURSUITS

An Athenian was identifiable as a member of a special social subgroup—even if he possessed no other elite attributes—if he belonged to one of the kinship associations (*genē*) that were made up exclusively of those Athenians who could claim a particularly noble lineage. Much remains obscure about the early history and nature of the *genē*, but by the fourth century, the *genē* had come to be defined as extensive "homogalactic" clans, each divided into various families (*oikoi*). The *genē* probably did not play as important a role in the early history of Athens as was once believed. Much of the evidence for the political power of archaic *genē* comes from the Atthidographers, fourth- and third-century chroniclers of local Athenian history who wrote (or rewrote) archaic Athenian history in accordance with the notion that all prominent political leaders of Athens' past must have belonged to important *genē*. But the question of archaic realities is of less moment here than the question of fourth-century perceptions. By the fourth century, all Athenians who belonged to a prominent *genos* were, by definition, nobly born. Therefore, despite the probability that the fourth-century Athenian view of the archaic origins of the *genē* was false in many particulars, the *gennētai*—individuals who could demonstrate that they were members of a *genos*—may be regarded as more or less coextensive with the aristocracy of fourth-century Athens.[13]

Some *gennētai* were not rich, and their lives were probably not very different from the lives of non-aristocratic citizens, but others continued to engage in the specific patterns of behavior that had long been associated with noble birth. "Well-born" Athenians of the fourth century retained their interest in the traditional activities of their (real or

---

[12] On the term *kaloi k'agathoi* and its use in oratory, see also Dover, *GPM*, 41–45.

[13] *Gennētai* as Athenian aristocracy: MacKendrick, *Athenian Aristocracy*; Bicknell, *Studies*. Roussel, *Tribu et cité*, 71–72, raises the possibility that not all *gennētai* were regarded as aristocrats and doubts that there was "un veritable ordre noble" in Athens. But his comments are directed against the concept of genuine ancient clans with genuine noble ancestors and fixed privileges, and he admits (74) that for Athenians membership in a *genos* "leur assuraient un réel prestige dans la société." On the history of the *genē* and fourth-century mythologizing, see Bourriott, *Recherches*, esp. 694–710, who demonstrates that in the fourth century some old "homogalactic" kinship groups in the countryside and some politically prominent *oikoi* began to be called *genē*; later Hellensitic and Roman historians assigned all the major political figures of earlier Athenian history to *genē* to fit this model.

imagined) ancestors.[14] The three great gymnasia outside the city—the Academy, the Lyceum, and Cynosarges—were centers where aristocrats could gather for physical contests and philosophical debate.[15] Xenophon's *Art of Hunting* emphasized the manly and aristocratic nature of the hunt. Horse raising and racing remained popular among those high-born Athenians who had managed to keep their ancestral wealth.[16] Plato's *Symposium*, though set in the late fifth century, gives a picture of idealized homoerotic love and of the sort of intellectual drinking party that continued to be popular in Athenian aristocratic circles.

B.2 ARISTOCRATIC PRIVILEGE: REALITY AND IMAGE

Some Athenian aristocrats enjoyed specific, socially sanctioned privileges which they possessed by virtue of birthright alone. Certain priesthoods had to be filled by members of particular *genē*.[17] Perhaps the most striking example of birth privilege, however, was the special status granted all descendants of the aristocratic "tyrant-slayers" Harmodius and Aristogeiton. Despite historians' doubts regarding the motives behind the assassination of Hipparchus and its political significance, the relatives of the two men remained exempt from most forms of taxation.[18]

Given that the aristocrats were an identifiable group whose special attributes qualified at least some of them for privileges that were recognized by the Athenians as legitimate and that some aristocratic values remained influential in Athenian ideology, we might expect aristocratic politicians and litigants to refer to their heritage when attempting to influence fellow citizens in the Assembly and courtroom. Various terms alluding to the general concept of "good birth" (*euge-*

[14] See, for example, Dem. 61.23: most sports are open to slaves and foreigners, but horsemanship is open only to citizens and so *hoi beltistoi* aspire to it. Isocrates (7.45), speaking of the good old days of Athenian ancestors, states that those with proper means turned to horsemanship, athletics, hunting, and philosophy. Thus some could become excellent and others could avoid evil.

[15] Athenian gymnasia and life there: Travlos, *Pictorial Dictionary*, 42–51 (Academy), 340–41 (Cynosarges), 345–48 (Lyceum); E. N. Gardner, *Greek Atheletic Sports and Festivals* (London, 1910), 468–82.

[16] Cf. J. K. Anderson, *Ancient Greek Horsemanship* (Berkeley, 1961), 128–39; Bugh, *Horsemen of Athens*.

[17] See Hignett, *HAC*, 64–65, 235, and esp. Roussel, *Tribu et cité*, 65–78 *bis*. Ps-Lysias 6.10 suggests that some unwritten laws had been in the hands of the Eumolpidai as late as the time of Pericles; cf. Sealey, "Athenian Concept of Law," 295.

[18] Doubts: Hdt. 5.55–61, 6.123.2; Thuc. 1.20.2, 6.54–59. Tax exempt: Dem. 20.127.

neia; cf. Aristot. *Rhet.* 1360b31–38) indeed come up in court cases. Isocrates' client Alcibiades the Younger (16.25) mentioned that his grandfather belonged to the *genos* of the Eupatridai "whose very name demonstrates their *eugeneia*" and that his father's wife was a daughter of Hipponicus, who was by birth (*genei*) second to none of the citizens (16.31). Demosthenes' client Euxitheus (57.46, cf. 62) noted in passing that he was nominated by his demesmen to draw lots for the priest-hood of Heracles, since he was "among the best born" (*en tois eugene-statois*),[19] and in the speech *Against Neaera* ([Dem.] 59.72) Apollodorus mentions Theogenes of the deme Kothokedai, who was chosen by lot as *basileus*, as he was a man of good birth (*anthrōpon eugenē*).[20]

There is little evidence, however, to suggest that their noble blood-lines translated directly into courtroom advantages for Athenian aris-tocrats in the fourth century. Lysias (30.1) claimed in a public trial of 399 B.C. that "in the past" there had been cases in which the accused appeared guilty but was acquitted due to his display of "the virtues of his ancestors" (*tas tōn progonōn aretas*) and his own beneficence (*euerge-sias*). We have seen (V.E) how references to personal and ancestral ma-terial benefactions to the state played upon the jurors' sense of grati-tude, but it is less clear that ancestral virtue per se was really much help to a fourth-century litigant. In the case just cited, Lysias brings up ancestral virtue only to give himself an opportunity to show that his opponent was a slave by ancestry and so should be scorned (cf. below, VI.D.1). Apollodorus ([Dem.] 59.116–17) mentions the case of the hierophant Archias, who, having conducted an improper sacrifice, was convicted in the courts despite the facts that he was "from the *genos* of the Eumolpidai" and that "his ancesters were *kaloi k'agathoi*." Demosthenes (21.182) mentions the conviction and execution of Pyr-rhus "one of the Eteoboutadai," and elsewhere (19.280–81) observes that "even a descendant of glorious Harmodius" was fined despite the weeping of his children with their "resplendent names."[21]

[19] Whitehead, *Demes*, 181n.25 (citing Haussoullier, *Vie municipale*, 137–38), sug-gests that in this context *eugenestatos* may mean no more than that he was a citizen on both sides.

[20] Cf. Lys. 18.11: the Thirty executed those who were especially worthy of honor because of *genos*, *ploutos*, or other *aretē*. Lys. 34.3: I am superior by wealth and birth to the proposers of the law, but I think that the safety of the polis requires that all Athenians have share in the *politeia*. Isoc. 7.37: in the good old days the Athenians put supervision of behavior in the hands of the Areopagus, which was composed uniquely of those who were *kalōs gegonosi*. But see also the "working man" of [Dem.] 59.50, 59, who was a member of the *genos* of Brytidai.

[21] For other references to those who were convicted despite their nobility, see Dem. 21.145–46: Alcibiades the Elder who was of the Alcmaeonidai on his father's

The "convicted, though high born" topos might be explained as a reflection of the genuine Athenian respect for aristocrats. On this assumption, we might suppose that the convicted aristocrat provided a powerful symbol of justice prevailing over privilege—even legitimate privilege—in the people's courts. But on the other hand, we might suggest that the jurors rather enjoyed the spectacle of seeing, or hearing about, high-born folk with famous ancestors who had been brought low by the votes of the masses. As in the case of topoi referring to the power of wealth to influence jurors (above, v.d.2), the "convicted aristocrat" topos points to a tension within Athenian ideology. Discussions of the punishments meted out to Athenian aristocrats who had been found guilty of wrongdoing probably played to anti-aristocratic prejudices, but such discussions assume that the jurors regarded respect for aristocrats to be the social norm.

In *On the Peace* (8.133) Isocrates complained that the Athenians wrongly considered sycophants to be democrats and regarded men who were *kaloi k'agathoi* as oligarchs. Although Isocrates, as usual, had his own bones to pick, several passages in Athenian speeches suggest that the demos distrusted and even actively disliked aristocratic pretension. Lysias (12.86) suggested that the jurors in the trial of Eratosthenes might well wonder whether Eratosthenes' supporters would speak for him "as *kaloi k'agathoi*, claiming that their *aretē* should be worthy of more than the criminality (*ponēria*) of the accused." Lysias wondered aloud why these men who spoke so glibly never brought up "those things that are just in regard to you [the people]." By contrasting the claims of *aretē* made for his aristocratic opponent with what is just in regard to the masses, Lysias hoped to persuade his jury that Eratosthenes' associates (and by implication, the defendant himself) cared more for aristocratic values than for popular justice. The jurors must, therefore, draw the conclusion that they should resist any tendency to be influenced by the aristocrats. In another speech, Lysias' client (10.28) used the notion of inherited attributes against his opponent by suggesting that his cowardice was congenital (*sumphutos*). Even his family's aristocratic beauty told against him: "The taller and more radiant they look, the more worthy of hatred they are, since it is clear that though strong of body, they are diseased in their souls" (10.29). Demosthenes (21.143) reminded his jurors that the attributes of birth, wealth, and power were intolerable if associated with hubris, and Isoc-

---

side and of the house of Hipponicus on his mother's; Din. 1.13–14: Timotheus, son of Conon, liberator of Greece. Cf. Lys. 14.24: if jurors allow defendants to talk about their ancestors' virtues, you must allow prosecutors to discuss the crimes of their opponents' ancestors.

rates (20.19) claimed that it was not just that retribution for unknown folk should be less than that for "those with double names" (*tōn diōnomasmenōn*). The double-named individuals Isocrates refers to are those who used the "x son of y" nomenclature, rather than the more egalitarian "x of deme y." He who used the former advertised that his primary identity was derived from his immediate family, rather than his ancestral place of residence.[22] Each of these passages implies that the jury was aware that aristocratic birth could be, or had been, used as a criterion that affected legal decisions. In each, the speaker attempted to demonstrate to the jurymen why they should reject such claims in the current instance.

Isaeus wrote a speech for a client that went so far as to dispute the status claims of a relative of one of the tyrannicides. Perhaps, he says, my opponent Dikaiogenes will claim to be "worth more than me" because of his ancestors, who slew the tyrant. The speaker is quick to assure the jury that he respects the tyrant-killers themselves, "but I do not believe you [Dikaiogenes] share their *aretē*" (5.46). Indeed, the speaker attacks the validity of the very notion of inherited virtue: "These heroes were honored not because of their birth (*ou dia to genos*) . . . but because of their manly courage (*dia tēn andragathian*), which you have no share in, Dikaiogenes" (5.47). This may be regarded as an extreme position, and the rhetoric conditioned by the difficulty inherent in legal action against a descendant of the tyrannicide. But in his *Rhetoric* (1390b19–31), Aristotle also specifically refutes the validity of the concept of inherited virtue, noting that although *eugeneia* leads its possessors to act haughtily, in fact most aristocrats are worthless (*euteleis*), and families that were once brilliant tended to breed maniacs and dullards. Whether this passage represents the philosopher's own views, or whether it was presented as an argument that could be used by orators to sway an audience, it suggests that claims of high birth could not be counted upon to stimulate a consistently positive response among fourth-century Athenians.[23]

If Athenian juries were at least potentially suspicious of claims based on high birth, we might also expect to find passages in legal orations

---

[22] On deme ties versus kinship and change/continuity in Athenian nomenclature, see Whitehead, *Demes*, 50, 71–72, 352; Osborne, *Demos*, 66, 72–74; cf. above, II.E.1.

[23] According to Aristotle F 91 (Rose), Lycophron also denied any validity to claims based on good birth. Cf. Aristot. *Pol.* 1271a16–21, 1286b23–25. For Aristotle on the other side of this question, cf. above, VI.n.7. Demosthenes has it both ways in 24.127, when he claims that he could easily demonstrate that an opponent's father was a thief, but that he is willing to assume that he is as worthy as his opponents will say. However, an evil son of a good father certainly deserves prison.

in which the speaker looks askance at the characteristic aristocratic attributes and patterns of behavior—especially those that conflicted with egalitarian principles. Here we must exercise some caution, since much of the aristocratic pattern of behavior was predicated on the possession of great wealth and so involves the ideology of class as well as that of status. But there are some passages that suggest that the Athenians may have associated certain forms of obnoxious behavior with aristocratic status per se. In the speech *Against Timarchus* Aeschines (1.41) describes his contemporary Misgolas as a *kalos k'agathos* and states that no one has anything to reproach Misgolas with, except pederasty, which he engages in "like mad" (*daimoniōs*). Incidentally, Aeschines goes on to point out, Misgolas always likes to have cithara players and singers about. Being a man of that sort, Misgolas hired young Timarchus as a live-in prostitute, despite the fact that the latter was a citizen and so was prohibited from prostituting himself. Aeschines' initial disclaimer—that no one has anything much to reproach Misgolas with—begins to ring false and can be read as rather heavy-handed sarcasm. Aeschines did not waste too much time attacking Misgolas, probably because depicting him as a paragon of evil might blur the emphasis on Timarchus' particular wickedness and crime (acting as a public speaker after having prostituted himself: above, III.B.2). Aeschines' tactic seems to be to allow the jury's innate suspicions of the *kalos k'agathos* and his pederastic ways to create the desired impression of an atmosphere of dissolution in which the decadent aristocrat and his hired lover lived.[24]

In the speech *Against Conon* Demosthenes relies more directly upon the presumption that the jurymen disliked and distrusted various aspects of the aristocratic pattern of behavior. The prosecutor in the case claims (54.13–14) that the defendant, Conon, will try to mislead the jurors by making his own and his sons' crime (battery) appear humorous. Conon will say that many sons of *kaloi k'agathoi*, when they are young, like to call themselves Ithyphalloi and Autolekythoi and run after prostitutes. Conon will try to portray the whole affair as a silly squabble over girls. But it would be an awful thing, says the prosecutor, if the jurors were to believe Conon's lies and discount the everyday life of "middling folk" (*metrioi*) like us (54.15). It is fine by me, he goes on, if Conon's sons want to call themselves Ithyphalloi and Autolekythoi—I only hope that the gods punish them for it (54.16). The prosecutor explains to the jury that his opponents are people

---

[24] For popular distrust of homoerotic relations, especially among the aristocrats, see Dem. 61.17–18. But cf. below, VI.E.1.

"who initiate each other with the phallus and do things that are too shameful to be spoken of, much less engaged in, by men who are *metrioi*" (54.17). Conon deserves no special treatment from the jurors. If he says, "We are members of the Ithyphalloi and in our love-affairs we can strike and strangle whomever we please, will you [jurors] let him off with a laugh?—I think not!" (54.20). The jurors must not be misled by those who speak on Conon's behalf. He had prepared as false witnesses his symposium friends (*sumpotai*) who share in his evil deeds. Of course these men will all deny their complicity, but "many of you [jurors]" know them—Diotimos, Archibiades, and Chairetimos—men who go about looking somber, speaking laconically, and dressed like Spartans, "but when they get together and are alone they leave nothing undone that is filthy (*kakos*) and shameful (*aischros*)." Conon's supporters are so evil that when the prosecutor demonstrates that they are all in cahoots, they will claim that it is just for men who are *hetairoi* and *philoi* to watch out for each other's interests (54.31–35).

Demosthenes' characterization of the behavior of Conon, his sons, and their supporters played upon a number of themes, all of which were intended to inflame the jurors' distrust and perhaps even their fear of the aristocrats. Like Alcibiades and the Profaners of the Mysteries, they gathered together in secret societies to do godless things. They engaged in "initiations" with blatantly homosexual overtones. Like hubristic Meidias in Demosthenes 21, they felt they had the right to attack anyone they wished. Like some of the counter-revolutionary oligarchs of the late fifth century, they imitated Spartan speech and dress. Furthermore, they were perfectly willing to perjure themselves in order to help their *hetairoi* and *philoi*. Demosthenes suggests here that the aristocratic value of loyalty to friends threatened the democratic process of the people's courts. Anyone who would perjure himself in front of the people (as represented by the jurors) in order to help his friends obviously put personal concerns above the public interest. Such individuals chose to stand outside the interest group of the demos, and so the masses must use their collective power—as jurors in the people's court—to redress the balance that aristocratic values and behavior patterns had threatened. The prosecutor takes for himself and his own family the role of *metrioi*—average citizens, whose interests and standing were identical to that of the ordinary-citizen jurors. The defendant and his supporters, on the other hand, chose not to live like other Athenians and thought that being *kaloi k'agathoi* gave them the right to act as they pleased, to anger the gods, to commit hubris against *metrioi*, and to perjure themselves in order to help their fellow nobles. Clearly, such men must be humbled lest their arrogance threaten the democratic order.

The Athenian demos' distrust of certain aspects of aristocratic behavior helps to explain why the Athenian nobleman who was involved in a trial might choose not to make much of his high birth. The prevailing egalitarian ideology made it safer for the aristocratic litigant, like the prosecutor in Demosthenes 54, to portray himself as a middling citizen of sober habits (*sophrosune*) whose public behavior conformed to that of other citizens. While the aristocrat might privately regard himself as a superior fellow, it was more politic to depict himself in court as one who saw himself as equal, not superior, to the rest of the Athenians.[25] In general, birth and behavior status seem to play lesser roles in private orations than considerations of class or ability. This may be in part because of the difficulty of separating status considerations from those of class, a problem Athenian aristocrats themselves may have worried about. The rewriting of early Athenian local history by fourth-century aristocrats and those closely associated with them was perhaps inspired in part by the aristocrats' concern with self-definition. Athenian *gennetai* seemed to need a historical validation of their own position, a concern more characteristic of a social group whose distinct existence and privileged standing is threatened than of a group whose standing is secure and universally acknowleged.[26]

C. Democratization of Birth Privilege

The apparent vagueness of appeals to or against the privileges associated with aristocratic status in the private speeches might seem to validate Ste. Croix's position that status is not a valuable category of social analysis. But a different explanation may go further in clarifying the evident concern of fourth-century aristocrats with defining themselves by fictionalized history: despite the apparent dissonance between aristocratic emphasis on superiority and demotic principles of equality, and despite some lingering popular distrust of the aristocrats as potential counter-revolutionaries, the concepts of *eugeneia* and *kalokaga-*

[25] For the "virtue" of *metriotēs*: Aesch. 1.42, 3.11, 218; Dem. 29.24; Is. 7.40; Din. 2.8; Hyp. 4.21. Of *sophrosune*: Dem. 24.126, 45.68; Lys. 21.19. Of *isotēs*: Isoc. 18.33, 50; Lys. 12.35.

[26] On the motives for the rewriting of Athenian history in the fourth century, Jacoby, *Atthis*, esp. 71–79, is seminal, although his emphasis on political "conservatism" is perhaps excessive; cf. discussion in Wallace, *Areopagos*, chapter 7. Connections of Atthidographers with *gennētai*: MacKendrick, *Athenian Aristocracy*, 24–25; but cf. the scepticism of Wallace, *Areopagos*, chapter 7.v, on the assumed relationship between Phanodemus and Lycurgus.

thia were democratized and communalized in the course of the fifth and fourth centuries and so made the common property of all citizens. Aristocratic claims of exclusive and personal birthright might therefore appear to deny the generalized nobility of the masses. The "true" aristocrats felt threatened precisely because their primary distinctive attribute—their high birth—had been "nationalized."

The democratization of the concept of *eugeneia* is hinted at in a Lysian speech in which the speaker states that although his father had had an opportunity to marry a woman who would have brought him a large dowry, he chose instead the daughter of a man who was considered excellent (*chrēstos*) in his private life and whom "you [the demos]" considered to be a worthy general (19.14). The father in turn refused to give his own daughters to certain very wealthy men (*panu plousiōn*) because he considered them "ill born" (*kakion gegonenai*). Instead, he married one daughter to a man whom "the many" judged to be better (*beltiō*) rather than richer, and the other to a man who became *penēs* through no fault of his own (19.15). The speaker thus makes the masses into the grantors and judges of *eugeneia*, a characteristic that is set above wealth as a criterion of value.[27]

In a similar fashion, *kalokagathia* could be transformed into an attribute at least potentially available to all Athenian citizens. Lysias (30.14) claims that his opponent Nicomachus had helped the Thirty Tyrants to convict Strombochides, Calliades, and "others of the citizens who were many (*polloi*) and *kaloi k'agathoi*." The association of the term *polloi*, typically used of the Athenian masses, with *kaloi k'agathoi* is deliberate. Lysias suggests that Nicomachus, a slave by birth, is the enemy of the Athenian citizen masses who were *kaloi k'agathoi* by birth. Aeschines (1.134) states that he expects that one or another of the opposing character witnesses at the trial of Timarchus will remind the jurors that all citizens pray that their unborn sons will "grow up *kaloi k'agathoi* in body and worthy of the polis." Aeschines demonstrates how the prayer will be perverted into a justification for shameful actions, but by arguing against the misuse—rather than the reality—of the prayer, he implicitly acknowledges that "sons beautiful and noble and worthy of the polis" were exactly what the common citizens desired. Aeschines' association of *kalokagathia* with worthiness in the eyes of the polis is reminiscent of the passage from Lysias 19, cited above; in both instances, the aristocratic attribute is linked with the common

[27] On excellence in public service as a common possession that is not limited to those of aristocratic status or to the wealth elite, cf. Pericles' Funeral Oration (Thuc. 2.37), with the comments of Loraux, *Invention*, 186–87; Carter, *Quiet Athenian*, 26–27.

good. Dinarchus (3.18) stated that his opponent lacked nothing that a *metrios* man might desire, but still took bribes, proving that his mask of *kalokagathia* was utterly false. In this passage the two ideal types of the *metrios* and the *kalos k'agathos* are merged; "moderateness" is equated with the old aristocratic virtue that had implied superiority.[28] *Kalokagathia* has become an attribute that any good citizen could manifest.

The tendency of the Attic orators to treat aristocratic attributes as communal and suitable to the masses is not particularly surprising in light of the standing of the citizenry. The citizen population of Athens was collectively a political elite vis-à-vis noncitizens, and a citizen's political status was normally inherited. Foreigners and slaves, who were excluded from citizenship, could be looked down upon by even the poorest and least well-educated citizen. The citizen "in-group" was, therefore, a hereditary aristocracy when compared to noncitizen "out-groups." All members of the in-group were equal insofar as their position was defined by their possession of a single attribute—citizenship—that was not possessed by any member of an out-group. Membership in a *genos* might bring enhanced social status, but citizenship itself conferred upon the Athenian the essential political standing without which there could be no legal or political privilege. Citizenship was the attribute which in and of itself distinguished the Athenian from those less-than-equal members of out-groups inhabiting Athenian territory. The citizenship group was thus the basic sociopolitical elite of which all other elite groups were necessarily subsets.[29] The value of the citizen's political rights, and hence of the social status based upon those rights, was measured by the exclusivity of the citizenship group, and therefore rights of citizenship and the means of cooptation into the in-group were jealously guarded by its members.

C.1 AUTOCHTHONY AND PATRIOTISM

Most Athenian citizens owed their citizenship to their parents, from whom they inherited a share (or at least a conditional share) in the government of the state. A citizen's parents, in turn, owed their citi-

---

[28] Cf. Aeschines' (2.150) description of the jurors as *hoi epieikestatoi*, who had come to the court for the good of the polis. Carter, *Quiet Athenian*, 12, notes that in some passages of Book 1, Thucydides seems to apply the ideal of the *agathos* to the demos.

[29] Lintott, *Violence*, 175, suggests that the Athenian law code "treated the members of the Athenian demos as aristocrats" by enabling them to protect their own *timē* as free men. And so "it is arguable that much of the motive power in Athenian democracy came from the fact that it was the rule of a people who were conscious that they were superior collectively and individually." On the citizenship group as elite, see also Davies, "Athenian Citizenship," esp. 106–107, 111–14; Dover, *GPM*, 39; Meier, *Anthropologie*, 7–26; Raaflaub, "Freien Bürgers Recht," 44–46.

zenship (considering women, for the moment, as place-holders of citizenship, that is, of citizen blood, though barred by their gender from political rights) to their own parents, and so on back through the generations to the time the first Athenians sprang from the soil of Attica. The myth of Athenian autochthony (e.g., Thuc. 1.2.4; Hdt. 1.56–58), despite the fact that even in historical times exogeny had been legal, allowed all Athenians to regard themselves as pure-blooded and thus, by definition, of well-born ancestry. As G. B. Walsh points out, "For an Athenian, to be earthborn (γηγενής) and indigenous (αὐτόχθων) was also to be well-born (εὐγενής), and so his national pride was tied closely to his sense of inherited personal status: if his city was free of racial impurity, so was he."[30] The formulaic funeral orations spoken over dead Athenian soldiers tended to emphasize the notion of communal aristocracy. Lysias (2.17) noted that their autochthonous ancestry gave the Athenians both a motherland and a fatherland, and he claimed (2.20) that the ancestors of the fallen were "of noble stock and with minds similarly noble."[31] Demosthenes (60.7) stated that the pride of the Athenians' ancestors was to be *kaloi k'agathoi* as well as the most just of men (*dikaiotatoi*). Hyperides also refers to common nobility in his *Funeral Oration*.

> Shall I first trace the ancestry (*genos*) of each one of these? To do so would, I think, be foolish. Granted, when praising certain other men who, though originating in various different locales, gathered together to live in a single polis, each one contributing his own bloodline, one must trace each man's separate ancestry. But in making speeches concerning Athenian men, born of their own land and sharing in common a lineage of unsurpassed nobility (*eugeneia*), I believe that to praise their ancestry on an individual basis is to be superfluous. (6.6–7)

Hyperides thus specifically contrasts and subordinates individual nobility of birth to the communal noble inheritance of the fallen soldiers, the representatives of the Athenian demos. The old aristocratic ideal

---

[30] Walsh, "Rhetoric," 301; cf. ibid., 309–10.

[31] Cf. Humphreys, *Family*, 121: it was the state burial of war dead "which first brought the honours of heroic burial within the range of every Athenian citizen." Loraux, *Invention*, esp. 148–53, 332, discusses the autochthony theme in funeral orations and the connection between autochthony and *eugeneia*. On the Lysias passage, see Loraux, *Invention*, 194–96, 211: Lysias might have, but did not attempt to free aristocratic terminology from its aristocratic values "in some 'democratic' attempt at redefining values" (196). This last seems to me an unsatisfactory reading; cf. below, VI.F.

of high birth as a possession of the privileged few has been appropriated and transformed into the inborn nobility of the citizen body as a whole.

The autochthonous and noble common ancestry of the Athenian people was a matter of considerable pride to the citizens and was frequently noted in orations as a distinguishing trait that rendered the Athenians superior not only to noncitizens living in Attica but to all other Greeks. Because their ancestors were born of the soil of Attica, all Athenians were, in effect, a single kinship group.[32] Demosthenes' client Euxitheus, in defending his citizenship, claimed that he had proved that his father was a citizen by the same tokens that "each one of you" have to prove citizenship: membership in a phratry, relatives, demesmen, and *gennētai* (57.24). Since each Athenian was tied to every other citizen by a common autochthonous ancestry, when in trouble he might ask his fellows to render him the aid and support blood relatives typically expected from one another. Andocides (1.148–49) evokes this conception of blood union when, after dwelling upon his relatives' prior services to the polis and stating that all members of his immediate family were dead and his sons as yet unborn, he demands that "you [jurors] must act as my father and brothers and children . . . and pleading with one another, you must save me." Antiphon (1.4) uses a similar tactic; the prosecutor stresses that he is an orphan and begs the jurors' aid, "for you are my kin (*anagkaioi*)." And since those who should have supported me are my opponents, "where is aid to be sought, where is there safe refuge, other than with you and with justice?" The idea of the citizen body as a kinship unit helps to elucidate the potential power of the rhetorical topos of claiming that an inappropriate obsession with wealth had destroyed in one's opponent the natural affection toward his kin that would normally lead him to come to their aid (above, v.b.3).

The Athenians, who shared a common lineage, also shared the glory of fine deeds done by their common ancestors. Lysias (18.12) reminded jurors of their ancestors, who had given their lives for the democracy. Lycurgus (1.108) noted how the victory at Marathon had demonstrated the superiority of aristocratic bravery (*andreia*) over mere wealth (*ploutos*) and of *aretē* over numbers (*plēthos*).[33] Aeschines

---

[32] E.g., Lys. 2.18; Lyc. 1.41. Aristotle (*Rhet.* 1415b28–30) notes that in epideictic oratory one must make the listener feel he shares in the praise, either personally or as part of his *genos*. On the importance of autochthony generally to Athenian thought, see Loraux, *Enfants*, esp. 35–70; in tragedy: Walsh, "Rhetoric"; Zeitlin, "Thebes."

[33] Is Lycurgus (a "true" aristocrat, of the *genos* Boutadai: above, iii.c) being sub-

(3.259) asked whether the jurors did not agree that "Themistocles and those who died at Marathon and Plataea and the very graves of your ancestors (*progonoi*) will all groan" at the crowning of traitorous Demosthenes. As with Hyperides' discussion of high birth, common ancestral glory could be specifically contrasted with individual aristocratic birth privilege. Lysias (14.18) asks the jurors whether it is not terrible if some men should be so fortunate (*eutucheis*) that when caught doing wrong, they should be let free because of their birth (*dia to autōn genos*), while if *we* (the masses in the infantry endangered by Alcibiades' maneuvering himself into the cavalry) should suffer misfortune (in battle), we would not be able to save a single man because of the virtues of *our* ancestors (*tas tōn progonōn aretas*).

Fourth-century Athenians tended to regard their ancestors as models of unobtainable excellence (e.g., Aesch. 3.178; Isoc. 12.198), but at the same time most Athenians remained convinced that all proper citizens had inherited from their forefathers not only citizen's blood but a patriot's love of fatherland and sense of personal responsibility toward the polis. Lycurgus (1.127) reminded his jurors that "you Athenians" had sworn an oath at Plataea (in 479 B.C.), and he told them that they had inherited the obligations imposed by the oath, just as they inherited the good fortune (*eudaimonia*) of the polis.

In his speech *On the Embassy* (2.152) Aeschines argued against a charge of traitorous conduct by asking a hypothetical question: "Would I have betrayed to Philip my homeland (*patris*), the common habits (*sunētheia*) of friends, my share in my ancestral altars and graves and these [my children] the dearest of all people to me?" Aeschines' question is an argument from probability that takes as given that Athenians with ancestral altars and graves and children to carry on their name would be unlikely to betray their heritage. If patriotism could be inherited, so too could its opposite and, in his definition of the ideal "demotic" politician (cf. above, IV.F), Aeschines argues that a political expert's ancestry should be taken into consideration by the masses: "He should inherit from his ancestors a sense of goodwill (*euergesian tina*) towards the demos, or at very least no hatred of the demos, lest he attempt to injure the polis in vengeance for the disabilities of his ancestors . . ." (3.169). In this passage Aeschines implies that native-born citizens might inherit either a love of or hate for the democratic form of government (cf. Lys. 14.40).

Aeschines' comment on patriotism suggests that along with the idea

---

versive here, by linking the term *plēthos*—ordinarily used by the orators of the masses in a positive sense—with Persian excess and arrogance?

that all Athenians inherited a generalized love of Athens went a parallel concept of the inheritability of more particularized sentiments toward the constitution that pertained there.[34] One might conceivably love Athens but hate the form of government under which the Athenian state operated. Such a one must be regarded as a potential enemy of the democracy. A litigant might hope to find an advantage in arguing that he had inherited a specific affection for the democracy from his forefathers. Isocrates (16.28), for example, stated that Alcibiades had inherited an ancient and genuine friendliness towards the demos (*philian ten pros ton demon*) from his ancestors. A similar argument was based on the presumption that the democracy-loving nature of a man's ancestors served as an example to him to act properly toward the demos. Andocides (2.26) claimed that the memory of his ancestors' resistance to the Pisistratid tyrants encouraged him to be *demotikos* himself. Litigants quite commonly brought up their ancestors' past service to the polis; the general notion of inheritability of attributes allowed the jurors to presume that a man with democratic and generous ancestors would be a good and generous citizen himself.[35]

The aristocratic litigant might make use of the latent Athenian respect for noble birth and yet avoid the opprobrium associated with haughty and traitorous aristocrats, by linking his ancestors' aristocratic behavior with the good of the state. Demosthenes' client (58.66–68) asked a jury to remember his ancestors who included his grandfather Epichares, who as victor in the boys' foot race at Olympia won a crown for the city, but also to remember Epichares' uncle Aristocrates, who helped knock down the fort at Eetioneia in 411 B.C. and so saved the democracy from the oligarchy of the 400. Presumably Aristocrates was particularly admirable, since he had rejected a form of government that had favored the privileged few over the many (cf. above, II.F.6). The speaker therefore can claim that for Aristocrates' sake you jurors would be right to save us, even if we were not "better men" (*beltious ontas*) than our opponents and speakers of the truth. One of Lysias'

---

[34] On the more specific link between autochthony and democracy (e.g., in Plato *Menexenus* 238e, 239a), see Loraux, *Invention*, 193–94. A. Saxenhouse, "Reflections on Autochthony in Euripides' *Ion*," in Euben, *Greek Tragedy*, 252–73, rightly points out the importance of the autochthony theme to national unity and legitimacy (255–56, 268), but wrongly (in my opinion) suggests that autochthony was rejected by the Athenians because it contrasted with the ideal of democratic openness (256–57, 272–73).

[35] On the notion that one's democratic ancestors stand in one's favor, see, for example, Is. 5.41–42; Lys. 10.27, 18.1–8, 21.

clients (19.63) made note of his father, a cavalryman who, whenever he spent more than was necessary, did so to bring honor (*timē*) to the polis as well as to himself. For example, he kept fine horses and was a victor in the games at the Isthmus and at Nemea. Because of his father's victory, the polis was proclaimed and he was crowned. The aristocratic pretensions of both speakers are tempered by the assurance that their ancestors were not only worthy exemplars of the aristocratic code of behavior but were also useful to the polis.

C.2 CITIZENSHIP AND *Charis*

Although just how much in the way of political loyalties could be inherited was open to question (cf. Lys. 25.8, 10), the Athenians clearly accepted the possibility of inheriting from one's ancestors a love of the polis, of the democracy, or both. The concepts of inborn patriotism and responsibility acted along with the communalized aristocratic values of *eugeneia* and *kalokagathia* to reinforce the conviction that the citizenship group must be kept pure. Individuals whose ancestors were not Athenians might be unwilling to make great sacrifices for the state; they were not autochthonous, they did not have ancestral altars and graves to defend, they did not inherit a love of the country. Thus it was the duty of all citizens to remain on guard against surreptitious infiltration by outsiders. Not only were the poorer citizens' various economic prerogatives diluted by the addition of noncitizens to the registers (cf. [Dem.] 59.113), but the inborn cohesiveness of the group itself was threatened. These concerns help to explain the periodic cleansing of the citizenship rolls of noncitizens and the various legislative programs enacted to ensure that restrictions upon creating new citizens were strictly enforced.[36]

Citizenship was terribly important to the Athenians, too important to be based solely on the criterion of parental lineage. In order to be recognized as a citizen, each young Athenian had to be accepted as legitimate by his fathers' demesmen at one of the annual meetings of the deme assembly.[37] The Athenian demos confirmed the citizenship of those Athenians who took the ephebic oath and thereby promised to protect their homeland from all external dangers. Aeschines made a point of his own ephebic service in *On the Embassy* (2.167); like his earlier reference to ancestral graves and altars (2.152, above VI.C.1), his two-years' service patrolling the *chōra* of Attica as an ephebe was

[36] On legislation to keep the citizen rolls "clean," see Patterson, *Pericles' Citizenship Law*, esp. 82–150; Osborne, *Naturalization*, IV.152, 155–64; Whitehead, *Demes*, 106–109, 259.

[37] See Whitehead, *Demes*, 97–108, 259; cf. above, II.E.1.

trotted out to demonstrate his full membership in the citizenship group and hence the legitimacy of his share in the common concerns and interests of the polis.[38]

The Athenians reserved the right to challenge the legitimacy of any individual's claim to group membership. The aspirant to any public *archē* might be called upon at his preliminary *dokimasia*, at his subsequent *euthunai*, or at both to prove that he deserved the title of citizen.[39] Furthermore, if an Athenian failed to fulfill certain duties, his rights of citizenship could be curtailed by the people's courts.[40] Since citizenship was subject to review by the group and could be legally restricted by the group, the right to citizenship cannnot be regarded as inalienable. An Athenian remained a full citizen only for so long as he was accepted by his fellows. Although he would have to be shown to have broken the law for his citizenship to be impaired, given the latitude of Athenian juries to interpret the law in terms of the good of society, this meant that in practice an Athenian (particularly one frequently involved in lawsuits) was secure in his possession of citizenhip only as long as his public behavior conformed to the norms of Athenian society.[41] Aeschines demonstrates his awareness of the importance of proper citizen behavior when, in *On the Embassy*, he capped his previous comments regarding group loyalty by proclaiming that "I grew up among you and I continue to live according to your ways" (*par' humin etraphēn, en tais humeterais diatribais bebiōka*: 2.182).

The citizenship group, which reserved the right to revoke the membership of any individual who acted extraordinarily badly, also had the corollary power to grant citizenship to any non-Athenian who acted extraordinarily well toward the polis. But, in light of the concerns discussed above, citizenship obviously could not be conferred lightly. Grants of citizenship were rare, and the process of conferring Athenian citizenship upon a foreigner was deliberately made complex. A preliminary vote by a quorum of 6,000 citizens at a meeting of the

[38] On the archaic nature of the oath, see Siewart, "Ephebic Oath." See also Pélékidis, *Éphébie*, esp. 103–117; Vidal-Naquet, "Black Hunter"; Winkler, "Ephebes' Song."

[39] On reviews of citizenship at *dokimasiai* and *euthunai*, see Ostwald, *From Popular Sovereignty*, index s.vv. Cf. Aesch. 2.182; Dem. 57.25, 46; and above, III.B.2, below, VII.F.2.

[40] On the laws and procedures associated with curtailment of citizenship rights (*atimia*), see Hansen, '*Apagoge*', 54–98; MacDowell, *Law*, 73–75; Sealey, *Athenian Republic*, 99–111, 116, 123; cf. above, III.B.2.

[41] Cf. the situation in colonial Massachusetts, where, according to Zuckerman, "Social Context," 534, "almost *any* taint on membership in the homogeneous community was a potential basis for derogation."

Assembly was required before the naturalization of an individual could even be considered.[42] Indeed, the scathing comments politicians made on the subject of those who were willing to make foreigners into Athenians suggest that the group was ambivalent about the wisdom of creating any new citizens at all.[43] In fact, citizenship was typically given only to individuals who had previously given a great deal to the polis and who were expected to be equally generous in the future.[44]

Since the Athenians regarded citizenship as so very important and dispensed it to foreigners with such reluctance, they expected that those who were honored with Athenian citizenship would be suitably and permanently grateful for the privilege that had been bestowed upon them and (potentially) upon their progeny. Apollodorus, the son of a naturalized slave, was well aware of the role he was expected to play. He admitted that he had less reason to feel pride (*phronein*) than "all of the rest of you [jurors]" (Dem. 45.82) and stated (45.85, somewhat insincerely, perhaps) that he did not expect any *charis* from the jurors for his material benefactions, but rather was under an eternal obligation to *them* for the share he had been given in the state. As in the case of monetary gifts, then, the concept of *charis* was operational in grants of citizenship. Therefore the individual who was made a citizen must be made to recognize that the honor was bestowed by the demos as a whole. If the new citizen believed that he owed his enhanced status to an individual, he might render his *charis* to that individual alone, rather than to the state (cf. Din. F XVI.5 [Conomis] = A.7.1 [Burtt]). In this case, the Athenian people would not benefit (in terms of future benefactions) for the sacrifice they had made in terms of dilution of their elite status.

The Athenian concern with citizenship, both as a source of the national unity that was thought to result from communal noble ancestry and as a special and *charis*-generating gift of the people, helps to explain the topos, common to several of the political orators, of claiming an opponent was not a citizen. Demosthenes was reviled as a Scythian (on his mother's side) and hence as being not a true Athenian by Aeschines (2.78, 180; 3.171–72) and by Dinarchus (1.15). Demosthenes in return claimed that Aeschines had only recently and mischievously become a citizen and had retroactively made Athenians of his parents

---

[42] Naturalization process: Osborne, *Naturalization*, IV.139–85; grants quite rare: ibid., IV.148–49, 204–206; cf. Hansen, "Demographic Reflections," 177–79.

[43] Attacks on those who would create new citizens: Dem. 23.185, 201, [13].24; Din. 1.44; Lyc. 1.41.

[44] See Osborne, *Naturalization*, IV.186–88. As he points out, the largest group of naturalized citizens were those living abroad and unlikely ever actually to enroll.

(18.130–31, 261).[45] Obviously, if the Athenians had believed the charges to be true, Demosthenes and Aeschines would have been deprived of political rights and their careers as rhetores would have come to an abrupt end. But probably none of the orators involved in this debate really expected legal actions to be brought against their opponents on the basis of a false claim to citizenship. Rather their intention was to plant a seed of doubt in the minds of the listeners about the inherited patriotism of the opponent. This is surely Aeschines' motive for stating that Demosthenes inherited a hatred of the demos from his grandfather and barbarian blood from his mother so that "his *ponēria* is not native to our land" (*epichōrios*: 3.172). Elsewhere (2.22), Aeschines scorned Demosthenes' claim to be full of concern for the "public salt and table" since, according to Aeschines, Demosthenes, not being a citizen, had no part in these things. If Aeschines' audience suspected the purity of Demosthenes' ancestry, they would hardly be surprised that the "barbarian" had no care for such civilized niceties as sacrifices, libations, or communal meals (Aesch. 2.183). In a similar passage, Demosthenes (21.149–50) insinuates that Meidias was born of a foreign woman, and so he is able to claim that Meidias' "genuine inbred barbarism" (*to tēs phuseōs barbaron alēthōs*) naturally rendered him incapable of abiding by Athens' laws.

It was a short rhetorical leap from inherited barbarous traits to naturally traitorous policies. Dinarchus (1.95) points out that since Demosthenes is not a citizen of the polis by birth (*genēi*), his policies and actions are not the sort that would normally be expected from a citizen politician. Dinarchus' attack on Demosthenes is reminiscent of Aeschines' (2.177) general castigation of certain men who had been illegally registered as *politai* and subsequently had encouraged by their policies all that was rotten in the polis. Such false citizens, according to Aeschines, paid court to the name of democracy not through their inborn nature (*ēthos*) but by base flattery. Aeschines implies that a born citizen, inherently respectful of the reality of the democracy, would naturally support policies that benefited the democracy (peace, in this case) rather than the policies that destroyed it. The politician with barbarian blood did not share the concerns, interests, and habits of true Athenians; his policies could not, therefore, be considered completely trustworthy.

The "my opponent is not a born citizen" topos also allowed the rhe-

---

[45] Among other attacks on political enemies as noncitizens, see Dem. *Letters* 4.1. Davies, "Athenian Citizenship," 112, notes the prevalence in Old Comedy of the denial that a politician is a citizen.

tor to invoke the powerful concept of *charis* and to use it against his enemies. Having stated that Aeschines had just the day before become simultaneously a rhetor and an Athenian (18.130), Demosthenes claims that his opponent was without *charis* and was a *ponēros*, since the Athenians had made him free although he had been a slave, and a rich man although he had been a pauper, yet still he plotted against them. Demosthenes hoped to convince the jury that Aeschines had been ungrateful to the demos on two counts. In order to show that his opponent was ungrateful for the wealth he derived from his political career, Demosthenes claims that Aeschines had been born poor; in order to demonstrate that he is ungrateful for his citizenship, Demosthenes claims that Aeschines was not born an Athenian.

D. Slavery and the Ideology of Labor

The topic of slavery takes us outside the world of the citizen and thus outside of the political domain proper. But in order to understand the political sociology of classical Athens and the ideological function of rhetoric in the Athenian state, we must look closely at passages in Athenian speeches that specifically contrast the ethos of the free citizen with the ethos of the slave.

D.1 SLAVE STATUS AND SLAVISH BEHAVIOR

In a passage cited above (VI.C.2: 18.129–30), Demosthenes not only claimed that Aeschines was not a natural citizen but furthermore that he was a slave. Aeschines had previously (2.79) said the same of Demosthenes, adding that the latter had almost been branded as a runaway.[46] Slaves stood at the bottom rung of Athenian society; their unfree status, their condition of being owned by and under the immediate control of another, was the antithesis of the position of the free citizen.[47] Since the laws and customs of the Athenian state kept slaves in bondage, the slave was a natural enemy of the political order, and he could be presumed to hate the system that maintained his servile status. This condition of hatred was regarded as endemic to slaves, part of a slavish ethos that could not be rooted out of the slave's nature by a simple change in status. Even slaves who were freed, according to Demosthenes (24.124), never felt anything but hatred toward their former masters and so could never really be trusted. Lysias (30.2, 5–6, 27–28, 30) repeatedly attacked the lowly status of Nicomachus, his

[46] Cf. Dem. 22.61, 68, *Letters* 3.29.

[47] On the low status of slaves generally, cf. Dem. 36.45–46, 45.73–75, 82. For a good review of the massive literature on the subject, see Finley, *Ancient Slavery*.

opponent in a public trial, emphasizing that he was a son of a public slave, therefore a slave himself by all rights, and completely without gratitude (*acharistos*) to the Athenians for the privileges they had granted him. It was, therefore, self-evident to the Athenians that if slaves were ordinarily allowed to become citizens the state would suffer. Some of the disasters of the past were conveniently attributed to slaves who had managed to get their names onto the citizenship rolls.[48]

If it was dangerous to give citizenship to slaves, it was *a fortiori* madness to allow former slaves to hold positions of political influence. Aeschines (3.169–70) states that the first condition for a *dēmotikos* politician was free birth: he must be free (*eleutheros*) on both his father's and his mother's side so as to avoid the misfortune of birth (*tēn peri to genos atuchian*) which would naturally make him resentful of the laws that preserved the democracy. The "my opponent is a slave" topos can be viewed as a variation and intensification of the more general "not a citizen by birth" topos. Both topoi were used to the same ends, to produce suspicion in the audience that one's opponent did not fully share the common background that united all true Athenians. The audience did not need to believe the slander; implanting a lingering doubt, which would allow the opponent's actions to be interpreted in a bad light, was enough.

An opponent could also be tarred with the slave brush by allusion to his mode of behavior. The Athenians clearly felt that certain types of behavior, suitable for a slave, were improper for a freeborn Athenian. The slave was naturally cowardly, the antithesis of the courageous aristocrat. Demosthenes (22.53) thought that no laboring man (*anthrōpos penēs*), nor even a rich man temporarily low on cash, should have to shame himself "in front of his wife . . . whom he married as a free man and a citizen of the polis" by fleeing the tax collector, running away over the rooftops, hiding under the bed, or doing other things "proper for slaves but not for free men."[49] It is hardly surprising, then, to find the orators attacking political opponents for their slavish actions. Demosthenes (19.210) claimed that Aeschines had "cowered like a slave" before Demosthenes' own rightful speeches and that opposing orators "had the habits of rascally, shame-filled slaves"(24.124). Hyperides (2.10) asked hypothetically whether it

[48] E.g., Aesch. 2.76–77, 173; [Dem.] 13.24.

[49] Note that here the shame at slavish activity is compounded by the citizen having to take the role of the slave in front of his wife, a somewhat higher status "outgroup" member. On the development of the idea of the slavish ethos as opposed to the ethos of the free man and the association of aristocratic values with the latter, see Raaflaub, "Democracy, Oligarchy," 533–34.

would be right for the jurors to spare his opponent Philippides because the latter was a *dēmotikos*. "But you [jurors] know that he has
chosen to be the slave of tyrants" (*turannois douleuein proelomenon*), and
yet he dared to consider himself worthy to give orders to the demos.
Aeschines (1.42) stated that Timarchus had become "a slave to the
most shameful lusts" and to other things that should never overpower
a man who was "well born and free" (*gennaion kai eleutheron*).

D.2 SLAVISH OCCUPATIONS AND
THE VIRTUES OF HARD WORK

Aeschines' comments on Timarchus come in the context of a charge
that the latter had illegally acted as a prostitute. Any number of factors
may have entered into the Athenian prohibition of male citizens who
publicly addressed the people in the Assembly from engaging in prostitution. The adult Athenian who prostituted himself might be per
ceived to be taking on the role of a child or a woman—in either case
not of a free citizen. But the prostitute was also engaged in a particularly lowly and degrading form of mercantile exchange, selling his
body for the use of another. This sort of activity was clearly too close
to slavery—in which the body of one individual is permanently at the
service of another—to be condoned.[50] Few other forms of personal
service were so self-evidently "slavish" as prostitution. But in his
speech *On the Crown* (18.258) Demosthenes claimed that Aeschines'
work at menial jobs in his own father's schoolhouse was the activity "of
a house slave (*oiketēs*)—not of a free-born boy." The implication that
manual labor was inherently slavish is striking. Most Athenians had to
work for a living, and some of them performed tasks as menial as
those Demosthenes claims were done by the young Aeschines. Citizens
who did menial work themselves might be expected to take umbrage
at this sort of remark.

Yet the political orators quite frequently attacked one another on
the basis of their present or former "servile" occupations. In both *On
the False Embassy* and *On the Crown*, Demosthenes returned time and
again to Aeschines' former employment in low-status jobs, mentioning
that he had helped not only his father in the schoolhouse but also his
mother at her initiations (19.199, 18.259–60, 265). After becoming a
man, Aeschines went on to "that finest of occupations," serving as a
"pestilent clerk" (*grammateus olethros*) for the magistrates of the state

---

[50] Cf., in general, K. J. Dover, *Greek Homosexuality* (New York, 1980), 19–39;
D. Cohen, "Work in Progress: The Enforcement of Morals, An Historical Perspec-
tive," *Rechtshistorische Journal* 3 (1984): 114–29; and esp. the insightful comments of
Golden, "Slavery," esp. 319–20.

(19.98, 200, 18.127, 209, 261, 265). He then changed jobs but chose one "that was no disgrace to his past": working as a bit actor (*tritagō-nistēs*) in the theater.[51] Incidentally, Aeschines was a rumor monger and agora loafer (18.127) and a logographer (19.250). His big voice was suitable for a public herald but not for an ambassador or politician in charge of serious public matters (19.337–38).[52] Demosthenes also attacked the occupations of Aeschines' relatives (19.281, cf. 19.249, 18.129), asking if, after having fined worthy men like Epicrates, Thrasybulus, and a descendant of Harmodius the Tyrant-slayer, the Athenians will choose to acquit Aeschines, the son of Atrometus the schoolteacher and of Glaucothea the priestess of the cult of Cybele. Demosthenes claims that Aeschines' brother Philochares was a painter of boxes and drums and that his other brothers were, like Aeschines himself, undersecretaries and errand-runners at various public offices (19.237, 249).

Although Demosthenes' wealthy background left him less open to attacks based on menial occupation, Aeschines attempted to reply in kind, labeling Demosthenes a juggler and a cutpurse (3.207) and harping upon his profession as a logographer (2.180, 3.173). Aeschines (3.255) implied that Demosthenes' youth had been rather less than aristocratic by suggesting that his audience inquire whether Demosthenes' supporters were "fellow hunters" and "co-gymnasts" of his youth. No, by Zeus, Aeschines replied to his own question, Demosthenes had not spent his boyhood hunting wild boar and cultivating the vigor of his body, but rather had practiced the trade (*epaskōn technas*) of pursuing other mens' wealth by sycophantic legal attacks. Elsewhere (2.93), Aeschines mocked Demosthenes for putting on airs (*semnologei*) as if the jurors did not know him to be the bastard son of a knife-maker.

Other orators also castigated their political opponents for their occupations, often employing terminology similar to that used by Demosthenes and Aeschines. Lysias (30.27–28) notes how Nicomachus not only went from slavery to citizenship and from poverty to wealth, but from the position of undersecretary (*hupogrammateus*) to Lawmaker. Iphicrates (Aristot. *Rhet.* 1405a19–20) called Callias a mendicant priest of Cybele (*mētragurtēs*). Both insults are reminiscent of those later used by Demosthenes against Aeschines. Lycurgus (F IV.2

---

[51] Dem. 18.129, 209, 261–62, 265, 19.200, 246–47, 337. Cf. Rowe, "Portrait," esp. 400–402; Kindstrand, *Stylistic Evaluation*, 19–22; Ghiron-Bistagne, *Recherches*, 158–60, 191–94; and above, III.E.6.

[52] On the duties and standing of the public heralds, see Vocke, "Athenian Heralds."

[Conomis] = A.3 [Burtt]) refers to an unnamed opponent who "will play other men's tragic parts" (*tous heterous tragōidous*), recalling Demosthenes' attacks on Aeschines' life as an actor. Dinarchus (1.92, 95), like Aeschines, called Demosthenes a juggler. Aeschines' slur on Demosthenes' father as a knife-maker finds parallels not only in Aristophanes' famous characterizations of fifth-century politicians[53] but in the works of other political orators. Andocides (F III.2 [Maidment]) claimed that Hyperbolus' father was a "branded slave" who worked in the public mint, while Hyperbolus himself, a foreigner and barbarian, made lamps for a living. Elsewhere (1.146), Andocides referred to Cleophon as "the lyre maker." Demosthenes (25.38) referred to two unnamed politicians as "the coppersmith from Piraeus" and "the tanner." Demosthenes (22.70) chided Androtion, who had melted down old honorary crowns, for being at the same time "rhetor, goldsmith, tax collector, and auditor of accounts." In a letter (4.1), Demosthenes suggested that Theramenes, who had attacked Demosthenes in public, was raised from childhood in a workshop.[54]

The slurs of Athenian politicians upon each others' menial backgrounds, along with the comments of their contemporaries who wrote for elite audiences—notably, Plato, Aristotle, and Xenophon—have led some scholars to conclude that the Athenians scorned industry, trade, and "banausic" occupations generally. The oratorical references are explained in terms either of mass acceptance of an aristocratic ethos scornful of manual labor, or by recourse to the theory that the Assembly and law courts were dominated by the well-to-do who did not have to work for a living.[55] Neither explanation is satisfactory.

[53] See Ehrenberg, *People of Aristophanes*, 120–21, 341; Connor, *NP*, 171–74; Ostwald, *From Popular Sovereignty*, 214–15.

[54] Aeschines (3.166) makes note of Demosthenes' "revolting and incredible words" to the effect that certain politicians were "pruning the polis," "trimming the tendrils of the demos," "cutting the sinews of affairs," and how Demosthenes had moaned that "we are being matted and sewn by them, [and] they are first drawing us, as if needles, into tight places." We might guess, in light of the preceding list of "craft insults," that Demosthenes had intended his audience to envision his political opponents engaged in the various menial tasks which he used as metaphors for their traitorous policies.

[55] Cf. Aristot. *Rhet.* 1367a32–33, 1381a21–23. Dover, *GPM*, 32–35 (cf. 40–41), for example, suggests that it is "remarkable" to find Demosthenes addressing a mass jury adopting a supercilious attitude toward low-status occupations and that it is even more remarkable to find Demosthenes contrasting himself, the man of leisure, with Aeschines, the working man. Dover argues that either the Athenian jurors were "fairly prosperous" (the hypothesis Dover prefers: cf. above, v.n.61) or they liked to be treated as if they were prosperous and adopted the values of the prosperous class. Hopper, *Basis*, 4, suggests that the prejudice (esp. in Aristotle)

Rhetorical discussions of an individual's occupations take on a some-what different tone once we leave the political arena. Certainly, the Athenians tended to distrust individuals who participated in certain occupations. No one loved professional money lenders (cf. Dem. 37.52–53), and many Athenians had deeply rooted suspicions about the honesty of the entire class of professional traders (e.g., Dem. 36.44). But the Athenian view of the "world of the emporium" is a question that must be kept separate from the question of citizens' oc-cupations that were not specifically linked to large-scale lending, buy-ing, and selling. The Athenian citizen who associated himself with the trading culture centered in Piraeus risked being identified with the less desirable traits Athenians ascribed to metics, especially lust for gain over honor.[56] Ps-Lysias (6.6, 26–29, 49) brought up Andocides' career as an overseas trader, perhaps because he hoped that the dis-taste the Athenians felt for traders would prejudice them against his opponent. Demosthenes (19.114) attacked Philocrates for openly en-gaging in trade and banking with money taken as bribes from Philip. Nevertheless, traders were not always regarded as completely heinous. Lycurgus (1.55–58) attempts to destroy Leocrates' excuse that he had left Athens after the battle of Chaeronea to engage in trade, by stating that was the very moment when all other traders had hurried home to aid the polis. No one, says Lycurgus, would have tried to increase his wealth at such a time. Lycurgus' comment implies at least a modicum of true patriotism for the trading community, albeit in contrast to Leo-crates' cowardice.

Attacks on the basis of nontrade occupations in private orations are very rare. Demosthenes' client Euxitheus, whose mother had served as a nurse and sold ribbons in the agora, claimed (57.30–36) that his op-ponent Eubulides had used the occupations of Euxitheus' mother in an attempt to prove that he, Euxitheus, was not a citizen. But this was not a fair argument, argued Euxitheus, and it was not right that jurors should consider those who worked for a living (*ergazomenoi*) to be for-eigners (*xenoi*), but rather they should realize that sycophants such as

---

against banausic professions was not altogether based on primitive aristocratic ide-als nor on the idea that yeoman farmers make the best soldiers. Rather, the preju-dice owed a great deal to the dislike of urban concentrations of people and their notorious instability. Hopper's hypothesis helps to explain Aristotle but not the Athenian jurors.

[56] See esp. Mossé, " 'World of the Emporium' "; Seager, "Lysias"; Whitehead, *Ide-ology*, 116–21. Of course one must keep in mind that a good number of the existing private orations, especially in the Demosthenic corpus, were maritime cases and so intimately involved with trade. But many were not, e.g., those by Lysias and Isaeus.

Eubulides were *ponēroi* (57.32). The defendant stated (57.35) that of course if his family were rich, they would not sell ribbons, but this has nothing to do with the question of citizen birth. Even if being a nurse is a lowly thing (*tapeinon*), Euxitheus goes on to say (57.45), the present trial was not about money or individual fortune, but birth, and many free men had in the past been forced by poverty to engage in slavish enterprises (*doulika pragmata*); such folk deserved sympathy, not disdain.

Euxitheus' argument accepts the premise that some occupations are regarded by Athenians as slavish, undesirable, and certainly to be avoided by anyone whose circumstances so allowed. However, he cites a *nomos* (57.30) that forbade anyone to reproach any Athenian, male or female, with working in the agora. The existence of such a law cuts two ways. It shows that the Athenians did not think such reproaches were fair in a court of law, but it also suggests that at some point in the past (unfortunately we do not know when) slander based upon occupation had been common enough to spark the concern of the lawmakers. In the present trial Euxitheus freely admits, even overstates (see above, v.D.2), his family's lowly status, and he expects the jurors to agree that he deserves sympathy for his plight, rather than scorn.

Euxitheus (Dem. 57.32) cites another law regarding idleness (*argias*) which he suggests his opponent Eubulides "who denounces us as workers" (*ergazomenous*) is liable to. The intentions of the idleness law remain obscure, but the context suggests that individuals who did not have a visible means of support were liable to its provisions.[57] This allows the supposition that the Athenians might in certain circumstances have considered hard work a virtue, a presumption that seems to be borne out by other rhetorical passages. Euxitheus (57.36) himself says that if *penētes* should not be dishonored, much less should "those who are willing to work (*ergazesthai*) and live by honest means" (*zēn ek tou dikaiou*). Aeschines (1.27) notes that the lawmaker who drew up the regulations concerning who might address the demos did not exclude anyone just because that person lacked ancestors who had served as *stratēgoi* or indeed if he worked at a craft to earn his daily bread (*oude ge ei technēn tina ergazetai epikourōn tēi anagkaiai trophēi*), but rather the lawmaker particularly (*malista*) invites these men to address the demos by repeatedly asking if anyone wishes to speak. Later in the same speech, Aeschines (1.195) suggests that the jurors tell Demosthenes' supporters who had wasted their patrimonies to "go to work" (*ergazes-*

---

[57] On the *graphai argias*, which may be as early as Draco or Solon, see Wallace, *Areopagos*, chapter 2.iii.a.

thai) and find some other way to make their living. Dinarchus (1.70) claimed it was not just, not in the communal interest (*koinon*), and not democratic that workers (*ergazomenous*) should pay *eisphora* while Demosthenes stole and plundered. Apollodorus ([Dem.] 59.50–51) describes the marriage of Neaera's daughter to Phrastor, a "working man" (*andra ergatēn*) who had collected a few goods by frugal living; the licentious daughter was unable to accommodate herself to his simple and decent way of life and so he threw her out. Clearly, the jurors' sympathies are to be on the side of the unlucky laboring man saddled with such a wife (cf. Aristoph. *Clouds* 41–55). In this context we may also recall the passages in which litigants claim to have obtained their fortunes through hard work; these were discussed above (V.D.1) as examples of attempts to deflect class resentment. These passages suggest that while popular ideology reflected an aristocratic ethos which regarded all manual labor as inherently slavish, the masses were also willing to regard working for a living—at least by poorer citizens—as respectable and proper.[58]

D.3 FREEDOM AND LABOR IN THE POLITICAL ARENA

Demosthenes 57 demonstrates that an attack upon the occupation of an opponent or on members of his family *could* be used in a private speech, but such attacks are uncommon in extant private speeches. They were, however, often used in the political arena. The underlying assumption of the rhetorical attack upon the occupation of one's opponent appears to be that working as a hired laborer limited the personal freedom of the hired man.[59] Aristotle noted in the *Rhetoric* (1367a32–33) that a man not carrying on a banausic trade (*technē*) was shown to be a free man (*eleutheros*) because he need not "live for the sake of another" (*pros allon zēn*). Later in the same work (1381a19–23), Aristotle claimed that "those whom we honor" are those who do not live upon others (*mē aph' heterōn zōntas*) but work for themselves. Among the latter are farmers and other "self-employed folk" (*autour-*

---

[58] Cf. Aymard, "Hiérarchie"; Mossé, *Fin de la démocratie*, 160–66; Markle, "Jury Pay," 284; Loraux, *Invention*, 182; and esp. M. Balme, "Attitudes to Work and Leisure in Ancient Greece," *Greece and Rome* 31 (1984): 140–52.

[59] For the idea that working for another implied a limitation on a man's freedom, see Finley, "Was Greek Civilization," 148; Dover, *GPM*, 40; Jones, *AD*, 11; Ste. Croix, *CSAGW*, 84–85. Cf. Zuckerman, "Social Context," 530–31, who suggests that in colonial Massachussets the vote could safely be withheld from tenants and dependent sons, since these classes of individuals could be privately coerced.

goi).[60] "Living for another" was no doubt an undesirable condition for any Athenian, but the masses knew that a citizen was not always able to live as he desired, and so they did not necessarily consider it despicable for an *idiōtēs* to work for another man in order to meet the needs of his existence.[61]

The rhetor, however, responsible for giving good advice to the people, could not fulfill his political function if he were another man's hireling. Demosthenes (18.284) scorned the relationship between Aeschines and Philip on the grounds that it was based not upon friendship (*philia*) or guest-friendship (*xenia*) but rather on servitude (*mistharnia*). The reference to *philia* recalls the aristocratic code. Demosthenes' comment contrasts the aristocratic norm of friendship between equals—by implication, a proper relationship for a politician—with an improper, servile relationship, one in which the hireling stands beneath his paymaster in the social hierarchy. Later in the speech, Demosthenes returns to this theme, claiming that after the battle of Chaeronea a call went out soliciting not advisers (*sumboulōn*) but rather "servants willing to take orders" (*tōn tois epitattomenois hupēretountōn*) and men willing to work for pay (*mistharnein*) against the good of the polis. This call was eagerly answered by Aeschines and his supporters (18.320). Demosthenes' opponents used similar language. Dinarchus (1.28) spoke of "Demosthenes the servant, the old retainer" (*misthōtos, misthōtos palaios*). Aeschines (3.218) said that Demosthenes spoke in the Assembly or stayed quiet according to what his paymasters (*misthodotai*) ordered him to do. Aeschines added (3.220) that constant oratory was the mark of a man who did it as work and for pay (*ergazomenou kai mistharnountos*).[62]

The hired orator was obviously not completely free to speak his own mind. The claim that one's opponent spoke for pay was therefore an attack on his status as a free citizen since, as Raaflaub has demonstrated, the right of free speech in the Assembly was an essential element in the Athenians' definition of themselves as a status group dis-

[60] Cf. Aristot. *Pol.* 1328b19–1329a2, 1337b18–22, 1341b8–18, *Nicomachean Ethics* 1131a24–29, and the discussion of Aristotle's concept of banausic in Ober, "Aristotle's Political Sociology."

[61] Raaflaub, "Democracy, Oligarchy," 528–34, *Entdeckung der Freiheit*, 304–11, suggests a hypothetical origin for the scorn for labor in elite attempts to respond to the democratic "monopoly" on the concept of freedom, and he notes that the "average Athenian citizen" may not have fully shared those views.

[62] Among other examples of "servile" imagery in the political orators, see Lyc. 1.138 (*philia* and *genos* contrasted to *mistharnia*); Lys. 29.6; Dem. 21.139, 23.147, 51.21, *Letters* 3.29.

tinct from the metics and slaves.[63] Furthermore, the Athenians recognized that the hired orator advocated in his speeches the policies his employers paid him to support. This was obviously a pernicious situation if the paymaster were an enemy of the Athenian state. Even if the political orator was hired by another citizen, however, the Athenians knew that his speech would reflect the opinions of the anonymous employer and not necessarily those of the speaker himself. As we have seen (especially III.E.5), Athenian jurors and Assemblymen felt it was important to consider the speech they were hearing in the context of their knowledge of the speaker. If the real "author" of the policies advocated by a speaker remained hidden, the Athenian demos could not use its knowledge of the life and character of the speaker in judging the probable worth of his proposals or the motives behind his prosecution of another politician. The hired orator was no more than a political logographer, differing from the private logographer only in that the hired politician was more dangerous and less honest.[64]

The public's distrust of the hireling political orator provides a context in which to view some of the attacks upon the earlier careers of political opponents. Demosthenes' work as a logographer, selling speeches to private litigants, could be seen as preparation for selling out the state's interests to his shadowy employers. Aeschines' jobs as an actor, speaking other men's lines for pay, and as a clerk in the *archai*, running errands for the magistrates and associating with public slaves, might be construed as leading naturally to a career as a hired speaker who recited whatever lines he was told to recite and who would remain at the beck and call of his Macedonian masters. As in the case of attacks upon opponents as noncitizens and as born slaves, the "occupational attack" may be read as an attempt to brand a political adversary with the suspicion of having engaged in past behavior that might be assumed to have some pernicious effect upon his present disposition.

E. Tensions within the Ideology of Status

The theory that the political orators referred to their opponents' former "servile" occupations in order to play upon the popular belief that "once a servant, always a servant" does not, however, provide a completely satisfactory explanation for the remarkably nasty attacks upon relatives and ancestors which the political orators engaged in with such

---

[63] Raaflaub, "Freien Bürgers Recht," esp. 16–20.
[64] See also Perlman, "Politicians," 331–33; Rowe, "Portrait," 399. Cf. below, VII.F.2.

apparent glee.[65] As we have seen, Demosthenes dealt viciously and individually with the professions and backgrounds of a variety of Aeschines' relatives, calling his father a shackled slave and his mother a common whore (18.129). Aeschines (especially 3.171–72) described Demosthenes' mother as a barbarous Scythian, his grandfather as a traitor, and his father as a knife-maker. Dinarchus (1.111) said that the jurors would soon discover that Demosthenes began life as an "unknown" (*agnōtos*) who inherited absolutely no ancestral fame (*patrikēn doxan*) from his ancestors, but indeed became famous (*endoxon*) only when the polis had fallen to a position completely unworthy of itself or of the Athenians' ancestors. Demosthenes (22.63) scolded Androtion for insulting the *eisphora*-payers, better men and better born (*beltious, ek beltionōn*) than himself. In another speech, Demosthenes called Meidias "nobody, son of a nobody" (*mēdena mēdamothen*), unworthy of *charis*, pity, or sympathy (21.148). The story of Meidias' birth was a "mock tragedy"; he was sold as an infant to a remarkably silly but wealthy Athenian woman, and he thereby got his hands on resources and citizenship which he in no way deserved as a birthright (21.149–50). Demosthenes (10.73) supposed that his opponent Aristomedes might try to claim that he had the fame (*doxa*) of a father or grandfather to uphold, "but your father was a thief, if he is like you!"[66]

E.1 Politicians' Aristocratic Pretensions

Unlike Euxitheus in Demosthenes 57, the political orators did not respond to their opponents' use of slanderous topoi based on their birth,

[65] Kennedy, *Art of Persuasion*, 229, characterizes Demosthenes' attacks upon Aeschines' background and Aeschines' replies as a kind of "perverted ethos," which reflects the fourth-century interest in personality. This is a good description of the attacks but hardly sufficient as an explanation of why such attacks would be acceptable to the Athenians, or why they were more acceptable in the political arena than in private orations. I agree with Markle, "Jury Pay," 283, that the Athenians expected influential speakers in the Assembly to be from a relatively high social stratum; but I do not agree with his suggestion that the attacks on Aeschines in Dem. 18 are to be interpreted as "comic interludes." Cf. the unsatisfactory attempt by Rowe, "Portrait," to show that Demosthenes attempted to portray his opponent as the comic type of the *alazōn*. Montgomery, *Way to Chaeronea*, 78–80, 103–104, discusses Demosthenes' and Aeschines' rhetorical attacks on one another's status and lifestyle and points out the importance of high status for the would-be politician. But he does not investigate the ideological context of Athenian attitudes toward status. Dyck, "Function and Persuasive Power," deals well with the rhetorical structure of Dem. 18 but has little to say on why particular images would have had a powerful effect upon Athenian audiences.

[66] Demades' father was called a sailor according to Suda D.414–15, and Demades himself was called a sailor, a shipbuilder, and a ferryman: Sextus Emp. *adv. Math.* 2.16, *Suda* D.414; cf. Davies, *APF* 3263. These labels may well go back to fourth-century rhetorical "occupation slander."

the status of their relatives, or their past occupations by suggesting that such attacks were unjust in principle. The political orators often attempted to show that their opponents had deliberately falsified the true facts of their background. But their failure to deny the validity of status-based slander, coupled with their willingness to engage in counter-arguments in the same terms, reveals an important element in Athenian political ideology.[67] The standard defense of an orator attacked on the basis of occupation, ancestry, or both was to refute the charges by demonstrating that his ancestors were highly reputable, even noble individuals and that his own life was consistently lived in accordance with the highest standards of the old-fashioned aristocratic code of behavior.

Aeschines, who suffered a particularly savage and skillful onslaught upon his status at the hands of Demosthenes, begins his defense by stating that the jurors were of course competent judges of his daily life, but he goes on to suggest that there were some things that remained hidden (*asunopta*) to the many (*hoi polloi*) but were considered most important (*megista*) by noblemen (*chrēstoi*). These things, says Aeschines, were to his advantage in the eyes of the law (2.146).[68] So, he continues, I will relate the story of my parentage truthfully, as I was educated to do (2.147). Aeschines states that his father, Atrometus, had competed as an athlete when a young man, before the Peloponnesian War destroyed his property. Atrometus then served as a soldier in Asia and proved his noble courage (*aristeuein*) when faced with danger. By birth he was of the phratry that shares the altars of the Eteoboutadai, from which *genos* comes the priestess of Athena Polias (2.147).

Aeschines thus attempts to demonstrate that his father was impoverished through no fault of his own and had engaged in the aristocratic pastime of athletic competition before the war. The challenges of battle proved that Atrometus was an aristocrat by nature, and he had cult associations with a noble *genos*. Elsewhere (3.191–92), Aeschines hints that his father lived a properly unservile life, claiming that "in his leisure" (*epi scholēs*) Atrometus had often lectured his son on

[67] The orators occasionally claim they will mitigate their comments. Cf. Dem. 18.256: I will be as moderate as possible in my remarks; Dem. 18.264: I will say about Aeschines only those things that are not shameful to say. Orators also might claim that slander per se was evil, but this comment typically precedes a character attack.

[68] Cf. Loraux, *Invention*, 183–84, who suggests that there are two levels operating in Pericles' Funeral Oration (Thuc. 2.40.2): one for a cultured elite audience (there is a place for aristocrats as leaders), the other for the masses (workers can acquire a sufficient knowledge to contribute to the political process).

the stern moral values of the old-fashioned jurors of his youth.[69] After
the war, during the reign of the Thirty, Atrometus—like all good
democrats—went into exile, and later he helped restore the democracy. Meanwhile, Aeschines' maternal uncle Cleobulus, son of Glau-
cus, served with "Demaenetus, a descendant of Bouzygos" (hence a
gennētēs) when he won a naval victory (2.78). Aeschines portrays his
mother herself as a free woman, who had accompanied her husband
into exile to Corinth during the rule of the Thirty (2.148). Hence,
Aeschines' inheritance from his parents is both noble (at least by association) and properly democratic. Aeschines' brother Philochares,
he asserts, was not a man of unaristocratic pursuits (*agenneis diatribas*)
as "you, Demosthenes, insultingly stated (*blasphēmeis*), but a man who
engaged in athletic pursuits (*gumnasiois diatribōn*), who had served as a
soldier with Iphicrates, and who had been *stratēgos* for the past three
years" (2.149). Aeschines' other brother, Aphobetus, served as ambassador to the Persian King and as state treasurer (2.149). Philon, the
brother of Aeschines' wife, is described as a hoplite sound of mind and
fit of body; her other brother, Epichares, whose excellent education
(*euagōgia*) Demosthenes had cast aspersions upon, was a man who was
"not unknown" in the city (2.151).

In view of his "peril" and Demosthenes' sarcastic references to him
as the "good soldier," Aeschines felt that he might also be permitted
to say a few words about his own military service. After his two years
as an ephebe (on which, see above, VI.C.2), he fought as a foot soldier
(*stratiōtēs*) in land battles whenever the polis required it of him (2.168–
70). The references to military service demonstrate Aeschines' patriotism and hoplite status. Aeschines' military record helped to place
him among the middling citizens, and he states (2.181, cf. 3.218) that
the jurors must remember that he is an *idiōtēs*, "the equal to the middling ones among you" (*tois metriois humōn homoios*).[70]

But Aeschines clearly implied rather more than middling status for
himself when he claimed that things about his background that were
hidden from the many were deemed important by *chrēstoi*, when he

[69] This passage may appear to belie the comment of Loraux, *Invention*, 179, that
the Athenian polis "condemned aristocratic leisure." But her context, unlike Aeschines', concerns those who preferred leisure to public life.

[70] Although it seems quite possible that by the mid-330s all Athenians served as
ephebes (above, IV.n.14), before the introduction of pay for ephebic service, most
ephebes may have been of at least hoplite status. On the lack of pay for ephebes
before 338, see Gauthier, *Commentaire des 'Poroi'*, 190–95. Rowe, "Portrait," 404,
points out that in *On the Crown* (esp. 18.62, 173, 211, 300) Demosthenes employs
the "modest metaphor" of the obedient soldier in referring to his own services as
statesman.

gratuitously dragged in his rather far-fetched links with the *genē* of the Eteoboutadai and Bouzygai, when he mentioned that his father was an athlete and his brother a man of "athletic pursuits." These comments allude to aristocratic associations, and Aeschines reinforces his pretensions to aristocratic culture by frequently employing athletic metaphors in his speeches. Apparently he hoped to be perceived as the sort of man who spent a good deal of time in gymnasia and so naturally used athletic turns of phrase.[71] As did other regular visitors to the gymnasia, Aeschines had developed an appreciation for boyish pulchritude, and in his speech *Against Timarchus*, despite his moralistic attack upon the evils of citizens prostituting themselves, he states quite openly that "I do not criticize correct boy-love (*erōta dikaion*) . . . and I do not deny that I have been a lover (*erōtikos*) and still am one; nor do I deny that I have been involved in the contests and squabbles that arise from this practice." Furthermore, "to be in love with those who are beautiful and self-controlled (*tōn kalōn kai sōphronōn*) is the experience of an open-hearted and generous soul." To engage in licentious acts for pay, on the other hand, is "the work of a hubristic and uneducated man" (1.136–37). Aeschines admits he was constrained to say something about his erotic adventures, since his enemies had got hold of some poems he had written to his lovers and planned to quote from them in court. Notably, Aeschines does not care to deny the authenticity of the verses—or at least of the less explicit of them. Indeed, he appears to have been eager to demonstrate that he was a participant in this most aristocratic of pastimes, and his "confession" is couched in self-consciously aristocratic terms.[72]

In short, Aeschines attempted to leave his audience with the impression that he was a member of an aristocratic family and that his behavior was consistent with several important aspects of the aristocratic code. Aeschines' pretensions to aristocratic status help to explain his claims that Demosthenes' supporters were not "fellow hunters" or "co-gymnasts." Aeschines is denying Demosthenes and his friends the sort of background he has created, by hint and innuendo, for himself.

In *On the Crown* Demosthenes not only attacked Aeschines' past but defended his own. Like Aeschines, Demosthenes introduces his life as well known to his audience: "I have always lived in your midst, so if you know me to be such a man as he alleges, do not now tolerate my

---

[71] E.g., Aesch. 2.183, 3.179–80, 206, 246. Aeschines (3.216) complained of Demosthenes' censuring him for visiting the gymnasia with the young men. Such censure does not appear in any extant Demosthenic speech.

[72] On pederastic *rhetores*, cf. Aristoph. *Ecclesiazusae* 112–13; Wilcox, "Scope," 129–30; Dover, *GPM*, 213–16, with other sources cited.

voice . . . but if you accept and know that I am a much better man than he and of better parents (*pollōi beltiō toutou kai ek beltionōn*) and that my family and I are in no way worse than the middling ones (*mē-denos tōn metriōn . . . cheirona*)—I put it this way in order not to say something grievous (*epachthēs*)—then refuse to believe his comments about me" (18.10). By emphasizing that he had always lived among the people, Demosthenes proves his conformity to popular values, but what is the "grievous" thing Demosthenes hints at but avoids saying outright? Surely it is that he is not only better and better born than Aeschines but also than most other Athenians. Demosthenes was under less constraint than Aeschines to dredge up aristocratic associations, because his background was in reality much more comfortable. Thus Demosthenes is able to claim that he restrains himself when discussing Aeschines' background: "Such topics are fitting for you [Aeschines], but to tell such stories is perhaps unbecoming to me" (18.129). But, of course, if Aeschines is determined to investigate Demosthenes' fortune, Demosthenes will, reluctantly, describe both their lives "from the beginning," attempting to be as moderate as possible (*metriōtata*: 18.256). We have considered some of the implications of Demosthenes' references to his good schooling and wealthy background above (IV.E, V.F.4), but it is instructive to review the general tone of the passages in which Demosthenes alludes to his own past: he went to suitable schools and had sufficient means, so that that he was not driven by need to do anything shameful (18.257). Obviously, therefore, he did not need to work for another man, as Aeschines had done. When he came of age, Demosthenes' "circumstances were in accordance with his upbringing," and he performed notable liturgies and "in no way renounced noble ambition" (*philotimia*) but aided both the polis and his *philoi* (18.257). The reference to Demosthenes' own *philoi* may be contrasted to his subsequent characterization of Aeschines' servile relationship to Philip, discussed above (VI.D.3). In short, Demosthenes was a man of leisure, an aristocrat by lifestyle, superior to his opponent by birth, a man who forbears to say all that he might about his superiority for fear of offending the sensibilities of his audience (18.258). In running through a step-by-step comparison of his own "fortune" with that of Aeschines (18.265–67), Demosthenes in effect asks the jurors to make their decision not only on the basis of his innocence but also on the basis of his superior social status. It was, he implies, unseemly that one such as himself should even be bothered with one such as Aeschines.

Demosthenes and Aeschines provide the best documented examples of politicians who defended themselves by laying claim to aristocratic attributes, but a few other passages suggest this line of argument was not rare in Athenian political rhetoric. Hyperides' client (3.25–26) stated, "I am not a perfume seller, nor do I work in any other trade (*allēn technēn ergazo[mai]*), but rather I farm the soil which my father left to me." Elsewhere (5.21), Hyperides declared that Demosthenes had no right to speak to him of the claims of *philia*, since Demosthenes' traitorous conduct had made him a laughing stock and had disgraced those who had formerly shared his policies: we might have been regarded as the finest of men by the demos (*lamprotatois [einai] para tōi demōi*) and enjoyed for the rest of our lives a noble reputation (*doxēs chrē[stēs]*) but for his shamelessness. Lysias' aristocratic client Mantitheus (16.18–19) begged his audience not to be offended by his long hair, arguing that they should judge his deeds, not his appearance. Mantitheus goes on (16.20) to say that some might be annoyed at such a young man attempting to speak in the Assembly, but he believed that he was not being overly ambitious (*philotimoteron*), "considering my ancestors who never ceased to be active in the affairs of the polis." Mantitheus' reference to his ancestors and their services to the polis might be explained partly in terms of the democratization of aristocratic ideology, but the fact that he kept his distinctive hairstyle (assuming that a budding politician would decide how to wear his hair not merely on the basis of personal vanity) suggests that he expected that this symbol of an aristocratic background would impress the *bouleutai* more than it irritated them. Later in the century, the politician Hegesippus was known as "Topknot" (Krobylos) because he too affected an aristocratic hairstyle (Aesch. 3.118, 1.64). Like Mantitheus, Hegesippus apparently believed that on the whole an aristocratic look was more of an asset than a hindrance to the politician's major goal of gaining the sympathies of his mass audiences.

E.2 *Ēthos* versus Achievement

The Attic political orators never developed a topos based on the notion that to have "pulled oneself up by the bootstraps" was a good thing for a potential leader of the people. The exception which proves the rule, the one example of an Athenian "Abraham Lincoln," might be Iphicrates. According to Aristotle (*Rhet.* 1365a28–29), Iphicrates lauded himself (*hauton enekōmiaze*) by asking his listeners to "look at what I started from" (*ex hōn hupērxe tauta*). Since Aristotle's context is people who accomplish things beyond what would naturally be expected of them (his other example is the Olympic victor who began as a fish carter), we may guess that Iphicrates indeed called attention to his humble past. Aristotle (*Rhet.* 1398a17–22) also states that when

Iphicrates desired to prove that the best man (*ho beltistos*) is the best born (*gennaiotatos*)—rather than vice versa—he said that Harmodius and Aristogeiton had nothing high born (*gennaion*) about them before they did a "high born deed" (*gennaion ti praxai*). Iphicrates tried to show that he was more closely related (*sungenesteros*) to Harmodius and Aristogeiton than his opponent when he said, "My deeds (*erga*) are more closely related at any rate to Harmodius' and Aristogeiton's deeds than are yours."

For Iphicrates, noble deeds were prior to, and evidence for, a noble nature. But Iphicrates' definition of his good deeds in terms of the vocabulary of noble birth demonstrates that he recognized the importance of birth to the Athenian public man. No Athenian politician whose works are preserved attempted to adopt Iphicrates' "humble origins" approach, but Iphicrates' placement of good deeds above good birth in the hierarchy of worth has echoes in other fourth-century political speeches. Demosthenes (20.57) notes that in private life (*idiai*) each man looks for some worthy (*axios*) man to be his son-in-law and that worthiness is determined by conventions (*nomoi*) and appearances (*doxai*). But, says Demosthenes, in communal affairs (*koinēi*) the polis and demos discover who of the politicians is their benefactor and helper, and this is not determined by birth (*genei*) or appearance but by deed (*ergōi*). Mantitheus (Lys. 16.19) urges that his aristocratic hairdo should not tell against him, by arguing that it is wrong to love or hate someone according to appearances (*ap' opseōs*) but proper to judge according to deeds (*ergon*). Many staidly dressed ones have harmed the state, and others, careless of their appearance, have done many good things—*polla k'agatha*—for you. In this last phrase Mantitheus is playing upon the term *kalos k'agathos*; he wants to claim that his deeds are good, but he reminds the jurors that his breeding is aristocratic even while telling them to ignore (and thereby calling attention to) his aristocratic looks.

Appealing to the ideology of status was a tricky business even for the most skillful orator. The tension of politicians caught between seemingly contradictory aristocratic and egalitarian ideologies is manifested in the sarcastic uses of the vocabulary of aristocratic privilege when attacking enemies. Andocides (1.133) sneered at Agyrrhios, "the *kalos k'agathos*" who embezzled state moneys when collecting taxes. Demosthenes (22.47) suggested that the Athenians look at the political policies (*ta politeumata*) of "this *kalos k'agathos*" Androtion—policies that show that he is depraved, impudent, a thief, and an arrogant fellow completely unfit to act as a politician in a democracy. Elsewhere (19.175), Demosthenes mocked Aeschines "the high born" (*ho gen-*

naios), who had accused Demosthenes of promising Philip to help overthrow the democracy while Aeschines himself was holding traitorous meetings with the Macedonian king.

The Athenian politician was clearly nervous about existing negative attitudes toward aristocrats and especially about the association of aristocrats with oligarchy. Both factors contributed to the hesitancy aristocratic *idiōtai* felt about playing upon their backgrounds when speaking in court. The politician who took on too many airs left himself open to attacks by his opponents. He could be accused of being excessively arrogant (Aesch. 2.22) or of thinking himself better than the many (Dem. 19.295, 26.15). The speaker in Demosthenes 51 attacked the orators who pleaded for his opponent in the *boulē* for their assumption of superiority. They act

> as if they were not members of a commonly-held state (*politeias koinēs metechontes*) in which, because of this fact, whoever desires to speak may do so—but as if instead they possessed this right as some personal, sacred privilege (*hierōsunēn idian*), so that if anyone else speaks to you about justice they claim they are suffering bad treatment (*deina*) and they call him an impudent person. Yes, they have become so deranged that they think if they call a man shameless who has spoken only once, they themselves will be thought *kaloi k'agathoi* all their lives. (51.19)

The Athenian politician therefore had to be careful not to leave himself open to the charge of regarding himself as a superior person deserving of special privileges in the state. Yet rhetorical attacks upon opponents for their inferior birth and lowly occupations, along with defenses based on the aristocratic background and behavior of the speaker, belie the notion that the Athenians were hostile to all displays of personal superiority by politicians. Although all Athenian citizens could be considered high born and better than noncitizens, certain politicians were evidently allowed and even expected to show themselves off as more aristocratic in birth and behavior than the average citizens. Although politicians who portrayed themselves as aristocrats put themselves at risk, their comments demonstrate that the Athenians of the fourth century did not wholly subscribe to the point of view that Isocrates attributed to their fifth-century ancestors.

> But when the polis became great and seized the empire, our forefathers, having become more self-assured than was good for them, began to envy those *kaloi k'agathoi* who had made the polis great because of their power. They began to desire instead ras-

cally (*ponērōn*) men full of insolence, believing that by their bra-
vado and quarrelsomeness these sorts of men would defend the
democracy and that because of the humbleness of their origins
(*dia de tēn phaulotēta tōn ex archēs autois huparxantōn*) they would not
be excessively prideful or be eager to establish a different *politeia*.
(15.316–17)

The conviction that the Athenians would be better off if they would
only learn to ignore base-born scoundrels was endorsed by Demosthenes (18.138), who reproached the Athenians for their past support
of Aeschines by claiming that "you [Athenians] have the habit (*ēthei*)
of giving to the first inferior type who comes along (*tini phaulōi . . .
boulomenōi*) a great deal of authority to overthrow and to attack in a
sycophantic fashion anyone who gives you good advice. . . ." Lysias,
for his part, claims (30.28) that one might indeed berate (*kategorēsai*)
the Athenians, whose ancestors chose as *nomothetai* men like Solon,
Themistocles, and Pericles, thinking their *nomoi* would match their
character, while the present generation chose (various politicians)
"and others who are undersecretaries." Lysias states that the present-
day Athenians knew perfectly well that such men destroy the *archai*,
yet they still trusted them.

The arguments of Isocrates, Demosthenes, and Lysias are based on
the aristocratic premise that a man's deeds (*erga*) are directly based
upon his character (*ēthos*) and that a man's character was inherited
from his ancestors. The Athenians were not willing to accept this
premise at all times and in all circumstances, but they were clearly influenced by it. The enduring influence of aristocratic ideology led the
Athenians to believe that some people really might be better or worse
than others by virtue of their birth. After all, citizens enjoyed rights
that were denied to noncitizens because of the accidents of birth.
Those who believed that it was possible to inherit love of a polis, or
even of a form of government, from one's ancestors could not easily
reject the notion that "better" men would make better policies and
"worse" men would lead the state to ruin by their inherent nature.
Although the Athenians were committed to egalitarian political ideals,
the tradition of aristocratic leadership was too deeply ingrained to be
discarded entirely. The Athenian politician had to demonstrate that
he was content to be the equal of his fellow citizens, but it was to his
advantage to show that he had consciously chosen to descend to that
position of equality. Isocrates (16.38), for example, suggested that the
Athenians would justly feel *charis* toward Alcibiades (the Elder) since,

although he had been powerful enough to be tyrant, he had believed so deeply in the *politeia* that he condescended to remain equal to all others (*ison . . . kai tois allois meteinai*).

We may contrast Isocrates' comment on Alcibiades with Demosthenes' on Aeschines and his brothers who were "undersecretaries and men of that sort of fortune." Demosthenes allows that these were not evil (*kakias*) professions but certainly not worthy (*ou . . . g' axia*) of generalships. Nonetheless, Aeschines and his brothers were made ambassadors and generals and given the greatest possible honors (19.237). Demosthenes informs Aeschines that he and and his brothers did not deserve the Athenians' *charis* because "we" (the Athenians) dignified (*esemnunomen*) "you," passing over many who were more worthy of being honored. Aeschines and his brothers should instead render *charis* to the Athenians for their elevation (19.238, cf. 19.249, 314). Hence, the aristocrat who descended to a position of equality deserved the demos' gratitude; the average citizen who was elevated by the demos was expected to be thankful to them. One might suppose that the Athenians would have been happy to have "low born" citizens serve in major military and political offices. Would not the grateful recipients of the offices remain loyal to the demos out of a sense of gratitude? But Demosthenes' aside, to the effect that people who were undersecretaries were unworthy of high office, suggests the opposite. A relatively humble citizen might succeed in ascending to high office and political influence in Athens, but once he had arrived, he must expect attacks on his background. If Aeschines may be taken as typical, he would attempt to meet his opponents' attacks by creating a past for himself that matched the Athenians' expectations about the credentials of a proper leader of the people: an aristocrat by birth and behavior who was simultaneously a middling citizen committed to the ideal of political equality for all Athenians.

F. Subversion of the Aristocratic Ethos

The evident desire of Athenian politicians to portray themselves in the role of aristocrats and their use of terminology that specifically recalls the aristocratic code of behavior surely demonstrate the continued importance of the aristocratic ethos in the political ideology of the democratic state. How should we interpret the sociopolitical significance of that continuing importance? Certainly, there can be no question of the existence of an actual ruling elite of *gennētai* in the fourth century. The number of politicians who can be demonstrated to have belonged to a *genos* is small (above, III.C), and there is no evidence to suggest that the limited privileges some *gennētai* retained in the religious sphere translated into political authority.[73] But direct domination by aristocrats is not the only way the aristocratic ethos could remain genuinely influential. Nicole Loraux has suggested that the deployment of aristocratic language in Athenian rhetoric, especially in the self-consciously democratic ritual of the public orations over the Athenian war dead, demonstrates that because the democratic ethos was ultimately "undermined from the inside by aristocratic values and representations, the official oration on democracy ultimately has no language of its own at its disposal." And since in the public funeral orations the "democratic features of the politeia"—such as equality and the political power of the masses—were constantly suppressed "under the declared dominance of arete, it seems clear that democracy never acquired a language of its own." Hence, Loraux agrees with M. Austin and P. Vidal-Naquet (among others) that in Athens, as in other Greek cities, "aristocratic values were without rival."[74]

[73] MacKendrick, *Aristocracy*, esp. vii–viii, supposes that *gennētai* were able to transform religious influence into genuine political power in the archaic period. Daviero-Rocchi, "Transformations," 34, citing MacKendrick, goes so far as to claim that in the fifth century the *gennētai* ran Athenian politics. She suggests that the decline of the *gennētai* in the fourth century was one of the major changes in the Athenian elite. Cf. also Bicknell, *Studies*. I do not think any scholar has seriously suggested that in the fourth century the *genē* were particularly powerful politically.

[74] Loraux, *Invention*, 52–56 (self-consciously democratic ritual), 172, 176, 180–202, 217–220, 334–35 (aristocratic ethos prevails), quotes: 217, 334. Without rival: Austin and Vidal-Naquet, *Economic and Social History*, 15–17; cited by Loraux, *Invention*, 334, from the second French edition (Paris, 1973), 30. But see, by contrast, the theoretical discussion of the origin and function of political discourse by Bowles and Gintis, *Democracy and Capitalism*, 152–75, who argue cogently (153) that "lacking an intrinsic connection to a set of ideas, words, like tools, may be borrowed. Indeed, like weapons in a revolutionary war, some of the most effective words are captured from the dominant class." See also the review of the original French edition of Loraux, *Invention* (Paris, 1981), by R. Seager in *JHS* 102 (1982): 267–68, who concludes (267) that "in general L[oraux] seems not to have grasped the elaborate and subtle process whereby the democracy took over the aristocratic language of individual achievement and redefined its key concepts in a manner consistent with the fundamental principle of the supremacy of the city." Seager (review of Loraux, 267–68) notes that the emphasis on *aretē* is "a further instance of the democratic pillaging of aristocratic values." Arnheim, *Aristocracy*, 131–32, 156, 163–64, would explain the apparent paradox of the egalitarian Athenians preferring "aristocratic" (and wealthy) politicians by the assumption that the Athenian polis was simultaneously anti-aristocratic in government and aristocratic in ethos; cf. also Adkins, *Moral Values*, 125–26, "Problems," 154–55; Carter, *Quiet Athenian*, 1–25; Raaflaub, "Democracy, Oligarchy," 535.

Undeniably, aristocratic values were incorporated into the political ideology of classical Athens. However, the aristocratic ethos and terminology did not serve to suppress or undermine egalitarian ideals, but rather aristocratic ideals were made to conform to the needs of the democratic state. The "nationalization" of the ideals of *kalokagathia* and nobility of descent does not represent a rejection of equality among citizens; rather, it demonstrates the power of popular ideology to appropriate and transvalue terms that had formerly implied the exclusivity of a few *within* the citizen group. Those "captured" terms were used to celebrate the equality of origin and the national unity that transcended differences between citizens.[75] The persons excluded from high status, upon whose existence the terminology still depended, were no longer merely inferior citizens, but noncitizens—especially metics and slaves. Furthermore, aristocratic behavior patterns were harnessed and used for the good of the masses. Competition was encouraged in the political arena between aristocratic or pseudo-aristocratic rivals, but political leaders were permitted to compete for the people's favor only so long as they publicly admitted that the masses were the only valid judges of their contests. The tendency for public speakers to link aristocratic value terms with terminology acknowleging the importance of the public good and the power of the masses is further evidence for the effectiveness of the people's ideological hegemony.

The result of the cooptation of the aristocrats and their ideals into the political realm of the democracy was similar in its effect to the ideological control exerted over the elites of ability and of wealth. In each case the members of the elite were allowed to retain their most valued personal assets: the wealth of the upper classes, the rhetorical

---

[75] Loraux, *Invention*, 334–36, considers the unity to be a function of ideology, but here she seems to be using the term to mean false consciousness, hence rather differently than I have ordinarily employed it. Donlan, *Aristocratic Ideology*, esp. 178, suggests that the aristocratic ethos was subject to constant pressure from below and changed in response to that pressure. But he sees the origin of the pressure largely in terms of the continued power of an ideology originating in the Ur-equality (my term) of the Dark Ages. Donlan's thesis seems to me to pay insufficient attention to the power of democratic ideology. Sealey, *Athenian Republic*, 134, seems to miss the significance of transvalued terminology, in stating that "the net result of the revolution of 404 was to discredit people who talked about 'gentlemen' and 'virtue.' Such language fled from the public oratory of the fourth century and found a home in the schools of philosophers." To the contrary, although the original *meaning* of the terms in question may have "fled," the terms themselves were (as we have seen) quite common in fourth-century political rhetoric.

skill of the educated, and the status, based upon birth and an exclusive code of behavior, of the aristocrats. But public display of elite assets was made contingent upon continuing mass approval. That approval was given only on the condition that elite assets were shared with the masses and so were demonstrably a benefit to the citizen body as a whole.

CHAPTER VII

CONCLUSIONS: DIALECTICS
AND DISCOURSE

Athenians of the fifth and fourth centuries B.C. believed in political equality, and their state organization reflected this basic principle. But all Athenians were not equal. Some citizens had superior abilities to communicate their ideas, were highly educated, possessed fortunes sufficient to free them from the necessity of laboring, belonged to noble clans, and were able to engage in a style of life inaccessible to most of their fellow citizens.

A. Political Equality and Social Inequality

Throughout the period of the democracy, Athenian society remained stratified along lines of ability, class, and status. Social stratification was not only a matter of relative degrees of material comfort. The possession of elite attributes by the few resulted in obvious power inequities, and when a conflict of interests between individuals resulted in legal action, the elite litigant enjoyed various advantages. The Athenian who had natural speaking skills and was educated in rhetoric was more likely than his less skilled opponent to present a convincing argument to the jury. The rich litigant could buy a finely honed speech from a logographer. Wealth also provided leisure for preparation and made a protracted series of litigations financially possible. The aristocrat could call upon influential friends and clansmen for support. Even after the jury had reached a decision, the "self-help" nature óf legal restitution favored the individual able to muster superior physical force.[1] The functional advantages enjoyed by members of the elite within the legal system posed a quandary for the non-elite political equals of the Athenian demos.

[1] On the power of the elite, cf. Dem. 21.45: force (*tēn ischun*) belongs to the few, laws to the many; Aristot. *Rhet.* 1372a11–17: those who are powerful speakers, experienced in affairs and in legal cases, those with many friends, and the rich believe they can do wrong and not be punished for it. On self-help in Athenian law, see Lacey, *Family*, 155–56; Hansen, '*Apagoge*,' 113–21; Finley, "Freedom of the Citizen," 11–12.

On the other hand, the existence of the democratic political order posed a quandary for the elite Athenian. As Aristotle noted (*Rhet.* 1378b26–1379a9; cf. *Pol.* 1283b34–1284b34), an individual who is superior to his fellows in any one way tends to believe he is entitled to a generally privileged position in society. He who considers himself worthy of privilege because of his social superiority may regard it as an injustice to be placed on equal political footing with average citizens. And yet, the Athenian form of government was predicated on the assumptions that all citizens were of equal political worth and that no citizen had an innate right to political privilege, regardless of his special attributes or attainments. Furthermore, the Athenians applied egalitarian principles in assigning many sorts of official duties. In modern democracies, in Britain and the United States, for example, the principle of representation and the process of election allow the politically ambitious elite citizen to use his or her functional superiority in gaining official positions from which he or she can legitimately wield political power. The Athenians did not delegate political power to representatives and tended to regard elections as undemocratic. Most offices were filled by lot, and in principle the elite citizen had no better chance than anyone else to serve as an officer of the state. Most officials held little real power in any case.[2]

The resolution of the competing demands of the elite for more legitimate privileges and of the mass for more complete equality was essential. On the one hand, the social advantages and individual power enjoyed by the elite threatened the rights of average citizens; on the other hand, elite citizens who became too irritated by their position of political equality might attempt a counter-revolution or refuse to participate in running the state.[3] Aristotle (along with other critics of the democracy) considered the enforced equalization of the elite to be one of the central injustices of the democratic form of government, but he also recognized that the only protection the masses had against the power of the elite lay in their numbers. Hence he attempted to devise a theoretical constitution based on a mathematical balance between the "arithmetical" principle of equality (one man-one vote) and the notion

---

[2] Lottery: above, II.F.1. On the lack of power of the magistracies, cf. Osborne, *Demos*, 9: Athenian officials were "little more than ciphers of a civil service" with no executive powers. Cf. also Maio, "*Politeia*," 21–22.

[3] Cf. Lys. 31.25: if the *chrēstoi* are honored no more highly than *ponēroi* they will no longer be eager to contribute materially to the state. On the importance of encouraging the rich to contribute liberally in the fourth century, see Daviero-Rocchi, "Transformations," 40; Whitehead, "Competitive Outlay." Cf. above, II.G, V.C.1.

that superior individuals deserved superior political powers.[4] Aristotle's idea of "proportionate equality" led him into a conundrum, from which he escaped only by a retreat to the elitist constitution of the "ideal state" of the *Politics* (Books 7 and 8). However, Aristotle's attempt to find a constitutional balance between the interests of mass and elite suggests that a solution to the problem *might* have been sought in the legal/constitutional domain. While the evolution of the Athenian constitution may be seen as an attempt to employ political equality as a counterweight to social advantages, the Athenians never achieved nor did they ever attempt, a final constitutional resolution of the dissonance between the relative social and political standing of masses and elites. The Athenian masses were not willing to compromise the principle of political equality in ways that might satisfy the ambitions of the elite, nor were the members of the elite willing to part peacefully with the conditions of their superiority in order to alleviate the apprehensions of the masses.

B. Liberty and Consensus

The limits of the Athenian ability to devise constitutional solutions to sociopolitical problems are elucidated by a consideration of two dichotomies that have concerned us throughout this inquiry: personal liberty/political consensus and popular sovereignty/rule of law. Aristotle considered freedom (*eleutheria*) to be the end (*telos*) that democracy was designed to foster,[5] and the Athenians were firm believers in at least some aspects of individual freedom. In his Funeral Oration, Pericles praises freedom in both its public and private aspects, proudly noting that the Athenians did not need to supervise the personal behavior of citizens (Thuc. 2.37.2).[6] Indeed, Athens did not have the official superintendents of private behavior that Aristotle (*Pol.* 1300a4–8, 1322b37–1323a6; cf. above I.A) considered proper to aristocracies. But the Athenians construed freedom more in terms of the positive right of the citizen to engage in political activity than in his

[4] Proportionate equality: Aristot. *Pol.* 1280a22–24, 1282b14–1284a3, 1287a13–17, 1296b15–34, 1301a25–1302a15, *Nicomachean Ethics* 1132b33–34. Cf. Finley, *PAW*, 137; Finley, "Aristotle," 5 with n. 9; Romilly, *Démocratie*, 49–52; Harvey, "Two Kinds," 113–20, 126–29; Ober, "Aristotle's Political Sociology."

[5] Aristot. *Rhet.* 1366a4, *Pol.* 1317a40–b16, cf. 1318a2–10; Ober, "Aristotle's Political Sociology."

[6] On the double (public/private) force of this passage, see Loraux, *Invention*, 180 with n. 30. Cf. also Thuc. 7.69.2.

"negative freedoms" from governmental interference.[7] The central freedom that the Athenians cherished, therefore, was *isēgoria*: the right of the citizen to address the sovereign Assembly of the people. This important right was reiterated at every Assembly, when, after a motion had been made, the "president" of the Assembly asked who among those present had advice to give to the Athenians. *Isēgoria*, literally "equality of public address," was a specifically egalitarian freedom, as Aeschines noted.

> He [the lawgiver] does not exclude from the bema the man who lacks ancestors who served as generals, nor indeed the man who works at some craft in order to earn his daily sustenance. Rather these men are most particularly welcomed and for this reason he [the president of the Assembly] asks repeatedly, 'who wishes to address the Assembly?' (1.27)

Athenian emphasis upon the importance of the freedom of public address led them to recognize (by the second half of the fifth century) a more generalized freedom of speech (*parrhēsia*) which implied the necessity and validity of individual freedom of thought. If one was to be free to offer one's advice to the Assembly, one must be free to think through that advice and to discuss it informally with others. Freedom of political speech furthermore implied the freedom *not* to speak out in public if one had no advice to offer, as Aeschines (3.220; cf. Dem. 22.30) reminded Demosthenes.[8]

Freedom—even the limited positive freedom of public speech with which the Athenians were particularly concerned—was not without its dangers. The freedom to speak or not to speak noted by Aeschines might imply the freedom of the citizen to contribute or not to contribute to the welfare of the state in other ways. If the upper classes decided to withhold their material contributions, the state would be in very serious trouble indeed. On the other hand, he who thrust himself forward to the bema, abandoning his place in the mass, had, by that act, declared an individuality that was potentially suspect. His motive

[7] On positive and negative freedoms in Athens, see Finley, "Freedom of the Citizen," 15–23; Lacey, *Family*, 154, 176; Holmes, "Aristippus"; Raaflaub, "Democracy, Oligarchy," 521–22, "Freien Bürgers Recht," esp. 44; cf. above, I.A.

[8] On *isēgoria* and *parrhēsia* in classical Athens, see Raaflaub, "Freien Bürgers Recht," 11–17 (*isēgoria*), 18–23 (*parrhēsia*), "Democracy, Oligarchy," 523–24, *Entdeckung der Freiheit*, 277–83, 325–26. Cf. Carter, *Quiet Athenian*, 13–14 and the studies cited in II.nn.44, 59. Link of freedom of speech to democracy: e.g., Dem. 21.124, 60.26 (*isēgoria*); Aesch. 3.6 (*parrhēsia*); Euripides *Suppliant Women* 430–42; cf. Raaflaub, "Freien Bürgers Recht," esp. 15, 34–38. On the general *absence* of these terms from the public funeral orations: Loraux, *Invention*, 175.

in choosing to address the people might be self-interest, rather than a desire to further the interests of the state as a whole. The skilled and trained speaker who used his *isēgoria* to address the Assembly might mislead the people into voting against the good of the state by employing the power of rhetoric.[9]

The inverse of freedom of speech and thought was the concept of *homonoia*: consensus, literally "same-mindedness." The glories of *homonoia* are celebrated with particular frequency by Isocrates and Lysias, and no doubt in the years after the democratic restoration of 403 the importance of consensus was very acutely felt.[10] But *homonoia* was always important to the Athenians and was praised as a central social virtue by Demosthenes (e.g., 9.38, 25.89–90), Hyperides (4.37), and Dinarchus (3.19) much later in the fourth century.[11] The term *homonoia*, as it was used by the political orators, generally implied a condition in which all citizens think the same thing, in which their social and political differences are submerged in a unified community of interest. Hence, the state becomes an organism with a single mind and a single will. The ideal nature of this condition is emphasized by Demosthenes (19.298) and Dinarchus (1.99), who refer to the advantages of the citizenry being "of one mind" (*mia gnōmē*) on important issues; similar sentiments are expressed by Andocides (2.1), Lysias (2.13, 17, 24), and Aeschines (3.208).

Consensus probably preceded freedom of speech as an operative principle in the development of the early democracy (see II.E). *Homonoia* is, on the face of it, the very antithesis of freedom. When the citizenry was "of one mind" there was no need for freedom of speech, thought, or action; everyone desired the same thing, and all could be expected to act with a unitary will. While this might be unattainable in practice, the ideal it represented was an important element in Athenian political ideology and provided the moral basis for a higher de-

---

[9] Maio, "*Politeia*," 19–20, notes that the fundamental Athenian values of personal freedom and political freedom were in conflict, because personal freedom offers the option of not participating in politics and was threatened by the Athenian failure to exempt privacy from government control. Cf. Finley, "Freedom of the Citizen," 9–10, *DAM*, 72–103; Meier, *Anthropologie*, 54–55.

[10] Isoc. 6.67, 7.31, 69, 8.19, 12.178, 258, 18.44, 68; Lys. 2.63–65, 18.17–18, 25.21–23, 30. Among other early fourth-century uses of the term: And. 1.106, 108. Cf. Finley, *DAM*, 62–64; Holmes, "Aristippus," 118–23; Funke, *Homónoia und Arché*, 13–26. Although elite writers sometimes spoke of *homonoia* as an ideal that was lacking at Athens (e.g., Xen. *Mem.* 3.5, 16), I do not agree with Loraux, *Invention*, 196, that *homonoia* was a "moderate" (as opposed to a democratic) political virtue.

[11] For other examples of *homonoia* in Demosthenes and Isocrates, see *Belegstellenverzeichnis*, s.v.

gree of regulation by the group of private behavior than Pericles' comment in the Funeral Oration might suggest.[12]

Why then, should the Athenians have bothered with freedom of speech at all? Presumably, because perfect and long-term political consensus was not only impossible but dangerous. If the citizenry is of a single mind, debate and discussion become irrelevant. But without debate, how could the Athenians be sure they had considered all options and selected the best policy? A politics of pure consensus could easily lead to stagnation and the loss of political initiative, since only simplistic or unimportant issues were likely to yield a complete consensus. Consensus decision making furthermore left the Athenians with no scapegoat and no easy way of revising policy when the consensus decision turned out to have unpleasant consequences. In this situation, the Athenians had no one to blame but the demos, and they might be forced to confront the fact that mass decision making did not always produce wise policy. Those who believed in the superiority of elite decision making would be vindicated and sociopolitical tensions exacerbated. Paradoxically, "same-mindedness" on a political plane threatened to tear the society apart.

Many Athenians no doubt could have grasped the antithetical nature of the concepts of individual freedom and political consensus, as well as the dangers that each concept entailed. And perhaps they could have come up with a set of laws that would have moderated the dangers of each. But most Athenians saw no need to resolve the issue constitutionally or philosophically. For them the two concepts were not so much antithetical as complementary. In his Funeral Oration, Lysias (2.18) discusses how the autochthonous ancestors of the Athenians threw out their rulers (*dunasteias*) and established a democracy, "believing that the freedom of all is the greatest consensus" (*tēn pantōn eleutherian homonoian einai megistēn*).[13] Far from facing the contradiction squarely and deciding which concept was of greater utility or how

---

[12] On the power of the demos to legislate concerning private action, see esp. Finley, "Freedom of the Citizen," 14–15. It is important to keep in mind that Pericles' comment about Athenian respect for privacy is in the context of an implicit comparison of Athens with Sparta. On the fundamentally undemocratic nature of a politics of pure consensus, cf. the comments of Zuckerman, "Social Context," 526–27, 533, 538–44.

[13] The context of *eleutheria* in the Lysias passage, the throwing out of the rulers, suggests that freedom here is meant to be construed as the freedom of the citizens to engage in political action, rather than freedom of the state from external domination. Cf. also Loraux, *Invention*, 202. On the more general linkage between freedom and equality in the fifth century, see Meier, *Entstehung des Politischen*, 297–98; Raaflaub, "Democracy, Oligarchy."

each might be moderated, the Athenians continued to believe that both freedom and consensus were simultaneously good, valuable to state and society, and attainable. That freedom was a good thing and worth defending and that consensus was a good thing and worth promoting were self-evident to the Athenians. Any attempt to limit either one by constitutional means might have been construed as an intolerable assault on basic Athenian values. No canny politician would willingly put himself in the position of attacking basic values. Hence, no constitutional solution (as far as we know) was attempted. The Athenians' willingness to maintain both principles, despite the philosophical contradiction this implied, allowed them to avoid the conflict between individual rights and the legitimate exercise of majoritarian power which is a major concern of modern democracies.

C. Rule of Law and the Sovereign Demos

A related pair of seemingly antithetical concepts was the sovereignty of popular will and the sovereignty of law and the courts. The attempt to demonstrate that the demos in Assembly was not sovereign is misdirected because the Athenians did not think in terms of a strict separation of powers (see especially III.E.4). Every Athenian knew that the people ran Athens and that their will was, in the normal course of events, law. The standard term for destruction of the political order used by the orators was "to overthrow the demos" (*kataluein ton dēmon*), rather than "to overthrow the laws."[14] Nevertheless, fourth-century Athenians also recognized the authority both of "The Laws" (those made by individual *nomothetai* of the past—especially Solon—and those more recently made by boards of *nomothetai*) and of the courts in which laws were applied to individual Athenians.[15]

There is indeed a philosophical and constitutional contradiction be-

---

[14] *Kataluein ton dēmon* (vel sim.): Lys. 20.13; Dem. 15.14.4, 19.175, 294, 24.144, 146, 149, 152, *Ex.* 42.2; Lyc. 1.147; cf. Thuc. 8.47.2; Aristoph. *Ecclesiazusae* 453, *Plutus* 948. *Kataluein tous nomous*: Dem. 24.22–23, 31. Neither list is comprehensive; cf. also Sealey, "Origins," 283 with n. 35.

[15] Cf. Dem. 21.223–25 and esp. 57.56. The modern debate on relative sovereignty of law, courts, and people seems to have been sparked (at least in the English-speaking world) by Hansen, *Sovereignty*. Hansen discusses the issue in several of the essays collected in *AECA* (esp. "Demos, Ecclesia") but has evidently moderated his views somewhat recently: *AECA*, 159–60. For other recent studies emphasizing the "separation of powers" and/or urging that by the fourth century the laws and/or courts were sovereign while the people were not, see above, I.n.48. Maio, "*Politeia*," is one of the most reasonable and judicious discussions of the issue known to me. Cf. above I.C.2, II.G, III.E.

tween sovereign laws and sovereign popular will, but modern discussions of the question of the relative sovereignty of law and demos in Athens, while interesting in terms of abstract legal theory, misrepresent the Athenian reality: most Athenians were not interested in resolving the contradiction. We have seen that the Athenian masses were perfectly capable of maintaining two philosophically contradictory concepts when they felt that each was valid and useful. And nothing prevented them from embedding contradictory concepts in the state "constitution." The law-making procedure included provisions for eliminating contradictory laws, but the decision about which laws were contradictory was made by the demos, not by philosophers schooled in logic or by legislative experts (above, II.G).

Demosthenes' client (42.15) expresses the simultaneity of popular and legal sovereignty when he tells the jurors that they would be right to "save those who believe that the voice of the laws is your [the people's] own voice." The lack of a formal police force in fourth-century Athens meant that the authority of the laws rested immediately on the ability of the populace to exert moral pressure upon individuals who broke the laws.[16] This is the thrust of a key passage in Demosthenes' peroration (21.223–24) to his speech *Against Meidias*. Demosthenes first asks the jurors what it is that makes them authoritative and masters (*ischuroi kai kurioi*) of all the affairs of the state. It is not their individual physical prowess, but "the authority of the laws" (*tēi tōn nomōn ischuï*). He continues,

> But what is the strength of the laws? For if one of you is wronged and cries out, will the laws come running up and offer aid? No; they are just inscribed letters (*grammata gar gegrammen' esti*), and they have no power to act independently. So what provides their power (*dunamis*)? You—but only if you support them and keep them masterful (*kurious*) in support of he who is in need. Thus, the laws are authoritative (*ischuroi*) through you, and you through the laws.

Consequently, "The Laws" never became truly externalized or abstract.[17] The cardinal principle of Athenian law remained that all laws should be in the interest of the Athenians. If Athenian political society

---

[16] Cf. Finley, *PAW*, 18–23.

[17] Cf. Humphreys, "Law as Discourse," 251: "Codification, as a form of rule-making, needs to be seen as an aspect of practice, a way of making assertions about social relationships, not as a description of practice or a blueprint existing on a different level of reality like a Platonic Idea."

would be harmed by the resolution of a constitutional contradiction, it was prima facie unnecessary to resolve it.

The interests of the Athenians were in fact protected by the simultaneous sovereignty of the people and the law. The immediate transmutation of the momentary will of the people into a policy or action that might have long-term ramifications could sometimes lead to serious difficulties, as the Athenians had certainly recognized by the early fourth century. The central problem was, as Aeschines (3.3–4) noted, that the masses might make a hasty decision in the Assembly on the basis of the emotions of the hour or because they were swayed by the rhetoric of an unscrupulous orator. The eventual consequences of a quick decision made under the influence of emotion or evil rhetoric might be disastrous, as was the case with the Sicilian Expedition of 415–13. Furthermore, the popular will might fluctuate with sufficient rapidity to obviate the possibility of establishing a decisive and cohesive policy; the classic example is the reversed decision on the fate of the Mytilenean revolutionaries in 427.[18] In that instance the reversal was no doubt salutary, but if the Athenians changed their minds on important matters with great frequency, they would soon cease to have a policy at all. Finally, while as a general rule Assemblies were more or less representative of the social composition of the Athenian citizen body (above, III.E.2), it was impossible that every Assembly could represent a full cross section of the demos. An Assembly that happened to be weighted toward one end of the social spectrum might come to an important decision that would not be in the best interests of the majority of citizens. The worst case scenario was played out at the Assembly held outside the city walls at Kolonos in 411, when the democracy was voted out of existence (Thuc. 8.67; cf. above, II.F.6).

No doubt the experience of the errors made by Assemblies under the stress of the Peloponnesian War brought home to the Athenians the dangers of unrestrained exercise of the popular will. Consequently, they enacted constitutional measures aimed at correcting the problem; the procedure of *graphē paranomōn*, the process of *nomothesia*, and the clarification of the distinction between *nomos* and *psēphisma* (above, II.G) must certainly be seen in this light. But there is no reason to suppose that these changes abrogated the ultimate authority of the demos. The comments of the orators on the relationship between demos and jury, discussed above (III.E.4), demonstrate that the demos

---

[18] Debate on the Syracuse expedition: Thuc. 6.8–30; disastrous outcome: 6.72–7.2; Mytilenean Debate and outcome: 3.36–50. Cf. Gomme et al., *Historical Commentary*, ad locc.

was still thought of as retaining fundamental political power. Rather, the reforms provided new ways of punishing *rhetores* who misled the demos in the Assembly (or were construed to have done so) and allowed the Athenians to reconsider important decisions at a remove, in light of their own established principles. The desired result was that politicians might become more circumspect in their proposals and more inclined to consider the basic and essential values and norms of the people, which could be expected to reassert themselves when the emotion of the hour had faded. The will of the people was still sovereign, but now that will was defined in broader chronological terms. The central and long-term political principles of the demos—some of which were now given written form as *nomoi*—were given primacy when they came into conflict with immediate desires.[19]

Turning over the power to set state policy to any group much more narrowly defined than the demos itself would have meant the end of the democracy. But in light of the perceived dangers of the unrestrained exercise of popular will, one might ask why the Athenians did not go somewhat further in broadening the constitutional locus of authority, perhaps by instituting an automatic judicial review of all major decisions made in the Assembly. Part of the answer is presumably that in the normal turn of events the short-term desires and long-term principles of the people did not conflict. This explains the apparent rarity (relative to the total number of *psēphismata* passed) of conviction under *graphai paranomōn*. Aristophon (Aesch. 3.194), for example, claimed to have been indicted seventy-five times and never convicted. Even if the number is an exaggeration, it may tell us something not only about political litigiousness but about the general unwillingness of Athenian juries to overturn the decisions made in the Assembly.[20]

[19] The relationship between the Athenians and their laws is clarified by Bowles and Gintis' (*Democracy and Capitalism*, 186) discussion of the ideal functioning of a "democratic dynamic": "The problem of building a democratic society is . . . one of a dynamic interaction of rules and actors, with the actors rendering the rules more democratic, and the increasingly democratic rules rendering the actors more firmly committed to and skilled at democratic participation and decision making." Cf. Harrison, "Law-Making," 35: "The question is not whether the sovereign people allowed itself to be robbed of full control of the law-making machine, but whether it deliberately invented a perfectly democratic brake to slow down the machine."

[20] The number 75 is surely not exact, as was pointed out by S. I. Oost, "Two Notes on Aristophon of Azenia," *CPh* 72 (1977): 238–40; but it must have been in the right general order of magnitude: D. Whitehead, "The Political Career of Aristophon," *CPh* 81 (1986): 313–19, esp. 313–14. Hyperides (5.29) suggests that the frequent acquittals of politicians by the *dikastēria* was proof of the confidence of the demos. But convictions were certainly far from unknown; e.g., Apollodorus' conviction over the *theōrika*, and that after a unanimous vote of the Assembly: Dem. 59.4–8; cf. Markle, "Jury Pay," 291; and Hansen, "Theoric Fund." On the fre-

Furthermore, the Assembly had to retain de facto sovereignty if Athens was to keep its ability to act quickly and decisively to new and sudden challenges, especially in the sphere of foreign policy. Late fifth- and fourth-century diplomacy was complex, and alliance structures shifted rapidly. For much of the fourth century, the Athenian democracy was threatened by powerful monarchies, and the Athenians were well aware of the advantages monarchs had in devising and quickly implementing policy decisions. The democratic decision-making process was by nature public and relatively time-consuming; the last thing Athens needed was to complicate and retard the process by requiring legal review of every decision of the Assembly.[21]

A detailed code of sovereign laws might be an advantage to the elites. It is hardly accidental that elite philosophers like Aristotle (e.g., *Pol.* 1292a3–38) considered the rule of law a good thing and something essentially different from the rule of the people, since the rule of law would favor the wealthy and educated. A highly complex law code might give rise to a professional class of lawyers.[22] Those who believed that a limited group of political experts should run the state might be expected to support such a development; the average Athenian would not. The more fully articulated the law code, the less leeway jurors would have in interpreting it. This would favor the elites who had the education and leisure to work through the legal niceties and would lessen their need to appeal to common interest and shared values when addressing a jury. Finally, complete articulation of the law was a denial of the collective wisdom of the masses. Aristotle (*Rhet.* 1354a31–b1) argued that laws properly should define matters as thoroughly as possible, because (inter alia) a few wise lawmakers are easier to find than many wise jurors. Since the Athenians believed in the wisdom of mass decisions, they drew the opposite conclusions: most laws should be general rather than specific, and juries should have much freedom in interpreting them. In this way their collective wisdom could be brought into play on the particularities of the case (cf. Dem. 24.193).[23]

---

quency of *graphai paranomōn*, see Hansen, *Sovereignty*, 25–26; of the 39 examples of the action collected in ibid., 28–41, 12 resulted in convictions, 15 in acquittals or in the action being dropped; the result of the other 12 cases is unknown. This is, of course, not a statistically meaningful sample.

[21] Complexity of fourth-century diplomacy: above ii.nn.108, 109. On the slowness of democratic decision making when compared to monarchies or oligarchies, see Dem. 19.185–86.

[22] On the conditions that led to the rise of an elite of legal specialists in Rome, see B. Frier, *The Rise of the Roman Jurists* (Princeton, 1985), esp. 269–87.

[23] On the advantages to the demos in keeping law vague, see E. Ruschenbusch, "ΔΙΚΑΣΤΗΡΙΟΝ ΠΑΝΤΩΝ ΚΥΡΙΟΝ," *Historia* 6 (1957): 257–74; Finley, *Ancient His-*

Raphael Sealey concluded a seminal article on the Athenian concept of law by stating that "the Athenians achieved something more valuable and more fundamental than democracy. They achieved the rule of law."[24] I imagine that the Athenians could have understood the opposition. And if required to choose between the two ideals, I think they unhesitatingly would have chosen democracy. We cannot put this proposition to the test and need not regret our inability to do so, because the Athenians never bothered themselves with the notion that democracy and rule of law were mutually exclusive. They saw that unrestrained popular will was dangerous, but they also saw that excessive constitutional checks and balances along with a fully articulated law code threatened the interests of the masses. Hence the constitutional settlement of the late fifth and early fourth centuries remained limited in scope and application. The Athenians maintained their belief both in the power of the law and in the power of the people. Lysias (14.10) noted that the elite cavalrymen acted properly because they feared both the laws and "you." The "you" referred to the jurors but also to the Athenian demos as a whole.

D. Ideology and the Balance of
Mass and Elite

The problems of balancing freedom against consensus, and the sovereignty of the demos against that of the law are linked to the general problem of the relationship between mass and elite. In each case the question is whether there is or should be any limit to the power of the collectivity—the demos—over any of its constituent parts, group or individual. In each case, the Athenians proved unwilling to deal with existing contradictions, at least on a constitutional plane. Constitutional resolutions might have proved dangerous and must have seemed unnecessary. The citizens more easily and safely embraced pairs of concepts that, if contradictory, were also complementary and that collectively served a useful function in the organization of state and society. The tensions generated by simultaneously maintaining social inequality and political equality therefore had to be resolved on the ideological plane.

The sociopolitical order operated smoothly as long as the social power of the elites was balanced by the political power of the masses. The trick was how this felicitous situation could be maintained, given

---

tory, 102. Cf. Maio, "*Politeia*," 40–43 (on the positivistic aspect of Athenian law); Osborne, "Law in Action" (on the "open texture" of Athenian law).

[24] Sealey, "Athenian Concept of Law," 302, cf. *Athenian Republic*, 91–106.

the limited efficacy of constitutional reforms. The balance absolutely had to be kept. The stability of the democratic state was dependent upon avoiding the concentration of political power in the hands of the elite on the one hand, and on the willingness of the masses to allow the elite certain privileges on the other; in short, upon maintaining a community of citizens' interests that overrode individual and subgroup differences. But tension between mass and elite remained; Athenians on either side remained suspicious of the other's privileges and intentions and jealous of their own prerogatives.[25] Hence, there was a continual and pressing need to deal with the question of the mass/elite antithesis.

Courtroom oratory played an important role in resolving the conflicting claims and desires of mass and elite Athenians. A series of ideological compromises, defined and referred to by legal rhetoric, helped to bridge the gap between the social reality of inequality and the political ideal of equality. These compromises mediated the superior power of the elite individual vis-à-vis the average citizen and protected the elite individual from the tyrannical exercise of collective power by the masses. Legal rhetoric was an obvious medium for compromise because the need for mediation was particularly acute in the law courts, where the people sat in collective judgment on the individual citizen. As an individual confronting the group, the litigant was in a high-risk position. The very fact of his appearance in court might arouse suspicion—every defendant had to explain why he, an honest citizen, found himself in court; every prosecutor had to explain why he should not be regarded a vicious sycophant. The elite litigant, who also possessed attributes that further differentiated him from the mass, was in a particularly delicate spot. Communication with the jurymen was his only way out of the dangerous individual-versus-community and elite-versus-mass situation.[26] The elite litigant who could persuade the jurors that, despite his elite privileges, his interests and theirs were identical, would win their sympathy and so save himself.[27] The rhetorical tactics of elite litigants, described above (IV–VI), are ex-

[25] Among the many passages cited above that illustrate the ongoing tension between mass and elite, the ongoing need of the masses for the contributions of the wealthy, and the fear of the wealthy that the masses will confiscate their wealth, see esp. Lys. 27.1–2; Dem. 21.66–67, 143, 210; Hyp. 4.33–36.

[26] On the opposition of the many and the one, see, for example, Lys. 3.9; Is. 5.38; Dem. 21.198. On the tension between the individual and the group in Greek tragedy, see Vernant, "Historical Moment," 2, 10, "Tensions," 10.

[27] Even if the litigant lost his case on its merits, a sympathetic jury would not be tempted to use the full extent of its punitive powers against him, so that the damage done him by the judgment would be limited.

amples of ways in which elites attempted to explain themselves and
their position in society to mass juries. Ultimately, the complex of rhetorical strategies successfully deployed by elite litigants over time
helped to create a vocabulary of social mediation which defined the
nature of mass-elite interaction for the Athenians and legitimated
both the power of the masses and the special privileges of the elites.

The degree of urgency of the litigant's need to employ tension-dif-
fusing tactics was a function not only of the innate strength or weakness of his case but also of the degree of his divergence from the
norm. The more obvious and extreme a litigant's elite attributes—the
greater his attainments in terms of ability, wealth, and status—the
more dependent he was upon ideological mediation. But, at least by
the fourth century, even a very obviously elite litigant was able to communicate with the jurymen through a well-established language; his
immediate task was to prove that his particular case should be judged
acccording to the accepted forms of mass-elite cooperation.

D.1 *Idiōtai* AND SOCIAL BALANCE

Mediation based on legal rhetoric worked—both on an individual and
a society-wide level—when everyone involved played his role correctly.
The elite litigant was expected to make clear to the jury his generalized adherence to egalitarian principles, his acceptance of the correctness of mass rule and mass judgment. By explicitly accepting the people's right to judge him, the litigant helped legitimate the legal
processes of the democratic government. This in turn removed the
trial from the realm of force and power, to the realm of peaceful adjustment of long-term mutual interests. By submitting gracefully to
the people's judgment, the litigant showed himself to be a good citizen, a *dēmotikos* (cf. Isoc. 18.62), the sort who would be likely to use his
elite attributes for the good of the demos.

The elite litigant further emphasized the community of interests he
shared with the jurors by resorting to dramatic fictions. The speaker
who was highly educated or had purchased an ornate speech from a
logographer begged forgiveness for his lack of eloquence. The
wealthy liturgist bemoaned his poverty. The well-connected aristocrat
asked the jury to act in lieu of his family. On other occasions, the elite
speaker addressed the jurors as fellow possessors of elite attributes:
the jurors became highly educated, taxpayers, and possessors of a
communal nobility of birth. By lowering himself and by elevating the
members of the jury in status, the speaker put himself on the same
social footing as his audience. He deemphasized his privileges, and/or
associated the jury in those privileges, in order to reduce the degree

of his differentiation. The elite litigant portrayed himself as an average Athenian who could naturally expect sympathy and support from his fellow citizens: he rejoined the mass. The jurymen, at least many of them, must have been able to see through these transparent fictions, but they chose not to call attention to them. The conspiracy of speaker and juror in maintaining the fiction helped to integrate the citizenry by encouraging *homonoia*. The metaphor of the theater helps to explain the relationship between the play-acting litigant and his audience. The juror's experience as a member of a mass audience in the theater, watching and hearing actors play their parts, reinforced the useful process of suspension of disbelief that he employed when sitting as a member of a mass jury, listening to the elite litigant plead his case.

Having established community of interest, the speaker in court might then attempt to demonstrate that certain of his elite attributes were valuable to the state. Especially important in this regard is the notion of *charis*. The wealthy man who contributed materially to the state in the correct spirit of generosity, patriotism, and *philotimia* could request that the jury return the favor. The jurymen were, in effect, given control of the litigant's wealth, since their decision would determine its disposition, but they were induced to "give it back" to the generous citizen, out of gratitude for his past benefactions and in expectation of future gifts. The well-born litigant played a similar game, by reminding the jurors of the fine deeds his ancestors had done and emphasizing his inborn love of democracy and state.

Each of these rhetorical ploys helped to smooth over power inequalities. The elite citizen diffused the jurors' suspicions about the dangerous power that his elite attributes afforded him by humbling himself, by dissimulating his rhetorical skill, by putting his power-producing wealth at the service of the state, by showing that his illustrious ancestors had been highly patriotic, and by affirming that all citizens were of noble birth. For their part, the jurors—and, on a society-wide level, the demos as a whole—were persuaded that there was no need to bring their collective political power to bear against the elite. The individual who played his role correctly was no longer perceived as a a threat, and hence there was no need to act preemptively against him. In short, having shown himself to be at the mercy of the masses, the individual had reason to expect merciful treatment from them (cf. Aristot. *Rhet.* 1380a12–b1).

The drama acted out by elite protagonists in Athenian courtrooms had many variations, but the theme was always the same: the community of interests and interdependence of mass and elite. The citizens were bound together more securely through the role playing on both sides. Social tensions within the citizen body were reduced, and the solidarity of the citizenry vis-à-vis noncitizens was upheld. The same community of interests the citizens experienced when sitting together in the theater and when voting in the Assembly could be achieved even in the contentious atmosphere of the courtroom, where the interests of mass and elite threatened to come into open conflict. The social stability that resulted from the development of a language of mediation allowed the Athenians to avoid the extreme forms of civil strife that tore apart many Greek states in the late fifth and fourth centuries.[28]

Public rhetoric not only *revealed* social tension, it was a primary vehicle for *resolving* tension. The evolving vocabulary of symbols of social mediation expressed in the topoi and other rhetorical tactics of legal orations was, therefore, a key ingredient in the maintenance of social peace at Athens. We need not assume that very many Athenians were consciously aware of the process. There is no way of judging how sensitive the ordinary litigant was to the ideological context of the courtroom. But the preserved speeches, written by and for elite Athenians, certainly show a high degree of awareness of that context. The rhetorical ploys described here are sophisticated and complicated; it seems unlikely that all elite citizens would have been fully aware of their efficacy or that unconscious awareness could have produced such highly elaborated mechanisms for playing to mass attitudes. The fact that most, if not all, of the private speeches we possess were written by logographers, whose job it was to fit the speech both to the individual litigant and to mass attitudes helps to explain the sophistication of the symbolic vocabulary in private orations. Indeed, the need to diffuse popular suspicion when appearing in court may have led the Athenian upper classes into an increasing dependence upon logographers.

The vocabulary of mediation was continuously being refined by the logographers, based on their reading of the ideological relationship between mass and elite, and their speeches helped to further define that relationship. As jurors became increasingly sophisticated "readers" of the logographers' "language," the elite litigant who wrote his own defense must have been more and more at a disadvantage. Juries

[28] Lintott, *Violence*, 179, notes that the absence of an oligarchic coup at Athens in the first half of the fourth century "is remarkable, inasmuch as the rest of Greece was plagued by revolution and counter-revolution during that period." He suggests that Spartan weakness after 378 might be part of the reason, but also notes (179–80) that, even with the rise of Macedon as a genuine power in the 340s and the Macedonian victory in 338, there was no upswing in oligarchic activity.

accustomed to communication through a highly elaborated vocabulary of symbols might discount or even resent those who did not employ it. Thus, while the masses never officially condoned the existence of the logographer, in fact the logographer became a necessary figure in the legal system, an interpreter who ensured that the needs and interests of his elite employer remained explicable to the mass jury. The willingness of the jurors to accept the fiction of the "unskilled speaker" topos became essential to the social order.

Ironically, the Athenians avoided the elaboration of law and the development of a class of professional lawyers but, through their concentration upon public speech, became dependent upon a class of expert speechwriters. It is, however, important to bear in mind that the speechwriters were never able to institutionalize their position in society and that their function remained one of social integration. The logographers, therefore, never formed the nucleus of the sort of oligarchy that Michels and the elitist philosophers thought must be the inevitable product of democratic societies.

D.2 POLITICIANS AND POLITICAL BALANCE

Turning from the question of social stability to decision making in the direct democracy, we move from the realm of private legal orations delivered by *idiōtai* to that of public legal and deliberative speeches delivered by rhetores. The Athenian politician was typically a member of various elites (see III.C), and his political activity put him in the position of facing judgment by the masses much more frequently than an average elite *idiōtēs*. Every time the political orator stood up to speak, he confronted the community as an individual, and as we have seen, that moment was fraught with tension and danger. Furthermore, when the politician spoke—whether in the Assembly or in court—it was typically in the context of open combat with opponents who were themselves skilled and experienced speakers. The people judged those contests; hence the political orator was intensely aware of the popular climate of opinion, and he was particularly eager to use mass attitudes to his own advantage and against his opponents. Not surprisingly, therefore, political orators employed many of the sophisticated rhetorical tactics that were used in private legal orations. It was to the politician's advantage to present himself as a *dēmotikos*, an individual fully in sympathy with the democratic government and with the egalitarian principles that underlay it.[29] Like the private litigant, he

[29] Orator as *dēmotikos*: Aesch. 3.168; Dem. 19.277; Hyp. 2.10, 5.5; Din. 1.44; cf. Hyp. 4.21.

attempted to show that his interests were identical to those of the community, while the interests of his opponents, who acted from selfish motives, were not.[30]

In order to demonstrate his conformity to popular norms, the political orator often attempted to obscure his own elite attainments and to spotlight those attributes that caused his opponent to stand out from the mass. Thus he might imply that his own education was no more elaborate than that of the average citizen, by claiming that he learned history from his elders and poetry in the theater. His opponent could then be portrayed as egregiously over-educated, the sort of elite sophist who engaged in specialized research with the goal of misleading the masses and who trained others to use rhetoric to pervert the mass will. He might stress too that his own style of life was simple, his needs few; this, in contrast to his opponent who could be cast in the role of the luxury-loving rich man who thought his wealth gave him the right to attack those who were less powerful than himself.

Yet there are significant differences between the overall rhetorical strategy of the elite politician and the elite *idiōtēs*. The politician avoided the topos of personal inability to speak well, and he might actually find occasion to brag about his superior education, wealth, and birth. His opponent was portrayed not only as someone whose elite attributes rendered him offensive in his personal habits and anti-democratic in his attitudes but also as someone who *lacked* elite attributes: a man who had to work for a living, who was ill educated, low- or foreign-born, a slave by nature and blood. The politician demonstrated his attainments and denigrated those of his opponent as part of the ongoing public competition between rhetores; each speaker tried to show the demotic judges of the contests that his own superiority made him useful to the state, while his opponent's inferiority rendered him useless or dangerous. The educated rhetor was an eloquent spokesman and insightful adviser for the demos; his ill-educated opponent was unable to make any lasting impression or to devise useful policy options. The wealthy political orator was immune to bribery; his opponent was cast as impoverished and hence a likely bribe-taker, or recently wealthy through having taken bribes. The politician who was materially generous deserved the *charis* of the people, while his opponent was *archaristos* since he did not appreciate the people's generosity in allowing him to drag himself up from the gutter at their expense. His own high birth made him particularly patriotic and

[30] E.g., Lyc. 1.140: the only people who would want to help Leocrates are those whose true interests are not those of the state.

a lover of democracy; his opponent's impure and servile blood rendered him a natural traitor who had unjustly insinuated himself within the citizen body, only to corrupt its ideals.

The political orator therefore played a double role, wore a mask with two faces. On the one hand, he was the perfect exemplar of the norms of society, an "average guy," a *metrios* in the most basic sense of the word. On the other hand, he was superior to the ordinary citizen, an elite in terms of his ability, wealth, and status. The two aspects of the politician's role are summed up in rhetorical discussions of the orator's proper character and function. The mix of elite and egalitarian virtues in these passages reinforces the impression we receive from more specific rhetorical comments on individual elite attributes: the speaker portrays the ideal orator as simultaneously of the mass and of the elite.[31] This situation may be seen as an elaboration of the dramatic role playing of elite *idiōtai* in private court cases. The difference is that the political orator was expected to demonstrate both egalitarian and elite credentials and to do so on a regular basis. The balance had to be maintained for as long as he was in the public eye, not merely for the duration of a trial. Maintaining this balance required, once again, consummate "acting" on the part of the speaker and a willingness on the part of the audience to accept the performance.

D.3 Origin of the Balance

The psychic mechanisms that allowed the Athenians to respect elitist claims in a political context, while rejecting them in most other contexts, were complex. Some of the political orators' elitist claims, especially to ability and education, may be explained by the assumption that the members of the audience would rationally choose to lend their attention to men who had proved their competence. But it seems absurd to suggest that the Athenians consciously decided to stymie the ambitions of the elite by forcing them to conform to a complex and contradictory code of public behavior and speech or that they consciously devised a symbolic language that would explain mass and elite to one another, along with a context for that language which would ensure that it was used frequently. Previous chapters have detailed the elaborate set of symbolic tactics that collectively formed the structure of a workable social and political strategy. But what is the etiology of those tactics, and how were they integrated into a coherent strategy?

[31] E.g., Thuc. 2.60.4–5 (Pericles' second speech to the Assembly); Isoc. 18.23 (on Thrasybulus and Anytus); Dem. 24.134–35 (on Agyrrhios of Kollytos), 18.171–72, 258, 320, 19.337–38; Aesch. 3.169–70.

A definitive answer to these important questions is beyond the scope of this study, but a review of the historical development of Athenian social attitudes and a consideration of audience response to elite speakers may allow us to formulate a plausible hypothesis.

Athenian popular culture in the classical period was strongly oral and remarkably public—the theater, courts, and Assembly provided its major forums. Hence, public speech was a natural medium of social mediation. The tactic of employing rhetorical topoi by public speakers was learned behavior on the part of persons who had been "taught" (directly or indirectly) what to say by several generations of Athenian audiences. The tendency of the audience in both the Assembly and courtroom to react immediately and vocally to the speaker's comments allowed the success or failure of each rhetorical ploy to be tested independently from the success or failure of the speech as a whole. Fourth-century logographers writing speeches for elite litigants in private court cases learned that blatantly elitist comments met with disfavor and that egalitarian comments would be regarded favorably, and so they used egalitarian topoi frequently. But political orators, in their turn, learned that elitist comments would be regarded favorably in certain contexts and so employed elitist topoi along with egalitarian ones. Each topos or ploy evoked a response, positive or negative, from the listener because it touched an existing sensibility—whether overt or latent—within the listener's value system. The origins of symbolic/rhetorical tactics and the key to their strategic integration might therefore be sought through a functionalist analysis of the historical evolution of Athenian modes of response to the stimulus of privilege claims based on elite attributes.

Athenian elitist ideals presumably originated at a time when the elite ruled. The basic principles of Greek elitist ideology may be traced back to the growth of a self-consciously aristocratic elite in the late Dark Ages and early archaic period. Within the generalized "panhellenic" aristocratic ideology, individual aristocracies in each coalescing state developed their own particularized set of ideas regarding the proper role of the elite in the state (cf. above, vi.b). The Athenian stress on birthright and on the aristocratic code of behavior may be traced to this early period. The ideology of the ruling elite continued to develop as the elite itself evolved. As the political position of the aristocrats was taken over by the wealthy and well educated, elitist ideology accumulated the other primary attributes discussed above. The long period of political dominance by the elite before the mid-sixth century ingrained in the masses a respect for elite attributes and a deferential pattern of behavior (above, ii.b). We may posit, therefore, that when a fourth-century Athenian political orator made the right elitist comment in the right context, he stimulated in his audience a deferential mode of thought and action. They responded by allowing him privileges somewhat similar to those a member of the ruling elite might have enjoyed before the development of the democracy.

From the mid-sixth century through the fifth century, the growth of national consciousness and the subsequent development of democratic political forms encouraged the growth of an egalitarian sensibility which, by the fourth century, clearly dominated Athenian ideology and had subverted some important aspects of the old aristocratic ideal. The dominance of the egalitarian sensibility explains why mass audiences responded favorably to topoi stressing equality. The elitist sensibility was, however, never completely suppressed. Some elite Athenians continued to advocate the adoption of an oligarchical form of government until the late fifth century. But the failed coups of 411 and 404 and the democratic victory of 403 spelled the death of oligarchy as a viable political alternative. Nevertheless, fourth-century political orators found that their audiences still responded favorably to elitist rhetoric. Why?

An evolutionary or behavioral/functional model seems to provide at least a partial explanation: the psychic mechanisms here called political ideology, like the physical and instinctive characteristics of a species, appear to have changed in reaction to events through a process of trial and error. After the establishment of the Assembly and court system as the primary decision-making apparatuses of the state, Athenian political ideology operated in an environment that encouraged relatively rapid evolution. Psychic mechanisms were reinforced and retained if they helped Athenian political society to function better (in terms of good decisions arrived at by the masses) in response to its broader environment. Mechanisms that damaged the society's ability to respond effectively—or which led to decisions harmful to society— were discouraged and discarded. The outcome may seem rational, but the process was not dependent on the conscious choices either of individuals or of the society as a whole.[32]

[32] An analogy is the set of mechanisms, developed within a species by evolutionary means, whereby instinctive actions by an animal can, under certain conditions, inhibit or release specific behavior patterns in members of the same species; see K. Lorenz, *On Aggression*, trans. M. K. Wilson (New York, 1966). Cf. the mode of chemical communication between mother and fetus, which inhibits and releases the normal activities of the maternal immune system at specific points in the gestation cycle in order to afford a "special privilege" to the fetus, which would otherwise be rejected: P. M. Johnson, quoted in *Science News* 130.15 (October 11, 1986): 234–35.

Thus, over the course of the fifth century, the Athenian masses' response to rhetorical symbols evolved according to how that response affected Athenian political society. The experience of the last third of the fifth century, especially the oligarchic counter-revolutions which had proved dangerous to the body politic, reinforced psychic mechanisms for the blocking or inhibiting of responses fostering respect for elites. An elitist comment therefore was not likely to evoke a favorable reaction in the hearer but, rather, suspicion and irritation. Yet the tribulations of the late fifth century also demonstrated that leadership was necessary to the survival of the state, that a complete suppression of all willingness to allow members of the elite a leadership position was deleterious to the functioning of Athenian society. Hence a psychic mechanism evolved that allowed the citizen's normal reaction that inhibited respect for elites to be suppressed under certain conditions and the surviving (but normally repressed) respect that Athenians felt for elite attributes to be released.

In sum: the Cleisthenic political order created a social environment conducive to the evolution of psychic mechanisms and of symbolic tactics to release those mechanisms. The mechanisms and symbols were integrated into a flexible sociopolitical strategy through an evolutionary process that selected mechanisms and tactics according to their functional efficacy. The result was that fourth-century Athenian private litigants and politicians were forced to perform the balancing act described above. If this etiological hypothesis is correct—and if the Athenian state did not run into an evolutionary dead end (and its survival in the fourth century suggests that it did not)— the balancing act of the elites should have been to the benefit of the citizenry as a whole. A review of the roles the politicians played in the Athenian state suggests that the act was indeed beneficial to the state.

E. Political Roles of the Rhetor

The function performed by the political orator in the democratic polity was multifarious. He was expected to express the unspoken will of the people, to defend the masses against their internal and external enemies, and to offer them sound advice. In some circumstances he might also serve in a more forthright leadership capacity. These several roles appear in some ways contradictory, but they were not mutually exclusive. The mode of their integration in the person of the individual rhetor can be explained in terms of the dialectic of mass and elite.

E.1 MOUTHPIECE OF PUBLIC OPINION

I discussed above (IV.B.4) the importance to the Athenians of the notions that mass decisions were likely to be wise and that what everyone believed was likely to be right. If these premises were applied consistently in the political arena, the orator's role would be a simple one: he would vocalize the will of the people, making manifest the *homonoia* of the demos. His function would be more or less that of a glorified herald. Demosthenes argued along these lines when he stated (18.280; see above, IV.C.1) that the worth of the orator was his preference for the same things as the people. And, from his own rather different perspective, Isocrates came to a similar conclusion. In the speech *To Nicocles* he suggested that the best orator was he who, like a poet, could collect what is scattered through the minds of men and say it most concisely.[33] Thus it might appear unnecessary, foolish, even perverse for the democratic political orator to oppose the will of the people, and, not surprisingly, Demosthenes (19.206) claims that, unlike Aeschines and his cronies, he had never tried to force the Athenians to do what they did not want to do. Other orators were similarly unwilling to oppose the clearly expressed will of the people.[34]

The role of the orator as mouthpiece of popular opinion was emphasized by ancient elitist writers; Plato, Aristotle, Thucydides, and Isocrates all condemn demagogues as mere crowd pleasers who said only what the people wanted to hear. Elitist writers, of course, typically considered mass decision making to be foolish, and the populace anything but wise. Therefore, they castigated the political orators for failing to exert a leadership role in the state, for failing to oppose the will of the mass, and for saying what everyone wanted to hear rather than what was good and salutary for the state.[35]

Athenian politicians were well aware of the climate of opinion in which they operated, and no public speaker could afford to contradict central principles of the Athenian belief structure very often (see I.E). Political orators did praise the demos, telling the people just the sorts of things we might imagine that they would want to hear: that the speaker himself was completely dependent upon the goodwill of the many (Dem. 18.5, 281), that Athenians had fine institutions, good hab-

---

[33] Isoc. 2.40–41, 43, 49. Cf. Jaeger, *Paideia*, III.104.

[34] E.g., Thuc. 8.92.10 (Theramenes). According to Plutarch (*Phocion* 16.2), one of Phocion's political opponents warned him against attempting to turn the Athenians from war when they already had arms in hand.

[35] Sources: above, I.n.102. Cf. Bolger, "Training," 36–37; and above, III.D.2.

its, were intelligent, just, free, and philhellenic by nature.[36] It was also common to attack an opponent on the grounds that he was a demos-hater (*misodēmos*: Lyc. 1.39, Aesch. 2.171), someone who despised the *politeia* (Din. 1.112), was contemptuous of the masses (Lys. 9.17), and thought them fools (Hyp. 3.23). In the speech *Against Meidias* (21.203–204, cf. 194) Demosthenes makes the point that Meidias' constant haranguing and berating of the masses in the Assembly was evidence that he nurtured a "secret hatred of you, the many." The attack seems to be based squarely on the notion that the orator's role was to enunciate mass opinion, not to oppose it.

E.2 Protector of the People

As Finley pointed out, however, the Athenian political orators did more than simply parrot the desires of the people and mouth vacuous niceties; rather, they served as a structural element in the functioning of the state.[37] One important function the orator fulfilled was to protect the masses—the term *prostatēs tou dēmou*, "he who stands before the people," meant not only one who stood first in the eyes of the people and who physically stood before the people in order to address them, but one who interposed himself between the people and dangers that threatened them.[38] Orators could be referred to as "guardians of the democracy" (Aesch. 3.250–51; cf. Lys. 27.3). Their guardianship lay in part in attacking internal enemies of the people in the courts.[39] They might also use their superior speaking abilities in court to aid citizens who were less able than themselves to speak persuasively (e.g., Hyp. 1.10). But the orator was also the protector of the people in the Assembly. Lysias (12.72) recalls the terrible Assembly of 404, called in order to name the Thirty Tyrants in Lysander's presence,

---

[36] E.g., Dem. 6.8, 8.40–42, 19.285, 330, 22.76, 23.109; Aesch. 1.178; Lyc. 1.51. Examples could easily be multiplied.

[37] Finley, "Athenian Demagogues," *PAW*, 75–84; cf. above, III.D.2.

[38] On the term *prostatēs* meaning "protector," see Connor, *NP*, 110–15. Cf. Lys. 13.7–8, 12: after Aegospotami the revolutionaries were only blocked by *tous tou dēmou proestēkotas*, along with the *stratēgoi* and taxiarchs. Therefore those who desired oligarchy had Cleophon put to death by a rigged jury. Aesch. 2.176: good government was restored when the demos came back from Phyle and the *prostantōn tou dēmou* were Archinus and Thrasybulus. Wilcox, "Scope," 155, cites the closure of the schools of rhetoric by the Thirty Tyrants (Xen. *Mem.* 1.2.31) as evidence that the oligarchs saw that "oratory is the life-blood of democracy." Attempts to distinguish the *prostatai* of the polis from the *prostatai* of the demos (Reverdin, "Remarques") or the *prostatai* from the rhetores (Ehrenberg, *People of Aristophanes*, 354–56) are futile and misleading.

[39] Court attacks salutary: e.g., Lys. 27.3; And. 1.136; Lyc. 1.3, 138; cf. Osborne, "Law in Action," 40–42; and above, III.B.1, below, VII.F.1.

when "no rhetor could oppose them [the Thirty] and you [the demos] could not overawe them."

E.3 ADVISER

The protective role of the political orators merged with an advisory function. As speakers in the Assembly, the rhetores presented the demos with a range of policy options that ordinary citizens might not have considered.[40] As Pericles noted in the Funeral Oration (Thuc. 2.40.2), speeches can help to instruct the people, and debate is salutary for a democracy. Each speech delivered in the Assembly was a public affirmation of the basic principle of *isēgoria*. Demosthenes (*Ex.* 44.1–2; see above, IV.B.4) bridges the gap between mass will and the orator's advisory function when he notes that he would not offer his own opinion in the Assembly if all were in agreement on the matter at hand, since he, being one man, would be more likely to be mistaken than "all of you." The implication is that since there *were* differences of opinion within the Assembly, Demosthenes felt he could legitimately offer his advice. The advisory role of the political orator is reflected in the term *sumboulos*, which politicians use of themselves and of "good orators" in general (e.g., Lyc. 1.11; Hyp. 5.28; Dem. 58.62; cf. above, III.B.2). Demosthenes sums up the advisory role of the political orators in the *First Olynthiac*.

> Oh Athenians, I believe that you would prefer it to great wealth if it could be made clear to you what would be the best policy in the matters now under discussion. This being the case, it is proper for you to listen intently to all those desirous of giving advice (*tōn boulomenōn sumbouleuein*). For not only might someone come forward with a carefully thought out proposal, and you, having heard it, might decide to adopt it, but I consider it part of your good fortune that other speakers may be inspired with suitable suggestions on the spur of the moment, so that from among many proposals it will be easy to choose the one most in your own interest. (1.1)

Demosthenes' comment leaves room not only for the expert public speaker who comes forward "with a carefully thought out proposal" but also for the ordinary citizen who might be "inspired with suitable

[40] As Plato *Theaetetus* 167b–c notes. Cf. Wilcox, "Scope," 146; Bryant, "Rhetoric," 412. Meier, *Anthropologie*, 50–51, discusses the advisory role of democratic leaders, arguing that leadership was acceptable only at the level of discussion rather than at the level of organization. I am in general agreement, but cf. Montgomery, *Way to Chaeronea*, 58–60, 91–94, 102–103; and below, VII.E.4.

suggestions on the spur of the moment." Certainly, ordinary citizens did sometimes take it upon themselves to address the people, and their contribution should not be underestimated (cf. above, III.B.2). But the regular speakers had a special part to play in the advisory process; the importance of their role is stressed by Demosthenes (19.285), who suggests that a conviction of Aeschines will improve the integrity of the politicians (*politeuomenoi*) "on whose shoulders rest the most important affairs of the state" (*ta megista kinduneuetai tēi polei*). Consequently, the political orator must give the best possible advice, and he must not allow anything, even fear of a possible negative reaction to his comments by the Assembly, to stand in the way of his oratorical service to the state (cf. Dem. 1.16, 8.71).

Dinarchus (1.40, 72, 74) seems to go even further in granting the politicians a special position in the decision-making process when he states that the advisers (*sumbouloi*) and the political leaders (*hēgemones*) are those who were responsible for all good or evil in the polis. In the same speech (1.17, 94, 97) he attacks Demosthenes for the latter's continual changes of policy which, Dinarchus says, neglect "the affairs of the demos" (*tas huper tou dēmou praxeis*; cf. Dem. 19.9–28; Aesch. 2.164). The emphasis upon the vital importance of expert public speakers, the recognition that good political orators must be willing to oppose the will of the people, the implication that a good politician stuck to one line of policy regardless of changes in the popular mood, and the conjunction of the terms "adviser" and "leader," all suggest that the rhetores might take a more active role in the state than merely offering the Assemblymen a smorgasbord of policy options from which the latter could pick and choose as they would.

E.4 LEADER, CRITIC, OPPOSER OF
THE PEOPLE'S WILL

Indeed, a political orator sometimes was willing to claim for himself a leadership role that went far beyond merely advising the demos on policy options. Demosthenes (18.320; see IV.E) claimed that at a key moment (in 339 B.C.) ". . . I revealed myself to be the best speaker, and all state business was conducted according to my decrees, my laws, and my diplomatic delegations. . . ." In a fragment that appears to be from a political trial speech in his own defense, preserved only in a Latin translation, Lycurgus strikes a similar note.

> When the young men (*iuventus*) in their enthusiasm had thoughtlessly taken up arms . . . I compelled the Council [*Senatum*] to use its authority to restrain their violence. I, by my threats to the

treasurers, forbade them to grant money for soldiers' pay. I stood firm when the armory was opened and refused to have arms taken out. It was thus entirely my doing, as you see, that an unnecessary war was avoided. (Lyc. F I.5 [Conomis] = A.1 [Burtt])

Both passages have an almost authoritarian tone, but I do not think that either Demosthenes, who notes that his leadership coincided with the freedom of the demos to decide policy, or Lycurgus intended to cast himself in the role of the tyrant. Their leadership was within the context of the democratic polity; therefore the Athenians apparently considered it acceptable and democratic for a politician to exercise a leadership role in times of emergency. The roles of adviser and leader were both parts of the essential "structural element" that the political orators provided to the state; and both required that the public speaker be willing to oppose the will of the demos.

The politicians' role in providing the state with thoughtful advice and leadership, and the necessity of their opposing the popular will in order to fulfill these functions, supply a general context for instances in which political orators actively castigate the demos for its failings. One particularly common topos of blame in political orations was the contrast between the Athenians of the present day and their illustrious ancestors. The "modern generation" was reproved for having fallen from the pinnacle of excellence achieved by its ancestors: in the past jurors were strict and enforced the law rigorously, unlike modern jurors who do not even pay attention when the clerk reads the law aloud (Aesch. 3.191–92). The ancestors lived in simple virtue and maintained equality among themselves (Aesch. 3.26); they did not give excessive honors to unworthy men (Aesch. 3.178, 182); they were on guard against traitors and were free from the laxity now common (Dem. 19.181). The ancestors had chosen excellent men as political leaders and advisers.[41] They attributed to the demos all that was good and fine, to the rhetores that which was evil (Aesch. 3.231). Unlike the ancestors, who had punished even Themistocles for making himself "greater than themselves," modern Athenians were not willing to bring malefactors to justice (Dem. 23.204–205); thus, whereas in the past the polis was master of the politicians, now the polis was servant of the politicians (Dem. 23.209).[42]

[41] E.g., Din. 1.40; Lys. 30.28; Dem. 58.62; Aesch. 3.181–82.

[42] Aristotle (Rhet. 1417b12–16) notes that in deliberative oratory one may relate things about the past so that the hearers will make better decisions in the future and that this may be done either in a spirit of praise or of blame. On the tendency

Other criticisms, while not mentioning the ancestors, take a similar tone: the contemporary Athenians were slack, failed to be on their guard, and idly awaited disaster (Dem. 18.149, 19.224); they made citizens of slaves and rabble ([Dem.] 13.24); they gave up their own control of offices, especially generalships, by allowing the same men to be reelected for years on end (Dem. *Ex.* 55.3). Their ideas on foreign policy tended to be too optimistic, and they left matters of war and peace to ambassadors, rather than deciding these matters for themselves (And. 3.35, cf. 41). Most particularly, they chose bad leaders. The Athenians gave political orators too much leeway, placed too much trust in them, and did not punish them strictly enough. They put their faith in rogues, while ignoring the good advice of genuine patriots.[43] They were misled, despite their native intelligence and good laws, because they chose to pay attention to speeches alone and ignored the lifestyle of politicians (Aesch. 1.179). They had fine judgment but did not apply it consistently, as shown by their unwillingness to be harsh enough toward bribe-taking politicians (Dem. 23. 145–46; cf. 24.172). On the other hand, the Athenians failed to appreciate the real worth of the orator (Lyc. 1.3); they did not recognize which politicians were their true benefactors, because each citizen was too concerned with his private concerns (Dem. 19.227–28).

Although each criticism had its particular context and was intended to put the speaker in the best light and his opponent in the worst, the thread running through the various topoi of blame is clear enough: the orator "attacks" the people for not living up to their own ideals. The people are accused of being too generous with grants of citizenship, of giving over their mass power into the hands of a few evil men, of ignoring their own laws, of trusting rhetoric instead of depending on their collective wisdom. Thus, when the political orator blamed the people, he typically did so by appealing to egalitarian principles. He took the position of reminding his audience of the pristine democratic code of thought and behavior from which they had strayed. The appeal is to an essentially reactionary sensibility which regarded the past as good, the present as a falling-away from that ideal, and the future as likely to be better only if it recapitulated the past.[44] The ideal past

---

of the orators to reproach their audiences for not living up to their ancestors' standard, cf. Dover, *GPM*, 23–25, "Freedom," 49.

[43] Too much leeway, too much trust: Lyc. 1.12; Dem. 9.54, 23.147, *Ex.* 55.2; Lys. 18.16. Insufficiently strict: Lys. 27.4–6; Dem. 23.206. Trust rogues, ignore patriots: Dem. 18.138, 19.226, 51.21, *Ex.* 42.1. Aristophanes' comic demagogues make similar comments: e.g., *Knights* 1340–44, *Ecclesiazusae* 173–207.

[44] Cf. the frequent allusions, by fourth-century writers and politicians of various

evoked by the rhetores was not, however, the idealized pre-democratic past longed for by Isocrates and other elitist writers, but the recent and "radical" democratic past. The orator called upon the Athenians to be the democrats their immediate forefathers had been; in so doing, the speaker payed court to an egalitarian climate of opinion.

Substantively, the blame topoi therefore have much in common with praise topoi, but when blaming the people the orator took on a didactic, quasi-paternal role. The orator who reproved the demos claimed for himself the remarkable privilege of setting his individual opinion and vision of the state in opposition to the ideas and current habits of the masses. Any one Athenian who deliberately set himself apart from and in opposition to the demos was taking a great risk. But castigating the people and opposing their will were central and expected parts of the political orator's function; this is amply demonstrated by the tendency of the rhetores themselves to attack the evils of public flattery and demagoguery.

In Assembly speeches, Demosthenes vigorously denounces both the practices of crowd-pleasing orators and the demos' tendency to listen to them. As he suggests in the *Third Olynthiac* (3.3), the popularity-hunting (*pros charin*) speeches of a few men led to the present crisis (of 348 B.C.). The true politician set the welfare of the state above the attempt to gain *charis* through his speeches (*tēs en tōi legein charitos*), and this is what the good *legontes* of the past, like Aristides, Nicias, Demosthenes the general, and Pericles had done. But now rhetores ask the demos: "What do you desire? What law should I propose? How can I please you?" (*ti humin charisōmai*). Hence, affairs of the state are frittered away for the sake of the pleasure of the moment (*tēs parautika charitos*: 3.21–22). The evil rhetores corrupt the demos by fawning upon "you," and they lead you to desire foolish things (like theoric payments), thereby "making you their prisoners" (*cheiroētheis hautois poiountes*: 3.31–32). Demosthenes concludes this last passage (3.32) by suggesting that he may get rough treatment from the Athenians, since there is not freedom of speech (*parrhēsia*) about all things in Athens; he was amazed indeed that the demos had allowed him to speak his mind so freely. In a similar vein, in the *First Philippic*, after having criticized the Athenians roundly for their laziness and indolence, Demosthenes concludes (4.51) that he had never said anything

---

political persuasions, to the "ancestral constitution" and its various "fathers": E. Ruschenbusch, "ΠΑΤΡΙΟΣ ΠΟΛΙΤΕΙΑ," *Historia* 7 (1958): 398–424; K. R. Walters, "The Ancestral Constitution and Fourth-Century Historiography in Athens," *AJAH* 1 (1976): 129–44; Mossé, "Comment." On the idea of progress generally, see Meier, *Entstehung des Politischen*, 435–99.

to gain the demos' *charis* which he did not believe was to its advantage. In the current instance he spoke bluntly (*haplōs*), using *parrhēsia*, although he was not sure his audience would like it. He strikes a similar note in the speech *On the Chersonese*: the politicians had prepared the demos to be difficult and fierce in the Assembly but lax and contemptible in war preparations, whereas they should have trained you to be gentle and humane (*philanthrōpous*) in the Assembly and fierce in military preparations (8.32–33).

> But now, by practicing demagoguery and pleasing you (*dēmagōgountes humas kai charizomenoi*), they have brought you to such a state of mind that in the Assembly you are elated by their flattery and lend a willing ear to their compliments, while in your public affairs and practices you currently run the gravest risks. (8.34)

Aeschines takes the same line in his political trial speech *Against Ctesiphon*: Aeschines chooses to speak the truth, rather than to please his audience, since it is the orators' bad habit of always speaking to please (*aei pros hēdonēn legomenon*) that has brought the polis to such an awful state (3.127). The many were in the process of giving over the democracy to the few, and the demos was fortunate in that so far no rhetores whose bravery matched their *ponēria* had sprung up to overthrow the demos, as had happened before (in the revolution of 404). At that time the demos had been thrown down because of its own love of flattery (*echaire gar kolakeuomenos*); the destroyers of democracy were those to whom the demos had willingly become prisoner (*hois heauton enecheirize*: 3.234).

The passages cited above suggest that the comments attributed by Thucydides to Diodotus and Cleon (Thuc. 3.38.4–5, 3.42.6) in the Mytilene debate, that the people were wrong to accept flattery and willingly became slaves to the orators, may reflect genuine statements by late fifth-century orators. Isocrates, who has often been accused of being out of touch with political realities, makes very similar sorts of comments in *On the Peace* (8.116, 121) and *Antidosis* (15.133). Both speeches purport to be genuine attempts to influence Athenian public opinion, and the similarity of the "attack" on the people's tendency to listen to flatterers, rather than true-hearted citizens who had the state's best interests in mind, shows that Isocrates here was working with topoi the Athenians were used to hearing from politicians.[45]

---

[45] For other examples of "blame" in oratory and in comedy, see Dover, *GPM*, 23–25, 28–30, who argues that both may be viewed within the context of a "didactic tradition" in which the speaker criticizes and instructs the audience. But traditions survive or die out according to the concerns and needs of the society. The specific

Like so many of the topoi employed by the political orators, the "Athenians corrupted by evil flattery" topos cuts two ways. On the one hand, it suggests that the Athenians really did like to be flattered in public oratory. And their pleasure in hearing dulcet phrases certainly explains the flowery praise with which the orators garlanded their speeches. But the topos also suggests that the Athenians were aware of their own tendency to listen to the pleasant and not to the necessary and were willing to be chided for it. While the line between telling the people what they wanted to hear and exercising a genuine advisory and leadership role was often a fine one, the "evils of flattery" topos suggests that Athenians mistrusted any orator who too overtly attempted to "please all of the people all of the time." The good orator not only praised the people, he also criticized and opposed them; orator and audience alike recognized that criticism and opposition to the will of the masses were central to the orator's political function.

The public speaker's position as critic and opponent of popular will was something of an anomaly in the egalitarian political order. Haranguing the people might well get a politician in trouble; as we have seen, Demosthenes attacked Meidias as a demos-hater on the strength of the latter's tendency to criticize the masses. The conviction of Socrates made clear the dangers of indulging in unrestrained public criticism. But a rhetor's willingness to go out on a limb, to oppose the will of the people in advocating a new and innovative policy, was the characteristic that made him useful. The political orators showed the Assembly the full range of possible policy options. Without the rhetores to develop and present reasonable proposals, the state might stagnate and drift. Without leadership in times of national emergency, the inherent slowness of democratic decision making could cause disaster.

Political power resided with the demos, but the demos was willing to "delegate" its powers in certain circumstances: power to lead the people in arms was delegated to generals in the field, power to make treaties to ambassadors, power to judge and to punish miscreants, as well as to reconsider decrees of the Assembly, to the *dikastēria*, power to review, confirm, and change the laws to the *nomothetai*. Similarly, the demos could, when it chose, grant to the orators the authority to advise the demos on a regular basis and even to lead the state in times of crisis. But the procedures by which specific powers were granted to generals, ambassadors, *dikastēria*, and *nomothetai* were clearly defined

---

uses of blame topoi by the political orators are of significance for understanding fourth-century political behavior. Cf. also Montgomery, *Way to Chaeronea*, 18–28, for a succinct discussion of Demosthenes' criticism of other orators and of the demos. See also citations above, I.n.111.

by the laws; the process of granting rhetores the authority to oppose
the mass will was not. What then was the mechanism that determined
when and to which individuals the political leadership of the people
should be entrusted?[46]

E.5 IMPORTANCE OF BEING ELITIST

Elitist statements by the political orators should be viewed in the context of the need for a nonconstitutional mechanism for delegation of
authority by the demos. The orator's elite attributes allowed him to
fulfill his political function. He had to be intelligent and well educated
in order to be able properly to analyze the problems of the state and
to formulate policy that might solve those problems. He had to be a
highly skilled speaker in order to render the complicated issues facing
the state clearly to the people and in order to gain support for his own
proposals. The orator's wealth provided him with the leisure to study
the challenges facing the state and (at least so the Athenians believed)
might help to make him impervious to bribery. Noble birth might provide him with connections among the Athenian elite generally, but
more importantly, citizen ancestors passed on to him the inborn sense
of patriotism and love of democracy that was a prerequisite to a political career. Furthermore, the Athenian politician could successfully attack Athens' enemies, internal and external, and so serve as a "protector of the people," only if he possessed attributes that rendered him
functionally equal to the state's enemies. Thus, he must be as well educated, as clever a speaker, as wealthy, and as well born as the various
malefactors he guarded the demos against. In short, elite attributes
were sine qua non for the political orator who hoped to compete in
the public arenas for the attention and respect of the people. An orator who was not elite could never be more than a mere "pleaser of the
people."

The Athenian system of government was based on mass decision
making following upon public discussion. By law, each of the 6,000–

---

[46] Hansen, "Demos, Ecclesia," 144–46, argues that the concept of delegation is
not useful in understanding the relationship between *ekklēsia* and *dikastērion*, on the
grounds that the superior body should be able to rescind delegated powers from
the delegatee. Hansen's legalistic argument is based upon his belief that only the
ekklēsia was regarded as embodying the will of the demos, but cf. above, III.E.4, VII.C.
The ideas, which I believe were commonly held by Athenians, that *nomothetai* and
jurors *were* expressing the will of the demos and that the demos reviewed decisions
by the jurors, seem to me to justify the use of the concept of delegation in analyzing
Athenian political behavior. In my other examples of delegation, the problem does
not arise, since the demos indeed had the right to rescind the powers.

8,000 citizens in attendance at a typical Assembly had the right to take an active part in the public discussion. But if even one in a hundred citizens chose to exercise his *isēgoria* at any given meeting, the volume of debate that would precede the vote would cause the system to founder. Many significant decisions had to be made every year; the Assembly had to come to some decision by the end of each meeting. Ancient and modern critics of democracy have pointed out that the time for deliberation in Assembly was very short.[47] Obviously, some procedure was required that would serve as a filter, to assure that those who addressed the Assembly at length on major issues had something worthwhile to say. The elite status of the orators provided such a mechanism. By alluding in his speeches to his own attainments, and by pointing out his opponent's lack of similar attainments, the orator demonstrated his "professional credentials" as adviser and defender and tested the credentials of his opponent. This filtering process stood in place of the more formal systems of representation and elections that allow elites in modern democratic societies to take legitimate roles of political leadership (cf. above, VII.A).

Through reiterated demonstration of his elite status in Assembly speeches and public trials, as well as by advocating successful policy, the politician developed in his audience a belief in his worthiness to advise them. His achievement of trusted adviser status was signaled by the willingness of the Assemblymen to hear him out when major issues were being discussed, to refrain from exercising their collective *isēgoria* by shouting or laughing him down. The politician who achieved this status was informally granted the authority to reprove and reprimand, to press for the adoption of his own policies even in the face of popular resistance to them. He might also be allowed to fail to convince the people of the rightness of his ideas from time to time. He could therefore continue to advocate a policy that had been at least temporarily rejected by the voters. The "vote of no confidence" represented by a speaker's failure to carry a proposal in the Assembly did not, therefore, necessarily stifle his voice, and the Athenians kept open the option of changing their policy (cf. Din. 1.13).

The accrediting process took time. It required perseverence and skill on the part of the prospective politician and a careful understanding of the role he was expected to play. Demosthenes himself failed to hold the Assembly's attention in his early attempts to address the peo-

---

[47] E.g., Aristot. *Rhet.* 1354b1–4; Cicero *Pro Flacco* 15ff.; Michels, *Party Politics*, 64–65.

ple (Plut. *Dem.* 5–8). His difficulties were no doubt the norm for a budding politician, since the Athenians could not afford to have too many elite political experts in contention (cf. Lys. 16.20; Dem. *Ex.* 13.1; Plato *Protagoras* 319b–323a). It was to the advantage of the demos to have a range of opinion presented in Assembly, but the available options had to be laid out in the course of a few hours. Too many speeches might muddle the issue, and not surprisingly, therefore, only a handful of "full-time" politicians operated in Athens at any one time (above, III.B.1).

The orator's elite status also facilitated his assumption of a more direct role in the government of the state. His demonstration that his superiority was directly linked to the public interest legitimated his claim to a position of leadership which might well appear anti-democratic in other circumstances. In a moment of crisis, the orator "revealed himself," in Demosthenes' words (18.320), as a leader. The theatrical metaphor clarifies the nature of this "revelation": the orator, normally playing a double role and balancing any elitist claims with egalitarian sentiments, stepped out of character (as the elite *idiōtēs* never did); he shed his double mask of "equal but better" and displayed himself to the audience as a superior being, worthy of rule. As such, he stood not only before, but above the people and so could lay claim to the delegated power of the demos. All state business might, for the duration of the emergency, safely be placed in his hands. Hence, Demosthenes, Lycurgus, and perhaps Thrasybulus, Callistratus, and Eubulus, among others, were able to promulgate consistent policies that allowed the Athenian state to get through difficult periods.[48] The elevation in status from adviser to leader was always temporary, the people's delegation of power always provisional. At the conclusion of the crisis, the leader was expected to revert to his normal advisory role. The obvious analogy is the Roman Dictatorship, but no-

---

[48] Humphreys, "Lycurgus," 201, suggests that Lycurgus' powers "diverged in some significant ways from the pure type of fifth-century democracy" and notes (218) the combination of democratic form and authoritarian content "which characterizes [Lycurgus'] political style." Although his control of finances gave Lycurgus an institutional base earlier politicians lacked, a similar combination of the democratic and the authoritarian characterized other Athenian politicians at certain points in their careers. Cf. Bowles and Gintis, *Democracy and Capitalism*, 183: ". . . effective political leadership and unanticipated innovation by individuals or groups other than 'the whole' is fully consistent with the ideal of popular sovereignty as long as both leadership and innovation are subject to effective ex post facto deliberation and accountability."

tably the Romans made emergency leadership a constitutional office; the Athenians never did.

F. Restraints on Politicians

In order to allow them to perform their political functions, the rhe-tores were freed from some of the ideological controls that bound other elite Athenians to the interests of the mass and that circum-scribed the public display of elite attributes. But the very fact that re-straints were loosened rendered the political experts potentially dan-gerous. Their occasional assumption of "delegated" powers increased the danger, as did the fact that they were not automatically accounta-ble to the state after their period "in office," as were all elected and lotteried magistrates. The elite politicians might appear to have been in a good position to evolve into an institutionalized ruling elite: many if not all of the factors that led to elite monopolization of power in other democratic societies were in place. Michels' Iron Law of Oligar-chy might, on the face of it, seem to be the inevitable end to which Athenian democratic government was tending.

Although they had not read Michels, the Athenians were well aware of the danger that politicians might come to dominate the state, and the political orators indeed played on this fear in their speeches. Juries in public trials were warned that evil politicians planned a revolution (Aesch. 3.225), regarded the *politeia* as their private possession (Aesch. 3.3–4; cf. Dem. 51.19), set themselves up as stronger than the decrees (Dem. 51.22), had taken diplomacy into their own hands so that am-bassadors from other places ignored the demos (Aesch. 3.250). Laws that dealt with orators should be harsh, so that they would be dis-suaded from harming the many (Dem. 24.193); treason should in fact be punished before the crime was committed, because afterward the traitors would be too strong (Lyc. 1.126). Allowing anyone or any group of people to become greater than the people and their laws presented the gravest of dangers. A proper ruling by the jury will make "them" equal to "you" (Lys. 12.35), will put political orators back under the power of the masses (Dem. 58.61), will free the Athenians and their governmental institutions from the grip of entrenched ora-tors (Dem. 22.37). A conviction of rotten ambassadors will show Philip of Macedon that those who claim to be the masters of the Athenians are not their masters (Dem. 19.301) and will lead Philip to deal with the many as directors of all affairs, rather than with the few (Dem. 19.341).

F.1 LEGAL CONTROLS

But in actuality the rhetores were closely controlled in a number of ways. First, they were a check on each other. There were many sorts of legal action to which the public speaker was liable (above, III.B.2). The thirty-four political trial speeches preserved in the corpus represent just the tip of the iceberg of legal competition among politicians. As noted above (VII.C), Aristophon commented he had been indicted, by *graphai paranomōn* alone, seventy-five times, and this figure must have been credible to his audience. Indeed, part of the protective role of the orator consisted in legal attacks upon other orators—acting as a viper-eating brown snake in Hyperides' striking image (above, IV.C.1). Of course, it was necessary to beware of vipers in brown-snake skins. Dinarchus (1.99) warned the Athenians against conspiratorial orators who pretended to abuse one another in the Assembly but who in private were united and so deceived the masses by their speeches. Rather than forming secret cabals, the duty of a traitor-hating *dēmotikos* rhetor was to do as Demosthenes' predecessors had done: indict one another by means of *eisangeliai* and *graphai paranomōn* (Din. 1.100; cf. Dem. 22.66).[49] The constant attacks of the orators on one another tended to prevent their developing into a cohesive ruling elite.[50] But legal restraints alone would not necessarily prevent the sort of informal and underhanded cooperation Dinarchus described. The existence of the *graphē paranomōn* did not prevent the conspiracy that led to the oligarchic coup of 411. At that time, as Thucydides notes (8.66.1), the major public speakers were in on the plot, and they agreed ahead of time on what to say to the Assembly. This conspiracy among the orators had effectively controlled the range of options available to the citizens, a serious and ongoing danger in the restored democracy.

Furthermore, although political trials provided exciting and useful sociopolitical theater, severe judicial punishments meted out to convicted rhetores were problematic since such punishments might actually rob the Athenians of a valuable source of advice. Diodotus (Thuc. 3.42.3–4) notes that attacks on good orators as bribe-takers led to unwarranted suspicions of them, and thus the state was robbed of advisers. Aeschines also complained about the slanders that stopped those with good ideas from offering their advice (3.226). Demosthenes (18.138) reproached the Athenians for allowing low types great powers to overthrow by sycophantic attacks anyone who gave good advice.

---

[49] Cf. Perlman, "Politicians," 343; Maio, "*Politeia*," 33–37.

[50] On the importance of cohesiveness for elite formation in classical elitist theory, see Marger, *Elites and Masses*, 82; cf. above, I.C.2.

F.2 CHARACTER AND POLICY

The Athenians were not limited to judicial punishments as a means of enforcing proper public behavior of politicians, nor were they completely dependent upon the rhetores controlling one another. Athenians considered accountability, both by the scrutiny of the prospective magistrate before he entered office (*dokimasia*) and by the formal review of his conduct in office after his term was up (*euthunai*), vital to the democratic polity. The orator's past political activity might be brought up at his scrutiny and review when he served in an *archō*.[51] But legal indictments, *dokimasiai*, and *euthunai* were only the most obvious and formal manifestations of the generalized power of the Athenian masses to review the actions, behavior, and political status of all citizens. Citizenship itself depended upon an individual's ability to persuade a deme assembly of his right to membership, and this could be challenged in court and in the occasional "cleansings" of the deme registers (VI.C.2). Every time an Athenian stood apart from the political in-group, he had to persuade its members that he was still in conformity with group norms.

The orator was scrutinized and reviewed every time he spoke in public. A sort of *euthunai* was held whenever the Assembly voted upon his proposal or when the jury in a political trial voted to acquit or convict, to accept or reject the arguments he had made as defendant or prosecutor. The Athenians' collective knowledge of the rhetor's life, character, and past history constituted an informal, but effective *dokimasia*.[52] Aristotle (*Rhet.* 1403b10–13) noted that the personal character of the speaker was one of the three "proofs" (along with affecting the emotions of the listener and logical demonstration) that yield persuasion. And Aeschines (1.179, 2.150, 3.174–75) made a point of arguing that an orator's entire life should carry more weight with the people than any individual speech. Public knowledge of an orator would be gained from the politician's own speeches, the comments of his adversaries, and rumor (see above, III.E.5). When he emphasized his elite attributes in a public speech, the orator was not only attempting to gain the momentary respect of his listeners, he was polishing and refining an image he hoped they already held of him. The orator might profess to be reticent to speak about himself (e.g., Dem. 5.4), but dis-

---

[51] Importance of accountability: Ste. Croix, *CSAGW*, 285; Roberts, *Accountability*; Adeleye, "Purpose"; Maio, "*Politeia*," 37–40. Orators formally accountable because of their service in *archai*: Roberts, *Accountability*, 168–71, "Athens' Politicians"; cf. above, III.B.2.

[52] Not to be confused with the formal *dokimasia rhētorōn*: above, III.B.2.

cussion of his own actions and character was a necessary and expected part of his political activity.

When the Athenians considered a proposal, they reviewed its merits, no doubt, but they also looked at it in light of their knowledge of the proposer. Many a proposal (especially in the area of foreign policy) was of necessity so complex that most Assemblymen might be unable to grasp its various ramifications. The ordinary Athenian voter might not understand all the technical arguments for or against a particular policy, but if he trusted the proposer, that trust alone might be sufficient to gain his vote. Once again, the time-limits that direct democracy placed upon decision making are important to keep in mind. The coincidence of complex proposals and limited time in which to discuss them led to the necessary conflation of man and policy; consequently, full differentiation of social and political roles, typical of modern society, was impossible (above, III.D.3). The orator who passed the *dokimasia* of community opinion on the subject of his life not only had an excellent chance of getting a hearing for his views in the Assembly but a better chance of having his proposal regarded favorably.

The orator was thus given special privileges, because the demos felt that he had something special to contribute to the state. But the unique position of trust he held entailed a grave responsibility. Demosthenes (19.298) reminded the Athenians of the oracles that warned them to beware of the leaders of the *politeia*, "for you have trust in them" (*toutois peithesth' humeis*) and so must not allow yourselves to be misled by them. The orator who withheld from the people his true opinion betrayed the pact between politician and demos. Demosthenes attacked Aeschines on the grounds that the latter did not address the people with sufficient frequency (e.g., Aesch. 3.216). But worse yet was the orator who chose to speak in public but did not speak his own mind. Demosthenes (18.282) argued that the worst crime a rhetor could commit was to believe one thing and say another in public. Dinarchus agreed; in his speech against Demosthenes he attacks the latter both for constantly changing his policy (above, VII.E.3) and for expressing ideas in public that he did not personally believe (1.17, 47). Other rhetorical passages express the same sentiment.[53] Clearly, when the Athenians paid a politician with the coin of their trust and their willingness to weaken ideological restraints, they ex-

---

[53] E.g., Thuc. 3.37.4–5 (Cleon on Mytilene), 6.8.2, 6.12.2 (Nicias on Sicilian preparations); Lys. 18.16; Dem. 19.184, 24.124; Hyp. 5.17; cf. Aristot. *Rhet.* 1399a30–32.

pected to be paid back in the form of the best and most heartfelt advice he could come up with. Anything less was treason.

There might be various motives for a rhetor not to tell the demos his true thoughts, but the motive for saying one thing while believing another most commonly alluded to in political trials was bribery. The bribe-taking politician was evil in various ways. He perverted the relationship of reciprocal gratitude that helped to bind together the interests of masses and elites (cf. esp. v.f.3). But the bribe-taker also subverted the link between character and policy. The Athenians' dependence upon conflating the character and lifestyle of the individual politician with the policies he publicly advocated helps to explain the prevalence and vehemence of attacks upon opponents as bribe-takers.[54] The bribed speaker advocated proposals favored by his paymaster, whose interests had not been demonstrated to be identical to the interests of the people and whose views were not necessarily even those of a patriotic citizen. Since the offerer of a bribe did not have to face the people himself but remained in the background, his life was not available for public scrutiny. The man who bought an orator was a genuinely unaccountable and uncontrolled element in the political process. By choosing a trusted adviser of the people to present his ideas, the covert employer purchased not only a glib tongue, but the backlog of trust the orator had built up by proper demonstration of his own credentials, elite and egalitarian, to the people over time. This consideration helps to explain why the orator who accepted a bribe for public speaking was liable to indictment under *eisangelia*, a legal process specifically designed for cases involving treason. *Eisangelia* was employed if anyone should attempt to "destroy the demos," attend a seditious meeting, form a conspiracy, betray the armed forces, or "if a rhetor should not say that which is most in the interest of the demos, because of having taken a bribe" (Hyp. 4.7–8; cf. above, iii.b.2).

Because the Athenians were often in the position of voting on an ad hominem basis, terrible effects were attributed to politically-motivated bribery: bribery is, for example, Philip's way of conquering great poleis (Hyp. 5.15). Dinarchus hits upon a number of common themes in his attack upon Philocrates, a *stratēgos* accused of having taken money

---

[54] Late fifth century: Thuc. 2.60.6 (Pericles), 3.38.2 (Cleon on Mytilene); early fourth century: Strauss, "Cultural Significance"; mid- to later fourth century: Dem. 9.54, 18.103, 114, 19.146–47, 265, 23.146, 24.172, 200, 203, 29.22, 51.21–22; Aesch. 2.79, 3.218, 220, 232, 257; Din. 1.1, 28, 42, 98, 3.19; Hyp. 5.21. J. Cargill, "Demosthenes, Aischines, and Crop of Traitors," *Ancient World* 11 (1985): 75–85, argues that Demosthenes' statements to the effect that Philip's supporters in Athens took bribes from him were true. Cf. also Harvey, "*Dona Ferentes*," and above, vi.d.3.

from Harpalus, the fleeing treasurer of Alexander the Great: the bribe-taker accepted gifts "against all of you, and your countryside, and children, and wives . . ." (Din. 3.2). Philocrates deceived all the Athenians, betrayed the trust (*pistis*) which he did not deserve to have received from "you" and so "did his best to destroy everything in the polis" (Din. 3.4, cf. 3.10). Clearly, bribe-takers are demos-haters (Din. 3.22). No doubt, speakers continued to accept money from individuals, but the extreme antagonism that the Athenians apparently felt toward the orator who betrayed his unique and trusted position perhaps made the orator less eager to take money "with some policy in mind" (Hyp. 5.24).

G. Ideological Hegemony of the Masses

The ideological control of the elite by the Athenian citizen masses was not a perfect system, but on the whole it worked remarkably well. Resentments and tensions remained between elite *idiōtai* and the ordinary citizens, but those tensions could be and were mediated through symbolic means in the law courts. The result was a relatively high degree of social harmony and a lack of overt class conflict. Equally important to the survival of the state was the system of granting elite politicians special privileges in the arenas of public debate which allowed them to serve as defenders, advisers, and sometimes leaders of the state. From the restoration of the democracy in 403 to the Macedonian overthrow of the democracy in 322, the Athenians had the use of the considerable personal abilities of thoughtful, well-educated, patriotic politicians who remained sensitive to the interests of the masses and helped to guide the state through difficult times. These individuals often held strongly opposing views and attempted to portray one another as traitors and lower-class rascals unworthy of the people's attention. Such attacks were part of the political contest system which in turn became part of the system of demotic control; it is not necessary for us to take any Athenian orator's assessment of his opponent's habits, background, or motives at face value.[55] Rather, these state-

---

[55] Of course it would be equally foolish to argue that the comments of the orators never had a basis in reality; no doubt many orators really did take bribes, perhaps some really were from lower-class families, and it is not impossible that a few were actually traitors to the democracy. There may well be a "nugget of truth" in these attacks, but we are seldom able to put the matter to the test, and so each modern writer is tempted to see as "nuggets" those comments that suit his or her own preconceptions. On the errors this approach led to in the reconstruction of archaic Greek history, see C. G. Starr, "The Credibility of Early Spartan History," *Historia* 14 (1965): 257–72.

ments allow us to analyze just how successfully the Athenian demos reserved for itself the right to judge the qualifications and character of its politicians. The ideological hegemony of the masses effectively channeled the fierce competitiveness of elites, a legacy of the aristocratic code, into patterns of behavior that were in the public interest. The vital shift occurred in the late sixth and early fifth centuries, when the elite competitors began to compete for the favor of the masses, rather than—or in addition to—the respect of their elite peers. The effect of the shift was that the abilities, wealth, and birthright of the elite politician (and to a lesser degree of all elites) were only valorized when he received public recognition by the demos. Thus, the continuing strength of the aristocratic code of competition and *philotimia* served the interests of the democracy.[56]

Athens' political leaders and advisers were unable to avert the Macedonian victory in 338 B.C. at Chaeronea or the subsequent loss of Athenian freedom of action in foreign policy. But that failure need not be laid at the door of the political organization of the state. Perhaps some solution to the "Macedonian problem" could have been found, perhaps the problem was insoluble given the inequality in resources. In any event, the mistakes the Athenians may have made in assessing and reacting to the military threat posed by Macedon were not the result of fatal flaws in the constitution, the gullibility of the people, or the treachery of the politicians.[57]

G.1 ATHENS AND THE IRON LAW OF OLIGARCHY

There was no major change in the Athenian sociopolitical order after Chaeronea, despite the new element in the sociopolitical equation represented by the power of Macedon to interfere in the affairs of the defeated Greek poleis. The bonds of interdependence between Athenian masses and elites might have been weakened by the alternative route to political power that cooperation with the Macedonians represented. Instead of humbling themselves before the masses, members of the Athenian elite might have chosen to court their conquerors in hopes that the latter would support a new political order that would offer them a more overt role in the government. There was indeed a good deal of fear in Athens that something of this kind might occur,

[56] Cf. Carter, *Quiet Athenian*, 10–17; Whitehead, "Competitive Outlay."

[57] I have attempted to define some of the errors in military policy made by the Athenians in *FA*, esp. 222. The central error that I believe the Athenians made, assuming the next conflict would be similar to the last, is hardly limited to antiquity, as the Vietnam War of the 1960s and 1970s demonstrated, or to democracies: witness the Russian war in Afghanistan of the 1980s.

and politicians publicly labeled their opponents Macedonian pawns. But the coup never came. On the other hand, if fourth-century Athens actually had been run by a crypto-ruling elite whose members successfully masked their real power behind a facade of democratic government, the facade could presumably have been dropped after 338. Yet no elite rulers emerged from the shadows after 338; the democracy remained strong and vital.

The solidarity of the Athenian democracy in the sixteen years between Chaeronea and the imposition of a puppet government by Antipater after the Lamian War supports the notion that no hidden governing elite had evolved in the course of the fourth century.[58] Therefore, Athens is an example of a direct democracy that achieved genuine, long-term, stable methods of decision making by the masses and that was not coopted by the growth of an internal ruling elite. The Athenian example may therefore be used to challenge the universality of Michels' Iron Law of Oligarchy.[59] Michels would, perhaps, respond that the Athenian politicians were merely play-acting; he noted that the elite "aristocrat" in modern society must appeal to the masses by seemingly democratic methods, hide his true motives, persuade the masses that his interests and theirs were identical: "He dissembles his true thoughts, and howls with the democratic wolves in order to secure the coveted majority."[60] This, I think, underestimates the power

[58] Hence, I disagree with de Laix, *Probouleusis*, 191–92, on this point and think that Whitehead, *Demes*, 248, is imprecise in speaking of an "Athenian governing class." See also Plato *Menexenus* 238d, who speaks as if there were a hidden elite: "Some call it democracy, others whatever name they please, but it is in reality government by the elite with the approval of the crowd." Loraux, *Invention*, 189, suggests that this is a deliberate revelation of what remains cryptic in Pericles' Funeral Oration (Thuc. 2.37–40). Perhaps so, but both Thucydides and Plato despised the "radical" democracy, and neither was willing to countenance the idea that the Athenian masses had the ability to rule themselves or to control their leaders. I remain in substantial agreement with Gomme, "Working," 25; and Finley, *DAM*, 25–26, *PAW*, 139–40. Bolgar, "Training," esp. 36, 47–49, also notes that "it would be wrong to describe them [politicians] as a ruling elite," and he attributes this "failure" to Athenian educational institutions.

[59] On the difficulty that opponents of elitist theory have had in adducing empirical counter-examples to the notion of the inevitability of elite domination of democratic institutions, see Marger, *Elites and Masses*, 81.

[60] Michels, *Political Parties*, 44–46; quote: 46. Field and Higley, *Elitism*, 19–20, postulate a revisionist paradigm of elites in political society which assumes that elites always require non-elite support and that elites are limited by the need to make political arguments "conform to the orientations and attitudes of the non-elites to whom they are addressed." Elites who fail to operate within these non-elite limits risk losing their power and tenure. So far this model might well suit the Athenian example, but I do not believe that their final tenet is valid: that non-elite orienta-

of ideology and rhetoric to define the values not only of the led but of the leaders themselves.[61] The actions of the Athenian politician were so carefully scrutinized, the privileges granted him so provisional, that he was constrained to act and speak in the best interests of the masses or not at all. No orator was given much of a chance to "howl with the democratic wolves" unless he could also sing a pleasant tune with a meaningful libretto. No orator was delegated true power before he had proved the sincerity of his patriotic adhesion to the principles of the democratic state.

The Athenian system for controlling elite politicians worked precisely because it was based on a series of contradictions. The orator had to be simultaneously of the elite and of the mass, and he was expected to prove his membership in both on a regular basis. The contradictions implicit in Athenian mass-elite ideology are exemplified in the intertwining meanings of *charis*: the wealthy orator gave material gifts to the people, protected them by attacking their enemies, worked hard to provide them with good advice, and hence they were grateful to him. But he was also grateful to them: every time they gave him their attention when he spoke in public, voted for him in a political trial or for a proposal he supported in the Assembly, or allowed him to profit materially by his political position, the orator was put in the demos' debt. *Charis* bound orator and audience together by reciprocal ties of obligation. But *charis* and the bonds it engendered could be dangerous. The orator who spoke only in order to please and win *charis* betrayed his function and *harmed* the people by binding them to himself: hence Aeschines' and Demosthenes' reiteration of the pun on *charis* (and its cognates) and *cheiroō*: to take someone prisoner.[62]

The contrariness of the expectations placed on the political orator clearly benefited the demos. Politicians competed for popular favor in public contests which were played according to certain conventions, but the details of the rules remained vague: when was *charis* good and when was it bad? when would an elitist claim be suitable and when would it constitute evidence of secret demos-hating tendencies? when

---

tions are only manifested in very general opinion tendencies and that therefore detailed treatments of political questions are largely left to elite choice. As I have attempted to demonstrate, Athenian "opinion tendencies," though not logically consistent, were quite specific. Athenian political questions were not necessarily left to elite choice, although the questions may have been framed by elite speakers.

[61] On the importance to eloquence of the speaker genuinely feeling the emotions he is attempting to portray, see Bryant, "Aspects II," 327–28.

[62] Dem. 3.31–32; Aesch. 3.234 (cited above, VII.E.4). Among other passages that allude to the *charis* relationship between orators and audience, see Aesch. 3.255; Dem. 18.131, 23.184; Hyp. 5. 28–30.

should one praise the citizens and when should one castigate them? None of the answers were spelled out, and so politicians always operated from a position of uncertainty. When the rules of a contest are ill defined, its judge is given a wide interpretive scope. The masses set the rules and always acted as combined referee and scorekeeper; the vague and internally contradictory rules they devised for those who would play the game of political influence allowed the demos to reserve for itself the right to cast its own judgments according to its own lights—and hence to keep control of the state.

As a result, the orators were never able to define a sphere of influence, authority, or power for themselves that was independent of the continued goodwill of the people. As Mantitheus noted (Lys. 16.21), since the Athenians considered as worthy only those who acted and spoke concerning the good of the polis, ambitious citizens were stimulated to do just that. The orator was constrained to lay up *eunoia* with the demos (as Hyperides [2.7–8] claims Philippides failed to do). The orator was forced to admit that he was privileged due to the democratic *politeia* (Dem. 21.63). He must recognize that any public speaker whose interests were not identical to those of the demos was an enemy of the polis (And. 2.3). Rather than being subverted by the elite politicians, the democracy was protected and advised by them, and in some periods the situation that Isocrates (7.27) describes as a lost ideal really pertained: "How can we find a more secure and just democracy than this, which places the ablest in charge of affairs and gives the demos authority (*kurion*) over them?" Isocrates, like Aristotle (*Pol.* 1281a2–1282b14; cf. 1277b25–30) wanted to give the "ablest" unique access to permanent and powerful magistracies. The Athenians realized this sort of legal reform would mean the end of real political equality and hence of true democracy. By granting the elite conditional privileges based on their rhetorical display, rather than inalienable legal/constitutional rights, the demos achieved social stability and political leadership in times of crisis without losing its control of political affairs or seriously compromising its egalitarian principles.

G.2 DISCOURSE OF DEMOCRACY

My investigation of the political sociology of democratic Athens began as an attempt to shed some light on a neglected facet of Greek history and incidentally to test the validity of some central tenets of the elitist school of political philosophy. But my conclusions may also call into question some interpretations of democracy, and of sociopolitical organization generally, that have been advanced by other schools of thought. As Finley, Ste. Croix, and Meier (among others) saw, a key feature of the Athenian democracy was the use of political power by political equals to counterbalance various social inequalities—especially the unequal distribution of wealth.[63] Consequently, democracy came to occupy a central position in Athenian society. This result was not inevitable from the beginning, as demonstrated by the peripheral position democratic process came to occupy in the society of colonial Massachusetts.[64] How then was the Athenian democratic political power deployed?

The most obvious manifestation of the power of the Athenian citizenry was the franchise. But ballot power was not the ultimate key to the success of the Athenian democracy. The modern world offers examples of states run by narrow elites in which a very high percentage of the citizenry votes in elections; voting is relatively meaningless when there are no genuine choices or when the results of the decision are unimportant. As noted above (III.E.2), it is unlikely that more than one- or two-fifths of the Athenian demos voted upon even the most important matters, and the demos itself remained "imagined" in that all franchise holders never assembled together in one place. On the other hand, every citizen who communicated with other citizens participated, directly or indirectly, in the creation and maintenance of the political ideology of the state. Consequently, the will of the entire "imagined" demos was manifest in the decisions of Assemblies and juries.

A democratic constitution creates an environment in which the masses *may* be presented with real alternatives and so have the chance to make real decisions. But only mass control of political ideology will ensure that elite advisers and leaders present to the voters real alternatives on important issues. Even in the direct democracy of Athens, many decisions, some of them very important (e.g., by ambassadors and by generals in the field), were in fact made by elites. Voting in the Assembly and courts may, therefore, have been most important as an enforcement mechanism, a means of reward and punishment, by which the masses reined in the tendency of elite political experts to diverge from the interests of the masses. The control of ideology was the key, voting merely the means of maintaining that control.

The overriding importance of the popular control of the ideological climate of opinion, along with the ambivalent and contradictory nature of Athenian political ideology, render futile any attempt to ex-

[63] Finley, *PAW*, 139–40; Ste. Croix, *CSAGW*, 96–97, 298, 317; Meier, *Anthropologie*, 7–26, 52–53; cf. Luhmann, *Differentiation*, 146.
[64] Zuckerman, "Social Context," 535; cf. above II.F.

plain the Athenian polity in terms of law and constitution alone. The
processes of social and political control described here were orderly
and efficient only in the long run; they were not rational in origin.
Consequently, ancient political philosophers tended to scorn the democracy as based on irrational principles. Much of the confusion in
modern debates over the Athenian conception of freedom and the
locus of sovereignty in the state seems also to be the result of misguided attempts to find an ordering principle that would render Athenian thought and governmental practice rational and internally consistent. Most Athenians were burdened by no such obsession. They
tolerated a degree of inconsistency in their legal and political systems,
because too much order was inimical to continued mass rule.

Some important "checks and balances" existed within the Athenian
legal and political systems, but of more fundamental importance was
the sociopolitical balance achieved on the symbolic plane. The demos
ruled, not so much because of its constitutional "sovereignty," as because of its control over significant aspects of the symbolic universe of
the Athenian political community. Athenian democracy—like all other
forms of political organization—was predicated on and functioned
through a network of symbols. At Athens, the key symbols were both
revealed and generated through the two-way communication of public
speech. Rhetorical communication between masses and elites, expressed through an increasingly rich vocabulary of topoi and images,
was a primary means by which the strategic ends of social stability and
political order were achieved. Communication was the tool the political equals used to exert their ideological hegemony over both social
and political elites.[65]

Athenian public rhetoric—with its complex mix of elitist and egalitarian tactics—was a key form of democratic discourse. It stood in the
place of an abstract theory of democracy and made theory unnecessary to the participants. It was arguably the failure of the elite to con-

---

[65] The concept of "ideological hegemony" was originally developed by Antonio
Gramsci in the *Prison Notebooks*, as an explanation for the origin of the "false consciousness" which leads exploited workers to conform to the ideals of the ruling
classes. See Gramsci, *Selections from the Prison Notebooks* (London, 1971); cf. Joseph
V. Femia, *Gramsci's Political Thought: Hegemony, Consciousness, and the Revolutionary
Process* (Oxford, 1981), 1–129. I have deliberately used Gramsci's term to describe
a situation which is in some ways an inversion of the one Gramsci himself saw as
pertaining in modern capitalist societies. For criticisms of Gramsci's (inter alios)
ideas of the function of false consciousness in sociopolitical relations, see Bowles
and Gintis, *Democracy and Capitalism*, 152–75, 231 n. 4. Cf. Wyatt-Brown, "Community," 179–80, 189–90, on the mechanisms of "social control by the poor over
the rich" among whites in the antebellum American South.

trol political ideology that led them to devise and write formal political theory which would explain what was wrong with the system they failed to dominate. The thesis that the masses controlled the upper classes through ideological means also inverts the traditional Marxist approach to ideology and raises the possibility that lower classes can achieve major changes in the organization of society without overt struggle on the material plane. Hence, the assessment of the nature of Athenian democracy offered here may present an alternative to both ancient and Marxist—as well as to modern elitist—conclusions on the fundamental relationship between politics and society.

Finally, the conclusions arrived at in this book may be seen as challenging the view that democracy never achieved a language or conceptual system independent of aristocratic ideas.[66] Democracy did, I believe, have its own language, created by the invention of new words (e.g., *dēmokratia, isonomia*), transvaluation of existing terms (*isēgoria, plēthos*), subversion and appropriation of the terminology and ideals of the aristocrats (*kalokagathia, aretē*), but above all by the elaboration of the vocabulary of rhetorical topoi and images described in the preceding chapters.[67] As long as the demos remained arbiter of public opinion and policy, the word *dēmokratia* was a name for a political society and culture in which the most basic and elemental human power—the power to assign meanings to symbols—belonged to the people.

[66] See esp. Loraux, *Invention*, 172, 176, 180–202, 217–20, 334–35, with literature cited.

[67] Cf. Meier, *Entstehung des Politischen*, 275–325, *Anthropologie*, 27–44, who suggests that in fifth-century Athens, as in the Enlightenment in Western Europe, there was a transformation in the entire conceptual universe, and as a result new words were invented and old terms redefined; and Washburn, *Political Sociology*, 257, who cautiously suggests that ideologies originating from elite sources have less effect on overall patterns of national behavior than do ideologies "which emerge from people's everyday social, economic, and political experiences."

CATALOGUE OF SPEECHES
AND CITATION INDEX

Section I catalogues the speeches of Antiphon, several passages in Thucydides, and texts by Plato that take the form of political or legal speeches. Section II lists extant speeches of the major fourth-century Attic orators. I have made use of various editions and translations of the corpus of Attic orators, particularly the Loeb, Oxford, Budé, and Teubner editions. The editors and publishers of fragments listed here are limited to those that have been cited in the text. I have included in section II speeches by major orators that were not cited in the text. Demades' *On the Twelve Years* is excluded, as I consider the extant speech to be a Hellenistic forgery. I have also omitted various fragmentary speeches and tracts by lesser orators; these are collected and edited by Sauppe in Baiter and Sauppe, *Oratores Attici*, II.128–355. The sub-categories of forensic speeches (I, P, R) reflect my reading of the context in which the speech was delivered and the status of the speaker (as *idiōtēs* or rhetor), rather than whether the speech was technically a *graphē*, some other sort of public action, or a *dikē*. Section III is the citation index to the speeches. This catalogue makes no claim to be an original contribution to the problems of the chronology or authenticity of individual speeches; further discussion of these issues can be found in chapter I(E), in the Loeb and Budé editions of the Attic orators, and in works by Adams, Blass, Cawkwell, Dover, Hansen, Jaeger, Jebb, Kennedy, Lavency, Lewis, MacDowell, Pearson, Schaefer, Sealey, Usher, Wallace, and Wyse; all are listed in the Bibliography.

KEY TO CATEGORIES OF SPEECHES

E = To the Assembly
B = To the *Boulē*
A = To the Areopagus
I = To a People's Court, no obvious political background
P = To a People's Court, political background
R = To a People's Court, spoken in *propria persona* by a major politician
F = Funeral oration
T = Political pamphlet, tract, or set of letters

D = Epideictic display speech
und. = undated

I. Fifth-Century Speeches, Fifth- and Fourth-Century Speechlike Texts

ANTIPHON

1. Against the Stepmother, for Poisoning	I 422–411
2. First Tetralogy	I/D mid-5th?
3. Second Tetralogy	I/D mid-5th?
4. Third Tetralogy	I/D mid-5th?
5. On the Murder of Herodes	I 422–411
6. On the *Choreutēs*	I 422–411

THUCYDIDES

On the relationship between speeches in Thucydides' *History* and the speeches as actually delivered, see above, I.E. Dates given refer to the original delivery.

Pericles: Funeral Oration (2.35–46)	F 431
First Assembly Speech (1.140–44)	E 432
Second Assembly Speech (2.60–64)	E 430
Cleon: Mytilenean Debate (3.37–40)	E 427
Diodotus: Mytilenean Debate (3.42–48)	E 427
Alcibiades: Sicilian Expedition Debate (6.16–18)	E 415
Nicias: Sicilian Expedition Debate (6.9–14, 20–23)	E 415
Hermocrates: Speech to Syracusan Assembly (6.33–34)	E/T 415
Athenagoras: Speech to Syracusan Assembly (6.36–40)	E/T 415

PLATO

Socrates: *Apology*	P 399
Socrates/Aspasia: *Menexenus*	D/F und.

II. Extant Speeches by the Major
Fourth-Century Attic Orators

AESCHINES

1. Ag. Timarchus	R 345
2. On the Embassy	R 343
3. Ag. Ctesiphon	R 330

ANDOCIDES

1. On the Mysteries	R 399
2. On His Return	E 409–408?
3. Peace with Sparta	E 391
[4]. Ag. Alcibiades	T/E und.

Fragments: collected by Maidment (Loeb)

DEMOSTHENES

Some of the deliberative speeches may not be by Demosthenes himself, but they are all arguably genuine fourth-century speeches. Likewise, some of the private orations may not be by Demosthenes, but they are still genuine speeches. I have generally avoided bracketing speeches as spurious unless the argument against Demosthenes' authorship seems to me very strong.

1. I Olynthiac	E 349/8
2. II Olynthiac	E 349/8
3. III Olynthiac	E 349/8
4. I Philippic	E early 351
5. On the Peace	E 346/5
6. II Philippic	E 344/3
[7]. Hegesippus?: On Halonnesus	E 343/2
8. On Chersonesus	E 342/1
9. III Philippic	E 342/1
10. IV Philippic	E 342/1?
[11]. Answer to Philip's Letter	T 340?
[12]. Philip's Letter	T 340?
[13]. On Organization	E ca. 353–348
14. On the Symmories	E 354/3
15. For the Liberty of the Rhodians	E 352–350

16. For the Megalopolitans   E 353/2

17. On the Treaty with Alexander   E 336–333?

18. On the Crown   R 330

19. On the False Embassy   R 343

20. Ag. Leptines   P 355

21. Ag. Meidias   R 348–346

22. Ag. Androtion   P 357–354

23. Ag. Aristocrates   P 352

24. Ag. Timocrates   P summer 353

25. Ag. Aristogeiton I   P 338–324

26. Ag. Aristogeiton II   P 338–324

27. Ag. Aphobus I   I 364

28. Ag. Aphobus II   I 364

29. Ag. Aphobus III   I 364

30. Ag. Onetor I   I ca. 364

31. Ag. Onetor II   I ca. 364

32. Ag. Zenothemis   I und.

33. Ag. Apaturius   I und.

34. Ag. Phormio   I *post* 335

35. Ag. Lacritus   I und.

36. For Phormio   I und.

37. Ag. Pantaenetus   I und.

38. Ag. Nausimachus   I und.

39. Ag. Boeotus I   I ca. 348?

40. Ag. Boeotus II   I *post* ca. 348?

41. Ag. Spudias   I und.

42. Ag. Phaenippus   I ca. 355?

43. Ag. Macartatus   I und.

44. Ag. Leochares   I und.

45. Ag. Stephanus I   I ca. 351

46. Ag. Stephanus II   I ca. 351

47. Ag. Evergus and Mnesibulus   I *post* 356

48. Ag. Olympiodorus   I 343/342

[49]. Apollodorus: Ag. Timotheus   I 362?

[50]. Apollodorus: Ag. Polycles   I 359?

51. Trierarchic Crown   B *post* 361

[52]. Apollodorus: Ag. Callippus   I und.

[53]. Apollodorus: Ag. Nicostratus   I und.

54. Ag. Conon   I und.

55. Ag. Callicles   I und.

56. Ag. Dionysodorus   I *post* 323

57. Ag. Eubulides   I 345?

58. Ag. Theocrines   I 340s?

[59]. Apollodorus: Ag. Neaera   I 349–339

60. Funeral Oration   F 338

61. Erotic Essay   D und.

Exordia (abbreviated *Ex.*)   E und.
A collection of genuine introductions for some of Demosthenes' Assembly speeches.

Letters   T
   1–4, 6 = 324–322; 5 = ca. 355

DINARCHUS

1. Ag. Demosthenes   R 323

2. Ag. Aristogeiton   R 323

3. Ag. Philocles   R 323

Fragments: collected by Burtt (Loeb), Conomis (Teubner)

HYPERIDES

Hyperides' speeches are known only from papyrus fragments. The references in the text are to the speech and section numbers of the Loeb edition, since this edition will likely be readily available to most readers. The speech numbers of Jensen's Teubner edition are given in parentheses.

1(2). For Lycophron I   P 333?

2(4). Ag. Philippides   R 338–336

3(5). Ag. Athenogenes   I 330–324

4(3). For Euxenippus   R ca. 330–324

5(1). Ag. Demosthenes   R 323
   Sections are cited in the text by column number.

6. Funeral Oration   F 322
Fragments: collected by Burtt (Loeb), Jensen (Teubner)

ISAEUS

His *floruit* seems (on basis of earliest and latest of his speeches) to be
about 389–344.

1.	Estate of Cleonymus	I und.
2.	Estate of Menecles	I ca. 355
3.	Estate of Pyrrhus	I und., but probably late in Isaeus' career
4.	Estate of Nicostratus	I soon *post* 374?
5.	Estate of Dicaeogenes	I ca. 389
6.	Estate of Philoctemon	I 364
7.	Estate of Apollodorus	I ca. 355?
8.	Estate of Ciron	I 383–363
9.	Estate of Astyphilus	I 371–355?
10.	Estate of Aristarchus	I 378–371
11.	Estate of Hagnias	I 396–378?
12.	For Euphiletus (fragment)	I 344/3

Fragments: collected by Forster (Loeb)

ISOCRATES

1.	To Demonicus	D/T 374–372?
2.	To Nicocles	D/T ca. 374
3.	Nicocles	D/T ca. 372–365
4.	Panegyricus	T ca. 380
5.	To Philip	T 346
6.	Archidamus	T ca. 366
7.	Areopagiticus	T ca. 357
8.	On the Peace	T 355
9.	Evagoras	D/T 370–365?
10.	Helen	D ca. 370
11.	Busiris	D 391–385?
12.	Panathenaicus	T 342–339

13. Ag. the Sophists   T ca. 390

14. Plataicus   T 373–371

15. Antidosis   T 354/3

16. De Bigis   P 397

17. Trapeziticus   I ca. 393

18. Ag. Callimachus   P 400/399?

19. Aegineticus   T ca. 403–393
    Speech was composed for delivery in Aegina, to a court of Aeginetans.

20. Ag. Lochites   I soon *post* 403

21. Ag. Euthynus   I soon *post* 403

Letters   T und.

LYCURGUS

1. Ag. Leocrates   R 330

Fragments: collected by Burtt (Loeb), Conomis (Teubner)

LYSIAS

Although some of Lysias' speeches are undated, his death in ca. 380 places all his speeches into the period before 377, as designated in Table 1, below. As with Demosthenes, I have only bracketed speeches that seem highly unlikely to be Lysian.

1. Eratosthenes   I und.

2. Funeral Oration   F 392?

3. Ag. Simon   A *post* 394

4. Wound by Premeditation   A und.

5. For Callias (fragment)   I und.

[6]. Ag. Andocides   P 399

7. Olive stump   A *post* 397

8. Accusation of Calumny   I und.

9. For the Soldier   I ca. 395–387

10. Ag. Theomnestus I   P 384/3

11. Ag. Theomnestus II
    Abstract of Lys. 10

12. Ag. Eratosthenes of the Thirty   P soon *post* 403

13. Ag. Agoratus   P ca. 399

14. Ag. Alcibiades I   P 395

15. Ag. Alcibiades II   P 395

16. For Mantitheus   B ca. 392–389
Speech of an aspiring politician who has been threatened with loss
of his bouleutic seat. Therefore, this speech has clear associations
with the P group.

17. Property of Eraton   I ca. 397

18. Property of Nicias' brother   P ca. 396

19. Property of Aristophanes   P 388–387

20. For Polystratus   P ca. 410

21. Defense Against a Bribery Charge   I 403/2

22. Ag. Grain Dealers   I 386

23. Ag. Pancleon   I 400/399?

24. On the Pension of an Invalid   B soon *post* 403

25. Defense Ag. a Charge of Subverting the   P ca. 399
    Democracy

26. On the *Dokimasia* of Evandros   B 382

27. Ag. Epicrates   P ca. 390

28. Ag. Ergocles   E 388
A rare case of a speech of accusation delivered in Assembly. The
overtones are clearly political, and so the speech is linked with the P
group.

29. Ag. Philocrates   P 388

30. Ag. Nicomachus   P 399

31. Ag. Philon, at a *Dokimasia*   B soon *post* 403

32. Ag. Diogeiton (fragment)   I 399/8?

33. Olympiacus   D 388 or 384

34. Ag. Subversion of the *Politeia*   T 403
Fragments: collected by Lamb (Loeb), Gernet and Bizos (Budé)

TABLE 1

Chronological Distribution of Extant Speeches

The letters in the column at the extreme left refer to the speech-type classifications used in the Appendix. Note that some classifications are rather arbitrary—e.g., in the distinction between category D and T for several of Isocrates' speeches (in each case the speech is tallied below under the first category). The periodization is based on major developments in Athenian foreign policy; other schemes, based, for example, on development of legal processes, could just as well be employed. This table is intended only to give a general idea of the chronological distribution of surviving speeches according to type across the course of the fourth century B.C. The totals may need to be adjusted as further work is done on dating individual speeches and on assessing their political content. Most of the undated speeches (below, n. f) would probably fall into the 355–338 period.

Type	450–404	403–378	377–356	355–338	337–322	Total
E	9	2	—	14	1	26
B	—	4	1	—	—	5
A	—	3	—	—	—	3
I	6	15	12	14	3	50
P	1	15	1	3	3	23
R	—	1	—	4	9	14
F	1	1	—	1	1	4
T	—	3	3	4	—	10
D	—	2	5	—	—	7
Total	17[a]	46[b]	22[c]	40[d]	17[e]	142[f]
Avg/yr	—	1.8	1.0	2.2	1.1	1.5[g]

[a] 450–404: Ant. 1, 2, 3, 4, 5, 6; Thuc. (9 speeches); And. 2; Lys. 20.

[b] 403–378: Plato *Apology*; And. 1, 3; Is. 5, 8, 11; Isoc. 4, 11, 13, 16, 17, 18, 20, 21; Lys. 1, 2, 3, 4, 5, 6, 7, 8, 9, 10, 12, 13, 14, 15, 16, 17, 18, 19, 21, 22, 23, 24, 25, 26, 27, 28, 29, 30, 31, 32, 33, 34.

[c] 377–356: Dem. 22, 27, 28, 29, 30, 31, 49, 50, 51; Is. 4, 6, 8, 9, 10; Isoc. 1, 2, 3, 6, 7, 9, 10, 14.

[d] 355–338: Aesch. 1, 2; Dem. 1, 2, 3, 4, 5, 6, 7, 8, 9, 10, 13, 14, 15, 16, 19, 20, 21, 23, 24, 39, 40, 42, 45, 46, 47, 48, 57, 58, 59, 60; Is. 2, 3, 7, 12; Isoc. 5, 8, 12, 15.

[e] 337–322: Aesch. 3; Dem. 17, 18, 25, 26, 34, 56; Din. 1, 2, 3; Hyp. 1, 2, 3, 4, 5, 6; Lyc. 1.

[f] To this total could be added Dem. 11, 12, 61, *Letters, Exordia*; Isoc. 19, *Letters*; and 16 undated speeches: Plato *Menexenus*; And. 4; Dem. 32, 33, 35, 36, 37, 38, 41, 43, 44, 52, 53, 54, 55; Is. 1; as well as fragments of various orators.

[g] Speeches from 403–322 only; the average per year for the period before 403 is meaningless, given the size of the sample.

III. Citation Index

The entries in this section are presented in the same order in which they appear in sections I and II of this appendix.

ANTIPHON

1. Against the Stepmother, for Poisoning
   4: 263
   14: 136n.83
2. First Tetralogy
   2.12: 221, 226n.47
   3,8: 230n.54
   4.1.: 165

3. Second Tetralogy
   2.1–2: 177n.39
5. On the Murder of Herodes
   1–7: 177n.39
   70–71: 181n.47
   80: 171n.29, 174n.35

THUCYDIDES

Pericles:
   Funeral Oration
      2.37.1: 194
      2.37.2: 295
      2.37: 260n.27
      2.40.2: 158, 280n.68, 317
      2.40–41: 157n.2
      2.41.1: 159
   Second Assembly Speech
      2.60.4–5: 311n.31
      2.60.6: 331n.54
Cleon: Mytilenean Debate
   3.37.3–5: 164n.22
   3.37.4–5: 330n.53
   3.38.2–7: 159, 177n.40
   2.38.2: 331n.54
   3.38.4–5: 322
   passim: 93, 301

Diodotus: Mytilenean Debate
   3.42.3–4: 328
   3.42.5–6: 189n.53
   3.42.6: 322
   passim: 301

Alcibiades: Sicilian Expedition Debate
   6.16.1–4: 93, 231n.56
   6.16.2–3: 206
   passim: 301

Nicias: Sicilian Expedition Debate
   6.12.2: 330n.53
   6.13.1: 14n.23
   passim: 301

Athenagoras: Speech to Syracusan Assembly
   6.39.1: 164, 194, 198

PLATO

Socrates: *Apology*
   17a–d: 175n.37
   24d–25a: 161
   26d: 179n.43
   passim: 160n.15

Socrates/Aspasia: *Menexenus*
   238e: 265n.34
   239a: 265n.34

AESCHINES

ANDOCIDES

DEMOSTHENES

HYPERIDES

SELECT BIBLIOGRAPHY

Works listed in the Abbreviations are not repeated here. Asterisks indicate works likely to be especially useful to the non-classicist.

Adams, Charles Darwin. "Are the Political 'Speeches' of Demosthenes to Be Regarded as Political Pamphlets?" *TAPA* 43 (1912): 5–22.

Adeleye, Gabriel. "The Purpose of the *Dokimasia*." *GRBS* 24 (1983): 295–306.

Adkins, A.W.H. *Merit and Responsibility: A Study in Greek Values*. Oxford, 1960.

*———. *Moral Values and Political Behaviour in Ancient Greece*. New York, 1972.

———. "Problems in Greek Popular Morality." Review of *Greek Popular Morality*, by K. J. Dover. *CPh* 73 (1978): 143–58.

Ancient Society and Institutions: Studies Presented to Victor Ehrenberg. Oxford, 1966.

Anderson, Benedict. *Imagined Communities: Reflections on the Origins and Spread of Nationalism*. London, 1983.

Andreades, A. M. *A History of Greek Public Finance*. 2nd ed. Translated by C. N. Brown. Cambridge, Mass., 1933.

*Andrewes, Antony. *The Greek Tyrants*. New York, 1956.

———. "Kleisthenes' Reform Bill." *CQ* 27 (1977): 241–48.

———. "The Mytilene Debate: Thucydides 3.36–49." *Phoenix* 16 (1962): 64–85.

Arnhart, Larry. *Aristotle on Political Reasoning: A Commentary on the 'Rhetoric'*. Dekalb, Illinois, 1981.

Arnheim, M.T.W. *Aristocracy in Greek Society*. London, 1977.

Audring, Gert. "Grenzen der Konzentration von Grundeigentum in Attika während des 4. Jh. v.u.Z." *Klio* 56 (1974): 445–56.

———. "Über Grundeigentum und Landwirtschaft in der Krise der athenischen Polis." In *Hellenische Poleis*, edited by E. C. Welskopf, vol. I: 108–31. Berlin, 1974.

*Austin, M. M., and Vidal-Naquet, P. *Economic and Social History of Ancient Greece: An Introduction*. London, 1977.

Aymard, A. "Hiérarchie du travail et autarcie individuelle dans la Grèce archaïque." In *Études d'histoire ancienne*, by A. Aymard, pp. 316–33. Paris, 1967.

Bachrach, Peter, ed. *Political Elites in a Democracy.* New York, 1971.

Badian, E. "Archons and *Strategoi.*" *Antichthon* 5 (1971): 1–34.

———. "Marx in the Agora." Review of *The Class Struggle in the Ancient Greek World* by G.E.M. de Ste. Croix. *New York Review of Books* 29:19 (December 2, 1982), pp. 47–51.

Baiter, G. and Sauppe, H. *Oratores Attici.* 2 vols. Turin, 1839–1850.

Beringer, Walter. "Freedom, Family, and Citizenship in Early Greece." In *The Craft of the Ancient Historian: Essays in Honor of Starr,* edited by J. W. Eadie and J. Ober, pp. 41–56. Lanham, Maryland, 1985.

———. " 'Servile Status' in the Sources for Early Greek History." *Historia* 31 (1982): 13–32.

Bicknell, P. J. *Studies in Athenian Politics and Genealogy.* Historia Einzelschrift 19. Wiesbaden, 1972.

Bloedow, E. F. "Pericles' Powers in the Counter-Strategy of 431." *Historia* 36 (1987): 9–27.

Boegehold, Alan L. "Toward a Study of Athenian Voting Procedure." *Hesperia* 32 (1963): 366–74.

Boersma, J. S. *Athenian Building Policy from 561/0 to 405/4 B.C.* Groningen, 1970.

Bolgar, Robert R. "The Training of Elites in Greek Education." In *Governing Elites,* edited by R. Wilkinson, pp. 23–49. New York, 1969.

Bonner, Robert J. *Aspects of Athenian Democracy.* Berkeley, 1933.

*———. *Lawyers and Litigants in Ancient Athens.* Chicago, 1927.

———. "Wit and Humor in Athenian Courts." *CPh* 17 (1922): 97–103.

Bonner, Robert J., and Smith, Gertrude. *The Administration of Justice from Homer to Aristotle.* 2 vols. Chicago, 1930, 1938.

Bourriot, F. *Recherches sur la nature du génos.* 2 vols. published as 1 vol. Lille and Paris, 1976.

Bowles, Samuel, and Gintis, Herbert. *Democracy and Capitalism: Property, Community, and the Contradictions of Modern Social Thought.* New York, 1986.

Brun, Patrice. *Eisphora, Syntaxis, Stratiotika: Recherches sur les finances militaires d'Athènes au IVe siècle av. J.-C.* Paris, 1983.

Brunt, P. A. "Athenian Settlements Abroad in the Fifth Century B.C." In *Ancient Society: Studies to Ehrenberg,* pp. 71–92. Oxford, 1966.

Bryant, Donald C. "Aspects of the Rhetorical Tradition, I (The Intellectual Foundation) and II (Emotion, Style, and Literary Association)." *Quarterly Journal of Speech* 36 (1950): 169–76, 326–32.

Bryant Donald C. "Rhetoric: Its Functions and Its Scope." *Quarterly Journal of Speech* 39 (1953): 401–24.

Buchanan, James J. *Theorika: A Study of Monetary Distributions to the Athenian Citizenry during the Fifth and Fourth Centuries B.C.* Locust Valley, N.Y., 1962.

Bugh, Glenn. *The Horsemen of Athens.* Princeton, forthcoming.

Burke, Edmund M. "Character Denigration in the Athenian Orators with Particular Reference to Demosthenes and Aeschines." Ph.D. dissertation, Tufts University, 1972.

———. "Lycurgan Finances." *GRBS* 26 (1985): 251–64.

Burn, A.R. *Persia and the Greeks: The Defense of the West, ca. 546–478 B.C.* 2nd ed. with postscript by D. M. Lewis. London, 1984.

Burnham, James. *The Machiavellians: Defenders of Freedom.* New York, 1943.

Burns, Alfred. "Athenian Literacy in the Fifth Century B.C." *Journal of the History of Ideas* 42 (1981): 371–87.

Buxton, R.G.A. *Persuasion in Greek Tragedy.* Cambridge, 1982.

Calhoun, George M. *Athenian Clubs in Politics and Litigation.* Austin, Texas, 1913.

Cantarella, Eva. *Pandora's Daughters: The Role and Status of Women in Greek and Roman Antiquity.* Translated by M. B. Fant. Baltimore, 1987.

Carawan, Edwin M. "*Apophasis* and *Eisangelia*: The Rôle of the Areopagus in Athenian Political Trials." *GRBS* 26 (1985): 115–40.

———. "*Eisangelia* and *Euthyna*: The Trials of Miltiades, Themistocles, and Cimon." *GRBS* 28 (1987): 167–208.

Carter, L. B. *The Quiet Athenian.* Oxford, 1986.

Cartledge, Paul A. "Trade and Politics Revisited: Archaic Greece." In *Trade in the Ancient Economy,* edited by P. Garnsey, K. Hopkins, C. R. Whittaker, pp. 1–15. Berkeley, 1983.

———, and Harvey, F. D., edd. *Crux: Essays in Greek History Presented to G.E.M. de Ste. Croix.* London, 1985 (= *History and Political Theory* 6.1–2, 1985).

Cawkwell, George L. "Eubulus." *JHS* 83 (1963): 47–67.

———. "Notes on the Social War." *CM* 29 (1962): 34–49.

———. *Philip of Macedon.* London, 1978.

Cloché, P. "Les hommes politiques et la justice populaire dans l'Athènes du IVᵉ siècle." *Historia* 9 (1960): 80–95.

———. *La restauration démocratique à Athènes en 403 av. J.-C.* Paris, 1915.

Cohen, Edward E. *Ancient Athenian Maritime Courts.* Princeton, 1973.

Connor, W. Robert. "The Athenian Council: Method and Focus in Some Recent Literature." *CJ* 70 (1974): 32–40.

———. *Thucydides*. Princeton, 1984.

David, E. *Aristophanes and Athenian Society of the Early Fourth Century B.C.* Mnemosyne Supplement 81. Leiden, 1984.

Daviero-Rocchi, Giovanna. "Transformations de role dans les institutions d'Athènes au IVᵉ siècle par rapport aux changements dans la société." *Dialogues d'Histoire Ancienne* 4 (1978): 33–50.

Davies, John K. "Athenian Citizenship: The Descent Group and the Alternatives," *CJ* 73 (1977–78): 105–21.

Davison, J. A. "Literature and Literacy in Ancient Greece." *Phoenix* 16 (1962): 141–56, 219–33.

Dewald, Carolyn. "Practical Knowledge and the Historian's Role in Herodotus and Thucydides." In *The Greek Historians, Literature and History: Papers Presented to A. E. Raubitschek*, pp. 47–63. Saratoga, California, 1985.

Donlan, Walter. *The Aristocratic Ideal in Ancient Greece: Attitudes of Superiority from Homer to the End of the Fifth Century B.C.* Lawrence, Kansas, 1980.

Dorjahn, Alfred P. "Some Remarks on Aeschines' Career as an Actor." *CJ* 25 (1929): 223–29.

Dover, K. J. "The Chronology of Antiphon's Speeches." *CQ* 44 (1950): 44–60.

———. "The Freedom of the Intellectual in Greek Society." *Talanta* 7 (1976): 24–54.

———. *Lysias and the* Corpus Lysiacum. Berkeley, 1968.

Dyck, Andrew R. "The Function and Persuasive Power of Demosthenes' Portrait of Aeschines in the Speech *On the Crown*." *Greece and Rome* 32 (1985): 42–48.

Eadie, John W., and Ober, Josiah, edd. *The Craft of the Ancient Historian. Essays in Honor of Chester G. Starr*. Lanham, Maryland, 1985.

*Ehrenberg, Victor. *The Greek State*. New York, 1964.

———. "Origins of Democracy," *Historia* 1 (1950): 515–48.

———. *The People of Aristophanes: A Sociology of Old Attic Comedy*. 3rd ed. New York, 1962.

*———. *From Solon to Socrates*. 2nd ed. London, 1973.

Ellis, J. R., and Stanton, G. R. "Factional Conflict and Solon's Reforms." *Phoenix* 22 (1968): 95–110.

Euben, J. Peter, ed. *Greek Tragedy and Political Theory*. Berkeley, 1986.

Field, G. L., and Higley, J. *Elitism*. London, 1980.

Figueira, Thomas J. "The Ten *Archontes* of 579/8 at Athens." *Hesperia* 53 (1984): 447–73.

*Finley, John H. Jr. *Thucydides*. Ann Arbor, 1963.

Finley, Moses I. "The Ancient City: From Fustel de Coulanges to Max Weber and Beyond." In Finley, *Economy and Society*, pp. 3–23.

*———. *Ancient History: Evidence and Models*. London, 1985.

———. *Ancient Slavery and Modern Ideology*. London, 1980.

———. "Aristotle and Economic Analysis." *Past and Present* 47 (1970): 3–25.

———. "Athenian Demagogues." *Past and Present* 21 (1962): 3–24.

———. *Authority and Legitimacy in the Classical City-State*. Danske Videnskab. Selbskab. Hist.-Filos. Meddel. 50:3. Copenhagen, 1982.

———. "Between Slavery and Freedom." In Finley, *Economy and Society*, pp. 116–32.

———. "Debt-Bondage and the Problem of Slavery." In Finley, *Economy and Society*, pp. 150–66.

———. *Economy and Society in Ancient Greece*. Edited with an Introduction by Brent D. Shaw and Richard P. Saller. New York, 1983.

———. "The Fifth-Century Athenian Empire: A Balance-Sheet." In *Imperialism in the Ancient World*, edited by P.D.A. Garnsey and C. R. Whittaker, pp. 103–26. Cambridge, 1978.

———. "The Freedom of the Citizen in the Greek World." *Talanta* 7 (1976): 1–23 (= Finley, *Economy and Society*, 77–94).

———. "Technical Innovation and Economic Progress in the Ancient World." In Finley, *Economy and Society*, pp. 176–95.

———. "Was Greek Civilization Based on Slave Labour?" *Historia* 8 (1959): 145–64 (= Finley, *Economy and Society*, pp. 97–115).

Fornara, Charles W. *The Athenian Board of Generals from 501 to 404*. Historia Einzelschrift 16. Wiesbaden, 1971.

Foucault, Michel. *The History of Sexuality. Vol. 1: An Introduction*. Translated by R. Hurley. New York, 1980.

Frost, Frank J. "Pericles, Thucydides, Son of Melesias, and Athenian Politics before the War." *Historia* 13 (1964): 385–99.

———. "Toward a History of Peisistratid Athens." In *The Craft of the Ancient Historian: Essays in Honor of Starr*, edited by J. W. Eadie and J. Ober, pp. 57–78. Lanham, Maryland, 1985.

Fuks, Alexander, "Patterns and Types of Social-Economic Revolution in Greece from the Fourth to the Second Century B.C." *Ancient Society* 5 (1974): 51–81.

———. "The Sharing of Property by the Rich with the Poor in Greek Theory and Practice." *Scripta Classica Israelica* 5 (1979–80): 46–63.

Funke, P. *Homónoia und Arché, Athen und die griechische Staatenwelt vom Ende des peloponnesischen Krieges bis zum Konigsfreiden*. Historia Einzenschrift 19. Wiesbaden, 1980.

Gabrielsen, Vincent. "ΦΑΝΕΡΑ and ΑΦΑΝΗΣ ΟΥΣΙΑ in Classical Athens." *CM* 37 (1986): 99–114.

———. *Remuneration of State Officials in Fourth Century B.C. Athens.* Odense University Classical Studies 11. Odense, 1981.

Gagarin, Michael. *Early Greek Law.* Berkeley, 1986.

Gallant, T. W. "Agricultural Systems, Land Tenure, and the Reforms of Solon." *Annual of the British School at Athens* 77 (1982): 111–21.

Garner, Richard. *Law and Society in Classical Athens.* New York, 1987.

Garnsey, Peter, ed. *Non-Slave Labour in the Greco-Roman World.* Cambridge Philological Society Supplement 6. Cambridge, 1980.

Gauthier, Phillipe. *Un commentaire historique des 'Poroi' de Xénophon.* Paris, 1976.

Gehrke, H.-J. *Phokion, Studien zur Erfassung seiner historischen Gestalt.* Zetemata 64. Munich, 1976.

Ghiron-Bistagne, Paulette. *Recherches sur les acteurs dans la Grèce antique.* Paris, 1976.

Gluskina, Lea M. "Zur Spezifik der klassischen griechischen Polis im Zusammenhang mit dem Problem ihrer Krise." Translated from the Russian by K. Schwarz. *Klio* 57 (1975): 415–31.

Golden, Mark. "Slavery and Homosexuality at Athens." *Phoenix* 38 (1984): 308–24.

Gomme, A. W. *The Population of Athens in the Fifth and Fourth Centuries B.C.* Oxford, 1933.

*———. "The Working of the Athenian Democracy." *History* 36 (1951): 12–28.

———, Andrewes, A., and Dover, K. J. *A Historical Commentary on Thucydides.* 5 vols. Oxford, 1959–1981.

*Gouldner, Alvin W. *Enter Plato: Classical Greece and the Origins of Social Theory.* New York, 1965.

Griffith, G. T. "Isegoria in the Assembly at Athens." In *Ancient Society: Studies to Ehrenberg*, pp. 115–38. Oxford, 1966.

Gruen, Erich S. *The Hellenistic World and the Coming of Rome*, 2 vols. Berkeley, 1984.

Hammond, N.G.L., and Griffith, G. T. *A History of Macedonia. Vol. 2: 550–336 B.C.* Oxford, 1979.

Hansen, Mogens Herman. Apagoge, Endeixis, *and* Ephegesis *against* Kakourgoi, Atimoi, *and* Pheugontes: *A Study in the Athenian Administration of Justice in the Fourth Century B.C.* Odense University Classical Studies 8. Odense, 1976.

———. "The Athenian *Ecclesia* and the Assembly Place on the Pnyx." *GRBS* 23 (1982): 241–49 (= Hansen, *AECA*, pp. 25–34).

———. "The Athenian *Nomothesia.*" *GRBS* 26 (1985): 345–71.

Hansen, Mogens Herman. "Athenian *Nomothesia* in the Fourth Century B.C. and Demosthenes' Speech Against Leptines." *CM* 32 (1980): 87–104.

———. "The Athenian 'Politicians,' 403–322 B.C." *GRBS* 24 (1983): 33–55.

———. "Demographic Reflections on the Number of Athenian Citizens, 451–309 B.C." *AJAH* 7 (1982): 172–89.

———. *Demography and Democracy: The Number of Athenian Citizens in the Fourth Century B.C.* Herning, Denmark, 1985.

———. "*Demos, Ecclesia* and *Dicasterion* in Classical Athens." *GRBS* 19 (1978): 127–46 (= Hansen, *AECA*, pp. 139–60).

———. "Did the Athenian *Ecclesia* Legislate after 403/2?" *GRBS* 20 (1979): 27–53 (= Hansen, *AECA*, pp. 179–206).

———. "The Duration of a Meeting of the Athenian *Ecclesia*." *CPh* 74 (1979): 43–49 (= Hansen, *AECA*, pp. 131–38).

———. *Eisangelia: The Sovereignty of the People's Court in Athens in the Fourth Century B.C. and the Impeachment of Generals and Politicians.* Odense University Classical Studies 6. Odense, 1975.

———. "Eisangelia in Athens: A Reply." *JHS* 100 (1980): 89–95.

———. "The History of the Athenian Constitution." Review of *A Commentary on the Aristotelian 'Athenaion Politeia,'* by P. J. Rhodes. *CPh* 80 (1985): 51–66.

———. "How Did the Athenian *Ecclesia* Vote?" *GRBS* 18 (1977): 123–37 (= Hansen, *AECA*, pp. 103–21).

———. "How Many Athenians Attended the *Ecclesia*?" *GRBS* 17 (1976): 115–34 (= Hansen, *AECA*, pp. 1–23).

———. "How Often Did the *Ecclesia* Meet?" *GRBS* 18 (1977): 43–70 (= Hansen, *AECA*, pp. 35–72).

———. "Initiative and Decision: The Separation of Powers in Fourth-Century Athens." *GRBS* 22 (1981): 345–70.

———. "ΚΛΗΡΩΣΙΣ ΕΚ ΠΡΟΚΡΙΤΩΝ in Fourth-Century Athens." *CPh* 81 (1986): 222–29.

———. "*Misthos* for Magistrates in Classical Athens." *SO* 54 (1979): 5–22.

———. "*Nomos* and *Psephisma* in Fourth-Century Athens." *GRBS* 19 (1978): 315–30 (= Hansen, *AECA*, pp. 161–77).

———. "The Number of *Rhetores* in the Athenian *Ecclesia*, 355–322 B.C." *GRBS* 25 (1984): 123–55.

———. "Political Activity and the Organization of Attica in the Fourth Century B.C." *GRBS* 24 (1983): 227–38.

———. "*Rhetores* and *Strategoi* in Fourth-Century Athens." *GRBS* 24 (1983): 151–80.

Hansen, Mogens Herman. "Seven Hundred *Archai* in Classical Athens." *GRBS* 21 (1980): 151–73.

———. *The Sovereignty of the People's Court in Athens in the Fourth Century B.C. and the Public Action against Unconstitutional Proposals*. Odense University Classical Studies 4. Odense, 1974.

———. "The Theoric Fund and the *graphe paranomon* against Apollodorus." *GRBS* 17 (1976): 235–46.

———. "Two Notes on the Pnyx." *GRBS* 26 (1985): 241–50.

———. "Two Notes on Demosthenes' Symbouleutic Speeches." *CM* 35 (1984): 57–70.

Hansen, M. H., and Mitchel, F. "The Number of *Ecclesiai* in Fourth-Century Athens." *SO* 59 (1984): 13–19.

Hanson, Victor D. *Warfare and Agriculture in Classical Greece*. Biblioteca di Studi Antichi 40. Pisa, 1983.

Harrison, A.R.W. *The Law of Athens*. 2 vols. Oxford, 1968.

———. "Law-Making at Athens at the End of the Fifth Century B.C." *JHS* 75 (1955): 26–35.

Harvey, F. D. "*Dona Ferentes*: Some Aspects of Bribery in Greek Politics." In *Crux: Essays Presented to Ste. Croix*, edited by P. A. Cartledge and F. D. Harvey, pp. 76–113. London, 1985.

———. "Literacy in the Athenian Democracy." *REG* 79 (1966): 585–635.

———. "Two Kinds of Equality." *CM* 26 (1965): 101–46; 27 (1966): 99–100.

Hasebroek, J. *Trade and Politics in Ancient Greece*. Translated by L. M. Fraser and D. C. MacGregor. London, 1933.

Haussoullier, B. *La vie municipale en Attique*. Paris, 1884.

Havelock, Eric A. *The Liberal Temper in Greek Politics*. New Haven, 1957.

Headlam, J. W. *Election by Lot at Athens*. 2nd ed. revised by D. C. MacGregor. Cambridge, 1933.

Holladay, A. J. "Athenian Strategy in the Archidamian War." *Historia* 27 (1978): 399–427.

Holmes, Stephen T. "Aristippus in and out of Athens." *American Political Science Review* 73 (1979): 113–28.

Hopper, R. J. "The Attic Silver Mines in the Fourth Century B.C." *Annual of the British School at Athens* 48 (1953): 200–54.

*———. *The Basis of the Athenian Democracy*. Inaugural Lecture, University of Sheffield, 1957.

———. " 'Plain', 'Shore', and 'Hill' in Early Athens." *Annual of the British School at Athens* 56 (1961): 189–219.

———. "The Solonian 'Crisis'." In *Ancient Society: Studies to Ehrenberg*, pp. 139–46. Oxford, 1966.

Humphreys, S. C. *Anthropology and the Greeks*. London, 1978.

———. "The Discourse of Athenian Law." *Law and History Review*, forthcoming.

———. "The Evolution of Legal Process in Ancient Attica." In *Tria Corda, Scritti in onore di Arnaldo Momigliano*. Biblioteca di Athenaeum 1, edited by E. Gabba, pp. 229–56. Como, 1983.

———. *The Family, Women and Death: Comparative Studies*. London, 1983.

———. "Law as Discourse." *History and Anthropology* 1 (1985): 241–64.

———. "Lycurgus of Butadae: An Athenian Aristocrat." In *The Craft of the Ancient Historian: Essays in Honor of Starr*, edited by J. W. Eadie and J. Ober, pp. 199–252. Lanham, Maryland, 1985.

———. "Social Relations on Stage: Witnesses in Classical Athens." *History and Anthropology* 1 (1985): 313–69.

Isager, Signe and Hansen, Mogens Herman. *Aspects of Athenian Society in the Fourth Century B.C.: A Historical Introduction to and Commentary on the* Paragraphe *Speeches and the Speech* Against Dionysodorus *in the* Corpus Demosthenicum. Odense University Classical Studies 5. Translated by J. H. Rosenmeier. Odense, 1975.

Jacoby, Felix. *Atthis: The Local Chronicles of Ancient Athens*. Oxford, 1949.

*Jaeger, Werner. *Demosthenes: The Origin and Growth of His Policy*. Translated by E. S. Robinson. Berkeley, 1938.

———. *Paideia: The Ideals of Greek Culture*. Translated by G. Highet. 3 vols. New York, 1939–44.

Jameson, M. H. "Agriculture and Slavery in Classical Athens." *CJ* 73 (1978): 122–45.

Jebb, R. C. *The Attic Orators from Antiphon to Isaeos*. 2 vols. London, 1875–1876.

Jordan, Borimir. *The Athenian Navy in the Classical Period*. University of California Classical Studies 13. Berkeley, 1975.

*Kennedy, George A. *The Art of Persuasion in Greece*. Princeton, 1963.

———. "Focusing of Arguments in Greek Deliberative Oratory." *TAPA* 90 (1959): 131–38.

Keuls, Eva C. *The Reign of the Phallus: Sexual Politics in Ancient Athens*. New York, 1985.

Kindstrand, Jan Fredrik. *The Stylistic Evaluation of Aeschines in Antiquity*. Studia Graeca Upsaliensia 18. Uppsala, 1982.

Kinzl, K. H. "Athens: Between Tyranny and Democracy." In *Greece and the Eastern Mediterranean in Ancient History and Prehistory: Studies Presented to F. Schachermeyr*, edited by K. H. Kinzl, pp. 199–223. Berlin, 1977.

Kraut, Richard. *Socrates and the State*. Princeton, 1984.

Krentz, Peter. "The Ostracism of Thoukydides, Son of Melesias." *Historia* 33 (1984): 499–504.

———. *The Thirty at Athens*. Ithaca, 1982.

Lacey, W. K. *The Family in Classical Greece*. London, 1968.

Laix, Roger Alain de. *Probouleusis at Athens: A Study of Political Decision-Making*. University of California Publications in History 83. Berkeley, 1973.

Larsen, J.A.O. "*Demokratia*." *CPh* 68 (1973): 45–46.

——— "The Judgment of Antiquity on Democracy." *CPh* 49 (1954): 1–14.

Lauffer, Siegfried. *Die Bergwerkssklaven von Laureion*. 2 vols. Mainz, Akad. der Wiss. und der Literatur. Abhandlungen der geistes- und sozialwissenschaftliche Klasse. 1955 no. 12, 1956 no. 11.

———. "Die Liturgien in der Krisenperiode Athens." In *Hellenische Poleis*, edited by E. C. Welskopf, vol. I: 147–59. Berlin, 1974.

Lavency, M. *Aspects de la logographie judiciaire attique*. Louvain, 1964.

Lawton, Carol. "The Iconography of Democracy in the Art of the Fourth Century B.C." Paper delivered at the Annual Meeting of the American Philological Association, December 30, 1986.

Lewis, David M. "Cleisthenes and Attica." *Historia* 12 (1963): 22–40.

———. "Notes on Attic Inscriptions." *Annual of the British School at Athens* 49 (1954): 17–50.

Lewis, J. D. "Isegoria at Athens: When Did It Begin?" *Historia* 20 (1971): 129–40.

Lintott, A. *Violence, Civil Strife, and Revolution in the Classical City, 750–330 B.C.* London, 1982.

Lipset, Seymour M. "Political Sociology." In *Sociology Today*, edited by R.K. Merton et al., pp. 81–114. New York, 1959.

Lipsius, Justus Hermann. *Das athenische Recht und Rechtsverfahren*. 3 vols. Leipzig, 1905–15.

Loraux, Nicole. *Les enfants d'Athéna: Idées athéniennes sur la citoyenneté et la division des sexes*. Paris, 1981.

———. *The Invention of Athens: The Funeral Oration in the Classical City*. Translated by Alan Sheridan. Cambridge, Mass., 1986.

Lord, Carnes. *Education and Culture in the Political Thought of Aristotle*. Ithaca, 1982.

———, trans. *Aristotle: The Politics*. Chicago, 1984.

———, ed. *Essays on Aristotelian Political Science*. Forthcoming.

Luhmann, Niklas. *The Differentiation of Society*. Translated by Stephen T. Holmes and Charles Larmore. New York, 1982.

MacDowell, Douglas M. "The Chronology of Athenian Speeches and Legal Innovations in 401–398 B.C." *Revue internationale des droits de l'antiquité*. 3rd ser. 18 (1971): 267–73.

MacDowell, Douglas M. *The Law in Classical Athens*. Ithaca, 1978.

———. "Law-Making at Athens in the Fourth Century B.C." *JHS* 95 (1975): 62–74.

MacKendrick, Paul. *The Athenian Aristocracy, 399–31 B.C.* Cambridge, Mass., 1969.

Mahaffy, J. P. *Problems in Greek History*. London, 1892.

Maio, Dennis Peter. "*Politeia* and Adjudication in Fourth-Century B.C. Athens." *American Journal of Jurisprudence* 28 (1983): 16–45.

Marger, Martin N. *Elites and Masses: An Introduction to Political Sociology*. New York, 1981.

Markle, M. M. "Jury Pay and Assembly Pay at Athens." In *Crux: Essays Presented to Ste. Croix*, edited by P. A. Cartledge and F. D. Harvey, pp. 265–97. London, 1985.

———. "Support of Athenian Intellectuals for Philip: A Study of Isocrates' *Philippus* and Speusippus' *Letter to Philip*." *JHS* 96 (1976): 80–99.

Marrou, H. I. *A History of Education in Antiquity*. Translated by George Lamb. New York, 1964.

Meier, Christian. *Entstehung des Begriffs 'Demokratie': Vier Prolegomena zu einer historischen Theorie*. Frankfort, 1970.

———. *Die Entstehung des Politischen bei den Griechen*. Frankfort, 1980.

———. *Introduction à l'anthropologie politique de l'antiquité classique*. Translated from German by Pierre Blanchaud. Paris, 1984.

*Meiggs, Russell. *The Athenian Empire*. Oxford, 1972.

Michels, Robert. *Political Parties: A Sociological Study of the Oligarchical Tendencies of Modern Democracy*. Translated by Eden and Cedar Paul. Glencoe, Illinois, 1915, reprinted New York, 1962.

*Mikalson, Jon D. *Athenian Popular Religion*. Chapel Hill, 1983.

Mills, C. Wright. *The Power Elite*. New York, 1956.

Mitchel, Fordyce W. "Lykourgan Athens: 338–322." In *Lectures in Memory of Louise Taft Semple*. 2nd ser. 1966–70, pp. 165–214. Norman, Oklahoma, 1973.

Montgomery, Hugo. *The Way to Chaeronea: Foreign Policy, Decision-Making and Political Influence in Demosthenes' Speeches*. Bergen, 1983.

Mossé, Claude. "Comment s'élabore un mythe politique: Solon, 'Père fondateur' de la démocratie athénienne." *Annales (E.S.C.)* 34 (1979): 425–37.

———. *La fin de la démocratie athénienne. Aspects sociaux et politiques du déclin de la cité grecque au IVe siècle avant J. C.* Paris, 1962.

———. "*Politeuomenoi* et *idiōtai*: L'affirmation d'une classe politique à Athènes au IVe siècle." *Revue des Etudes Anciennes* 86 (1984): 193–200.

———. "Les symmories athéniennes." In *Points de vue sur la fiscalité antique*, edited by H. van Effenterre, pp. 31–42. Paris, 1979.

———. "The 'World of the Emporium' in the Private Speeches of Demosthenes." In *Trade in the Ancient Economy*, edited by P. Garnsey et al., pp. 53–63. Berkeley, 1983.

*Murray, Oswyn. *Early Greece*. Atlantic Heights, New Jersey, 1980.

Nagy, Gregory. *The Best of the Achaeans: Concepts of the Hero in Archaic Greek Poetry*. Baltimore, 1979.

North, Helen. "The Use of Poetry in the Training of the Ancient Orator." *Traditio* 8 (1952): 1–33.

Ober, Josiah. "Aristotle's Political Sociology: Class, Status, and Order in the *Politics*." In *Essays on Aristotelian Political Science*, edited by Carnes Lord, forthcoming.

———. Review of *Demes of Attica*, by D. Whitehead, and *Demos*, by R. Osborne. *CPh* 83 (1988): 70–76.

———. "Thucydides, Pericles and the Strategy of Defense." In *The Craft of the Ancient Historian: Essays in Honor of Starr*, edited by John W. Eadie and Josiah Ober, pp. 171–88. Lanham, Maryland, 1985.

———. "Views of Sea Power in the Fourth-Century Attic Orators." *Ancient World* 1 (1978): 119–30.

Osborne, M. J. *Naturalization at Athens*. 4 vols. published as 3 vols. Brussels, 1981–1983.

Osborne, Robin. Demos: *The Discovery of Classical Attika*. Cambridge, 1985.

———. "Law in Action in Classical Athens." *JHS* 105 (1985): 40–58.

Ostwald, Martin. "The Athenian Legislation against Tyranny and Subversion." *TAPA* 86 (1955): 103–28.

———. *From Popular Sovereignty to the Sovereignty of Law. Law, Society, and Politics in Fifth-Century Athens*. Berkeley, 1986.

———. *Nomos and the Beginnings of the Athenian Democracy*. Oxford, 1969.

Patterson, Cynthia. *Pericles' Citizenship Law of 451–50 B.C.* Salem, New Hampshire, 1981.

Pearson, Lionel. "Apollodorus, the Eleventh Attic Orator." In *The Classical Tradition. Literary and Historical Studies in Honor of Harry Caplan*, edited by L. Wallach, pp. 347–59. Ithaca, New York, 1966.

———. "Historical Allusions in the Attic Orators." *CPh* 36 (1941): 209–29.

———. "Party Politics and Free Speech in Democratic Athens." *Greece and Rome* 7 (1937): 41–50.

Pélékidis, Chrysis. *Histoire de l'éphébie attique, des origines à 31 av. J.-C.* Paris, 1962.

Perlman, S. "The Historical Example, Its Use and Importance as Political Propaganda in the Attic Orators." *Scripta Hierosolymitana* 7 (1961): 150–66.

———. "Political Leadership in Athens in the Fourth Century B.C." *Parola del Passato* 22 (1967): 161–76.

———. "The Politicians in the Athenian Democracy of the Fourth Century B.C." *Athenaeum* 41 (1963): 327–55.

———. "Quotations from Poetry in Attic Orators of the Fourth Century B.C." *AJP* 85 (1964): 155–72.

———, ed. *Philip and Athens.* New York, 1973.

Pickard-Cambridge, Arthur W. *Dramatic Festivals of Athens.* 2nd ed., revised by J. Gould and D. M. Lewis. Oxford, 1968.

Pilz, Werner. *Der Rhetor im attischen Staat.* Dissertation, Weida, 1934.

Pritchett, W. Kendrick. *The Greek State at War. Part 4.* Berkeley, 1985.

Raaflaub, Kurt A. "Democracy, Oligarchy, and the Concept of the 'Free Citizen' in Late Fifth-Century Athens." *Political Theory* 11 (1983): 517–44.

———. *Die Entdeckung der Freiheit. Zur historischen Semantik und Gesellschaftsgeschichte eines politischen Grundbegriffes der Griechen.* Vestigia 37. Munich, 1985.

———. "Des freien Bürgers Recht der freien Rede: Ein Beitrag zur Begriffs- und Sozialgeschichte der athenischen Demokratie." In *Studien zur Antiken Sozialgeschichte: Festschrift F. Vittinghoff.* Kölner historische Abhandlungen 28, edited by W. Eck et al., pp. 7–57. Cologne, 1980.

Ranulf, Svend. *The Jealousy of the Gods and Criminal Law at Athens: A Contribution to the Sociology of Moral Indignation.* 2 vols. London and Copenhagen, 1933–1934.

Raubitschek, A. E. "Demokratia." *Hesperia* 31 (1962): 238–43.

Reinhold, Meyer. "Human Nature as Cause in Ancient Historiography." In *The Craft of the Ancient Historian: Essays in Honor of Starr,* edited by John W. Eadie and Josiah Ober, pp. 21–40. Lanham, Maryland, 1985.

Reinmuth, O. W. "The Spirit of Athens after Chaeronea." *Acta of the Fifth International Congress of Greek and Latin Epigraphy (1967).* Oxford, 1971. 47–51.

Reverdin, Olivier. "Remarques sur la vie politique d'Athènes au Vᵉ siècle." *Museum Helveticum* 2 (1945): 201–12.

Rhodes, P. J. *The Athenian Boule.* Oxford, 1972.

———. "Athenian Democracy after 403 B.C." *CJ* 75 (1980): 305–23.

―――. "ΕΙΣΑΓΓΕΛΙΑ in Athens." *JHS* 99 (1979): 103–14.

―――. "Ephebi, Bouleutae and the Population of Athens." *ZPE* 38 (1980): 191–201.

―――. "On Labelling 4th-Century Athenian Politicians." *LCM* 3 (1978): 207–11.

―――. "*Nomothesia* in Fourth-Century Athens." *CQ* new series 35 (1985): 55–60.

―――. "Political Activity in Classical Athens." *JHS* 106 (1986): 132–44.

Ridley, R. T. "The Hoplite as Citizen: Athenian Military Institutions in their Social Context." *L'antiquité classique* 48 (1979): 508–48.

Riley, John W., and Riley, M. W. "Mass Communication and the Social System." In *Sociology Today*, edited by R. K. Merton et al., pp. 537–78. New York, 1959.

Roberts, Jennifer T. *Accountability in Athenian Government*. Madison, Wisconsin, 1982.

―――. "Athens' So-Called Unofficial Politicians." *Hermes* 110 (1982): 354–62.

Romilly, J. de. *Problèmes de la démocratie grecque*. Paris, 1975.

―――. *The Rise and Fall of States According to Greek Authors*. Ann Arbor, 1977.

Roussel, Denis. *Tribu et cité: Etudes sur les groupes sociaux dans les cités grecques aux époques archaique et classique*. Annales littéraires de l'Université de Besançon 193. Paris, 1976.

Rowe, Galen O. "The Portrait of Aeschines in the *Oration on the Crown*." *TAPA* 97 (1966): 397–406.

Ruzé, Françoise. "*Plethos*. Aux origines de la majorité politique." In *Aux origines de l'hellénisme . . . Hommage à H. van Effenterre*, pp. 247–63. Paris, 1984.

Ryder, T.T.B. *Koine Eirene*. London, 1965.

Ste. Croix, G.E.M. de. "The Character of the Athenian Empire." *Historia* 3 (1954/55): 1–41.

―――. "Demosthenes' TIMHMA and the Athenian Eisphora in the Fourth Century B.C." *CM* 14 (1953): 30–70.

―――. *The Origins of the Peloponnesian War*. Ithaca, 1972.

Salkever, Stephen G. "Tragedy and the Education of the *Dēmos*: Aristotle's Response to Plato." In *Greek Tragedy and Political Theory*, edited by J. Peter Euben, pp. 274–303. Berkeley, 1986.

Saller, Richard P. *Personal Patronage under the Early Empire*. Cambridge, 1982.

Sattler, William M. "Conceptions of *Ethos* in Ancient Rhetoric." *Speech Monographs* 14 (1957): 55–65.

Schaefer, A. D. *Demosthenes und seine Zeit.* 3 vols. Leipzig, 1856–1858.

Seager, R. "Elitism and Democracy in Classical Athens." In *The Rich, the Well Born, and the Powerful,* edited by F.C. Jaher, pp. 7–26. Urbana, Illinois, 1973.

———. "Lysias against the Corndealers." *Historia* 15 (1966): 172–84.

Sealey, Raphael. *The Athenian Republic: Democracy or Rule of Law?* University Park, Pennsylvania, 1986.

———. "Athens after the Social War." *JHS* 75 (1955): 74–81.

———. "Callistratos of Aphidna and His Contemporaries." *Historia* 5 (1956): 178–203.

———. "Dionysius of Halicarnassus and Some Demosthenic Dates." *REG* 68 (1955): 77–120.

———. "Ephialtes." *CPh* 59 (1964): 11–21.

———. "How Citizenship and the City Began in Athens." *AJAH* 8 (1983): 97–129.

———. "On the Athenian Concept of Law." *CJ* 77 (1982): 289–302.

———. "The Origins of *Demokratia.*" *California Studies in Classical Antiquity* 6 (1973): 253–95.

———. "Probouleusis and the Sovereign Assembly." *California Studies in Classical Antiquity* 2 (1969): 247–69.

———. "Regionalism in Archaic Athens." *Historia* 9 (1960): 155–80.

———. "The *Tetralogies* Ascribed to Antiphon." *TAPA* 114 (1984): 71–85.

Segal, Charles. "Greek Tragedy and Society: A Structuralist Perspective." In *Greek Tragedy and Political Theory,* edited by J. Peter Euben, pp. 43–75. Berkeley, 1986.

Shaw, Brent D. " 'Eaters of Flesh, Drinkers of Milk': The Ancient Mediterranean Ideology of the Pastoral Nomad." *Ancient Society* 13/14 (1982/83): 5–31.

———. "Social Science and Ancient History: Keith Hopkins *in Partibus Infidelium.*" *Helios* 9.2 (1982): 17–57.

Siewert, P. "The Ephebic Oath in Fifth-Century Athens." *JHS* 97 (1977): 102–111.

Small, David. "Social Correlations to the Greek Cavea in the Roman Period." *Annual of the American Schools of Oriental Research,* forthcoming.

Smith, Billy G. "Inequality in Late Colonial Philadelphia: A Note on Its Nature and Growth." *William and Mary Quarterly* 41 (1984): 629–45.

———. "The Material Lives of Laboring Philadelphians, 1750–1800." *William and Mary Quarterly* 38 (1981): 163–202.

*Snodgrass, Anthony. *Archaic Greece: The Age of Experiment*. London, 1980.

Solmsen, Friederich. "Aristotle and Cicero on the Orator's Playing upon the Feelings." *CPh* 33 (1938): 390–404.

Sommerstein, A. H. "Aristophanes and the Demon Poverty." *CQ* 34 (1984): 314–33.

Stanton, G. R. and Bicknell, P. J. "Voting in Tribal Groups in the Athenian Assembly." *GRBS* 28 (1987): 51–92.

*Starr, Chester G. *The Awakening of the Greek Historical Spirit*, New York, 1968.

*———. *The Economic and Social Growth of Early Greece, 800–500 B.C.* New York, 1977.

*———. *Individual and Community: The Rise of the Polis, 800–500 B.C.* New York, 1986.

Staveley, E. S. *Greek and Roman Voting and Elections*. London, 1972.

*Stone, I. F. *The Trial of Socrates*. Boston, 1988.

Strauss, Barry S. "Aristotle and Athenian Democracy." Forthcoming.

———. "The Cultural Significance of Bribery and Embezzlement in Athenian Politics: The Evidence of the Period 403–386 B.C." *Ancient World* 11 (1985): 67–74.

Thompson, Homer A., and Wycherley, R. E. *The Agora of Athens*. The Athenian Agora 14. Princeton, 1972.

Thompson, W. E. "The Athenian Investor." *Rivista di Studi Classici* 26 (1978): 403–423.

Thomsen, Rudi. *Eisphora*. Copenhagen, 1964.

Trade in the Ancient Economy, edited by Peter Garnsey, Keith Hopkins, C. R. Whittaker. Berkeley, 1983.

Traill, John S. *The Political Organization of Attica. A Study of the Demes, Trittyes, and Phylai, and their Representation in the Athenian Council.* Hesperia Supplement 14. Princeton, 1975.

Travlos, John. *Pictorial Dictionary of Ancient Athens*. New York, 1971.

Usher, S. "Lysias and His Clients." *GRBS* 17 (1976): 31–40.

Vernant, J.-P. "The Historical Moment of Tragedy in Greece: Some of the Social and Psychological Conditions." In *Tragedy and Myth in Ancient Greece*, by J.-P. Vernant and P. Vidal-Naquet, pp. 1–5. Atlantic Heights, New Jersey, 1981.

———. "Remarks on the Class Struggle in Ancient Greece." Translated by R. Archer and S. C. Humphreys. *Critique of Anthropology* 7 (Autumn 1976): 67–81.

———. "Tensions and Ambiguities in Greek Tragedy." In *Tragedy and*

Myth in Ancient Greece, by J.-P. Vernant and P. Vidal-Naquet, pp. 6–27. Atlantic Heights, New Jersey, 1981.

Vernant, J.-P., and Vidal-Naquet, P. *Tragedy and Myth in Ancient Greece.* Translated by J. Lloyd. Atlantic Heights, New Jersey, 1981.

Vidal-Naquet, P. "The Black Hunter and the Origins of the Athenian Ephebeia." *Proceedings of the Cambridge Philological Society.* new ser. 14 (1968): 49–64.

———. "La tradition de l'hoplite athénien." In *Problèmes de la guerre en Grèce ancienne*, edited by J.-P. Vernant, pp. 161–81. Paris, 1968.

Vlastos, G. "ΙΣΟΝΟΜΙΑ ΠΟΛΙΤΙΚΗ." In *Isonomia: Studien zur Gleichheitsvorstellung im griechischen Denken*, edited by J. Mau and E. G. Schmidt, pp. 1–35. Berlin, 1964.

Vocke, W. F. "The Athenian Heralds." Ph.D. dissertation, University of Cincinnati, 1970.

Wade-Gery, H. T. "Eupatridai, Archons, and Areopagus." *CQ* 25 (1931): 1–11, 77–89.

Wallace, Robert. *The Areopagos Council.* Baltimore, forthcoming 1988.

———. "Undemocratic Ideology in Athenian Politics, 355–336 B.C.: Demosthenes' Areopagos-Decree." Paper delivered at the Annual Meeting of the American Philological Association, December 30, 1986.

Walsh, G. B. "The Rhetoric of Birthright and Race in Euripides' Ion." *Hermes* 106 (1978): 301–15.

Washburn, Philo C. *Political Sociology: Approaches, Concepts, Hypotheses.* Englewood Cliffs, New Jersey, 1982.

Webster, T.B.L. *Greek Theatre Production.* London, 1956.

Welskopf, E. C. "Elitevorstellung und Elitebildung in der hellenischen Polis." *Klio* 43/44 (1965): 49–64.

———, ed. *Hellenische Poleis.* 4 vols. Berlin, 1974.

Whitehead, David. "Competitive Outlay and Community Profit: ΦΙΛΟΤΙΜΙΑ in Democratic Athens." *CM* 34 (1983): 55–74.

———. *The Demes of Attica, 508/7–ca. 250 B.C.* Princeton, 1986.

———. *The Ideology of the Athenian Metic.* Cambridge Philological Society Supplement 4. Cambridge, 1977.

———. "A Thousand New Athenians." *LCM* 9.1 (January 1984); 8–10.

Wilcox, Stanley. "Isocrates' Fellow-Rhetoricians." *AJP* 66 (1945): 171–86.

———. "The Scope of Early Rhetorical Instruction." *HSCP* 53 (1942): 121–55.

Will, Edouard. "Histoire grecque." *Revue Historique* 245 (1971): 85–150.

Will, Wolfgang. *Athen und Alexander. Untersuchungen zur Geschichte der Stadt von 338 bis 322 v. Chr.* Munich, 1983.

Winkler, John J. "The Ephebes' Song: *Tragōidia* and *Polis*." *Representations* 11 (1985): 26–62.

Winkler, John J., and Zeitlin, Froma I., edd. *Nothing to Do with Dionysus: The Social Meanings of Athenian Drama*, forthcoming.

Wolff, H. J. *Normenkontrolle und Gesetzesbegriff in der attischen Demokratie.* Heidelberg, Akad. der Wissenschaft. Philol.-Hist. Klasse. Abhandlung 2, 1970.

Wood, Ellen M. "Agricultural Slavery in Classical Athens." *AJAH* 8 (1983): 1–47.

Woodbury, Leonard. "Aristophanes' *Frogs* and Athenian Literacy: *Ran.* 52–53, 1114." *TAPA* 106 (1976): 349–57.

Woodhead, A. G. "ΙΣΗΓΟΡΙΑ and the Council of 500." *Historia* 16 (1967): 129–40.

Wyatt-Brown, Bertram. "Community, Class, and Snopesian Crime: Local Justice in the Old South." In *Class, Conflict, and Consensus: Antebellum Southern Community Studies*, edited by Orville V. Burton and Robert C. McMath Jr., pp. 173–206. Westport, Connecticut, 1982.

*Wycherley, R. E. *The Stones of Athens*. Princeton, 1978.

Wyse, William, ed. *Isaios: The Speeches of Isaeus with Critical and Explanatory Notes*. Cambridge, 1904.

Zeitlin, Froma I. "Thebes: Theater of Self and Society in Athenian Drama." In *Greek Tragedy and Political Theory*, edited by J. Peter Euben, pp. 101–41. Berkeley, 1986.

Zuckerman, Michael. "The Social Context of Democracy in Massachusetts." *William and Mary Quarterly* 25 (1968): 523–44.

INDEX

References in boldface indicate page(s) on which terms are defined.